Banned in the U.S.A.

BANNED
IN THE U.S.A.

A Reference Guide to Book Censorship in Schools and Public Libraries

Revised and Expanded Edition

Herbert N. Foerstel

GREENWOOD PRESS
Westport, Connecticut • London

Library of Congress Cataloging-in-Publication Data

Foerstel, Herbert N.
    Banned in the U.S.A. : a reference guide to book censorship in schools and public
libraries / Herbert N. Foerstel.—Rev. and expanded ed.
        p.   cm.
    Includes bibliographical references and index.
    ISBN 0–313–31166–8 (alk. paper)
        1. Censorship—United States.   2. Textbooks—Censorship—United States.   3. Public
libraries—Censorship—United States.   4. Public schools—Censorship—United States.
5. Book selection—United States.   6. Public libraries—Book selection—United States.
I. Title: Banned in the USA.   II. Title: Banned in the United States of America.
III. Title.
    Z658.U5F64   2002
    025.2'13—dc21   2001055620

British Library Cataloguing in Publication Data is available.

Copyright © 2002 by Herbert N. Foerstel

Library of Congress Catalog Card Number: 2001055620
ISBN: 0–313–31166–8

First published in 2002

Greenwood Press, 88 Post Road West, Westport, CT 06881
An imprint of Greenwood Publishing Group, Inc.
www.greenwood.com

Printed in the United States of America

The paper used in this book complies with the
Permanent Paper Standard issued by the National
Information Standards Organization (Z39.48–1984).

10 9 8 7 6 5 4 3 2

Contents

Preface to the Second Edition   xi

Acknowledgments and Dedication   xiii

Introduction   xv

Chapter 1: A Survey of Major Bookbanning Incidents   **1**

    Kanawha County: West—By God—Virginia   1

    Godless Textbooks in Washington County, Virginia   7

    Island Trees v. *Pico*: A First Amendment Victory   11

    Conflict and Compromise in Prince George's County   15

    Hawkins County, Tennessee: My Way or the Highway   23

    Graves County: Kentucky-Fried Faulkner   31

    Panama City, Florida: Darkness in the Sunshine State   39

    Blasphemy in Cheshire, Connecticut   50

    Impressions: The Textbook That Brought Paganism to
    California Public Schools   55

    Nappy Hair: It Took a Book to Lose a Teacher   58

    Black and Banned: Books by African Women Cause a
    Furor in Maryland   62

Chapter 2: The Law on Bookbanning   **73**

    Background   73

    Appropriate Means and Legitimate Purposes   74

    The Right to Receive Ideas   79

    Secularism and Sex: The Twin Threats to America   94

    Hazelwood: A Chill Wind for the 1990s   97

    Improving on the First Amendment: States Seek
    Remedies to *Hazelwood* Restraints   103

    Positive Impressions: Courts and Schools Find Common
    Ground   108

    Legislative Attacks on the Internet: Implications for
    Bookbanning in Schools and Libraries   112

    Hit Man: The Courts Say the Book Made Him Do It   122

Chapter 3: Voices of Banned Authors   **131**

    Judy Blume   131

    Daniel Cohen   142

    Robert Cormier   148

    David Guterson   156

    Lesléa Newman   161

    Katherine Paterson   165

    Jan Slepian   171

**Chapter 4: The Most Frequently Banned or Challenged
Books, 1996–2000**   **179**

    The *Harry Potter* Books, by J.K. Rowling   180

    The Adventures of Huckleberry Finn, by Mark Twain
    (Samuel Clemens)   188

    I Know Why the Caged Bird Sings, by Maya Angelou   194

    Of Mice and Men, by John Steinbeck   197

    The Chocolate War, by Robert Cormier   201

    *It's Perfectly Normal: A Book about Changing Bodies,
    Growing Up, Sex, and Sexual Health*, by Robie H. Harris   204

The Color Purple, by Alice Walker 206

My Brother Sam Is Dead, by James Lincoln Collier and
Christopher Collier 208

*Kaffir Boy: The True Story of a Black Youth's Coming of Age
in Apartheid South Africa*, by Mark Mathabane 210

The Catcher in the Rye, by J.D. Salinger 212

Daddy's Roommate, by Michael Willhoite 214

The House of Spirits, by Isabel Allende 216

Native Son, by Richard Wright 218

Fallen Angels, by Walter Myers 219

Beloved, by Toni Morrison 220

Goosebumps Series, by R.L. Stine 222

Snow Falling on Cedars, by David Guterson 224

We All Fall Down, by Robert Cormier 225

Go Ask Alice, by Anonymous 226

Bless Me, Ultima, by Rudolfo Anaya 228

The Handmaid's Tale, by Margaret Atwood 229

The Bluest Eye, by Toni Morrison 230

Flowers for Algernon, by Daniel Keyes 231

To Kill a Mockingbird, by Harper Lee 233

Iceman, by Chris Lynch 234

The *Alice* Series, by Phyllis Reynolds Naylor 235

Brave New World, by Aldous Huxley 237

One Fat Summer, by Robert Lipsyte 238

Always Running: La Vida Loca: Gang Days in L.A., by Luis
A. Rodriguez 239

Slaughterhouse-Five, by Kurt Vonnegut 241

The Joy of Gay Sex/The New Joy of Gay Sex, by Charles
Silverstein 243

Forever, by Judy Blume 244

Heather Has Two Mommies, by Lesléa Newman 245

Two Teenagers in Twenty: Writings by Gay and Lesbian Youth, edited by Ann Heron   246

The Drowning of Stephen Jones, by Bette Greene   247

Women on Top: How Real Life Has Changed Women's Sexual Fantasies, by Nancy Friday   248

The Giver, by Lois Lowry   249

The Witches, by Roald Dahl   250

Blubber, by Judy Blume   251

A Day No Pigs Would Die, by Robert Newton Peck   252

Ordinary People, by Judith Guest   253

Julie of the Wolves, by Jean Craighead George   254

Jack, by A.M. Homes   255

Being There, by Jerzy Kosinski   256

Captain Underpants Series, by Dav Pilkey   257

Fool's Crow, James Welch   258

Cujo, by Stephen King   259

A Wrinkle in Time, by Madeleine L'Engle   260

Crazy Lady, by Jane Leslie Conly   261

Black Boy, by Richard Wright   262

Appendixes   271

A(1). Office for Intellectual Freedom: The 100 Most Frequently Challenged Books of 1990–2000   271

A(2). OIF Censorship Database 1990–2000: Initiator of Challenge (Chart)   275

A(3). OIF Censorship Database 1990–2000: Institution Being Challenged (Chart)   275

A(4). OIF Censorship Database 1990–2000: Challenges by Type (Chart)   276

A(5). OIF Censorship Database 1990–2000: Challenges by Year (Chart)   276

B. Office for Intellectual Freedom: The Most Frequently Challenged Books and Authors of 2000   277

C. Office for Intellectual Freedom: The Most Frequently
Challenged Books and Authors of 1999   278

D. Office for Intellectual Freedom: The Most Frequently
Challenged Books and Authors of 1998   278

Selected Bibliography   281

Index   283

Preface to the Second Edition

Like the first edition of *Banned in the U.S.A.*, published in 1994, this revised and expanded second edition examines the landscape of book censorship in American schools and libraries, but there is much new material and analysis presented. Significant new developments in bookbanning are reflected in the updated Introduction to the second edition and in two new, in-depth accounts of censorship in Chapter 1, "A Survey of Major Bookbanning Incidents." Recent cases have been added to the legal analysis of Chapter 2, "The Law on Bookbanning," including Supreme Court decisions involving censorship on the Internet and in book publishing as they relate to schools and libraries. As we saw in the first edition, legal precedent with respect to bookbanning more often than not addresses broad questions of administrative authority rather than specific censorship guidelines. That same tangential application to bookbanning is true in many of the new cases.

Chapter 3, "Voices of Banned Authors," has been augmented to include new interviews with two of the most censored authors of the new millennium, David Guterson and Lesléa Newman. Guterson's *Snow Falling on Cedars* is ranked number 17 in my list of most banned books; Newman's *Heather Has Two Mommies* is number 33.

The fourth and final chapter of *Banned in the U.S.A.*, "The Most Frequently Banned or Challenged Books, 1996–2000," has, of necessity, been entirely rewritten to reflect the fifty most banned books from 1996 through the year 2000. The new list contains a number of titles that did not appear among the first edition's fifty most banned books, most prominent among them the Harry Potter books, tops on the banned list. There are, of course, many holdovers from the earlier list, which covered the years 1990 through 1992. These include traditional censorship targets like Mark Twain's *The Adventures of Huckleberry Finn*, J.D. Salinger's *The Catcher in the Rye*, John Steinbeck's *Of Mice and Men*, and Robert Cormier's *The Chocolate War*.

The most obvious conclusion to be drawn from the second edition of *Banned in the U.S.A.* is that book censorship in the United States continues apace. The older conservative organizations continue to seek out hints of vulgarity and mysticism in books for children and young adults, but liberal groups have also attempted to ban books containing violence and racial epithets. This emerging censorship combination bodes ill for free expression.

Acknowledgments and Dedication

For most of the documentation in this book, I have relied on the important and continuing work of the American Library Association's Office for Intellectual Freedom (OIF). By monitoring the disturbing tide of censorship and by organizing social and political action against it, the OIF leads the way for librarians, educators, and First Amendment advocates.

This book is dedicated to my grandchildren, Herbert, Lauren, and Anna, who are encouraged to read whatever appeals to their minds and imaginations.

Introduction

The arrival of Y2K brought none of the social, environmental, or technological catastrophes predicted by the tabloids, but neither did the new millennium bring relief from the persistent impediments to free expression that characterized the twentieth century. Arthur Schlesinger, Jr., reminds us that throughout most of human history, authority, "fortified by the highest religious and philosophical texts, has righteously invoked censorship to stifle expression." He cites the Old Testament proscription: "Tell it not in Gath, publish it not in the streets of Askelon; lest the daughters of the Philistines rejoice, lest the daughters of the uncircumcised triumph." Schlesinger also offers the injunction of Plato: "The poet shall compose nothing contrary to the ideas of the lawful, or just, or beautiful, or good, which are allowed in the state; nor shall he be permitted to show his compositions to any private individual until he shall have shown them to the appointed censors and the guardians of the law, and they are satisfied with them."[1]

The issue of banned books has been escalating since Guttenberg introduced the printing press in 1455. Once speech could be printed, it became a commodity, to be controlled and manipulated on the basis of religion, politics, or profit. After Pope Leo X condemned Martin Luther's *Ninety Five Theses* in 1517, both Catholics and Protestants began censoring materials that they found dangerous or subversive. Religious censorship quickly led to political censorship when Luther defied the Pope, bringing an immediate response from Emperor Charles V. On May 26, 1521, the emperor issued the Edict of Worms, containing a "Law of Printing," which prohibited the printing, sale, possession, reading, or copying of Luther's works.

In 1564 the papacy promulgated its *Index librorum prohibitorum*, defining those books and authors that Catholics were prohibited from printing or reading. In addition to individual banned titles, the *Index* listed authors whose entire works were prohibited. It also provided guidelines for expurgating books that were generally acceptable and broad rules for the regulation of the book trade. As papal decrees banned new books, the *Index* was revised to keep it up to date.

Protestant censorship followed the same pattern as Catholic censorship, with one important exception: Because most Protestant religious leaders accepted substantial state authority over the church, the *state* became the source of most censorship. For example, in England the crown defined heresy, issued censorship regulations, and authorized civil agencies to enforce them. Nonetheless, despite joint efforts of church and state to impose censorship throughout Europe, printed works were surprisingly protected from effective control owing to a clandestine network of distribution. In addition, throughout the sixteenth and seventeenth centuries, Europe's heterogeneity and lack of political cooperation allowed authors to avoid local censorship by having their books printed in other countries.

In the eighteenth century, the breakdown of political power in France made censorship virtually unenforceable. By 1762, when Jean-Jacques Rousseau published the controversial *Émile*, there was a flood of European novels depicting the decadence and debauchery of the aristocracy and monarchy. The police did their best to suppress these books, but without success. In fact, despite the frequent use of police informers to identify the novels and punish their readers, a censored book in Europe was almost always commercially successful.

However, in the United States and England, a social consensus on censorship was emerging that would be far more repressive than overt state or church power. By the 1830s, this new ideology was proclaiming the necessity for propriety, prudence, and sexual restraint. During the remainder of the nineteenth century, private virtue became public virtue, and American and British editors, publishers, writers, and librarians felt obliged to examine every book for crude language or unduly explicit or realistic portrayals of life. In her introduction to the 1984 New York Public Library exhibition on censorship, Ann Ilan Alter said that there may have been more censorship, self-imposed or otherwise, during the nineteenth century in England and the United States than during all the preceding centuries of printed literature.[2] The twentieth century in America has seen the emergence of pressure groups that maintain an uneasy balance in the struggle to interpret our First Amendment rights. The federal government tips that balance in whatever direction the winds blow, and since 1980, those winds have been chilling. Arthur Schlesinger, Jr. notes: "[T]he struggle between expression and authority is unending. The instinct to suppress discomforting ideas is rooted deep in human nature. It is rooted above all in profound human propensities to faith and fear."[3]

Indeed, in the early years of the twenty-first century, faith and fear are still prominent in determining our right to free expression. The most spectacular international act of bookbanning in the twentieth century was surely Iran's death sentence on the British author Salman Rushdie, and America's response to it has not been encouraging. Rushdie went into hiding in 1989 when his novel *The Satanic Verses* offended Iran's Ayatollah Khomeini, who called for his execution and placed a $1 million bounty on his head. The Tehran underground publisher of *The Satanic Verses* had already been killed.[4] "The real book is struggling to get out from under all the rhetoric," says Rushdie. "But I've always said that the best defense of the book is the book itself, when people read it openly and realize that some terrible injustice has been done not only to me, but to the book." Rushdie warns:

I have tried repeatedly to remind people that what we are witnessing is a war against independence of mind, a war for power. The case of *The Satanic Verses* is, however—and I hope this can be conceded without argument—at present the most public battle in that war. It is a battle that can only be won, because the consequences of losing it are horrendous."[5]

In the spring of 1992, Rushdie made a five-day trip to Washington— his longest time "out of the box," as he put it—to plead for help. The State Department and the White House refused to speak to Rushdie. Margaret Tutwiler, the State Department spokesperson, said there had been no meeting with Rushdie "because at this time we felt that such a thing could and possibly might be misinterpreted." Marlin Fitzwater, speaking for the White House, said: "There's no reason for any special relationship with Rushdie. I mean, he's an author, he's here, he's doing interviews and book tours and things that authors do. But there's no reason for us to have any special interest in him. . . . He doesn't write about government policies."[6]

Art Buchwald reported a fanciful conversation about the incident with his imaginary White House contact Charlie, who explained the president's snub of Rushdie. "If we let him in to see the President, we risk losing the Hezbollah vote this year. . . . The White House never takes sides between a writer and those who pass a death sentence on him." When Buchwald asked Charlie how we could ignore Rushdie's plight at the hands of the nation that took more American hostages than any other country, he was told:

That doesn't compare with someone who writes a satire containing blasphemous statements about a religion. The White House disapproves of people being sentenced for what they write. At the same time, you don't rub a book in a nation's face. . . . Americans don't understand other people's cultures. In some countries they kill you for reading a book and in others they kill you for writing one.[7]

In September 1990, the Thomas Jefferson Center for the Protection of Free Expression announced the results of the most comprehensive opinion survey ever conducted on free expression and declared the First Amendment to be "in perilous condition across the nation." The survey revealed that nearly a third of all Americans believe that constitutional protection of free speech does not extend to the media and arts. Robert O'Neil, the center's founding director, cited evidence of an "alarming double standard—a sense that the First Amendment protects what the speaker wants to say, but not equally the expressions of others." Forty-eight percent of those surveyed mentioned some non–national security aspect of the media or the arts in which they felt government should have the power of censorship. Only one quarter of those questioned would support use of their tax dollars to fund art they found offensive. "Obviously," said O'Neil, "Congress is not required to fund any form of art, or to fund art at all. . . . But it is one thing for government simply not to be a patron of the arts; it is quite another for government to say it will support only individual works or artists it does not deem objectionable."[8]

The American compulsion to censor government-subsidized expression can be seen in the trials and tribulations of the National Endowment for the Arts (NEA), whose director, John Frohnmayer, was forced to resign in 1992 after he complained of pressure from the Bush administration to function as a "decency czar." Acting chairman Anne-Imelda Radice, appointed by President George H.W. Bush, quickly rejected two grants for exhibits containing sexual themes, overruling the NEA review panels and advisory council that had traditionally judged whether works were appropriate for funding. The next day, Stephen Sondheim, the Tony Award–winning lyricist and composer, turned down the 1992 National Medal of the Arts administered by the NEA. To accept the award, he said, "would be an act of the utmost hypocrisy." He charged that the NEA "is rapidly being transformed into a conduit and a symbol of censorship and repression rather than encouragement and support."[9]

Under overt political pressure from the White House and conservative members of Congress, Radice dutifully testified on Capitol Hill that she would avoid funding sexually explicit or "difficult" work. In an unprecedented protest, the entire NEA peer review panel for visual arts resigned, complaining that the process of peer review had been "severely compromised and placed in great jeopardy." Panel member Susan Krane said, "We have no desire to participate in a puppet process." In another 1992 protest, Artist Trust of Seattle turned down an NEA award, declaring, "Radice's actions are so reprehensible that artists whose work has been approved by the NEA are forfeiting their grants in a show of solidarity for censored artists."[10]

The issue of government funding is increasingly invoked to cloud the First Amendment aspects of censorship. Just as Jesse Helms can glibly claim that Congress has the right, indeed the obligation, to censor state-funded art in the name of the people, so do various pressure groups insist that the public funding of most schools and libraries makes them subject to "community censorship." This view does not conform to America's cultural or legal history. It may be true that federal and state legislators have the right to arbitrarily withhold funds to the National Endowment for the Arts or to public schools and libraries. But once that money is allocated, whether it be for NEA exhibitions or public library books, we enter First Amendment territory. There is no more constitutional authority to censor public-funded expression than private expression.

At the 1991 annual meeting of the National Society of Newspaper Editors, John Seigenthaler, publisher of the *Nashville Tennessean*, outlined the disturbing results of a new national survey on free expression that confirmed the previous year's report by the Jefferson Center. In a 281-page report analyzing the survey, Robert Wyatt, a journalism professor at Tennessee State University, and David Neft, research chief for Gannett, Inc., stated, "After nearly a year of surveying, it is apparent that free expression is in very deep trouble." The report noted that the respondents displayed an inability to distinguish between what the law protects and what they dislike personally. It concluded that Americans display "an alarming willingness to remove legal protection from forms of free expression they disagree with or find offensive. . . . That is, they only believe that they believe in free expression."[11]

The 1991–1992 report, *Attacks on the Freedom to Learn*, prepared by People for the American Way (PAW), declared,

> The last several years have witnessed an apparent diminution of Americans' appreciation and willingness to defend freedom of speech and expression. . . . The result has been a series of compromises on freedom of expression, each of which has sent the message to Americans that speech and expression are free, but only within certain parameters. That message, badly at odds with the First Amendment, has fed the wave of curricular attacks in our public schools.[12]

The American public's propensity to suppress expression with which it disagrees is most visible in schools and public libraries, where books are often removed by school and library boards that are vulnerable to local pressure groups. The PAW report revealed that censorship in classrooms and school libraries had increased to the largest single year total in the ten-year history of their report. Some 376 attacks on the freedom to learn, including 348 demands that curricular or library materials be removed, were reported in forty-four states. Nearly one fifth of all challenges to school and library materials came from conservative political groups, some of which have successfully run candidates for school boards.

The count of challenges to materials each year is underestimated, because school systems often seek to avoid controversy by quietly acceding to the censors' demands. PAW notes that, in the past, educators often had to defend their curricular choices against media and lobbying campaigns, including letter-writing drives, petitions, and even paid advertising.

The PAW study found that the three most common reasons for challenging schools' materials in 1991–1992 were:

1. The materials were "anti-Christian," "Satanic," "New Age," or generally contrary to the challengers' religious views. Of the 376 documented censorship attempts in 1991–1992, 140 of them were based on this sectarian point of view. Typical challenges were to books like *Of Mice and Men* and *Catcher in the Rye*.

2. The materials contained profane or otherwise objectionable language. Almost one third of the challenges were on this basis, including books like *The Chocolate War* and *Blubber*.

3. The materials' treatment of sexuality was considered offensive. Over one fifth of the challenges were on this basis, including books like *The Grapes of Wrath* and *Slaughterhouse-Five*.

PAW found that the success rate of the censors in the 1991–1992 school year was disturbingly high, with 41 percent (144 instances) of requests to remove materials succeeding in some measure. During the previous year, only 34 percent of the challenges were successful. "The unfortunate conclusion," states the PAW report, "is that while school systems have grown better equipped to deal with censorship attempts, challengers have more than kept pace in terms of their ability to apply political pressure to achieve their ends."[13]

The power of pressure groups to suppress whatever they find objectionable is reflected on Capitol Hill where ill-advised legislation imposing censorship on broad categories of expression has dangerous implications for schools and libraries. The badly flawed Child Pornography Act was found unconstitutional in 1989 by a U.S. district court, but a modified version was resurrected during the 1990 Congress. In

May 1992, after heavy opposition from the American Library Association and the National Association of Artists' Organizations, that bill was also declared unconstitutional by U.S. District Judge Stanley Sporkin for the District of Columbia who said it would chill the exercise of constitutionally protected First Amendment rights to free expression.

Undaunted, Congress introduced an even more disturbing bill, the Pornography Victims Compensation Act (S.1521), which would impose civil liability on commercial producers of "obscene material" if a plaintiff demonstrates that the material "inspired" or "incited" a crime. Thus, a victim of an assault could file suit against a publisher, claiming that expressive material somehow led the criminal to commit the assault. Because of the court's "community standard" definition of obscenity, publishers would have no way to predict what materials a given jurisdiction would consider "obscene" and subject to such a lawsuit. The result would be a kind of prior restraint by uncertaintly, with publishers avoiding the possibility of costly litigation by electing not to publish important works.

In a *New York Times* article, Teller (of Penn and Teller fame) wrote:

Producers, writers, directors and actors who depict rape are not rapists. They are makers of fiction. To punish them is insane. We might as well punish Agatha Christie for murder and John Le Carre for espionage. . . . It's a death knell for creativity, too. Start punishing make-believe, and those gifted with imagination will stop sharing it. A writer's first thought will be, 'If I write anything original or bold, a reader could get me sued.' We will enter an intellectual era, even more insipid than the one we live in.[14]

The bill did not pass, though it was favorably reported by the Senate Judiciary Committee and actually adopted by the Republican party into its platform. Nonetheless, its sponsors were prescient in anticipating chilling political and legal winds. On May 11, 1995, just a few weeks after a right-wing extremist killed 168 people by blowing up a building complex in Oklahoma City, Oklahoma, a Senate subcommittee held hearings on legislation to criminalize Internet information about bombmaking. Frank Tuerkheimer, a professor at the University of Wisconsin Law School, told the subcommittee that he was able to acquire twelve manuals from the library that contained the same information on bombs that was on the Internet. He noted that the readily available *Blaster's Handbook* tells exactly how to prepare the mixture used in the Oklahoma City bombing.

"I share your concern that there is material on the Internet that I would rather not see," said Tuerkheimer. "[T]here are things in newspapers I would rather not see. There are books I would rather not see printed.

However, I believe in a society such as ours, the answer to ideas we don't want to see . . . are ideas that we do want to see."

Senator Dianne Feinstein (D-Calif.) disagreed emotionally with Tuerkheimer. "I have a hard time with people using their First Amendment rights to teach others how to go out and kill and to purvey that all over the world," she declared.[15] Feinstein's sentiment currently pervades the American judiciary, where federal courts, including the U.S. Supreme Court, have recently established the liability of publishers and motion picture producers for the criminal acts of readers and viewers. In *Rice* v. *Paladin Enterprises* (1999), the Court upheld a judgment against the publishers of the book *Hit Man*, after a real-life hit man committed murder following guidelines suggested in the book. In *Byers* v. *Edmondson* (7125.2d 681 [La.Ct. App. 1998]), the Louisiana Supreme Court upheld an appeals court decision allowing the family of a clerk shot during a robbery to sue director Oliver Stone and the producers of his film *Natural Born Killers*. The film allegedly "incited" the crime (see Chapter 2). As the judiciary strikes at the freedom of the publishing industry, Congress has produced a bevy of laws censoring the Internet in ways that may have profound implications for book publishing. In July 1995, the Senate Judiciary Committee convened the first congressional hearing on Internet pornography, at which a number of witnesses urged Congress to take action to control "cyberporn."

On February 1, 1996, Congress passed the Communications Decency Act (CDA) and President Bill Clinton promptly signed it into law. The act, which criminalized "indecent" expression on a "telecommunications device" was challenged in court by a coalition that included the ACLU, the Electronic Frontier Foundation, and the American Library Association. On June 26, 1997, the Supreme Court struck down the CDA as an abridgement of freedom of speech.

Conservatives in Congress were infuriated by the Court's ruling, and they quickly declared their intention to pass a new, more carefully drawn law. A number of new bills were drafted, but the most popular of these "Sons of CDA" was the Child Online Protection Act (COPA), introduced in April 1998 by Rep. Michael Oxley (R-Ohio).

The COPA retained many of the provisions of CDA, but its sponsors hoped to avoid First Amendment problems by defining the proscribed expression as anything "harmful to minors." The COPA was passed by Congress in September 1998 and signed into law by President Clinton the following month. A coalition of seventeen plaintiffs led by the ACLU immediately challenged the law, and on November 20, U.S. District Judge Lowell Reed granted a temporary restraining order. On February 1, 1999, Judge Reed reaffirmed the restraining order pending a trial on the merits. The Justice Department filed an appeal, leading the COPA down the same path that took the CDA through the federal courts to the U.S. Supreme Court.

A subtle and perhaps more insidious legislative approach to Internet censorship in schools is through the installation of software "filters" on computers that would block student access to inappropriate Internet sites. A flurry of congressional bills were introduced in 1999 and 2000 that would withhold federal funding from schools that did not install filters on their computers. During President George W. Bush's campaign appearances in October 2000, he said he would require libraries to install such filters to prevent children from accessing sexually explicit or violent material. Indeed, a national survey conducted at about the same time revealed that 92 percent of those polled favored filters on school computers to block pornography, and 79 percent said filters should be used to bar hate speech. Behind such support for filters was the more disturbing revelation that 74 percent of those surveyed supported a total government prohibition of online pornography, and 75 percent favored a government ban of online hate speech.[16]

National educational organizations have directed their criticism at federal mandates that would impose filtering on schools, and Internet advocacy groups oppose any form of filtering as an abridgement of First Amendment rights. Marc Rotenberg, executive director of the Electronic Privacy Information Center (EPIC), believes that installing filters on school computers is akin to banning books from a library. "We've described filters simply as censorware," he says. "They can exclude political opinion, medical information and information on sexuality. You essentially rely on someone else's unknown list" to determine what is blocked.[17]

Organizations like the ALA's Office for Intellectual Freedom (OIF) provide an essential public service by documenting censorship incidents around the country and suggesting strategies for dealing with them. Unfortunately, such organizations are finding it difficult to compete with well-financed conservative pressure groups. People for the American Way (PAW) has ceased publishing its highly regarded annual survey of censorship, *Attacks on the Freedom to Learn*. Even the Office for Intellectual Freedom, the nation's best source of news about censorship controversies, announced in its March 2001 newsletter that it could no longer afford the commercial clipping service that provides much of its information. Under the headline "READERS! We Need Your Help!" the newsletter admitted that it would have to place greater emphasis on materials sent in by its readers. It concluded, "Our readers—librarians and free expression advocates nationwide—are now our clipping service."[18]

Despite such budgetary problems, the OIF will continue to document bookbanning and prepare its annual lists of most-banned books. An ironic and unfortunate testimony to the power of banned-book lists was seen during 2000 when a Virginia high school principal ordered teacher Jeff Newton to remove two such lists from his classroom door. Newton had been posting the lists without incident for five years until a parent complained that some of the books on the list had sexual and mature themes. In a letter to Newton, the principal said, "A teacher's door is not . . . a billboard or a vehicle for the promotion of such books."[19] The ACLU intervened, urging the school board to investigate the violation of Newton's First Amendment rights. When the board took no action, the ACLU filed suit on Newton's behalf. In June 2000, Newton resigned under protest after nearly nine years at the school, leading the school board's attorney Douglas Guynn to declare that the case against the school was now "without a vehicle" because Newton was no longer employed there.

Robert O'Neill, director of the Thomas Jefferson Center for the Protection of Free Expression, said, "We felt that constraining a public school teacher's choice of materials, not simply in the classroom, but in this case, materials on the classroom door . . . does in fact abridge a teacher's First Amendment rights." Speaking for the school board, Guynn responded, "He didn't have any First Amendment rights to be violated."[20]

Teachers and librarians are clearly in the line of fire when books are censored, a fact recognized and appreciated by all banned authors. Nonetheless, authors are typically ambivalent about their own role in the principled struggle for freedom of expression.

Kurt Vonnegut, a frequently banned author, says, "I hate it that Americans are taught to fear some books and some ideas as though they were diseases. . . . Well, my books have been thrown out of many libraries. . . . My publisher and I have two agreements on this. One is that we will not seek publicity about the banning of the book. . . . And the other is to see if the individual librarian or teacher is in a jam and whether we can help."[21] Yet Vonnegut admitted that when parents of the "disturbed rich kids" he was teaching in Cape Cod complained of his assignment of *The Catcher in the Rye*, he agreed to change the assignment to *A Tale of Two Cities*. "My job was to teach," he explained, "not to defend the First Amendment."[22] Though most authors may not be so blunt, a surprising number of those I interviewed for this book (see Chapter 3) expressed emotional exhaustion and growing anger at having to divert so much of their time from writing to defending their works, or those of others, against the censors.

In modern society, the censorship of books can be initiated by the federal or state government, by local bureaucrats, or by community pressure. It may occur at any stage of publication, distribution, or institutional control. America's federal government has been inclined to cast its national security veil over massive amounts of scientific, diplomatic, and historical documents, invoking the classification system and export controls to withhold information, the espionage and sedition laws to punish communication, and even prior restraint to prevent publication.

Today, despite the end of the Cold War, the federal government persists in imposing national security censorship, but the overwhelming majority of bookbanning is local, not federal. Community censorship, particularly in schools and libraries, has targeted books, periodicals, newspapers, films, videos, and even the performance of school plays. This "institutional" censorship prohibits or restricts access to books already published, distributed, and even approved by school or library boards. Such materials may already be on library shelves or part of the teaching curriculum, and the pressure to remove them usually comes from groups outside the institution in question. All too often, the strident demands of a well-organized minority are accomodated by politically sensitive school and library boards or harried teachers. As we have seen, the major grounds for such censorship are sex, profanity, and religion, but they are often intertwined to cover a broad range of "unacceptable" attitudes or ideas.

Chapter 1 of the revised edition of *Banned in the U.S.A.* analyzes several major bookbanning incidents from 1976 through 1999. Some of these disputes were extended and quite violent, leaving the community torn and exhausted, with the conflict essentially unresolved. Others revealed the ability of school or library officials to establish an uneasy truce with the bookbanners through compromise and consensus. Some of these conflicts entered the courts to challenge existing law or community standards, whereas others generated new, often ill-conceived legislation. Some focused on a single book; others attacked a broad range of authors and subjects. All the incidents described in Chapter 1 were difficult and instructive for the individuals and communities involved. Most of the "local" censorship occurred in schools and their libraries, rather than in public libraries, a pattern seen consistently throughout this book.

Chapter 2 analyzes the court cases that comprise the body of precedent concerning First Amendment rights in schools and libraries, revealing the evolving status of constitutional protection against bookbanning. What are the limits on bureaucratic and administrative authority to determine what may be read in public schools and public libraries? The case law in this area is unsettled and often ambiguous. Adding to the confusion, the legal precedents controlling school and library censorship often address such disparate sources of expression as the Internet and the publishing industry.

Chapter 3 presents the voices of some frequently banned authors and their responses to censorship. Although many of their books have won national awards, these authors find their works suppressed in schools and libraries around the country. Who are these dangerous writers whose work must be kept from our impressionable youth? How actively do these authors enter the fray to defend their books against the censors? What pressure is brought to bear on them by their editors and publishers? Are they tempted to adjust their writing to avoid the continuing controversy?

Chapter 4 surveys the fifty most banned books during the five-year period 1996 through 2000. The challenges to these books are summarized to reveal the bases for their controversy. The ranking of the books was calculated primarily from censorship incidents reported by the ALA's Office for Intellectual Freedom from 1996 through the year 2000.

Among the new appendices to the second edition of *Banned in the U.S.A.* are the American Library Association's annual lists of Most Banned Books and Most Banned Authors for the years 1998 through 2000 and its comprehensive list of most-banned books for the period 1990 through 2000.

NOTES

1. Arthur Schlesinger, Jr., preface to *Censorship: 500 Years of Conflict*, by New York Public Library (New York: Oxford University Press, 1984), p. 7.

2. New York Public Library, *Censorship: 500 Years of Conflict*, p. 19.

3. Schlesinger, in ibid., p. 7.

4. In 1999, the Iranian government lifted the "fatwa" or death sentence on Rushdie, but he is still accompanied by plain clothes security whenever he appears in public.

5. "Rushdie Comes to Seek U.S. Support," *New York Times*, March 25, 1992, p. A8.

6. Al Kamen, "Senators Back Rushdie at Hill Lunch," *Washington Post*, March 26, 1992, p. A6.

7. Art Buchwald, "The White House's Rushdie Brushoff," *Washington Post*, April 2, 1992, p. D1.

8. Office for Intellectual Freedom, *American Library Association Memorandum*, September 1990, Attachment I.

9. "New NEA Chair Comes Out Shooting," *Newsletter on Intellectual Freedom*, July 1992, p. 114.

10. "NEA Storm Grows as Panel Quits in Protest," *Washington Post*, May 16, 1992, pp. B1, B8.

11. "Survey Finds Weak Support for Free Expression," *Newsletter on Intellectual Freedom*, July 1991, p. 122.

12. People for the American Way, *Attacks on the Freedom to Learn: 1991–1992 Report* (Washington, D.C.: PAW, 1992), pp. 9, 21.

13. People for the American Way, *Attacks on the Freedom to Learn: 1990–1991 Report* (Washington, D.C.: PAW, 1992), p. 15.

14. Teller, "Movies Don't Cause Crime," *New York Times*, January 17, 1992, p. A29.

15. *The Availability of Bomb-Making Information on the Internet*, Hearing before

the Subcommittee on Terrorism, Technology, and Government Information, Committee on the Judiciary, U.S. Senate, 104th Congress, 1st Session, May 11, 1995. Washington: U.S. Government Printing Office, 1996, pp. 50–51.

16. "Survey Shows Support for Filters," *Newsletter on Intellectual Freedom*, January 2001, p. 5.

17. Ibid.

18. *Newsletter on Intellectual Freedom*, March 2001, p. 43.

19. "ALA Joins Suit over Banned Books Week Pamphlet," *Newsletter on Intellectual Freedom*, March 2000, p. 45.

20. "Banned Books List Teacher Resigns," *Newsletter on Intellectual Freedom*, September 2000, p. 133.

21. *Censorship or Selection: Choosing Books for Public Schools*, transcript of a videotape produced by Media and Society Seminars, Columbia University, 1982, pp. 27, 41.

22. "Vintage Vonnegut," *Johns Hopkins Magazine*, February 1992, p. 8.

| | | |

A Survey of Major Bookbanning Incidents

KANAWHA COUNTY: WEST—BY GOD—VIRGINIA

Charleston, West Virginia, is the state capital and the urban center of Kanawha County, which contains some of the most depressed rural society in America. The entire county forms a single school district, within which was waged the mother of all school censorship battles. In December 1973, a West Virginia Board of Education resolution directed all school districts to select school materials that accurately portray minority and ethnic group contributions to American culture and that illustrate the intercultural character of our society. In Kanawha County the English Language Arts Textbook Committee, composed of four teachers and one principal, was authorized to make recommendations for textbook purchase. On March 12, 1974, the Textbook Committee recommended 325 titles for adoption by the board, and neither the local citizenry nor the media took notice. Among the basic texts ratified by the board were the Heath Company's *Communicating* and *Dynamics of Language*, Scott Foresman's *America Reads* and *Galaxy*, and Silver Burdett's *Contemporary English*. Among the supplemental texts adopted were McDougal-Littell's *Language of Man* and Houghton Mifflin's *Interaction*.

Board member Alice Moore, wife of a fundamentalist minister, took some of the books home for examination. She then telephoned Mel and Norma Gabler, self-appointed textbook evaluators operating a corporation called Educational Research Analysts out of Longview, Texas. Many of the Kanawha texts were under consideration within the Texas school system, and the Gablers, famous since the 1960s for their well-financed textbook protests, airmailed their "reviews" of the Kanawha titles to Alice Moore. Mrs. Moore passed her concerns, and the Gablers' evaluations, to other board members and to a local newspaper reporter. Community grumbling and rumor soon reached the point where the school board decided to schedule a meeting to "explain" the textbook selections. At the heated May 23 meeting, Mrs. Moore charged that the textbooks were filthy, disgusting trash, unpatriotic and unduly favoring blacks. Some parents and a fellow board member at the meeting supported her, and a June 27 meeting was scheduled to continue discussion and finalize the actual purchase of the already approved books.

Alice Moore chose to take her cause to the public, appearing on television and reading passages from the challenged texts in churches and community centers. As a result, the local PTA was moved to oppose several of the textbook series, claiming: "Many of the books are literally full of anti-Americanism, anti-religion, and discrimination. Too, these books are woefully lacking in morally uplifting ideas. Many of the statements flout law and order and respect for authority. Several passages are extremely sexually explicit." The Magic Valley Mother's Club joined the fray by circulating a petition to ban from the schools any materials that "demean, encourage skepticism or foster disbelief in the institutions of the United States of America and in western civilization."[1]

A coalition of ministers from the West Virginia Council of Churches and from Catholic, Jewish, and Protestant clergy soon issued a statement in support of the textbooks:

> Any treatment, especially in the schools, of questions like war and peace, racism—black and white—religion and patriotism, is bound to raise disagreements and stir emotional response. . . .We know of no way to stimulate the growth of our youth if we insulate them from the real issues. We feel this program will help our students to think intelligently about their lives and our society.[2]

The June 27 board meeting was held before an audience of more than 1,000 people, with crowds overflowing into hallways and outdoors into the rain. After hours of stormy debate, the board voted to purchase all the disputed books, except for eight titles from the *Interaction* series. But the conflict was far from over. A new organization, Christian-American Parents, sponsored letter-writing campaigns, newspaper advertising, rallies, picketing, and demonstrations in opposition to all the books. Still another new antibook group, Concerned Citizens, picketed the Board of Education and sponsored a Labor Day protest rally where the Reverend Marvin Horan exhorted a crowd of 8,000 to boycott the schools when they opened the next day.

New fliers containing purported excerpts from the books were being circulated throughout the community, some containing blatantly sexual material that had no connection with the textbooks adopted by the Kanawha County schools. The fliers contained excerpts from books like Kate Millet's *Sexual Politics* and a book titled *Facts about Sex for Today's Youth*. Such fliers inflamed the controversy tremendously. During the first week of school, when parents examined the textbooks brought home by the students, they were, of course, unable to find the passages they had seen in the fliers. Ironically, they accused the administration of hiding the books containing the advertised excerpts.

Boycotts, strikes, and pickets became the primary tactic to force the offending books out of the schools. During the first week of school, 9,000 of the county's 45,000 students were kept home by their parents. Miners from all the mines in the county also stayed home rather than cross picket lines set up by parents. Sympathy strikes closed down mines in adjoining counties. Picketing spread to mines, schools, school bus garages, industry, and trucking companies. City bus drivers soon honored the picket lines, closing down service to about 11,000 people.

As a result of these tactics, as well as illegal demonstrations outside the Department of Education building, the board announced on September 11, 1974, that they were withdrawing the offending textbooks from the schools to allow a thirty-day review by a committee of citizens selected by board members. But at a large ballpark rally, the Reverend Marvin Horan repudiated any such compromise, demanding a continuation of the boycotts and picketing until all the challenged books had been permanently removed and the school superintendent and board members who voted "the wrong way" were dismissed.

The antibook campaign soon reached the boiling point. Reverend Horan, who was later sentenced to three years in prison for conspiracy to blow up two elementary schools, was soon joined by other fundamentalist ministers. Reverend Ezra Graley and Reverend Avis Hill were soon sentenced to thirty days in jail for defying a court injunction, and Graley received an additional sixty days for contempt of court. The Reverend Charles Quigley shocked the county by asking Christians to pray that God would kill the three board members who voted to keep the books.

Many of the students in whose name the fundamentalists terrorized the county found the furor ironic. One pointed out, "They're shooting people because they don't want people to see violence in books." Violence escalated further in September during the second week of school. As the number of wildcat mine strikers reached almost 10,000, two men were wounded by gunfire at a picket line. A CBS-TV crew was attacked, and car windows were smashed. Threats of violence were leveled at the school superintendent, board members, and parents who tried to send their children to school. Kanawha's sheriff joined other county officials in asking West Virginia Governor Arch Moore to send in state troopers, but the governor said he would not interfere in local political disputes. By September 13, 1974, Superintendent Kenneth Underwood ordered all 121 public schools closed for a four-day weekend, during which all extracurricular activities were banned. Underwood and several board members, including Alice Moore, quietly slipped out of town. Moore said, "I never dreamed it would come to this."[3]

A *Charleston Gazette* article revealed: "A few extremists among the churchmen who wanted 'godless' textbooks removed from the schools became so fanatical they discussed bombing carloads of children whose parents were driving them to school in defiance of a boycott called by book protesters." Assistant District Attorney Wayne Rich stated that one of the convicted bombers testified that he and others had discussed ways to stop "people that was sending their kids to school, letting them learn out of books when they knew they was wrong." One method discussed was to place a blasting cap in the gas tank of a car, hooking the wire to the brake or signal light. When the brake was applied or the signals used, it would blow up the car.[4]

The protesters' hysterical attacks on "the books" quickly extended beyond particular titles or passages, to all 325 books approved for the curriculum and then to many of the world's most respected literary works, including Plato's *Republic*, Herman Melville's *Moby Dick*, John Milton's *Paradise Lost* and *Paradise Regained*, and even *The Good Earth*, the Pulitzer Prize novel by Pearl Buck, West Virginia's most renowned author! By now the dispute had attracted the national media. From magazines like *The New Yorker* and *U.S. News & World Report* to scholarly journals and the national press and television, the significance of this controversy over school books was dramatically acknowledged.

The controversy forced the resignations of the president of the school board and Superintendent Underwood, and when the new Textbook Review Committee began its deliberations on September 24, it came under heavy pressure from community organizations, some of which now had national support. The Business and Professional People's Alliance for Better Textbooks, led by businessman Elmer Fike, published antibook ads and pamphlets with the support of the Washington-based Heritage Foundation. On the other side, the Kanawha County Association of Classroom Teachers passed a resolution denouncing the removal of the textbooks and censuring the school board for abdicating its legal responsibilities under public pressure. The association voted to oppose any recommendation of the Textbook Review Committee that would revoke the original approval of the texts.

During the Review Committee's deliberations, one local elementary school was dynamited and another fire-bombed. Other schools were vandalized and attacked with gunfire. School buses were stoned, as were the homes of parents whose children attended school. Two school buses were hit by shotgun blasts, and eventually the county's fleet of buses was virtually inoperable. Even Alice Moore was threatened by phone, and after shots were fired outside her house, she was accompanied by guards at all times.

On November 8, 1974, amid fears of violence, the school board met to make a final decision on the recommendations of the Textbook Review Committee. The board heard testimony from the majority and minority factions of the Committee, one recommending return of virtually all the books and the other rejecting them all. The board then unanimously passed resolutions to protect students from the imposition of any books that their parents found objectionable. It was agreed that a form would be sent to parents, on which they could indicate any books they did not want their children to read. With only Mrs. Moore dissenting, the board voted to authorize the return of all the basic and supplemental books to the classroom except the elementary school series *Communicating* and the senior high school portion of the series, *Interaction*, which was confined to the library only. The board's vote actually imposed more severe restrictions than the majority recommendation of the Textbook Review Committee, which would have approved *Communicating* for classroom use.

The long-awaited board decision did little to defuse the conflict. Protesters intensified their boycotts, bomb threats increased, and one Kanawha town had Superintendent Underwood and two board members arrested for contributing to the delinquency of minors. Only after two police cars were fired upon as they escorted a school bus did the West Virginia State Police commit itself to enforcing the law against the protesters.

On November 21, 1974, the board passed a resolution setting guidelines for future textbook selection. Those guidelines closely followed the requirements that the Gablers' Texas organization had sent to Mrs. Moore. The National Education Association asserted that these guidelines, "if given the interpretation obviously meant by their proponent, would not only bar the disputed books from Kanawha County classrooms, but would proscribe the use of any language arts textbooks."[5]

On January 30, 1975, the U.S. District Court in Charleston considered a lawsuit brought by a group of Kanawha County citizens who complained that their religion required them to place their children in private schools to avoid the use of the controversial textbooks. The plaintiffs claimed that the texts were not only offensive to Christian morals, but defamed the nation and attacked civic virtue. Alleging that they and their children would suffer irreparable harm unless the court enjoined the school board from violating their constitutional rights, the plaintiffs sought an injunction restraining the schools from using the challenged textbooks. District Judge K.K. Hall dismissed the plaintiff's action, ending the legal phase of the Kanawha battle.

On February 10, 1975, operating under new West Virginia procedures for textbook selection, a Kanawha County screening committee of fifteen lay members and five teachers rejected parts of all four textbook series under consideration. After the West Virginia Department of Education ruled that the Textbook Selection Committee was not bound by the screening committee, the board approved one of the series by a vote of 4 to 1, Mrs. Moore dissenting. Technically, the dispute over the books had been resolved, but demonstrations and boycotts continued until April 1975, when the Reverend Marvin Horan was tried and sentenced to three years in prison for conspiracy to bomb schools. Finally, shortly after school began in the fall of 1975, the board restored to Kanawha classrooms the *Communicating* series that had been dropped in November 1974. Ironically, this textbook series had been the most violently opposed of all the challenged books, yet it was now approved without objection.

The war was over, but in its wake remained an atmosphere of caution. Though technically reinstated, the controversial textbooks were never reordered. The new books that eventually replaced the offending texts came from intimidated publishers who provided only the most sanitized subjects and bland authors. The retrenchment led some of Kanawha's schools to reintroduce the textbook series they had used in the 1940s.

Looking back, education professor George Hillocks, Jr., called the Kanawha County dispute "the most prolonged, intense, and violent textbook protest this country has ever witnessed." A few years after the conflict had been subdued, Hillocks visited the Kanawha County school system and observed:

> Children whose parents granted permission must use the controversial books only in the library, not in the classroom where other children might overhear discussions of them. Or teachers must make special provisions for use of the books. The result is that many do not use them at all. Many of the texts sit in the board of education warehouse. One elementary principal told me that she will not order the books. . . . She does not want to disrupt the school again. . . . Some teachers are looking for ways out of education, many others are angry at the vilification to which they feel they have been subjected, and many say they will never feel the same about teaching again.[6]

James Moffet, author/editor of Houghton-Mifflin's *Interaction* series, one of the most vilified of the texts in Kanawha County, concludes:

> The fact that nothing like it has occurred since gives a good indication of how effective it was: no publisher has dared offer to schools any textbooks

of a comparable range of subjects and ideas and points of view to those the protesters vilified and crippled on the market. Theoretically returned to the Kanawha County schools, they may as well not have been. In many other ways the bitter controversy closed up its own school system as much as it did textbook editorial offices.[7]

GODLESS TEXTBOOKS IN WASHINGTON COUNTY, VIRGINIA

In February 1974, a customer came to Bobby's Market, a small grocery store in the rural community of Benhams, Virginia, and told the proprietor, Bobby Sproles, about the profanity he had discovered in his son's high school English textbook series. When the customer showed him one of the volumes in Ginn and Company's *Responding* series, Sproles was outraged. Upon returning home, Sproles examined his daughter's English text, also from the *Responding* series, and he found it equally objectionable. Soon the word had spread from Bobby's Market that "dirty" books were being used in the local schools.

Sproles was never very clear on the "dirty" language in the stories presented in the *Responding* series. He complained of words like "damn" and "hell," but these are not normally considered "dirty" words. He identified particular stories like Erskine Caldwell's "Indian Summer," which describes a mud bath given to an adolescent girl by two young boys. But there was no profane or vulgar language of any kind in that story. Sproles did cite a particular passage in John Updike's "A & P" in which a character refers to a girl's "sweet soft broad-looking can." This was apparently representative of the "filth" that made the *Responding* series unacceptable.

Sproles advised his customers to contact Dr. R.G. Raines, acting superintendent of schools for Washington County, and the complaints began to mount. When Raines failed to take action against the books, several angry parents decided to take their grievance to the school board. On March 2, 1974, Sproles spoke at the school board meeting, presenting his group's objections to the *Responding* series as well as other books in the school libraries. Sproles passed out copies of the books for the board members to examine, and the board agreed to look into the matter. This satisfied Sproles, who told his supporters that he was confident that the board would not tolerate dirty books in the school system.

At the next board meeting, D.M. Cooke, the director of instruction, described the justification for continuing to use the *Responding* series. He stressed that the primary aim of the language arts program was to get the students to love to read. To accomplish this, the schools would need to accept occasional profanity, because "the students like these books and they read them because they reflect the student's world and his language of the present." Cooke did, however, promise that an alternative to the *Responding* text would be sought, though this would involve a lengthy process. Sproles was shocked at the board's decision. He asked all children to leave the board room, and proceeded to read from the offending books. The Reverend Tommy Tester of the Gospel Baptist Church led a prayer asking that the devil be defeated. "The demons of Hell have entered into the bodies of our educators," he said.[8]

Sproles soon organized the first of many public meetings to oppose the books. The 200 people who attended the meeting at the Baptist church in Benhams later came to call themselves the Concerned Citizens for Better Government, and Sproles became their spokesman and leader. At that first meeting, Sproles demanded the resignation of Acting Superintendent Raines, Director of Instruction Cooke, the school board, and the Textbook Adoption Committee. His demands were communicated to Virginia's governor and attorney general.

Though Sproles had complained of the profane language in *Responding*, he now seemed more concerned that the books were unpatriotic and irreligious, "communist inspired" and un-American, undermining love of country and parental authority. But attacking the books on the basis of profane lanaguage was an easier public task than analyzing their political implications. In an interview, Sproles admitted: "I think there's things in the books that to me, personally, is more damaging psychologically than the words is. Now I've played on the profanity, I've fought the issue on the profanity, simply because I guess I didn't know any other way to do it."[9]

On April 17, 1974, Sproles and the Concerned Citizens took their case before the board of supervisors, where they requested that the school budget be reduced as a tactic to effectively remove the books. The board then considered a motion to oppose the use of *Responding* in Washington County schools, but after heated debate, the motion failed by a vote of 3 to 2.

The following day, a disappointed Sproles chose to begin a petition drive, circulating copies in churches and schools throughout the county. On May 4, 1974, the school board met again to hear the Concerned Citizens' complaints and receive the petition. On May 10, Sproles received the board's reply to his complaint. The letter from Acting School Superintendent R.G. Raines reiterated the board's policy that whenever parents object to a book such as the *Responding* series, their children may be assigned alternative reading materials. When Sproles notified the Board that the Concerned Citizens could not accept such an arrangement, Raines requested that the case be put on the docket of the Washington County Circuit Court.

When the matter came to trial, Sproles himself acted for the plaintiffs. He argued that the school board had denied the citizens of Washington

County their freedom of religion by teaching doctrines contrary to their beliefs. Sproles also said the board had acted corruptly in failing to warn parents of the books' offensive contents. But Judge Aubrey Matthews decided in favor of the board, concluding that its actions were neither corrupt nor beyond its jurisdiction. After Court was adjourned, Sproles accosted the newly appointed superintendent of schools, W. Grant Tubbs, saying that the Concerned Citizens would back candidates for the Board of Supervisors who were more sympathetic to their aims. The following day, Sproles began distributing 10,000 copies of a list of alleged profane words that he had culled from *Responding*. The list was immediately printed in the *Bristol Herald-Courier*, along with a sympathetic editorial and instructions on how to contact Sproles and receive his materials. On July 26, 1974, Acting Superintendent Raines announced that two books would be offered as possible alternatives to *Responding*. Those books were made available for public inspection at the local library, after which a public hearing was held on their acceptability. At that hearing, Sproles and his supporters dominated the audience and opposed both of the proposed series, claiming that they also contained profanity such as "by God." More important, Sproles said *any* alternative books would be unacceptable so long as *Responding* was used by *any* child in the school system.

The August 10 school board meeting was attended by about 500 persons, assembled not in the usual boardroom, but in the large high school auditorium. Eight of the speakers, including one minister, defended the books. Twelve speakers, eight of them ministers, were opposed to the books. Reverend Tom Williams, an emerging fundamentalist leader within the Concerned Citizens, described the *Responding* series as a symptom of and a contributing factor to a collapse of morals and traditional values that endangered America's survival. As a result of his speech, Williams was soon receiving as much media attention and publicity as was Sproles. Interviewed at his home, Reverend Williams said the disputed books were wrong religiously, wrong morally, and wrong constitutionally. He warned: "There will be no peace in the school system as long as the present Board sits and as long as these books remain and as long as our libraries are not cleaned up. We're determined to clean up the libraries too. All these filthy books have been brought into the library. They're going out."[10]

Not to be outdone, Sproles promised:

We're still going to try to get the books out, but at the same time we're going to try to get some of the people out of the school system too. . . . Some of these teachers that approved these books, they need to go. I think really that we're going to have to get rid of the Superintendent, the Assistant Superintendent and the School Board and some of these teachers before we can get rid of the books.[11]

After the August 10 school board meeting, Sproles and Reverend Williams met with board members and Superintendent Tubbs. Tubbs attempted to negotiate a compromise, but Sproles would accept nothing short of removing the books entirely from the schools. Another board meeting was arranged for the following week, at which the protesters were told that the board was willing to have offending portions of the *Responding* texts "blocked out." Sproles again rejected the board's offer, claiming that the children might find some way to circumvent the excisions. The board then offered to restrict the texts to classroom use only, under the supervision of a teacher. Reverend Williams agreed to present that proposal to the Concerned Citizens.

Feeling his leadership challenged, Sproles soon decided to move toward more extreme tactics, including a school boycott. Through the local newspapers, Sproles announced an August 20 meeting of the Concerned Citizens to develop plans for the boycott. Before the meeting, Washington County Sheriff Robert Clendenen visited Sproles to warn him of the grave consequences of a boycott, including the growing possibility of violence, and Sproles agreed to allow Clendenen to speak at the meeting. Clendenen told the Concerned Citizens that any parents participating in the boycott would be arrested. As a result, the Concerned Citizens concluded that, rather than organize a formal boycott, parents should decide independently whether to enroll their children in school.

On September 5, the school board announced a compromise proposal. Teachers would select inoffensive portions from both *Responding* and *Adventure*, a proposed alternative text, using the established criteria for book selection. Parental input would be sought in choosing the excerpts, and even these sanitized selections could be used only in the classroom under teacher supervision, unless a parental consent form was signed. Sproles was suspicious of the compromise and continued to threaten boycotts.

At the first board meeting of 1975, Sproles read from a Virginia statute that called for "moral education" in the public schools, and Reverend Williams demanded the resignation of Tubbs and Raines. The board said it would respond at an appropriate time, but after the protesters had left the meeting room, the board gave a unanimous vote of confidence to Tubbs and Raines.

At the next Board meeting, a motion was made to remove one of the books in the *Responding* series and to appoint a committee to review the entire series. Superintendent Tubbs objected, saying this would deny the books not only to the protesters' children but to all children. He noted that school officials, board members, and teachers had been threatened by protesters, and he asked, "What will be next? Where will the witch-hunt end?" When Tubbs finished speaking, the board unanimously approved the motion.[12]

The Textbook Advisory Committee, appointed to evaluate the *Responding* series and recommend a resolution to the conflict, filed its final report on March 13, 1976. The official report vaguely declared that the books may be inappropriate for use in public schools but that the dispute was a complex issue with no simple answer that would be acceptable to all. The committee report offered two possible courses of action: Remove the *Responding* series entirely from the school system, or cease its use as the basic text while retaining it as supplemental reading. In addition to its "official" report, the Textbook Review Committee provided the board with an "unofficial" report, which made no pretense of objectivity. That report criticized *Responding* for encouraging disobedience, disrespect for authority, disrespect for God, and contempt for American institutions and the free enterprise system.

Perhaps on the basis of the Committee's "unofficial" report, the school board, at its next meeting, voted 5 to 2 to remove the *Responding* series entirely from the Washington County School System. A school bureaucracy had thus consummated a bookbanning, and a fundamentalist group had established permanent influence over the process of textbook selection in Washington County, Virginia.

ISLAND TREES v. *PICO*: A FIRST AMENDMENT VICTORY

In September 1975, in Long Island, New York, the seven members of the Island Trees School Board, including the board president, Richard Ahrens, attended a conference sponsored by a conservative organization called Parents of New York United (PONYU). The Island Trees board members heard a speech on the subject of controlling textbooks and library books in the public schools, and they obtained a list of books that PONYU opposed. At the top of the list was the heading "Objectionable Books," followed by thirty-three titles, along with excerpts from those books and editorial comments. Most of the excerpts concerned sex, but some of the editorial comments were political in nature. For example, one book was described as objectionable because it "equates Malcolm X, considered by many to be a traitor to this country, with the founding fathers of our country."[13]

After the conference, when the board members returned to Island Trees, they decided to examine their own library's collections. On a night when the school was closed and the building empty, the board members entered the library. Steven Pico, the student who later led the opposition to the Island Trees censorship, recalls the episode:

> Now please don't ask me why book banners feel more comfortable working during the night. . . . I guess they decided that is how censors should act. So, they had the janitor unlock the library, proceeded to go through

the card catalog, and found that our district had eleven of the books on that list.[14]

Several weeks later, at its February 1976 meeting, the board ordered the principals of the junior and senior high schools to immediately remove all copies of the eleven books: *The Fixer*, by Bernard Malamud; *Slaughterhouse-Five*, by Kurt Vonnegut; *The Naked Ape*, by Desmond Morris; *Down These Mean Streets*, by Piri Thomas; *Best Short Stories by Negro Writers*, edited by Langston Hughes; *Go Ask Alice*, anonymous; *A Hero Ain't Nothin' but a Sandwich*, by Alice Childress; *Black Boy*, by Richard Wright; *Laughing Boy*, by Oliver LaFarge; *Soul on Ice*, by Eldridge Cleaver; and *A Reader for Writers*, edited by Jerome Archer. At that time, Malamud's *The Fixer* was not only in the library but was assigned reading in a senior literature course in the Island Trees district.

When the Superintendent of Schools Richard Morrow discovered what had been done, he publicly objected and wrote a memo to the board stating his opposition to banning the books on the basis of a list from an unknown source and with no criteria specified. "[W]e already have a policy," said Morrow, "designed expressly to handle such problems. It calls for the superintendent, upon receiving an objection to a book or books, to appoint a committee to study them and make recommendations. I feel it is a good policy—and it is board policy—and that it should be followed in this instance." The board responded to the superintendent's memo by repeating its directive that "*all copies* of the library books in question be removed from the libraries to the Board's office" [emphasis in original].[15]

In March 1976, the board agreed to form a Book Review Committee consisting of four Island Trees parents and four school staff members, to be appointed jointly by the superintendent and the board. The committee was to read the books in question and make recommendations to the board concerning their educational suitability, good taste, appropriateness, and relevance. The board then held a public meeting on the book dispute, at which it distributed copies of excepts from the offending books. Superintendent Morrow once again expressed his concern in writing, saying it was wrong for the board or any other group to remove books without following established procedure and without considering the views of the parents whose children read the books and the teachers who use them. He also said it was wrong to judge any book on the basis of brief excerpts taken out of context and from a list prepared by someone outside the Island Trees community. Morrow recommended that, pending review by a committee, the challenged books should be returned to the shelves.

In July, the Review Committee made its final report to the board, recommending that five of the listed books be retained and that two others be removed from the school libraries. As for the remaining four books, the committee could not agree on two, took no position on one, and recommended that the last book be made available to students only with parental approval. The Board overruled the committee's report, deciding that only one book (*Laughing Boy*) should be returned to the high school library without restriction, that another (*Black Boy*) should be made available subject to parental approval, but that the remaining nine books should be removed from elementary and secondary libraries and from use in the curriculum. The board gave no reasons for rejecting the recommendations of the committee that it had appointed, nor did it justify its disregard for the concerns of School Superintendent Morrow. Within a year, Morrow had left the school district, replaced by an administrator from California with ties to former Governor Ronald Reagan's administration. The head librarian in the Island Trees schools, who like the superintendent had opposed the book removals, was demoted and transferred to a small elementary school.

The Island Trees book dispute attracted considerable news coverage. The fact that two of the school board members were running for reelection further heightened tensions. So began a seven-year First Amendment struggle, during which the books remained banned from the library shelves. When the controversy reached the media and the community at large, the board issued a press release explaining that while at the PONYU conference, they had learned of books in schools throughout the country that were "anti-American, anti-Christian, anti Sem[i]tic, and just plain filthy." The board said that after finding some of those books in their own libraries, they verified that they contained "obscenities, blasphemies, brutality, and perversion beyond description." The press release concluded: "[I]t is our duty, our moral obligation, to protect the children in our schools from this moral danger as surely as from physical and medical dangers."[16]

Students at the high school and junior high school, led by seventeen-year-old Steven Pico, sued the board in U.S. District Court, claiming a denial of their First Amendment rights. The plaintiff in *Island Trees* v. *Pico* (see Chapter 2) was an Island Trees student who recently recalled this epic legal conflict in a speech before the Missouri Association of School Librarians. Pico said he remembered quite clearly his first reaction to the book banning:

> I could not believe the hypocracy of the censorship of books in the United States. In school, year after year, I had been told how books were banned in communist countries and burned in Nazi Germany. I could not believe that it was happening in the United States in the 1970s. . . . I found it hard to believe that students didn't care and that every single teacher remained silent. For the first time in my life I felt that I understood what happened

during the McCarthy era. After twelve years of schooling, my education had in many ways finally begun.[17]

Steven Pico told the assembled librarians that the events in Island Trees were not unusual, but in fact represented the norm in schools around the nation. He noted that in this case, as in many other censorship incidents, the books had not been read by the censors and were praised by educators and reviewers. In the Island Trees case, two of the books were Pulitzer Prize winners, yet the opinions of professionals were ignored, the attitudes of students were never sought, and those who defended the books were ostracized.

Before initiating his suit, Pico conferred with representatives of the American Library Association, but realizing that he needed the support of a group with the resources to sustain protracted litigation, he turned to the American Civil Liberties Union. Pico's attorneys began by taking depositions from the school board members to establish a record of their objections to each book. The board members claimed that *The Fixer* was anti-Semitic because derogatory terms were used to describe Jews. Yet the book was written by a Jewish author who was simply describing the persecution of Jews. The board gave two reasons for banning *A Hero Ain't Nothin' but a Sandwich*: First, because "ain't" appears in the title; and second, because George Washington was identified as a slaveholder. *A Reader for Writers* was banned because, among selections like the Declaration of Independence and President John F. Kennedy's inaugural address, the editors included a satirical essay by Jonathan Swift. The bookbanners said *Go Ask Alice* glorified sex and drugs, though it was simply a moving account of the horrors of drug addiction.

The district court found in favor of the school board, but the students appealed to the U.S. Court of Appeals, which reversed the decision and remanded the case back to the district court for trial. The school board then appealed to the U.S. Supreme Court which granted a review in 1982. Pico and his fellow students asked the Court for a declaration that the board's actions were unconstitutional and that it should return the nine books to the school libraries and refrain from interfering with their use in the schools' curricula.

By the time the case reached the Supreme Court, the school board was no longer claiming that they had banned the books because they were anti-American and antireligious. Now they simply said the books were "vulgar." But one of these books, *A Reader for Writers*, contained no vulgarity at all. When the school board attorney appeared before the Supreme Court, Justice Stevens asked him why *A Reader for Writers* was banned, because it contained no vulgarity. The attorney answered that the board considered the book to be in bad taste. An incredulous Justice

Stevens then asked whether "bad taste" was really an appropriate basis on which to ban books in the United States.

The Supreme Court ruled 5–4 in favor of Pico and his fellow students, but Pico says they won by the skin of their teeth. The case came to the most conservative court in sixty years at a time when the Reagan administration and groups like Moral Majority were fueling anti-intellectualism. Asking that Court to recognize a First Amendment "right to know," which had no firm history in constitutional law, was risky business. (For an in-depth discussion of the legal implications of this case, see Chapter 2.)

The Supreme Court decided that the case should have been tried to determine the board's *motivation* in banning the books, and so the case was remanded for trial. The Island Trees School Board considered their options, and then, rather than go to a trial that they might lose, they voted to return *all* the disputed books to the library shelves to be used without restriction.

Stephen Pico believes that since that decision school officials have been reluctant to have their motives examined at trial and scrutinized in the press. They are also less willing or able to justify to taxpayers the hundreds of thousands of dollars in legal fees which would be necessary to ban a library book. But Pico remains disappointed at the passive community response to the bookbanning:

> Not one parent in Island Trees ever complained about these eleven books. Not one teacher, not one student, ever objected to these books. A group of activists from around the country . . . succeeded in keeping these books off the shelves for seven years. . . . I do look back now and then and recall how it felt to be called a "communist" in public because I was defending the right to read a book. That's sad and ironic, but I can easily brush it off. What I shall never forget is the silence of my teachers during the book banning. Only one of my teachers ever commented to me about the book banning. . . . One day after class she whispered to me, "Steve, you're doing the right thing." I will never be able to forget that she felt the need to whisper.[18]

CONFLICT AND COMPROMISE IN PRINCE GEORGE'S COUNTY

In September 1977, the rumbling of an approaching censorship storm could be heard in Maryland's Prince George's County when County Executive Winfield Kelly received a letter complaining about a book, *Our Bodies, Ourselves*, that was owned by the local public library. The letter was signed by C. Paul, a member of the Coalition for Children, a local religious group headed by Beth Trotto. Ms. Paul claimed that the book described and illustrated sexual acts that were illegal in the state of Maryland. She said that exposure to books like *Our Bodies, Ourselves* made it difficult to raise Christian children with the hope of eternal life with their Creator. She opposed the use of her tax dollars for the purchase of "pornography" produced by "feminist degenerates," and she warned the county executive that if even one more cent of her taxes was spent on such "smut," she would be forced to read aloud from *Our Bodies, Ourselves* at the county executive's next town meeting.

County Executive Kelly wrote to Ms. Paul, informing her that the Prince George's County Memorial Library System was an autonomous body and that the county government had no control over a library's internal policy, including material selection. He advised her of the library's procedure for handling complaints, and enclosed a blank complaint form. Ms. Paul filled out the form, stating that the book encouraged sexual activity among adolescents, including lesbianism, birth control, and abortion, all of which were against her religious convictions. A member of the library staff responded to the complaint, explaining why the book was in the library's collections.

Perhaps disappointed with the library's response, Ms. Paul sent a letter to the editor of the *Prince George's Journal*, attacking sex education in the schools and taking particular aim at *Our Bodies, Ourselves*. The letter stated:

> *The Wanderer*, in its February 23, 1978 edition, called this literary effort "a veritable litany of the most disgusting and outrageous sexual immorality available today." ... Currently 184 copies of the book reside in the 18 branches of the County library system—enough for everyone to have at least one peek. Additionally, the paperback may find its way into the classroom (remember, it is not approved for school use) as a resource material used by teachers. It also is used as a major reference work in many sex and psychology texts. . . .
>
> It advocates abortion, lesbianism, and masturbation. . . . With such volumes as this available and in use by our youngsters, are our children really discouraged from becoming sexually active at an early age or are we merely piquing their curiosity to experiment with that which they ordinarily would not if alternatives were not provided at taxpayer expense?[19]

In 1977, *Our Bodies, Ourselves* was a hot item in Prince George's County libraries. In response to the complaints, County Executive Kelly asked the State's Attorney's Office to review the book's original (1970) and revised (1976) editions. The review, expressed in an internal memo from Stephen Orenstein to State's Attorney Arthur Marshall, said:

> The text is occasionally explicit but is done so to develop the thought espoused. The explicit language is minimal. Vulgar words and phrases are

also minimal. . . . The text does deal with some controversial subjects such as abortion and homosexuality and one could conclude that the authors espouse or condone certain unpopular views regarding these subjects. In my view it is clear that these books are not obscene under the law of Maryland. The dominant theme of the material taken as a whole does not appeal to a prurient interest in sex. . . . There is much contained in each volume that has significant social value. . . . Since the books are not obscene in my view, the distribution is not a crime. Another issue presented is whether a public library should offer these books for loan and to whom. This is both a political question and a first amendment censorship question not for the State's Attorney for Prince George's to decide.[20]

Based on Mr. Orenstein's review, State's Attorney Marshall wrote to Beth Trotto, nominal leader of the Coalition for Children, assuring her that the distribution of *Our Bodies, Ourselves* did not violate the obscenity laws and that decisions on its use in the public library system were up to the county executive.

By now, William Gordon, Director of the Prince George's County library system, had been informed of the growing controversy, and on September 21, 1977, he sent a memo to the library board members, warning,

Mr. Kelly is understandably concerned about C. Paul's threat to read portions of the book at the Town Meeting scheduled for September 28. We will work with Mr. Kelly's office to attempt to avoid a public confrontation. . . . In any event, I am sending selected staff members to the Town Meeting. They will be prepared to defend the selection of the book, and advise those who wish to submit complaints that a routing for such complaints has been established.[21]

Gordon recently looked back on the origins of this bookbanning struggle:

The main challenge was directed toward *Our Bodies, Ourselves*, but growing from that were complaints about *all* the Norma Klein books and *all* the Judy Blume books. The controversy grew through the activities of an organization headed by a woman named Beth Trotto. It was called Coalition for Children, the sort of name that would make people feel cozy and good. The organization was formed to see to it that *Our Bodies, Ourselves* and other "objectionable" material was removed from the library.[22]

On October 13, 1977, two county councilmen wrote to the president of the board of library trustees to protest *Our Bodies, Ourselves*, expressing their strong objection to making the book available to county youngsters. The councilmen claimed that most adults would consider the book objectionable and would indeed find portions of it thoroughly disgusting. They declined to quote any particular passages from the book in order to spare their secretary the indignity of typing the material. The councilmen then urged the board to investigate the appropriateness of placing the book in county libraries.

A prompt response from the board of trustees described the library's selection policy and its reevaluation procedure, already under way as the result of Ms. Paul's written complaint. Further problems or inquiries were to be referred to William Gordon, director of the library system. But the threatened town meeting confrontation occurred nonetheless. At two consecutive town meetings, complaints were voiced about a number of books in the county libraries, and Gordon discussed the matter face-to-face with Beth Trotto.

In the meantime, the widely circulated *Newsletter* of the Coalition for Children had printed isolated quotes from *Our Bodies, Ourselves*, which, taken out of context, caused more members of the community to complain to William Gordon. In his written response to these people, Gordon explained the exhaustive research done by his staff to verify the book's objectivity and medical authority. He urged parents to continue to exercise responsibility over their own children, but said the library must provide information for a multiplicity of interests.

On December 2, County Executive Kelly wrote to William Gordon, asking him to "personally review" *Our Bodies, Ourselves* for appropriateness in the libraries. Gordon formed an Ad Hoc Reconsideration Committee to examine the book, asking its members to be "as objective as possible and approach your review as though you were considering it for the first time." The committee subsequently delivered a positive evaluation of the book to Gordon, who then wrote County Executive Kelly to express his official judgment. In his letter to Kelly, Gordon said that he had carefully reviewed and approved *Our Bodies, Ourselves* several years earlier when working at another library. He noted that *Our Bodies, Ourselves* had been available and in use in the Prince George's County libraries for over four years, with no complaints until now. Gordon concluded:

Now that I have re-examined the book word-for-word, I can only say that my attitudes toward it are unwavering, and that I support its being available in the young adult and adult sections of the library. *Our Bodies, Ourselves* is not sensational; it does not appeal to one's prurient interest. It is a straightforward presentation which deals with the physical and sexual realities of the female body. Any information about human sexuality is going to offend someone. For too long, the tendency has been to withdraw from making sexual information available, particularly to young people who, during their developmental years, are most desperately in need of such information. . . . But it is in opposition to our philosophy that freedom of access to information is basic to public library service.[23]

Gordon enclosed a letter from Dr. Murray M. Kappelman of the University of Maryland School of Medicine, attesting to the medical accuracy of the book. He also attached the American Library Association's 1976 list of best books for young adults, on which *Our Bodies, Ourselves* appeared.

But the dispute was not yet resolved. On January 19, 1978, Councilman Casula wrote to Mrs. Lucille Zugay, president of the board of library trustees, asking that *Our Bodies, Ourselves* and other "adult" materials in the library's collections be physically sequestered so that younger persons could not browse through them. Mrs. Zugay wrote Councilman Casula that it would be awkward logistically to restrict physical movement from one section of the library to another. She said it would be difficult for her to accept any suggestion that the library "lock up" certain materials to restrict their use, because such restrictions would stand in the way of general access and freedom of information. Zugay emphasized the parental responsibility to guide a child's reading, noting that if the library refused information to a child whose parents had approved access to the information, the library would have failed that child. She said the reverse was also true, confirming the importance of the parent in guiding a child's reading, whether it is done at home or in a library. Zugay concluded that it was impossible to expect library personnel to police the reading that people do in the library.

In January 1978, Beth Trotto's Coalition for Children began to recruit political support for a campaign against local bookstores, and Ms. Trotto's organization was soon able to to persuade the county council to introduce legislation concerning "obscene reading matter," not just in bookstores, but in libraries as well. That initiative received considerable media attention. County Bill 42 (1978), entitled "An Act concerning Obscene Matter," would have made it

unlawful for any person knowingly to sell or loan to a juvenile, or to display in a manner whereby juveniles can or may examine, peruse or otherwise view any picture, photograph, drawing or other graphic . . . image of a person or portion of the human body which depicts nudity, sexual conduct, sexual excitement or sadomasochistic abuse and which is predominantly harmful or potentially harmful to juveniles.[24]

When the bill was initially proposed, William Gordon warned that the law, if strictly interpreted, would ban from public display any art books that depict nudes, as well as some health books, encyclopedia volumes, magazines like the *National Geographic*, or even the *Smithsonian* or *Sports Illustrated*. He told the *Prince George's Journal*, "We're concerned about how this law could be interpreted. It makes no distinction as to the type of book."[25]

When the bill was introduced, Gordon expressed his concern. "It would be extremely difficult for us to operate effectively [with this bill]," he said. "The law is so broad in definition it would restrict access to a substantial part of our collection to people under 18." Gordon said the law could also affect the thirty-five students, called "pages," employed by the public libraries. "If the bill were to pass in its present form," said Gordon, "the library board would have to meet to decide what to do about the pages, and about parts of our collection."[26] Gordon predicted that even the less controversial books purchased for the county libraries would fall prey to the new law, noting that "nearly every publication selected, even with the elaborate set of criteria, is going to offend someone, whether it's on the basis of religion, philosophy or sex. We attempt to fulfil the needs and wishes of over 600,000 people." Gordon warned that if a child checked out a book on home medicine and his mother discovered that it had a drawing of the female reproductive system, the proposed bill would leave the library open to a lawsuit.[27]

County council member Francis Francois insisted that the concerns raised by librarians and teachers were "simply not valid issues." He acknowledged, however, that the bill was "confused" and would probably be further amended. As written, the bill would have prevented doctors and nurses from handing out to juveniles anything classified as obscene, but Francois said the Council would discuss exempting the doctors and nurses, as well as schools and libraries. He was confident that people could "tell what is bad and what is good. This is the kind of bill that requires a lot of common sense to administer."[28]

The bill came under attack by county librarians and teachers. Toby Rich, president of the Prince George's County Educators Association, said it amounted to bookburning. He explained that the county schools already had procedures by which to decide the books to be used by students, and the teachers objected to allowing the council to decree what materials may be used by the public.

Gordon told me:

> We understood that the penalties would apply to the Head of the library personally, or that it could apply to the library's public service staff individually. The first thing we were able to accomplish was a change to the bill, adding a clause excluding from the penalties any person operating or employed by any public or research library. . . . Even then, we opposed the bill. The legislation was eventually defeated, but it was not an easy process. We sent out information to some of the library's customers in an attempt to rally them around the issue and to write their legislators. Ms. Trotto's organization charged that we had used public money to oppose the county legislation. We had not, but we had failed to indicate on our fliers and informational materials that the items were being paid for with private money, not tax money. That created a great furor.

Gordon attended a hearing on the bill in the county council chambers, but he told me:

> I did not testify against the bill at that hearing. Our interests were so vested, we believed at that point that testimony from me, or from a library board member for that matter, would not be as effective as testimony from residents of the community. We had solicited testimony from people who were informal friends of the library, people whom we knew were library users. Only four of them were allowed to testify, but when the chairman of the County Council asked for a show of hands from the audience, many people raised their hands against the bill. On the other side, all who spoke in support of the bill were from Beth Trotto's group, and they probably did as much to damage their case as anything. They proclaimed that God had spoken to them and told them to testify. One woman had seen a vision while she was eating her oatmeal, telling her that she should testify. But Beth Trotto was very articulate and effective. She was absolutely superb, and frankly that gave us some concern.
>
> Fortunately, the anti-pornography bill was defeated in its entirety, amendments and all. The struggle had gone on for about a year and a half, and eventually the bookbanners simply wore out. The defeat of the legislation was really the benchmark of when their activity dramatically began to decline. Mrs. Trotto did not go away. She took up other campaigns dealing with censorship. She hassled the board of education over similar censorship issues for a very long time afterwards, and appeared regularly at the board's media center, complaining about school materials. But after the legislation was defeated, even she pulled back from the harassment of public libraries. She regarded me as a problem and knew that I was in some respects vulnerable, because I had only been Director here since April 1977. I had not really developed the kind of base that one needs to respond quickly and effectively to censorship pressure. During that period, Winfield Kelly was the County Executive, and he held regular Town Meetings throughout Prince George's County. Mrs. Trotto's group would appear at every one of those meetings for more than a year, and they would lay on each seat copies of excerpts from *Our Bodies, Ourselves*. The excerpts were chosen, as you can imagine, such that the audience would become very upset.

I asked Gordon if he had changed any of the library's policies as the result of this extended bookbanning incident. "No, we didn't," he said.

> We already had in place, and still do, a policy that some libraries may not agree with. That is, we have a parental consent clause on our library card, authorizing children to have access to all of our collections. The parent has to be proactive in the process of acquiring a child's library card. The child's card is valid anywhere in the library, unless the parent takes action to restrict it. We believe that parents want some supervision over what their children view or read. Of course, we also have a book selection policy.

That's critical for institutional buying. We feel censorship should not play a role in selection, but there is a fine line between censorship and selection in the minds of many, because choices must be made. Choosing between book A and book B can be terribly difficult, particularly on a tight budget. But we believe when we choose not to buy a book, it's because it does not meet the standards established in our selection policy.

Gordon described the bureaucratic pressure a public library director feels when community pressure groups attempt to impose censorship. "I report to a library board," said Gordon.

Whatever actions we take have to be justified to the board, which can function as a voice for the community. We didn't have any trouble with the library board during the controversy with Mrs. Trotto. They were very supportive, and that was very important to us. The kind of people who apply to be members of the library board tend to have an understanding of the issue of censorship. I never felt caught in the middle, never felt pressure there. The next level above is the County Council and the County Executive, the legislative and executive branches of the county government. They made no demands on the library to remove the challenged materials. What they really wanted was for this problem to simply *go away*. It was an election year and people were running for office, and they did not want a library book that talks about female masturbation to be the pivotal point on which their success as candidates would rest. So I was expected to make this thing go away, however that might be accomplished. If that meant taking the book off the shelf, so be it. Of course, none of them came out in favor of censorship.

But what are the appropriate limits of community control over public library collections? To what degree must public librarians respond to the loudest voices in the community? Gordon said:

Libraries, particularly of this size, do not bend very easily to these strident demands. We are more likely to fight the necessary battle. I've been in smaller settings where we have dealt with vaguely similar situations, but none where the group was so well organized. I don't believe that public libraries give in to the demands of the censors, but the director becomes involved in a kind of political whirlwind that has to be played out very carefully. You've got to try to see that no elected official gets hurt or blamed. You've got to be sure that your board of trustees doesn't get hurt or blamed, and that your staff comes out feeling that, without bending, you have been supportive of them and at the same time you have somehow generally met the grievances of the community. Public librarians must still exercise professional discretion in these matters. I believe in a very strong exercise of professional judgment, but you certainly don't ignore the politics or demographics of the community. The demographics are important in collection development, but that does not mean that censorship is appropriate to collection development.

A decade and a half after the furor over *Our Bodies, Ourselves*, Bill Gordon assessed today's pressures for censorship in the Prince George's County Public Library:

> We have a regular trickle of complaints or challenges. Not a stream, but a trickle. So far we have been able to resolve them. . . . With respect to books, the kind about which we now receive the greatest number of complaints are the books about witches and goblins and the like . . . , and we have lots of them. It seems the devil is lurking behind every bush and under every stone.

HAWKINS COUNTY, TENNESSEE: MY WAY OR THE HIGHWAY

The 1983 edition of the *Basic Reading* series, published by Holt, Rinehart and Winston for use in grades K through 8, differed very little in content from the previous editions, but it used a new approach, teaching reading, writing, spelling, and language as a unified language arts program. In late 1982, Tennessee's State Textbook Committee, consisting of five elementary school teachers and five middle school teachers, had formally recommended the 1983 edition of the Holt series to the Hawkins County School Board for adoption at the beginning of the following year. The new Holt readers replaced eleven-year-old readers.

In late August 1983, Vicki Frost's oldest daughter asked for her mother's help in answering questions at the end of a story in the Holt series. Mrs. Frost noticed a mention of mental telepathy, which she considered contrary to her religious beliefs. To Frost, a devout fundamentalist, such mental powers belong to God alone, and attempting to share them suggests that man is aspiring to rule the world apart from God. Indeed, Frost regarded any use of fantasy or imagination as a temptation that could lead a Christian away from biblical truths. Frost was also concerned that any communication without language barriers could contaminate Americans with foreign ideas or, even worse, lead to global unity, one-world government, the end of the free enterprise system and America's prosperity.

Frost examined the other textbooks used by her children in the first, second, and seventh grades, and concluded that none of these Holt readers fostered American Christian values like patriotism and the American family. She was disturbed that the books spoke of minorities, foreigners, environmentalism, and women in nontraditional roles.

Soon afterward, she contacted Bill Snodgrass, the county school supervisor, who suggested that perhaps the offending stories could be excised, but Frost did not consider that an acceptable solution. She called Jay Salley, principal at the Church Hill Middle School, and requested a meeting with interested parents, teachers, and school officials to air her concerns. That meeting, held on September 1, 1983, was the first public discussion of the dispute, at which Frost and others warned of an educational conspiracy, beginning with John Dewey, that was destroying the parents' role in raising their children. In particular, Frost charged that the Holt readers were promoting idolatry, demon worship, gun control, evolution, and feminism while opposing free enterprise, the military, lawful authority, and Christianity.

About a week later, Frost called Mel Gabler, the famous textbook protest leader based in Longview, Texas. Soon the Hawkins County parents were receiving literature from the Gablers indicating that the Holt series had not been approved by the Gablers' organization. The Gablers' *Parental Guide to Combat the Religion of Secular Humanism in the Schools* warned: "As long as the schools continue to teach ABNORMAL ATTITUDES and ALIEN THOUGHTS, we caution parents NOT to urge their children to pursue high grades or class discussion, because the harder students work, the greater their chance of brain washing."[29] These organizational materials were subsequently shared with school officials and others in Hawkins County, giving the impression that the local protest was in fact under the influence and direction of the Gablers.

Early in the the textbook dispute, Vicki Frost was the chief spokesperson for the complaining parents. She identified herself as "born again" and a "fundamentalist Christian," explaining that her faith extended beyond her home and church into the school. Frost and other protesting parents officially presented their objections at the September 8, 1983, meeting of the school board, which had unanimously adopted the Holt series four months earlier. Now the board heard claims that the texts taught telepathy, witchcraft, black magic, sorcery, astrology, Hinduism, and Shintoism. The charge was also made that the Holt series taught children to use mind control over their parents. Mrs. Frost asked that the books be removed and replaced with texts that do not teach these concepts and religions. The discussion was concluded when board chairman Harold Silvers stated that because the Holt series had been selected by a committee of teachers and unanimously approved by the board, it would be taught in Hawkins County schools until either the State Department of Education or the courts prohibited it.

After failing to convince the school board to ban the Holt readers, Frost went to see Jay Salley, principal of Church Hill Middle School, where two of her children were students. As the result of that meeting, Frost and several other parents were allowed to use alternate readers acceptable to them. These alternative reading arrangements may have seemed like a reasonable compromise, but they conflicted with the state's obligation to teach reading effectively. For one thing, the alternative readers were twenty-five years old, providing a very narrow and dated glimpse of American culture. In addition, the children using these readers were from different grades and had their reading classes at different times. They spent their time in isolation, reading stories and answering assigned questions. These children were supervised by any adult who happened to be in the area, including cafeteria workers. But their parents were satisfied, so long as their children did not read the Holt books.

On September 22, 1983, the *Rogersville Review* printed a large advertisement stating the religous and social beliefs of an organization identified as Citizens Organized for Better Schools (COBS). Local citizen Bob Mozert was soon revealed to be the director of COBS, and under that title, Mozert began submitting "Letters to the Editor" each week. In these letters he "reviewed" various volumes from the Holt series, claiming that his reviews would better inform the taxpayers and parents in the area about the corruption of public education. In the October 6 issue, a letter appeared as part of Mozert's review series, complaining about *The Three Little Pigs* and *Goldilocks*, as presented in the Holt readers. In that letter, Mozert complained that punishment was meted out in *The Three Little Pigs* without a crime being committed. Even worse, in *Goldilocks* the little girl commits the crime of trespassing on the private property of the three bears, yet she is not punished. This, claimed Mozert, was a deliberate attempt to preach "secular humanism" to impressionable minds.

As the result of the Goldilocks letter, the fundamentalist parents became the target of considerable public ridicule. In a letter to the *Kingport Times-News*, the principal of the Valley Elementary School mocked the parents' objections to "Satan-oriented" stories such as *The Three Little Pigs* and *Goldilocks*.

County School Superintendent Bill Snodgrass complained that such "narrow thinking" was tearing up a good school system. "I think they are too far right of center for Hawkins County people," he said. "Most of the people here are moderate conservatives. I don't think you're going to turn Hawkins County folks against the three pigs and the three bears."[30]

The national media soon discovered the Hawkins County dispute. A *USA Today* editorial began, "Goldilocks is on trial in Greenville, Tennessee. So are the three little pigs, Jack and Jill, and a little boy who cooks. . . . What have they got against Goldilocks? Well, she didn't go to the slammer for breaking and entering. What's wrong with *The Three Little Pigs*? Well, dancing around a kettle promotes witchcraft. And the jollity of Jack and Jill suggests satanism, and the lad who cooks advances feminism. That's so ridiculous it's hard to take seriously."[31]

In a letter to a local newspaper, Mozert defined *secular humanism* as a "lethal religion" that denies God and morality by endorsing evolution, self-authority, situation ethics, distorted realism, sexual permissiveness, anti-Biblical bias, anti–free enterprise, one-world government, and death education. Mozert presented new demands at the October 13 school board meeting, including a mandatory moment of silence in the schools, a mandatory Pledge of Allegiance, and a dress code. The board took the demands under advisement and formed a committee to look into them. At the November 10 school board meeting, the board declared that teachers must use only textbooks approved by the board of education, ruling out any future assignment of alternative reading materials. Board members expressed the belief that anything other than a uniform textbook would place an undue burden on the schools, their teachers, and students. Middle school principal Jay Salley then met with the protesting parents and made clear that no student would be allowed to use any reader other than the Holt series. The next day, several students were suspended from school for three days when they refused to attend reading class or read the Holt books. Upon their return to school, the students still refused to use the Holt readers, and Salley suspended them for another ten days.

Vicki Frost had planned to take over her daughter Sarah's reading instruction by removing her child from class each day and taking her to another part of the school building. Principal Jean Price told Frost that she was not allowed to teach reading on school property, but Frost nonetheless went to Sarah's reading class, removed her, and took her to the school cafeteria. When Principal Price once more told Frost that she would have to leave the premises, the mother and daughter simply relocated outside the building but still on school property. When Frost returned the next day, she was ordered to leave the school grounds. When she refused, a police officer read her the trespassing law and took her into custody. Frost was subsequently released on her own recognizance but was told to stay away from the school until the matter came up for trial.

Around this same time, conservative religious groups nationwide were complaining that Supreme Court decisions had introduced secularism and humanism to the schools, threatening the social values associated with religious faith. Moral Majority cofounder Tim LaHaye charged that the public schools had exposed American youth to atheism, evolution, amorality, human autonomy, and a socialist one-world concept. LaHaye's wife Beverly, who headed Concerned Women for America (CWA), not only played a significant role in the Hawkins County textbook controversy but simultaneously initiated a federal lawsuit—*Grove v. Mead School District No. 354*—over a similar textbook controversy in Washington State (see Chapter 2). The district court dismissed the case, and the dismissal was upheld on appeal, largely because the child had not been compelled to read the disputed book. Because the Hawkins County schools *were* requiring students to use the Holt readers, CWA had high hopes for victory in *Mozert* v. *Hawkins County*.

Hawkins Countian David Wilson was a typical spokesperson for the local opponents of the Holt books.

> [T]he textbooks promote equal rights for women. . . . They promote peaceful coexistence between nations. . . . They are pro-gun control. . . . [T]hose are some of the social values that are promoted in the textbooks. And those values are not values that are held by Hawkins Countians. . . . Religious values involved in the textbooks promote a[n] understanding of other people involved in other religious beliefs from other cultures. . . . But when it comes to Baptists accepting the religious beliefs of Islamic people or Buddhists, that is beyond the value system of rural East Tennessee.[32]

But a large majority of Hawkins County residents supported the school board and its choice of the textbook series. Hawkins County is overwhelmingly white, native Tennessean, conservative Republican, and strongly Baptist. The teachers, school administrators, and members of the school board were seen as trustees of the local culture. One mother wrote to the *Kingsport Times-News*, saying she had read the Holt books and found nothing that was humanistic, feminist, or self-authoritative. Branding COBS as a bunch of fanatical troublemakers, she told them that if they didn't like the local public schools, they should take their chidren out and go elsewhere. She concluded by warning COBS to keep their fanatical beliefs within their own group and stay out of her children's education.

School board member Conley Bailey had a similar view: "I think that COBS is trying to dictate education regardless of textbooks or anything else. If textbooks were not the issue, they'd bring up something else." He claimed, "Every tactic they've used so far has come out of Longview, Texas."[33]

On December 2, Jean Price sent a letter to the parents of all children at her school, asking them to attend a meeting to counter the COBS demands. In her letter, Price said: "As principal of your school and a mother, I now feel that we must stand for your child's rights. It is not appropriate for a few local people controlled by outside sources to try to impose their beliefs on all, and be allowed to disrupt the education of our boys and girls in Church Hill."[34] Price also announced the formation of a support organization, Citizens Advocating the Right to Education (CARE), which was to become the voice for the anticensors against COBS. CARE distributed a written declaration opposing the disruptive tactics of COBS and the censorship attempts of a fanatical minority.

Almost 1,000 people met at the December 1983 CARE rally. Speakers included Jean Price, School Board Chairman Harold Silvers, and School Superintendent Bill Snodgrass, who characterized the protesters as extremists, outsiders, and a threat to local institutions. Snodgrass said:

> My message to extremists groups is to become a carpenter and help us build a great school system. If you cannot do this and insist on being a wrecking crew, take your unsound ideas to Washington, D.C . . . or Longview, Texas. The right to have challenging and interesting material must not be taken away by outside agitators with their fat wallets and attorneys from Washington, D.C.[35]

On December 2, 1983, Robert and Alice Mozert, represented by the national conservative organization Concerned Women for America (CWA), filed suit in federal district court seeking injunctive relief and money damages for the alleged violation of their First Amendment right to free exercise of religion. Mozert, Frost, and the others claimed that the Holt series violated their religious beliefs, promoted the breakdown of the family and the denial of the primacy of Christ, and advocated a one-world government.

Mozert v. *Hawkins County Public Schools* was assigned to Federal District Judge Thomas G. Hull and was heard without a jury. Though the protesters had originally attempted to remove the Holt books totally from the public schools, the plaintiffs now chose to focus on the need for alternative readers for their children. In February and March 1984, Judge Hull dismissed eight of the plaintiffs' nine complaints, including allegations that the Holt readers promoted disrespect for parents, the Bible, and Jesus Christ, and that it advocated witchcraft, situational ethics, idol worship, humanistic values, and evolution. The one complaint that Hull said should be examined in court was the claim that the Holt books teach that any faith in the supernatural is an acceptable means to salvation.

In their replies to Judge Hull's ruling, the plaintiffs insisted that mere exposure to the ideas in the Holt books was a violation of their First Amendment rights, whereas the school authorities argued that leaving children ignorant of and hostile to any ideas outside of a single religious group was not proper education. After reading the briefs submitted by CWA and PAW, Judge Hull dismissed the case without trial, saying the Holt books presented religion in a "neutral" manner and were well calculated to equip today's children to face our diverse society with sophistication and tolerance. The plaintiffs immediately appealed, and in July 1985, the Sixth Circuit Court of Appeals ordered Judge Hull to try the case. The appeals court instructed Hull to determine whether the mandatory use of the Holt books violated the plaintiffs' religious rights and, if so, whether there was any compelling state interest to justify that burden. Accordingly, the plaintiffs tried to convince Judge Hull that the Holt readers promoted the religion of secular humanism and that reading the books violated their own religion.

In their pretrial depositions, the plaintiffs presented more than 400 objections to the Holt readers, many of them relating to the books' inadequate patriotism. Any criticism of America's founders, its policies, or its history would allegedly offend God and promote a communist invasion by discouraging young boys from fighting for their country. According to the plaintiffs, war was God's way of vindicating the righteous and punishing the wicked. The protesters regarded kindness to animals as another form of support for diversity, which could lead to religious tolerance, world unity, the reign of the anti-Christ, and the destruction of the world. An empathy toward animals could also soften children, discouraging hunting, war, and violence in general.

The plaintiffs attacked everything in the Holt readers that could conceivably relate to world unity, nontraditional gender roles, family democracy, moral relativity, the brotherhood of man, nonreligious views of death, imagination, reason, neutral descriptions of religion, socialism, social protest, magic, environmentalism, kindness towards animals, vegetarianism, fear of nuclear war, disarmament, or gun control. They did not want Hispanics to be mentioned in schoolbooks, because most Hispanics are Catholic and Catholics are not real Christians. They opposed stories that discussed poverty or social justice, claiming that the poor and unemployed were simply lazy. They challenged *The Wizard of Oz* because it promoted self-reliance and personal responsibility. The Lion wanted courage, the Tin Man wanted a heart, and the Scarecrow wanted brains, but none of them prayed to God. *The Wizard of Oz* thus promoted secular humanism by suggesting that goodness and salvation can be acquired through human effort. It also promoted Satanism by showing a good witch Glenda.

The school board rebutted such arguments, and noted that the state had a compelling interest to teach children to read, to uphold the authority of school officials, and to avoid the expense of alternative reading programs. The school authorities noted that the Supreme Court had repeatedly ruled that public education cannot function in a pluralistic society if it must avoid all information and ideas that might be offensive to any religion.

On October 24, 1986, to the surprise of all who followed the case, Judge Hull ruled in favor of the plaintiffs, focusing on their demand that they not be forced to choose between their religious beliefs and a free public education. He ruled that the state's obligation to teach children to read did not require that all children read the same books. He therefore ruled that the plaintiffs could teach reading to their children at home, while their children would continue to participate in the rest of the school curriculum. Hull did caution that his ruling did not require the school system to make alternative reading arrangements to any other persons or to these plaintiffs for any other subject. By this time the children who were involved in the suit had transferred to private schools, where they intended to remain, and Hull ruled that the plaintiffs were entitled to reimbursement for that expense and for lost wages during the trial.

The school board promptly appealed Hull's decision, claiming that home schooling would encourage religious divisiveness. They also questioned whether Hull's ruling could be restricted to one school subject and one group of parents. On August 24, 1987, the Sixth Circuit Court of Appeals overturned Hull's ruling by a 3–0 vote, with each judge addressing a different aspect of the case. Writing for the court, Judge Pierce Lively stated:

> The only conduct compelled by the defendants was reading and discussing the material in the Holt series, and hearing other students' interpretations of those materials. This is the exposure to which the plaintiffs objected. What is absent from this case is the critical element of compulsion to affirm or deny a religious belief or to engage or refrain from engaging in a practice forbidden or required in the exercise of a plaintiff's religion.

Lively rejected the claim that certain ideas were being inculcated rather than simply being mentioned in the books. He stated: "The plaintiffs did not produce a single student or teacher to testify that any student was ever required to affirm his or her belief or disbelief in any idea or practice mentioned in the various stories and passages contained in the Holt series."[36] Lively concluded that the plaintiffs' definition of religion was too broad to be accomodated within the public schools.

Judge Cornelia Kennedy agreed with Lively that reading the Holt books did not violate the plaintiffs' religious rights, but she said, in any case, there was an overriding state interest in teaching children to draw conclusions, express opinions, and deal with complex and controversial social and moral issues. Kennedy also said the state had a compelling interest in promoting cohesion among a heterogeneous democratic people, something that could not be accomplished through religious segregation. The third member of the appeals court panel, Judge Danny Boggs, accepted the board's overriding authority to forbid the use of alternative readers, basing his ruling entirely on a school board's right to control the curriculum.

The appeals court's reversal of Judge Hull's ruling dismissed the plaintiffs' complaint, leaving the Hawkins County School Board free to forbid alternative reading instruction and removing any obligation to compensate the protesters. On December 5, 1988, the U.S. Supreme Court denied certiorari on the last of Mozert's two appeals, effectively ending the attempt to ban the Holt readers. The plaintiffs petitioned the Supreme Court to hear the case, but their petition was denied.

On the surface, *Mozert* represented a defeat for fundamentalist attempts to censor textbooks, but on closer view, the repercussions of the case are disturbing. Keith Waldman in the *Rutgers Law Journal* compared the 1983 and 1986 editions of the Holt books and found that passages opposed by the *Mozert* plaintiffs had been removed from the 1986 edition. For example, a reference to the humanistic ideals of the Declaration of Independence was no longer in the 1986 edition. In her book, *What Johnny Shouldn't Read*, Joan DelFattore observed:

> If the *Mozert* plaintiffs' children attend public school, they now have to read the books school officials select. School officials, however, have to choose from what is on the market; . . . Since the textbooks produced by America's largest publishers were more in keeping with the Gablers' beliefs in 1986 than they were in 1980, it is not at all clear that the *Mozert* plaintiffs were on the losing side.[37]

GRAVES COUNTY: KENTUCKY-FRIED FAULKNER

Graves County, Kentucky, four hours from Louisville, has a population of about 30,000 people. A third of them live in Mayfield, the county seat, where the county school board administers a single school, the Graves County High School. In late August 1986, sixteen-year-old Chris Hill returned from school and told his mother that he was being asked to read a book on reincarnation. The boy's mother, LaDone Hill, read the book, William Faulkner's *As I Lay Dying*, and concluded that it was an example of "secular humanism." At first, Mrs. Hill accepted the school's offer to assign a different book, *Moby Dick*, to her son, but after deciding that the other students required protection from Faulkner's dangerous novel, she complained to a school board member, Johnny Shelton.

In early September 1986, as the Graves County School Board was concluding its regular monthly meeting, chairman Jeff Howard asked if there was any other business. Board member Johnny Shelton held up a paperback book and demanded to know why it was being taught at Graves County High School. In addition to the five board members, the board room contained Superintendent of Schools Billy Watkins, school board attorney Dan Sharp, high school principal Jerald Ellington, several local media representatives, and a few spectators. They watched as Shelton waved a copy of William Faulkner's *As I Lay Dying*, pointing to passages that he had highlighted with a yellow marker.

"This is the kind of book you'd pick up in a backways place and read," said Shelton. He held the book in front of Jerald Ellington, the principal of Graves County High School, and demanded that he read some of the underlined passages out loud. Principal Ellington tried to decline, but Shelton insisted. Finally Ellington shrugged, took the book, and turned to one of the highlighted passages. He read aloud from the words of one of Faulkner's characters, the son of a dying woman: "If there is a God, what the hell is he for?" Ellington continued to leaf through the book, reading aloud any passage marked in yellow. Some of the passages referred to God, or to abortion, and some used curse words like "bastard," "goddamn," or "son of a bitch." Ellington found nothing wrong in Faulkner's words when he read them aloud. He told the board that his teachers did not necessarily condone some of the language in the book, but that it had to be seen in the context of the character's personality. Ellington also explained to the board how the high school selected its books, following the recommendations of the American Library Association. But the board was disdainful of such niceties.[38]

The meeting room was suddenly alive with tension. Principal Ellington realized that by reading the passages aloud he had ignited the emotions of the board members. He tried to defuse the situation by explaining that a review procedure existed that allowed administrators and parents to express their opinions and if necessary, appeal to the superintendent and the board of education. And parents always had the right to request that a different book be assigned to their children. Ellington warned that none of this procedure had been followed in this case, and the board was therefore encroaching on First Amendment rights. The board was unimpressed. Bob Spaulding declared that it was wrong to ban the sale of "pornography" while teaching it in the schools. Another board member, ignoring Ellington's caution, stood up, pointed his finger at the principal, and demanded that the book be removed from the shelves by the next day. A motion was made that William Faulkner's *As I Lay Dying* be banned from the Graves County High School. The Board voted unanimously in favor of the motion, the meeting was adjourned, and Ellington subsequently had the book removed from the school and its library.

None of the board members had read the book, though a few said they had thumbed through it. Dan Sharp, the school board attorney, estimates that the school board's discussion of Faulkner's book lasted about five minutes.

> The board member who brought this up very definitely caught everyone by surprise. He said, "I want it banned, I want it out of this school, trash and filth, let's have a vote on it." Without much discussion at all, the motion was passed unanimously, and I was kind of scratching my head about it. It happened so fast I'm not sure everyone realized the significance.[39]

Lonnie Harp, a reporter for the *Mayfield Messenger*, was present at the board meeting, and he recalls that there was no discussion of the merits of the book or why it was used in the high school. The board's vote was taken so fast that the reporters present were not sure what had occured. Harp examined Johnny Shelton's copy of the book and wrote down the seven or eight passages highlighted in yellow ink, all of them dialogue. Harp recalls, "At that point we—the radio reporters and I—said to ourselves, *They've just banned a book!* We knew it would be big news."[40]

On the morning after the board's vote, the Mayfield radio station, whose reporters had attended the board meeting, opened its seven o'clock news show with a description of the bookbanning. The story was repeated on the local news each hour thereafter, and it soon was carried nationally on the Associated Press (AP) wire.

Mike Turley, editor of the *Mayfield Messenger*, said the school board's action caught him by surprise. He ran the story on the bookbanning the next day, no larger than a normal school board story would be, but he led with the headline "County Bans Faulkner Book." When reporter Lonnie Harp began work on his story of the bookbanning, he telephoned Principal Ellington, who told him he was very disappointed that the board didn't follow "appropriate channels" in removing the book. Ellington pointed out, "A sentence or paragraph out of about every book in print can be taken out of context." Harp then called Delora English, the teacher in whose class *As I Lay Dying* had been assigned. English had been forced to retrieve all thirty-three copies of the book from her sophomore students. She defended the book, saying it was a fine example of "stream of consciousness" literature and something that her students should read. She concluded firmly that discussions on the book would begin in her class the following week.[41]

The bookbanning had a devastating effect on the teachers involved. The English Department consisted of twelve people, most of them Sunday school teachers, and one of them a minister. Delora English, the teacher most directly involved in the book dispute, took it very personally when the chairman of the school board criticized her judgment in using *As I Lay Dying*. The entire department felt abandoned by the school board. Ellington said he felt caught in the middle as he tried to hold his faculty together. He met with them and told them that he supported them 100 percent, and that he was not going to side with the board. School Superintendent Billy Watkins called Dan Sharp, the board's attorney, to express his concern and ask for advice. Sharp told him that there were First Amendment questions involved, matters of free speech and censorship that could become embarrassing.

Johnny Shelton, the board member who had proposed the book ban, held to his position. "The book may be literature, but there's some literature you use on the street about midnight," said Shelton. "We don't allow students to use that language in school and then we give them that stuff to read."[42] A reporter from the *Paducah Sun* called school board chairman Jeff Howard, who admitted that he had read "only portions" of the book and didn't know if other board members had read it. Still, he didn't think the book should be required reading. "God's name is used in vain in several places," he said. "In there, a young girl goes to a so-called doctor to get an abortion. . . . We had hoped the teacher would select a book more appropriate for the sophomore class." The *Paducah Sun* newsroom then called Bob Spaulding, who had seconded the motion to ban Faulkner's book. "There's a lot better literature for students to read than to learn how to curse," Spaulding said. He admitted he had not read *As I Lay Dying*, but said his own daughter had been assigned the book the year before. "It just didn't make sense to her why she should have to study it," he said, describing his daughter's discomfort with both the language and content of the book. He added that none of his five children were allowed to read the book.[43]

When Suzanne Post, director of the Kentucky branch of the American Civil Liberties Union, heard of the Mayfield bookbanning, she commented, "This one is pretty extreme. We rarely get a Nobel prize winner thrown out of a public school."[44] Ironically, her major area of study in graduate school had been the work of William Faulkner. She told the *Paducah Sun* that the board's action was "certainly an infringement on academic freedom and probably is unconstitutional." Claiming that the board was "on some thin ice," she added, "I would hope that a school board would have more respect for issues that involve academic freedom."[45]

Elwin Abrams of the Kentucky Council of Teachers of English complained that the school board's decision allowed one parent to impose her tastes on all parents. He said the board had acted contrary to "what a free society should be doing. We should be exchanging ideas freely, not banning books."[46]

Two days after the school board vote, LaDone Hill wrote a letter to the *Mayfield Messenger*, identifying herself as the parent who had complained to Johnny Shelton about *As I Lay Dying*. She wrote that her son did not want to read the book because of some of the words in it, and she said she was shocked by its contents. Principal Jerald Ellington had explained to her that her son would be allowed to read an alternative book, but she wanted to protect every child from this blasphemy. She said she wanted to remove *As I Lay Dying* because of her "concern for other students and to make other parents aware of the content of the material in this book and perhaps other books." LaDone Hill placed her full faith and confidence in the board members, characterizing their action as "the hand of God working in a few people." She asked, "Can we not stand without compromise not only regarding this, but also against other things which lower morals, weaken character and usher in secular humanism?"[47]

Simultaneously, more than 200 miles away, Suzanne Post of the ACLU was writing her letter to the Graves County School Board. Post's letter called the board's action unconstitutional, a violation of the First Amendment's guarantees of free expression. Post phoned Lonnie Harp at the *Messenger*, expressing unrestrained indignation. She said the board had followed improper procedures in removing the Faulkner book from the Graves County schools. After formally requesting that the school board rescind its action, she told the *Paducah Sun*:

> We are asking that they rescind their action, which we consider unconstitutional. We have had an outpouring of offers of free legal assistance from a number of well-established attorneys. People are angry about this. Our fear is that if one school district gets away with this, it will have a ripple effect—it will send a message to other thoughtless people.

She said she had sent a copy of the ACLU letter to school board attorney Dan Sharp, who admitted that the school board was "off base."[48]

As the battle escalated in the media, the executive committee of the Graves County Baptist Association held its regular monthly meeting and agreed to set forth in writing its support for the school board's action. Reverend Al Cobb was chosen to write the letter for the association. He had read *As I Lay Dying* and said it was dull, uninteresting, and unworthy of a Nobel Prize. The letter, addressed to the Graves County School Board, commended the board for removing *As I Lay Dying* from the libraries, and concluded: "We urge you to continue to take measures which will safeguard our children from being forced to read and study filthy literature in the classroom."[49]

The editorial in the September 11 *Paducah Sun* began:

> Usually, when we comment on "book-banning" incidents, we take the side of the school board. . . . In the case of the Graves County school board's ban on the novel "As I Lay Dying," however, there's a sad difference. The board wasn't merely deciding not to include some writer's glitzy trash in its list of approved readings. It was denying its students the opportunity to read one of the milestone works of one of the finest writers America has produced. It has denied them, then, a part of their heritage.

The editorial concluded, "It's bewildering to see the book attacked by *a member of the school board* as pornographic. It suggests that the board not only doesn't know what literature is, but it doesn't know what pornography is."[50]

On the evening of September 11, 1986, the Graves County School

Board met once more to determine the fate of *As I Lay Dying*. This time the meeting room was packed with spectators, including at least half a dozen Baptist ministers. When Chairman Jeff Howard called the meeting to order, he described the letters of support the board had received and read into the minutes the letter from the Graves County Baptist Association.

When the agenda reached the item titled "pending or proposed litigation," Chairman Jeff Howard announced that the meeting would now go into closed session. The room was quickly emptied of all but the five board members, attorney Dan Sharp, and school administrators. Sharp immediately addressed the ACLU's letter and the threat of a lawsuit. He explained that by banning *As I Lay Dying*, the school board had challenged the First Amendment. "You are clamping down on what people can read," he said. "You're interfering with the right to free expression." He read from Kentucky law books and demonstrated how other school boards had run afoul of the Constitution. "Unless you provide due process and right of appeal," he explained, "it's going to make trouble." One board member insisted that it was simply "our opinion against theirs." But Sharp replied, "I don't think the ACLU is kidding around. That book should go back on the shelves. All they need is one parent to come forward and agree to be the plaintiff."[51]

The board remained unconvinced. The closed session ended, and the crowd filed back into the meeting room. Superintendent Billy Watkins then offered a compromise. He recommended that the teachers in the Language Arts Department review the books selected for use as assigned reading and that they consider replacing any book that would not serve the best interest of students. He also recommended that a seven-member review committee be established to consider any complaints about the books. Watkins said the committee would first review the Faulkner book and report at the next regular board meeting. All five board members approved the recommendation.

The Graves High School English teachers met on Friday afternoon and decided to stand by their list of approved novels, including *As I Lay Dying*. "We felt we had spent many hours prior to the [board] meeting working on those novels and choosing what we thought were the best," said Alicia Brown, Language Arts Department chair. "We still feel the list intact is in the best interest of our students."[52] The next morning came the first sign that the board might be willing to compromise. Board member Andrew Goodman told Lonnie Harp that he expected the board would go along with whatever the review committee suggested. Even Board Chairman Jeff Howard said that the committee's recommendations would weigh heavily in the board's decision. Attorney Dan Sharp had recommended that the board establish the committee and return the book to the library. "It was not placed back," complained Sharp, who warned that the school board was "constitutionally vulnerable on the issue as it stands right now."[53]

Lonnie Harp recalls that preachers and church types were still anxious to get their moral position on the record. Baptist minister Terry Sims called the Faulkner book pornography. "As a parent, I wouldn't want my daughter reading this book," he said. "I feel like somewhere along the line people have to make a stand against this kind of thing." Minister Ronnie Stinson said, "It's something that if I caught my kid reading out of literature class, I would have to discipline him for it."[54]

Harp described another Baptist preacher, "a moral-majority type," who claimed that he and some of the others saw the bookbanning as a way to step into the limelight and get in front on "the march for decency." Reverend Charles Simmons was particularly anxious to tell the press how distasteful he found As I Lay Dying. "If you hear that type of language, you would associate it with a rough, unruly group that is involved in a more worldly type of life than living a Christian life with the Lord. . . . Not only the Baptists but most all the religious groups would be against the blasphemy in the book where they take the name of the Lord in vain."[55]

But Bridges Holland, a junior high school teacher and minister, questioned whether removing books from the shelves wasn't an "infringement of a person's rights." He warned, "I think it is a very dangerous procedure, because who decides? Where do you draw the line? Are you going to pull out every Faulkner book? Is every book that has a cuss word in it going to be pulled off the shelf?"[56]

When the ACLU's Suzanne Post discovered that despite the board's conciliatory language, As I Lay Dying remained banned from the school library shelves, she described the board's action as "illegitimate, mindless, anti-intellectual, authoritarian and extremely dangerous. . . . Rational people ought to be flying the flags at half mast for the Graves County board of education." Post said the board's action represented a "pre-fascist mindset—the kind of mind set that led to what the Nazis did in Germany."[57]

The Lexington Herald-Leader editorialized that the board's bookbanning was "an excuse in the kind of wanton logic that keeps so many Kentuckians from managing even the reading skills necessary for comic books."[58] Jim Paxton, editor of the Paducah Sun, wrote:

[T]he action by the Graves board was ridiculous. It has already become state-wide news, and newspapers and editorial cartoonists are making a mockery of our region as a result of it. I predict that if the people of Graves County do not yank the board's chain soon, it's going to become national news and a national embarrassment for the state's educational system.[59]

A seventeen-year-old senior at the high school said that the school board wanted to prevent students from reading *As I Lay Dying*, but they would soon discover that the bookban produced the opposite effect. "It is idiotic. You can tell the guy [Johnny Shelton] who proposed it isn't in school. If they tell us we can't read something, everybody is going to read it."[60] Indeed, almost overnight, area bookstores and libraries were deluged with requests. "It's unreal," said a clerk at a local bookstore. "We're getting probably about 20 [requests] a day. Everybody wants to read it and we are sold out."[61] The same heavy demand was seen in the local public libraries, where all copies of the book were on loan, with two or three requests each day.

Juanita Davis Elliott, a local resident, wrote to the Graves County Board of Education asking that the book be returned to the Graves County High School Library and curriculum. She warned that if the board did not lift its ban against *As I Lay Dying*, she would not rule out a suit against the board. "I want to handle it the right way," she explained. "But if they won't put it back, I'll take it from there." She called the book banning "an embarrassment," saying the board "reacted like a bunch of adolescent boys reading dirty words that had been printed on the outhouse wall."[62] Elliott added, "William Faulkner's book is not the main item here. The main item is that [the board members] are messing with our minds and our kids' minds. They are trying to control our minds. People got on boats and came over here a long time ago to get away from that."[63]

The school board decided to call a special meeting for the evening of September 18, 1986, at which time a "superintendents report" was to be presented. Once more, the meeting room was filled to overflowing. Chairman Jeff Howard opened by acknowledging Superintendent Billy Watkins, who began to read a prepared statement. After describing the school's book selection policy, Watkins recommended that the board's action to ban *As I Lay Dying* be rescinded. From the calm response of the board members it was clear that this recommendation had been discussed in advance of the meeting. Board member Andrew Goodman quickly moved that the recommendation be accepted. Robert Spaulding seconded the motion but explained that he had been advised to do so by Dan Sharp and Billy Watkins. He added that his second was not intended to endorse the use of books with foul language.

The board quickly voted 4 to 1 to rescind the banning of *As I Lay Dying*. Only Johnny Shelton voted to continue the ban, saying, "I still stand by what I said before. This hasn't changed my opinion."[64] After the vote, Chairman Jeff Howard read a prepared statement explaining the board's action and reassuring the audience and the media that he was still against indecent literature in schools. "We believed then as we believe now that books containing abusive language not be taught in our school system," stated Howard.

> However, since taking our actions we have been severely criticized by those who seem to feel that children may study any material available, so long as someone says it is valid or beneficial. The criticism does not bother us when we feel we are right. . . . Most significantly we have contacted constitutional lawyers throughout the state of Kentucky who tell us that our actions in excluding the book from our school were ill-advised. For this reason we have serious doubts as to successful litigation. . . . We therefore have made a motion rescinding our previous action taken on September 4 concerning the book "As I Lay Dying." We do feel, however, that our actions have brought attention to the books being taught in our schools. . . . We do believe that literature can be found which passes to our children all the ideas of Western Civilization that do not border on obscenity or in fact are obscene.[65]

The next day, *As I Lay Dying* was returned to the library shelves at Graves County High School, but LaDone Hill, the parent whose complaint initiated the ban, said the battle against the book would continue. "I'm not disappointed," she said, "but in my opinion the Graves County schools stand for better morals than this. I don't see it as being over; it's just starting. God has started moving and the book will come out."[66]

PANAMA CITY, FLORIDA: DARKNESS IN THE SUNSHINE STATE

One of the nation's more disturbing bookbanning incidents occurred in Panama City, Florida, a beach town within what is called the "Redneck Riviera." Greater Panama City has a population of about 120,000, served by over 125 churches that advertise their healing powers in the Yellow Pages. This Bible Belt town was to witness the familiar battle between religious fundamentalists, who wanted to teach children *what* to think, and teachers, who wanted to teach children *how* to think.

Gloria Pipkin was an eighth-grade English teacher in Panama City. When she first arrived at Mowat Junior High School, the English Department had the students spending most of their time identifying nouns and verbs in grammar workbooks, and the few textbooks that were used ignored all twentieth-century literature. Pipkin says the kids hated this arrangement, and so did the teachers. But then a new chairman of her English Department, Ed Deluzain, arrived from Florida State University (FSU), bringing with him new ideas for teaching English to kids, ideas that encouraged children to read and write, not just to learn grammar by rote. Gloria Pipkin and her friend ReLeah Hawks had heard of these teaching techniques, which utilized books that children actually enjoyed reading, including "young adult novels" written for and about adolescents. Soon all eleven teachers in the Mowat English Department were enthusiastically reading and discussing the novels.

In 1982, Gloria Pipkin became the chairman of the Mowat English Department, and under her leadership, the teachers introduced books by Mark Twain, George Orwell, Anne Frank, and Robert Cormier, while organizing paperback book swaps and book fairs at the school. The teachers created minilibraries within each classroom, purchased with their own money or income they earned from selling soft drinks at football games. Books from the classroom libraries were passed out to kids, allowing them to sample books at random and replace them as they wished. The students in Pipkin's eighth-grade class even wrote and bound their own novels. In a countywide writing contest, Mowat students won all five first-place prizes, and eleven of fifteen prizes overall. Mowat ninth-graders soon achieved twelfth-grade reading comprehension, vocabulary, and grammar, well ahead of students at any other junior high school in the county. In 1985, the National Council of Teachers of English designated the Mowat English Department a "Center of Excellence," one of only 150 secondary schools in the United States and Canada to be so designated, and the only one in Florida.

Then the censors descended. In 1985, Marian Collins, grandmother of a Mowat Junior High School student, wrote to Bay County School Superintendent Leonard Hall, complaining that the novel *I Am the Cheese*, by Robert Cormier, contained vulgar language and advocated humanism and behaviorism. *I Am the Cheese* tells the story of a teenage boy whose family is put in a witness protection program after his father testifies against members of the Mafia. The book had been named as one of the best young adult books of 1977 by *Newsweek*, the *New York Times*, and *School Library Journal*. Hall immediately ordered Mowat principal Joel Creel to ban the book. Two months after Collins's original letter to Hall, she wrote again, complaining that *I Am the Cheese* was still being used at Mowat. She also wrote Principal Creel, asking why he had not complied with the superintendent's order to remove the book. Collins's daughter, Claudia Shumaker, then joined her mother's censorship campaign, and now mother, daughter, and granddaughter were in the fray. The Shumakers objected to the book's occasional profanity and the "subversive" suggestion that government agents could be involved in a murder plot.

Soon a few other parents began complaining about vulgarity in some of the books their children had acquired from the book fairs or borrowed from the classroom libraries. During the summer of 1985, the Mowat teachers did their best to accommodate them without altering the curriculum or their classroom libraries. They met regularly with concerned parents to explain their programs. They encouraged students whose parents objected to a book used in class to choose an alternative book. Also, written parental permission was required before any student could attend a book fair or read challenged books. But none of this could placate Claudia and Robert Shumaker, whose daughter was in ReLeah Hawks's English class. When they saw the classroom, with books lining the walls, they were dismayed. "It's like walking into a B Dalton with desks," complained Claudia Shumaker, who described some of the books as "immoral" and "blasphemous."[67] She said she didn't allow her children to see any movie they wished, so why should she have them exposed to books they shouldn't see?

The previous April, when ReLeah Hawks had assigned *I Am the Cheese* to her class, she sent a letter to parents, warning that the book was "difficult" and asking permission for their children to read it. If they disapproved of the book, an appropriate alternative would be assigned. When all parental responses were received, eighty-eight parents gave permission, and four, counting the Shumakers, rejected the book. Teacher Hawks saw the vote as an endorsement of Cormier's novel, and she anticipated no difficulty in assigning alternative reading for the other four students. Later she reflected, "How could I know that this was the first step in a long and terrible process that would lead to full-scale censorship and the virtual dismantling of our program?"[68]

The Shumakers were not willing to accept alternative books. They claimed that if their daughter read an alternative book, she would be ostracized. Therefore, on the advice of Superintendent Hall, Claudia Shumaker filed an official complaint against *I Am the Cheese* and another novel used at Mowat, Susan Pfeffer's *About David*. Creel immediately withdrew both books from use in all schools in the county, pending judgment by a review committee.

The teachers felt personally offended. "There was a lot of hurt and a lot of rage too," recalls teacher Sue Farrell.[69] ReLeah Hawks had to tell four classes that they couldn't read the book she had been touting all year. Gloria Pipkin warned, "If they take our books away and start giving us the books they want, then the kids won't read. We want to make them literate, life-long readers. We're co-learners. We're participating with the kids in the process of reading and writing."[70] But Pipkin was not discouraged. "I was really pleased," she says. "At last it was in the open, and there was a forum where it could be heard and we could respond."

In her formal challenge to *I Am the Cheese*, Claudia Shumaker stated that "the theme of the book is morbid and depressing. The language of the book is crude and vulgar. The sexual descriptions and suggestions are extremely inappropriate. Our children's minds are being warped and filled with unwholesome attitudes by reading worthless materials." She attached photocopies of offending passages containing words like "hell," "shit," "fart," and "goddamn." Her challenge to *About David*, a book about teenage suicide, said the subject should be handled through prayer at home, rather than in school. She added, "If the teaching of Christian morals and code of decency is illegal in the school system, then the teaching of the Humanist religion's code of immorality is also illegal."[71]

On May 20, 1986, the review committee issued its report, describing *I Am the Cheese* as a high-interest young adult novel that encourages reading, critical thinking, and class discussion. The committee recommended that the use of *I Am the Cheese* be continued with young adults. But the final judgment was left in the hands of Bay County School Superintendent Leonard Hall, who was in no hurry to make a difficult decision. He allowed the school year to pass without action on the challenge, thus effectively keeping *I Am the Cheese* out of the classrooms.

Even so, Charles Collins, Claudia Shumaker's father, was enraged over the recommendations of the review committee. Collins, a wealthy beachfront developer and former school board member, called the novels used in the Mowat schools "trashy" and "obscene," recommending instead the Nancy Drew mysteries and the Bobbsey Twins books. He regarded Mowat's book fairs and classroom libraries as part of the humanist conspiracy to take over American education. After the review committee recommended retention of *I Am the Cheese*, Collins stepped up his attacks on Mowat's schools, taking out a large ad in the local newspaper that began: "Your child's textbooks—Have you read them?" The ad printed a few excerpts from *I Am the Cheese* and another Cormier novel, *The Chocolate War*, and concluded by saying, "If you believe these books should be banned, mail in the attached coupon." School officials were quickly inundated with letters and phone calls.[72]

In a newspaper interview, Collins complained: "There's no respect in this county any more. You cannot go down the halls of the high schools and junior highs without hearing the dirtiest language you ever heard in your life. I believe these filthy little books are the cause."[73]

The teachers responded by calling a meeting on May 27, 1986, inviting all students, teachers, and parents. On the morning of the meeting, Superintendent Hall stormed into the Mowat English Department, accusing the teachers of inflaming the students. Hall told the teachers not to discuss the First Amendment with their students and not to answer any questions on the book controversy. He ordered the teachers to tell the students not to attend the meeting. "The issue is a parental issue," said Hall. "It is not a student issue. I think the parent should speak for his or her child. . . . We feel like they're at an impressionable age. They're not mature enough to recognize that the books are an invasion of their rights to have literature that is not full of obscenities in the classroom."[74] The meeting was attended by nearly 300 parents and an unexpected TV crew. There were some protesters present, but two thirds of the speakers expressed support for the school's English program. Many parents thanked the teachers for inspiring their children to read. One father told the crowd, "A strange thing has happened to my son since he's been going to Mowat. I've caught him reading. Sometimes on weekends. I also caught him writing a letter to his grandmother without my telling him to do it."[75] After the meeting, the teachers were optimistic, but they had no way of knowing what was in store for them.

On June 5, 1986, as summer vacation began, Hall announced that despite the review committee's recommendation to accept *I Am the Cheese*, the book could not be used in Bay County schools, nor could any other material not specifically approved by the board be used in the future. Hall's announcement began with the statement that the school district would not use instructional materials that contain vulgar, obscene, or sexually explicit material. His proposal specifically required that all materials not formally adopted by the state be approved by the school superintendent and the principal before use in the schools. Even after approval, a challenged book would automatically be withdrawn from use until a series of review boards had decided its fate.

The edict not only banned the Cormier novel but eliminated virtually every book that had been used during the past year, as well as all classroom libraries. Even literary classics that had been taught for years were excluded under the new policy. All that remained for classroom use were a few old English textbooks. Many teachers were left with no books that could legally be used. ReLeah Hawks recalls: "Eleven dumbfounded, award-winning English teachers sat listening to our Superintendent tell us our program no longer existed. There was an overpowering feeling of helplessness as we realized that everything not on the state-adopted textbook list was being banned."[76]

In opposition to Hall's proposal, Gloria Pipkin organized a group of teachers, librarians, and book lovers calling themselves CHOICE (Citizens Having Options in our Children's Education). To Pipkin, the forces recruited by Collins were fighting the concept of critical thinking. "They want kids to read well enough to follow directions and write well enough to take dictation," she said.[77] On the other side, Charles Collins began working full-time with church women circulating petitions against "obscene books."

On a hot August evening in 1986, the school board met to consider Hall's proposal and make the ultimate decision on the challenged books. Several hundred people packed the room, made all the hotter by the TV lights. After the board's attorney read the proposal, Hall himself presented the board with a stack of antiobscenity petitions that he claimed contained 9,000 signatures. Pipkin told the board of the successes of the English program. Another teacher pointed out that Bay County's program for children with learning disabilities used thousands of "unapproved" materials, each of which would now require a laborious review. The president of the teachers union noted that under the proposed guidelines, teachers would spend most of their time writing justifications for their books. An FSU professor read a long list of authors—from Shakespeare to Tennessee Williams—whose works would be banned under Hall's proposal. Several Mowat students spoke in defense of their teachers and the controversial books. But a woman opposing the challenged books rose to declare that she and her followers had prayed two hurricanes away during the previous year and there would be grave consequences if the schools continued to profane the name of God.

After almost five hours of haggling, the board voted to approve Hall's policy, with a minor modification. Any books used during the previous year could be used in the coming year, after which they would all be subject to title-by-title official approval. Even that concession would not apply to two books—I Am the Cheese and About David. Those books remained banned.

Gloria Pipkin decided to submit a request to reinstate I Am the Cheese in ReLeah Hawks's class. She wrote a rationale and submitted it to principal Creel. Creel rejected her request, saying the book was not appropriate for the age group, that it contained vulgar or obscene language and might tend to encourage seventh- or eighth-graders to rebel against parental authority. Pipkin then wrote to Hall, asking him to override Creel, and when Hall refused, she wrote to the school board requesting a hearing.

But in the meantime, the bookbanning process proceded apace. When the school year began in September 1986, Hall appeared in the library of the Lynn Haven Elementary School and browsed through the periodicals, looking for a magazine called Young Miss. Hall had heard that one issue of the magazine contained a story on abortion. After Hall left, the librarian received a phone call from the assistant principal, saying that Hall wanted the magazine removed from the shelf. The librarian picked three issues of Young Miss off the shelves and threw them in the trash. Librarians at other elementary schools did the same. When the teachers' union protested the arbitrary removal of library materials, the local TV station, an NBC affiliate, assigned reporter Cindy Hill to cover the story. When her report was aired on TV, Hill received several irate phone calls, demanding that she drop the story. She was told to stop bothering Leonard Hall, a good, God-fearing man.

But Hill smelled a good story. She went to the school board to check on the 9,000 signatures Charles Collins had claimed during his petition drive. She reported that there were only 3,549 signatures, many of which were not registered Bay County voters. She also discovered that many people had signed the petition three or more times. In some cases, heads of family had signed the names of all family members, including children.

Immediately after Hill's report aired on the evening news, calls came in attacking her as a "Communist," "atheist," and the "daughter of Satan." One caller recited: "Roses are red, violets are black. You'd look good with a knife in your back."[78] The calls continued for several days, and on the morning of October 25, when Hill stepped out of her apartment, she noticed a gasoline-soaked carpet with a burned match atop it. The following morning, at about 3:00 A.M., Hill was awakened by her smoke alarm to find her living room filling with smoke. She fled her apartment and called the police, who concluded that a flammable liquid had been poured under her door and then lighted.

A nervous Cindy Hill called Gloria Pipkin, who invited the young reporter to move in with her family for a few days. Soon thereafter, Pipkin's husband noticed the hood of Hill's car open in the driveway, and discovered evidence of tampering. A few nights later, Hill's car suddenly stalled on a dark stretch of highway. When a policeman examined the engine, he noticed that three of the four sparkplug wires had been pulled loose.

After Hill received a phone call telling her, "Satan will get revenge," Pipkin staked out Hill's apartment to catch any intruders. She did surprise someone tampering with Hill's car, but the intruder fled to his car in the adjoining parking lot and disappeared. A note had been left on Hill's car warning, "Beware of the bomb." When the police arrived, they found a tape-covered device sitting on the engine, ticking. The police evacuated several apartments, sealed off the area, and summoned the bomb squad. The "bomb" turned out to be a fake, but that did not calm Pipkin's nerves. Charles Collins ridiculed the incident, first saying, "It may have been a practical joke."[79] He then announced, "I don't believe anything. The thing in her car was just a joke. The fire didn't burn anything. It just smoked. That's a good way to get your apartment painted by the landlord. I'm thoroughly disgusted with these trite little people in this county." Referring to the Mowat teachers, Collins said, "They ought to be fired, run out of the county and gotten rid of for insubordination."[80]

On a November afternoon, after a long day teaching and coaching the school's "Knowledge Bowl" team, Gloria Pipkin checked her school mailbox. There, amid the departmental notices and memos, Pipkin noticed an envelope addressed with letters crudely cut from magazines. She opened the envelope and unfolded a note, again written in letters cut from magazines. The note read:

Woe to those who call evil good and good evil, who put darkness for light and light for darkness, who put bitter for sweet, for they have revoked the law of the Lord. For this you all shall DIE. One by one. Hill, Hawks, Farrell, Pipkin.[81]

Pipkin took the letter to the Panama City police. She later showed it to the other women threatened in the note. They were terrified. Hill talked of moving, and Farrell, a divorced mother of a teenage daughter, was worried that there was no one to protect them. Hawks, who was pregnant, wondered if she should send her five-year-old son to his grandparents. Pipkin said: "Three-quarters of me, the rational side, realizes that it's probably a trick to scare us, but part of me is afraid." After reflection, she concluded, "I'm in this to the bitter end."[82]

On November 12, 1986, when the school board met to consider her request to reinstate *I Am the Cheese*, Collins and the Shumakers were in the front row. There was some doubt about whether Pipkin would even be allowed to speak. The board chairman asked her if she was going to be speaking as a citizen or as a teacher, and Pipkin said it would be difficult for her to separate those roles. The chairman reminded her that she was obliged to follow the edicts of the principal and superintendent. Only after Pipkin said she had followed those edicts did the acting school board attorney state, "I think that since she's on the agenda, she has a right to speak." Pipkin then told the board, "Despite the fact that the board attorney . . . recently informed me that no right of formal appeal exists under the new policy, I am here today requesting that you restore this powerful tool to our curriculum. Make no mistake about it, *I Am the Cheese* has been banned in the Bay County School System because the ideas in it are offensive to a few." Charles Collins then attacked the book and suggested that Pipkin's actions might be cause for dismissal. "If teachers are unhappy then they should resign," said Collins. "We would ask this board to reprimand the teachers." Collins warned that if the teachers continued to oppose the bookban, "the board should dismiss the teachers and let them find another job."[83]

When all speakers had finished, the board chairman denied Gloria Pipkin's request to reconsider *I Am the Cheese*. In addition, the board approved a policy requiring all nontextbook materials to be formally approved by the principal, the superintendent, and the school board.

The next morning, Pipkin returned to her eighth-grade classroom. One of her students asked her if they could talk about censorship. Pipkin said they could if they wanted to. A number of students asked if Pipkin was going to be fired, and she assured them that a teacher couldn't be fired for simply talking to the school board. One student said, "I think they ought to keep you, not in spite of what you're doing but *because* you're doing it." Some students criticized Principal Creel, but Pipkin defended him, saying he was under enormous pressure.

"We lost *I Am the Cheese* and we're mad," said one girl.
"What would happen if we just started reading the book next Monday?" asked another student.

"I'd be fired," said Pipkin.

"I think you should take us to another state and teach us the book," suggested a girl.

"The sad thing about it," said Pipkin, "is that similar things are happening all over the country."

"About *I Am the Cheese*?"

"About a lot of different books," Pipkin said.[84]

Indeed, Superintendent Hall was not finished with his plan to cleanse the Bay County schools of "bad language and ideas." Early in 1987, Hall cited a single vulgarity in Farley Mowat's *Never Cry Wolf* as sufficient reason for banning it. "If you say a single vulgar word, you've said it," proclaimed Hall. "If you steal a penny, you're still a thief, or is it only when you steal $500,000?"[85]

In May 1987, Hall extended this purist notion of vulgarity by announcing a new three-tier book classification system by which all school books would be judged. Hall's new system divided all the world's literature into three categories: books with no vulgarity; books with a "sprinkling" of vulgarity; and books with "oodles" of vulgarity. Hall declined to define "sprinkling" or "oodles," but he quickly issued a list of sixty-one books in Category III, claiming they either contained vulgarity or the word "goddamn" and must henceforth not be taught or discussed in Bay County classrooms. Banned titles included classics by Sophocles, Shakespeare, Dickens, the Brontë sisters, Hemingway, Chaucer, Orwell, Steinbeck, Tennessee Williams, and a host of other prominent writers.[86]

There was widespread concern that Hall's continuing crusade would finally destroy Bay County's acclaimed English program. Some students wore black arm bands to school as a protest, and the Panama City Commission unanimously urged that the bookban be lifted. The Bay County Public Library decided to assemble a "Banned Books" display, prominently featuring the books that Hall had banned from classroom use. The public librarian said Hall had moved his censorship to a new level that required some response from the community. "[H]e's gone beyond imaginative fiction for young people to the classics of our culture. The censorship craze has definitely moved from amusement to concern, grave concern."[87]

On May 12, forty-four Bay County teachers, parents, and students chose to file a class action suit in federal court against Superintendent Hall, Principal Creel, and the school board, arguing that the bookban was a violation of their First Amendment rights. A student, Jennifer Farrell, was first among the plaintiffs, and the case was named *Farrell* v. *Hall*. The day after the suit was filed, People for the American Way (PAW), which provided legal representation for the plaintiffs, met with the school board in an attempt to negotiate changes in the school's book review policy. A subsequent board meeting produced a revised policy, allowing teachers to assign any books that had been used in 1986–1987, so long as they were recommended by the principal.

Farrell v. *Hall* asked the court specifically to restore *I Am the Cheese* and the other books still excluded and to declare the ban on classroom libraries to be unconstitutional. The board claimed that their compromises on the book review policy now rendered *Farrell* moot, but the plaintiffs pointed out that *I Am the Cheese* and other books were still banned at Mowat because of Hall's earlier prohibitions. The plaintiffs noted that the new policy provided no time limits for board response to requests to use particular materials, thus allowing officials to effectively veto requests by delaying a decision. For example, while *Farrell* was in progress, Gloria Pipkin resubmitted a rationale for teaching *I Am the Cheese*. This time, Creel and the county curriculum officials approved the book, but Hall again rejected it, and the board upheld his action. The plaintiffs therefore asserted that it was disingenuous for Defendant Hall to claim the controversy over *I Am the Cheese* was moot or that the defendants' minds were open on these matters.

In particular, the plaintiffs argued that Hall had excluded books solely because they conflicted with his religious beliefs, and the new policy would not prevent such actions in the future. Hall's *motivation* in banning books thus became essential to the case, and the plaintiffs brought witnesses before the court to testify on Hall's religious agenda in the schools. Hall's public statements were cited to demonstrate his intention to bring Christian values to the schools of Bay County and remove library books and curricular materials that involve subjects such as feminism, consumerism, environmentalism, and racism. Hall had earlier stated that he had removed *I Am the Cheese* because it gave a negative picture of a department of the U.S. government, prompting a local journalist to ask, "What will they protect Bay County Children against next? The depressing knowledge of the size of the federal debt?"[88] Even when Hall claimed to be banning books solely because of "vulgar" language, he failed to define what he meant by that characterization, allowing him to use language as a pretext to ban books on religious grounds. The plaintiffs concluded that the school board had acted improperly in allowing the superintendent to exercise such broad authority over the selection and rejection of books.

On July 18, 1988, Judge Roger Vinson of the U.S. District Court for the Northern District of Florida issued an order that supported some of the plaintiffs' claims while rejecting others. Judge Vinson said Hall had admitted that his actions were motivated by his personal conservative beliefs, such as an obligation to restore Christian values to the county's schools. Vinson noted:

Hall thinks that one vulgarity in a work of literature is sufficient reason to keep the book from the Bay County school curriculum. Hall's opposition to *I Am the Cheese* arises solely from his personal opposition to the ideas expressed in the book. He believes it is improper to question the truthfulness of the government. Thus, students should not be presented with such ideas.[89]

Vinson ruled that the school board's use of the revised policy continued most of the activities to which the plaintiffs objected. On the other hand, Vinson expressed the traditional support for broad school board authority, finding that the removal of books on the basis of a single vulgarity was within the board's authority. Vinson said the review policy itself was acceptable to the court because school boards have the right to regulate the content of school libraries, including classroom libraries, in any way they wish. Their decisions can be challenged if they are made for illegal or arbitrary reasons, but the policy itself is legal. On the other hand, Vinson did *not* dismiss the complaint that *I Am the Cheese* and other books had been removed in an effort to suppress the ideas in them.

As both sides began preparing their arguments for trial, Leonard Hall announced that he would not run for reelection as superintendent, and on December 31, 1988, his term expired. Judge Vinson ruled that Hall's successor, Jack Simonson, automatically replaced Hall as a defendant, and a suspension was granted to attempt a resolution of the dispute out of court. By this time, the community was beginning to turn against Hall's draconian censorship. The Panama City mayor complained, "New business will not want to come to a place like this." The influential *St. Petersburg Times* warned:

Local control of schools is an important part of public education, but it has limits of reasonableness. Depriving students of knowledge by the widespread banning of books is not a reasonable element of local authority. Unless the book banners are stopped in Bay County, there's no telling how far they'll go.[90]

After three years of settlement negotiations between the school board and PAW, a further revision of the policy for approving instructional materials was approved by all. Time limits were set for each stage of the review process, and teachers were allowed to appeal denials of their requests for new materials. The new policy detailed a procedure for handling challenges to materials already in the classroom and ensured that parents would be notified of any complaints against materials in time for them to respond. The settlement negotiated under Vinson's order had the appearance of compromise, but the board's review policy was changed in a direction favorable to the *Farrell* plaintiffs only because the board agreed to it. In reality, Vinson's order had followed the decisions of other courts involved in textbook controversies, affirming the board's almost unlimited power over the curriculum.

Soon after Superintendent Hall left office, the terms of two of the five school board members expired, and their successors gave the board a potential 3–2 majority for a more liberal textbook policy. The reconstituted board countermanded Hall's exclusion of sixty-four literary classics in time to allow their use when classes began in September. But the educators who had endured this protracted censorship struggle were not around to savor the victory. Principal Creel had left Mowat Junior High School to head a brand-new junior high school in Bay County, and all eleven English teachers who had earned their department national awards had resigned. Today, the Mowat English Department is no longer listed as a "Center of Excellence" by the National Council of Teachers of English.

BLASPHEMY IN CHESHIRE, CONNECTICUT

On November 7, 1991, irate parents at a Cheshire, Connecticut, Board of Education meeting demanded that two award-winning books be removed from the Highland Middle School because of offensive language. The offending books were *The Alfred Summer*, by Jan Slepian, and *The Great Gilly Hopkins*, by Katherine Paterson. The most vocal parent, Sharon Kuehlewind, claimed that the books were filled with profanity, blasphemy, and obscenities. Kuehlewind also told the board that the authors had "dragged God and the church in the mud and slyly endorsed unwholesome values such as stealing, smoking, drinking and simply rebelling against authority." When Kuehlewind demanded an investigation into "who was pushing this filth on our kids," she received loud applause from supporters at the board meeting. Another parent said, "We don't need any more bureaucratic baloney. Pull it and pull it now. . . . I'd like to know who willfully introduced these books into our system."[91]

Board Vice-Chairman George Bowman was even more rash in his response, proclaiming that he would personally pull the books from the school library the next morning if something were not done. "I'll take them out myself, and you can arrest me," Bowman said. "Some of this language I hear on construction sites. I'm shocked these books are in our school. I want this trash removed from our school system, and find out who brought it in here and fire them. And I don't want to hear some warm fuzzy words about liberal ideas—it's trash."[92] Bowman concluded that the books had been written by perverted minds. Ironically, Paterson's book had received the 1980 American Book Award, the Newbery Medal, and the 1977 Christopher Award for novels representing the "highest human spiritual values." Slepian's book had been runner-up for the American Book Award.

Bowman waved copies of *Playboy* and the *National Enquirer*, asking if they too would be accepted for fifth-graders. Though he had not read the books he was attacking, Bowman did say that he could safely recommend alternative books such as *Snow White and the Seven Dwarfs*. In response to the complaints, Board Chairman William P. Meyerjack announced that effective immediately a "moratorium" would be placed on the Paterson and Slepian books in all school libraries until the board could review the matter. The two books were therefore "temporarily" pulled from the language arts curriculum at Cheshire's four elementary schools.

Under cooler circumstances the following day, the complaining parents admitted that the books had positive themes, but they maintained that the language used made them unacceptable. Kuehlewind said she became aware of the problem books when her fifth-grader told her that he was reading a "bad book" in school. She later discovered that a neighbor's child was reading the other offending book. At that point Kuehlewind and two other parents met with Highland Principal Diane Hartman, the principal of grades 3 to 6 at the Highland School, filled out the complaint forms, and listed the words that offended them. Hartman told them that she understood their point of view, but it was a district issue, not just a Highland one. Kuehlewind was not satisfied.

School Superintendent John Barnes said the offending words were "very much a part of reality for fifth-graders, and that using a book which contains them does not mean the school system is promoting obscene language."[93] He said the complaints were the first they had heard since the books were selected in 1987 by the school system's Language Arts Committee. He said no books had ever been pulled from the shelves in the Cheshire School District, but he gave assurances that the complaints would be reviewed. "I'll either come out and say they should be returned as literature in grade five, or the books are not appropriate for that grade," said Barnes.

> I read the books, and frankly it gave me some pause when it came to the language. But I also felt the books had strong messages about the lives the children lead and issues children need to come to grips with. I'm a realist. I know what language children this age use. The question is whether they should encounter this language with people their age in the classroom or in the back of the bus.[94]

Barnes emphasized the seriousness of the issue, warning that it would be regarded as censorship if the books were removed on the basis of personal biases or prejudices instead of good academic values.

Mrs. Kuehlewind insisted that parents had received forms at the beginning of the year saying there would be no swearing allowed on the school bus or on the playground, yet profanity and blasphemy were being read in the classroom. She said, "No matter what 'phenomenal metaphors' or 'excellent themes' could be taught through these 'prize-winning' books, they are totally inappropriate and unacceptable for our public school system. They are filled with profanity, blasphemy and obscenities and utter gutter language."[95] She maintained that there were basic philosophical issues at stake in the book dispute. "We have the right to send our kids to public schools without having them bombarded with language and concepts counter to the moral standards upon which the country was founded," she said. "Who would have used books like these in the fifth grade, or any grade, 30 years ago?"[96]

Superintendent Barnes convened a special review board to assess the books' educational value before taking further action. "It could be," said Barnes, "that we don't want these books used because of these words, but I want to try to get a sense of perspective on this. The parents had a rather intense, emotional reaction to the books and I want to make sure they're not pulling the naughty words out of context."[97] Barnes invited board of education members, parents, PTA members, child psychologists, and others to attend the review board meeting, at which the Kuehlewinds submitted a complete list of the offending words, specifying book and page number.

Jan Slepian, who wrote *The Alfred Summer* in 1980 for an audience of nine to twelve year olds, said she was saddened by the parents' reaction to her work. "These pitiful people who would point to a phrase and judge a whole book," Slepian said from her New Jersey home. "That's just what we don't want children to do." She said the main theme of the book—about the friendship of four boys, two of them handicapped—is acceptance and understanding. Slepian said the characters in her book are based on real children, including her retarded brother Alfred, and they talk the way real children do. "For them to say 'Gosh, darn,' it just wouldn't be true," she said.[98]

Katherine Paterson, author of *The Great Gilly Hopkins*, was similarly disappointed by the Cheshire controversy. "I'm sorry people are offended," she said, "but they're offended when they don't see what I'm trying to do." Paterson, the daughter of a missionary, said that her book about an eleven-year-old foster child was being misinterpreted by Cheshire parents who overlooked the book's positive themes. She said the book was "for those children who don't know if they have a place. . . . Gilly is a foster child who is very angry about being treated as a disposable commodity in the world. She lies, steals, bullies the handicapped and is racially prejudiced. Her mouth needs to reflect her state of anger and lostness."[99] Paterson said she wouldn't change a word in the book, her favorite of the eighteen she has written. As to the appropriateness of the language, she says fifth-graders should be the judge of that. She points out that virtually every time the main character, Gilly, curses, the other character, Trotter, corrects her.

Most of the Cheshire children reading the two books had no objection to them. Ten-year-old Elizabeth Abbate said of *The Great Gilly Hopkins*, "I really thought it was a good book. It was interesting, and it told kids how to behave. Most of those words you hear every day. They didn't really bother me."[100]

Highland School Principal Diane Hartman said both novels had been in the elementary schools' reading program since 1987 and were widely used in other schools and systems. Hartman said a curriculum committee had selected the books because they were outstanding examples of contemporary children's fiction and because they espoused strong values. She said the committee was aware of the language in the books, but the committee's goal was to get books for the children that have a strong message of acceptance of other people.

The *Meriden Record-Journal* editorialized:

> Clearly, the situation with these books is not black and white. The issue, really, is tolerance for rough if realistic language used at a given grade level. To one person, expressions seem blasphemous or obscene; to another, such usages shock no more than the casual use of "gosh." The attempt to remove such volumes from Cheshire's school libraries should be stoutly resisted. These books were not written to titillate or shock but to help kids work through problems and situations not unusual in real schools.

The editorial recommended that the children of the complaining parents be offered different reading assignments, but it concluded:

> In the long run, no significant book in the 4,000 years of Western civilization has failed to offend someone. The Bible contains some pretty racy scenes; Shakespeare has a number of gross physical jokes; racial language in Mark Twain can give offense; *The Wizard of Oz* has offended not only because it is fantasy but also because it deals with magic and witchcraft. If one were to start removing offending volumes from libraries upon the application of anyone who objected, it wouldn't be long before libraries no longer faced a space problem.[101]

Representatives of educational organizations around the state soon became involved in the Cheshire dispute. Mary Pellerin, president of the Connecticut Educational Media Association, said that books, like people, should be given a fair trial and not censored without a thorough review. Harriet Selverstone, member of the Connecticut Educational Media Association (CEMA) and head of the group's Intellectual Freedom Committee, said she had notified other watchdog groups like The National Coalition against Censorship and People for the American Way. On November 21, Selverstone wrote to School Superintendent John Barnes to urge that the books not be pulled from the schools' libraries or curricula. Selverstone said that parents have a right to keep certain materials away from their children but not to prevent others from being exposed to the same material.

On December 4, Leanne Katz, head of the New York–based National Coalition against Censorship, sent a letter to Superintendent Barnes, expressing concern over the removal of the books before any inquiry had been made into the complaints. She stated that proper procedures were being ignored and that the professional opinions of educators were not being respected. Katz asked that her letter and an accompanying list of book selection procedures and principles be shared with the school board members and review committee. She urged the school board not to "cave in" to demands for bookbanning.

Connecticut's state historian Christopher Collier wrote:

> Parents of Cheshire school children who see no beauty but only blasphemy and obscenity in a pair of books read by their fifth-graders should look again. And so should the hysterical Board of Education member who compared the books to a copy of Playboy which . . . he waved at citizens gathered at a Board meeting. Far from obscene or blasphemous, these books deal with family, love and mutual respect. They are exactly the books that parents concerned about old-fashioned family values should want their kids to read.

Collier, himself an author of historical novels for young adults, said that the words some have cited as objectionable in these books were being read out of context. To construct the dialog in any other way, says Collier, would have left teenage readers "bored, uninvolved, and unmoved." He concluded, "Children lucky enough to have teachers perceptive enough and wise enough to choose such books as *The Alfred Summer* and *The Great Gilly Hopkins* should count their blessings."[102]

Most Connecticut schools have book selection policies and step-by-step procedures for handling complaints about books. If complaints cannot be resolved by the school principal or library media specialist, a review and decision by a Library Media Advisory Council would follow. If the complainant does not accept the council's decision, the school superintendent or, ultimately, the board of education would make a final review and decision. Materials are supposed to remain in use or on library shelves until a complaint is resolved. Such was not the case in the Cheshire incident, where the books were impounded, pending the recommendation of the supervisor's review panel.

The review panel was made up of about a dozen members, including school staffers, a board of education member, a parent, and a consultant on children's literature. The first two meetings of the panel were closed, and the third allowed public discussion of the issues. As the committee review of the Paterson and Slepian novels approached its conclusion, more books came under attack. Parents at a January 1992 school board meeting condemned the Newbery Medal–winning *Slave Dancer*, by Paula Fox, claiming it spoke disparagingly of blacks. Another novel, *My Brother Sam Is Dead*, by state historian Christopher Collier, was attacked for its "graphic violence" and "inaccurate depiction of the Revolutionary War." The board took no action on the request to remove these books from Cheshire schools. One parent, a former board member, said, "I understand the great fears parents have, but I submit that we have become a hysterical society when we review every single book and every single word."[103]

On February 6, 1992, the attempt to ban the Paterson and Slepian books came to an official end when the board of education, in response to the review panel's recommendation, voted unanimously to restore the two books to elementary school classrooms. In front of 300 residents packed into the council chambers at the town hall, the board voted 6–0 to approve School Superintendent John Barnes's recommendation to retain the books. *The Great Gilly Hopkins* was retained as a fifth-grade reader; *The Alfred Summer* was moved from the fifth- to the sixth-grade level.

The board's decision came after a final two-hour public debate on the books, during which about twenty people spoke. Those parents who spoke against the books at the final board meeting expressed disappointment at the outcome. "I am very concerned for the children of Cheshire," said Sharon Kuehlewind, "because what we teach at home will not be reinforced in the schools." She felt that the board's decision implied approval for the use of profanity in the classroom. But board member Robert Bown said the books were age appropriate, positive, and enriching. The audience responded with a standing ovation when he concluded, "Should a parent or well-organized group of parents dictate what should or should not be in the curriculum? I submit the answer is clearly no. Parents have no right to impose moral judgments and values on the children of others."[104]

IMPRESSIONS: THE TEXTBOOK THAT BROUGHT PAGANISM TO CALIFORNIA PUBLIC SCHOOLS

The *Impressions* language arts textbook series is a literature-based reading series from Holt, Rinehart and Winston intended for kindergarten through sixth grade. During the early 1990s, it became the most banned book in the nation, as religious groups charged that it was introducing American children to paganism, satanism, and New Age religion.

Impressions is a series of fifty-nine books containing approximately 10,000 literary selections and suggested classroom activities. It teaches reading, speaking, and writing through exposure to poetry, folklore, myth, songs, and fictional and factual narrative. *Impressions* implements a "whole language" approach to reading instruction that has the goal of inducing children to read more quickly and with greater enthusiasm through the use of high-quality literary selections. The text contains works by many award-winning authors, including C.S. Lewis, Laura Ingalls Wilder, Martin Luther King, Jr., Rudyard Kipling, A.A. Milne, and Dr. Seuss. Literary selections reflecting a broad range of North American cultures and traditions are followed by suggested learning activities, such as having children compose rhymes and chants, act out the selections, and discuss the selections' characters and themes.

During the early 1990s, *Impressions* was in use in thirty-four states and 1,500 schools nationwide. Despite its popularity, it was challenged hundreds of times throughout the nation, with particular controversy occurring in California. Among the California districts challenging *Impressions* were: Amador County, Ballard, Bella Vista, Black Butte, Buckeye, Campbell, Castro Valley, Dixon, Enterprise, French Gulch, Grant, Grass Valley, Happy Valley, Hayward, Lawndale, Lincoln, Los Banos, Napa, Nevada City, New Haven, Pleasant Ridge, Redding, Redondo Beach, Ripon, Saratoga Union, Willits, Winters, Woodland, and Yucaipa.

In Yucaipa, some parents complained in 1990 that the face of the devil could be seen in the illustrations in *Impressions*. When a school official was unable to detect the devil's face as described by complaining parents, he was instructed to photocopy the illustration, turn it upside down, and hold it up to a mirror. He did as instructed but was still unable to see the devil that was tormenting the parents.

Also in 1990, the Winters, California, School Board heard allegations that *Impressions* emphasized witchcraft and the occult, promoted disrespect for parents and other authorities, and had a Canadian bias, the latter charge deriving from the publisher's corporate connection. The source for most of these complaints appeared to be a packet of material circulated by several ultraconservative religious groups, including Educational Research Analysts (ERA) and Citizens for Excellence in Education (CEE). ERA is the Texas-based textbook review organization formed by the notorious Mel and Norma Gabler. CEE was founded by Robert L. Simonds, who lists the National Education Association among his enemies.

After the Winters school district made the *Impressions* series available for public review, a number of parents complained about its content. One local parent, after reading a story about trolls under a toll bridge, said she and her children could never again cross a toll bridge. Other parents complained of the frequent appearance of rainbows among the illustrations, a symbol supposedly associated with New Age religion. However, many parents, teachers, and scholars in the area spoke up for the book.

Dr. John Boe, who teaches literature at the University of California at Davis and has served as a consultant on the therapeutic use of children's literature, wrote to the superintendent and board of trustees, saying that *Impressions* represented an admirable trend in recent education, that of giving children "real literature" rather than "hack work" written for specially produced textbooks. Dr. Boe subsequently testified before the school board and has written of that experience:

> I'd always thought Mark Twain had it right: "First God made idiots. That was for practice. Then he made school boards." But after a recent school board meeting in Winters, I'm not so sure. The issue was whether to adopt a textbook series, Holt's *Impressions*. Some townsfolk, spurred on by national Christian organizations, had protested that this series was literally the work of the devil and was as well a foreign product (that is, Canadian). There were three TV cameras in the crowded auditorium, one of them from CBS' *48 Hours*. . . .
>
> My turn came early. I talked of my experience with a project at St. Mary's Hospital in San Francisco, where the kind of fantasy literature people were objecting to in *Impressions* was actually used as part of the *treatment* for disturbed children, including children abused by real Satanists!
>
> Having read one of the texts in question, I simply couldn't understand the bizarre allegations: the books supposedly promoted drug and alcohol abuse (the troll princess in *Beauty and the Beast* puts a sleeping tablet in the prince's wine), cannibalism (the story of the *Gingerbread Man*), satanic ritual (encouraging the children to "chant" rhymes), black magic (in one story musical instruments control the colors of the sunset), New Age religion (references to rainbows), the practice of witchcraft (various fictional witches, including the one from *The Lion, the Witch and the Wardrobe*, by C.S. Lewis, one of modern literature's most passionate Christians), and the Wicca religion (this is not the worship of furniture, as I first thought). I also couldn't understand the fear that the texts promoted Canadian culture. Is there some International Canadian Conspiracy I'm simply not aware of? . . .
>
> Finally, the vote. We anxiously awaited the words of Michael Roberts, the Superintendent of Schools. . . . He recommended *Impressions* be adopted. To the surprise of most in the audience, the rest of the board unanimously voted to adopt the books. It turned out they weren't really convinced by the various speakers, many of whom, on both sides of the issue, were intelligent, passionate, and eloquent. The crucial factor was that most of the board members had test marketed the books, simply trying them out on their own kids. Their kids had all loved *Impressions* and hadn't turned into either Satanists or Canadians.[105]

Most school districts throughout the country dealt with challenges to *Impressions* in the same way that folks in Winters, California, did. They approved the books. But in several of these districts, the religious organizations leading the challenge to *Impressions* had the will and resources to file lawsuits attempting to reverse the acceptance of the text. In Woodland, California, a 1991 decision by the school board to adopt the *Impressions* series resulted in a suit filed by Douglas and Katharine Brown, whose children attended the Woodland Joint Unified School District. The suit was originally sponsored by the American Family Association, headed by the Reverend Donald Wildmon, but was subsequently taken over by the American Center for Law and Justice, affiliated with the Reverend Pat Robertson.

District Judge William B. Schubb of the Eastern District of California ruled in 1991 that the use of *Impressions* in Woodland did not violate the United States or California Constitutions. The Browns appealed. The U.S. Appeals Court for the Ninth Circuit addressed *Brown* v. *Woodland Joint Unified School District* in 1994, just a few months after another legal challenge to *Impressions* was decided in a federal appeals court in Illinois. That case, *Fleischfresser* v. *Directors of School District 200*, would be used as precedent in deciding the Woodland case (see Chapter 2).

Though the decisions in *Fleischfresser* and *Woodland* reassured California school boards that they would ultimately prevail in court when challenged on the use of *Impressions*, the hue and cry in local California communities continued unabated. Indeed, only after the publisher began to market a new series as an alternative to *Impressions* did the controversy recede.

NAPPY HAIR: IT TOOK A BOOK TO LOSE A TEACHER

Attempts to ban books in the United States can proceed under formal, bureaucratic cover, or they can work through mob psychology and the threat of violence. A recent episode of bookbanning hysteria in Brooklyn, New York, hounded a frightened elementary school teacher out of town. Virtually all the enraged bookbanners had one thing in common: They had not read the book in question, nor did they have children in the teacher's class.

Ruth Sherman first came to work in the rough Brooklyn, New York, neighborhood of Bushwick in 1997 as a volunteer reading assistant at Public School 75. The school was under review by the State Education Department for poor performance, and the new principal, Felicita Santiago, was searching for highly motivated young educators who could raise test scores and reading levels at P.S. 75. When Sherman's students showed dramatic improvement, Santiago invited her to join the regular teaching staff. Sherman accepted without hesitation and proceeded to help double the number of third graders reading at or above the state proficiency level.

In September 1997, Sherman began using *Nappy Hair*, a critically acclaimed book by Carolivia Herron, a black professor at Chico State University in California. The heroine of the book is a little black girl named Brenda who has the "nappiest, most screwed up, squeezed up, knotted up" hair. The book, which had sold more than 30,000 copies, had been celebrated nationally as an excellent teaching tool for black self-esteem and for broader social acceptance of racial differences.

Author Herron says that *Nappy Hair* began as a lecture based on stories her uncle had told her. "When I was younger, I tape-recorded my Uncle Richard at one of my birthday parties," she said. "I am Brenda, the little girl in 'Nappy Hair.' I can remember him saying, 'Carol, you sure do got some nappy hair on your head.' And that's the opening line in the book." The kids in Sherman's class embraced *Nappy Hair* like no other book they had encountered. "These were children who hated reading, that never opened a book and had difficulty reading," recalls Sherman. "I'm talking about comprehension and even word recognition. Some of them couldn't read the word 'the' and for them to be enthusiastic and excited about reading, that was really something."[106]

Indeed, the children were so delighted with *Nappy Hair* that they begged Sherman for their own copies. She obliged them with photocopies. Then one day in early November a parent walked into Sherman's class waving a handful of photocopied pages from the book. "The first I knew of the problem was when this parent came into my room and said she was surprised she didn't see a white [Ku Klux Klan] hood on my desk,"said Sherman.[107]

Sherman was shocked and confused. She asked the school's assistant principal to arrange a meeting with the woman to resolve her concerns, but it was too late for damage control. Selected pages of *Nappy Hair* had been copied and circulated throughout the community, accompanied by a note warning that racist literature was being foisted on the school's children by a "white teacher." An angry protest was brewing.

On the Monday before Thanksgiving, as Sherman was conducting a lesson in class, she was summoned by the principal to appear immediately in the school auditorium before a group of parents who were upset about her use of *Nappy Hair*. Sherman promptly left her class, telling the children that she would be back in ten minutes. She had no way of knowing that she would never see them again.

As Sherman approached the auditorium, she could hear a loud commotion. She briefly ducked into the principal's office and called her fiancé. "I think something bad is happening," she told him. "Please come get me."

Sherman then proceeded to the auditorium. The moment she entered, pandemonium erupted. "It was an ambush," recalls principal Santiago. "They turned into a lynch mob."[108]

"They started getting in my face, asking me who I thought I was reading that book, calling me a cracker. Nobody would let me, or the principal, or the librarian . . . talk," said Sherman. A woman told Sherman that she had "better watch out." When Sherman asked if that was a threat, the woman said "it was no threat, it was a promise."[109]

Sherman's attempts to defend the book were, of course, drowned out. "They would not let me speak," she recalls. "They would not let me explain the book. They never took the time to find out anything about it."[110]

Angry parents shouted racial epithets and threats at Sherman. "We're gonna get you," shouted one as she lunged at Sherman, poking her fingers in her face. The principal and a security guard intervened and rushed Sherman out of the auditorium.

"It was like a trial," says Sherman. "A very violent trial."[111]

Local school board president Dennis Herring, who is black, recalls, "The people in the community who had seen the copies [of selections from Nappy Hair], but who had no knowledge of what they were all about or what the teacher's intentions were, were the most upset. The majority of the parents who had students in that class were fully supportive of the book."[112]

A distraught Sherman was escorted from the meeting and sent home by district superintendent Felix Vazquez. "He told me he heard people saying they wanted to do me bodily harm," recalled Sherman. "And that was it. I never saw my students again."

The next day, Vazquez made a perfunctory defense of Nappy Hair, but said Sherman should have asked permission from the principal before using it as extracurricular reading. Dennis Herring said, "We're not censoring the book. We're not saying it should be banned. . . . The Superintendent wants to make sure that staff review material with the principal."[113]

School officials continued to express concern that Sherman had used a "sensitive" book in class without first requesting permission, but they insisted that Sherman had been removed from her class for her own safety. Pending further investigation of the book, Sherman was ordered by the district superintendent to perform desk work at district headquarters instead of teaching in her class.

Then, just twenty-four hours after Ruth Sherman had been suspended from her teaching duties, she and Nappy Hair seemed to be vindicated. A second, more orderly meeting of parents showed a change in attitude, as more parents had an opportunity to read the book in its entirety. The school district offered to reinstate Sherman and to provide her with extra security, including an escort from her car to the school door. Rudy Crew, chancellor of the New York City Schools, wrote Sherman to personally commend her performance and ask her to return to P.S. 75. Police continued to investigate threats against Sherman, but she told detectives that she did not wish to increase tension by pressing charges against anyone. The ugly incident seemed to be moving toward a resolution.

Chancellor Crew said, "This is a case of parents rushing to judgment of a teacher without knowing the facts or the context at all. It's a misguided deed that these people did.... At the same time [that] we are trying to give children strong images of themselves, we're also sending a message that you better not do it if you are a white teacher."[114]

Black community leaders attempted to calm the furor. Reverend Herbert Daughtry, national administrator for the House of the Lord Pentecostal churches, was called in to help mediate. " 'Nappy' is a word that has and always will have negative connotations because of its origins," he explained. Daughtry said that some parents "felt that children were being taught to hate themselves" and that the book "stirred up the whole feeling of self hate, self rejection."

How could a book specifically designed to combat those very feelings have caused the uproar?

"The idea that the book is racist is ridiculous," said author Herron. "This book is a wonderful celebration of nappy, African-American hair." She said Sherman "could have taught 'Mary Had a Little Lamb' or some other books that had nothing to do with the African-American culture. Instead, she tried to relate to the culture of the children she was teaching."[115]

Some in the Bushwick community were candid in admitting that the book was not the source of the problem. "It had to be because she's white," said one parent who had a child in Sherman's class. "If she were a black teacher teaching that book, it wouldn't have been no problem."[116]

In the end, Sherman could not bring herself to return to P.S. 75. "At first I wanted to get back to the kids when this happened," said Sherman. "But when I woke up to go to the district office, I froze. I couldn't even think of driving there by myself.... I just wanted to crawl into a hole because I was afraid. I can't live like this, day by day. I can't have people at my door or people escorting me from my car to the school because that just totally depreciates the whole idea I was trying to teach my kids about getting along and loving one another."[117]

Sherman released a statement saying that support from the school administration came too late. "You were criticizing me instead of investigating the people who were threatening my life," she told district superintendent Felix Vazquez. "I have experienced abuse and tremendous fear brought on by an angry group, and I strongly feel that I am in danger."[118]

On December 1, school officials approved Sherman's request for a transfer to another school. A week later she began teaching at P.S. 131 in Queens, New York. Parents with children at the multiethnic school welcomed Sherman and dismissed the *Nappy Hair* controversy as uncalled for.

"I don't think it should have happened," said an African American parent with sons in the first and second grades. "If the parents didn't like it, there are ways they should have gone about it. They didn't have to threaten her."

"I am glad she is coming to this school," said another black parent with a daughter in the fifth grade. "I saw the book and I didn't think it would be a problem at all. Nappy hair is part of the black culture, and if you have nappy hair, there is nothing wrong with it. I think her motive was good."[119]

In the months since the furor over *Nappy Hair*, its black author, Carolivia Herron, and its white teacher, Ruth Sherman, have appeared together on numerous television talk shows and educational conferences, and they have begun work on a study guide instructing teachers on how to effectively use the book. Even Principal Santiago at Bushwick's P.S. 75 announced that *Nappy Hair* would be made required reading for grades 3 through 5. Indeed, Santiago invited Herron to speak at P.S. 75 to help the school's children understand the book and the wild episode surrounding it. Unfortunately, the principal subsequently decided to "uninvite" her, as Herron put it. "I always thought that I would get to talk to those children," said Herron sadly. "They are essentially cut out of what happened to them, what happened to their teacher and what happened to their reading. Is this what happens when you like a book a lot?"[120]

BLACK AND BANNED: BOOKS BY AFRICAN WOMEN CAUSE A FUROR IN MARYLAND

During 1998, schools in two Maryland counties attempted to ban books by Maya Angelou and Toni Morrison, America's two foremost black female authors. Indeed, the books in question, *I Know Why the Caged Bird Sings* and *Song of Solomon*, are celebrated as modern American classics. Complaining white parents said the books were "trash" and "anti-white," leading black parents to characterize the bookbanning as racially motivated. The white parents who challenged the books insisted that vulgarity, not race, was the major problem, but Marjorie Heins, head of the ACLU's Arts Censorship Project, said, "For someone to demand the removal of a book from a curriculum because it is anti-white raises an implication of racial motivation."[121]

In Maryland's Anne Arundel County, School Superintendent Carol S. Parham ordered Angelou's book removed from the ninth-grade English curriculum; St. Mary's County School Superintendent Patricia Richardson had Morrison's *Song of Solomon* removed from the list of approved texts. In both cases, the superintendents overruled faculty committee recommendations to maintain the books, giving in to the demands of small groups of parents.

The Morrison novel describes the spiritual journey of a young black man named Milkman Dead. Bernadette Williamson, the mother of a sixteen-year-old high school student in St. Mary's County, said she was disturbed by Morrison's depiction of a mother who nurses her son well past infancy and appears to get sexual pleasure from it. In her complaint to school officials, Williamson called the book "trash."

"It's just way too graphic," she said. "There are so many other things kids could read to teach them how to interpret literature."

As the result of a small number of similar complaints, *Song of Solomon* was banned from the curriculum throughout the school district. The African American community in St. Mary's County was angered by what it considered censorship of the book.

"The decision was bigoted," said Everland Holland, a local nurse. "*Song of Solomon* showed black people in a human perspective, with all the problems and emotions of genuine people. . . . What it did was put a human face on African Americans . . . and that makes people nervous."[122]

St. Mary's County commissioners were quick to approve Superintendent Richardson's decision to ban *Song of Solomon*, voting unanimously to remove the book from the curriculum. Calling the novel "filth" and "trash," the county commission voted to draft a letter of support for Richardson. None of the five commissioners had read the book, basing their review on just two pages that Richardson had provided them. Commission President Barbara Thompson insisted that the commission's objections to the book were not racially motivated, but were based on concerns about sexually explicit language. She would not say what objectionable language the two selected pages contained, but said it was so "vulgar" that she tore up the pages and threw the scraps away. "I may be naive, but I'm no spring chicken either," she said. "The book was repulsive." Other commissioners were similarly unwilling to identify the offending text. "I'm not going to repeat it," said Commissioner Paul Chesser.[123]

At the same time that St. Mary's County officials were effectively disposing of Morrison's novel, a similar action against Maya Angelou's *I Know Why the Caged Bird Sings* was causing a furor in Maryland's Anne Arundel County, where some parents complained of vulgar language and sexually explicit passages. Attempts to ban Angelou's acclaimed book angered not only community activists but local students and teachers as well, who saw the action as an attack on African American literature. Angelou's autobiographical work is a stark yet poetic look at the author's childhood in segregated Arkansas. It won a National Book Award when it was published in 1970 and has become a staple in high school English classes across the country. It provides students with a firsthand account of a dark period in history, and in that regard it has been compared with *The Diary of Anne Frank.*

An Anne Arundel faculty committee had reviewed *Caged Bird* in November 1997 and decided overwhelmingly to recommend keeping it in the ninth-grade curriculum. Nonetheless, School Superintendent Parham acceded to the demands of about a dozen vocal parents and sent a departmental memo two days before Christmas announcing her decision to remove the book from the ninth-grade curriculum. County spokesperson Annelle Tuminello explained, "The atmosphere created by the parents made our ability to continue teaching the book difficult. I think she [Superintendent Parham] felt removing it from the ninth grade and retaining it for the 11th grade was a reasonable compromise, because the book is worth teaching."[124]

Other county officials made it clear that the superintendent's action against *Caged Bird* had been taken without consulting the county school board. "As a board we have not discussed it," said Vaughn Brown, a school board member. "It's a decision made within the authority that the superintendent has. This situation and the publicity caused me to go out and get the book to read. I'm glad I did—It's a wonderful piece of literature. I don't see a problem with it being in the schools."[125]

Jane Doyle, a spokesperson for the schools, said the parents were concerned over both content and language, and she added, "I don't have the feeling that it was related to a racial issue."[126]

Gerald Stansbury, president of the county chapter of the NAACP, disagreed. "I really feel it's racially motivated," he said of the decision to remove the book. "I think they should put it back. We read about the white culture all the time. . . . But when someone writes about our culture—and that's what Maya has done—that's not OK."[127]

Julie Pruchniewski, a high school teacher in Anne Arundel County, said it was "ridiculous" that she could no longer use *Caged Bird* in her ninth-grade classes. She said this was the first time in her twenty-year teaching career in Anne Arundel that a book was removed from the curriculum because of parental objections. "It's one thing to read about segregation from a history textbook, another to read it in a teenager's young voice," said Pruchniewski. "It's much more vivid."[128]

Sheila Finlayson, who had taught the book in her ninth-grade class for two years, said the county action had removed a teaching tool that caught the interest of virtually every student. "I think it's pretty sad," she said. "Both years my ninth-graders totally enjoyed the book. It teaches a wonderful lesson about overcoming obstacles."[129]

Dr. Ronald Walters, professor of African American studies and political science at the University of Maryland, expressed concern that a small number of vocal parents could exert such influence on the curriculum.

"What the school system has appeared to do is be sensitive to a few individuals, and that's a bad way to run a school system," said Walters. "I couldn't imagine them doing this to classics that were boosting white self-esteem to which black parents objected."[130]

Anne Arundel school officials insisted that they had not banned the book, because it would continue to be taught in the eleventh grade and would remain in school libraries. But anger over the removal of the book from the ninth grade continued to grow.

About 80 percent of Anne Arundel's public school enrollment is white, and less than 20 percent is black. Though the group of white parents protesting *Caged Bird* was small, they thought of themselves as representing the county's majority. Sue Crandall, leader of the protest, defended the school board's action. She said the book was sexually explicit and gave an out-of-date and negative image of white people. "It is perfectly understandable for it to be anti-white, because it was written in 1969," she explained. Still, she complained that Angelou portrayed white people as "horrible, nasty, stupid people. I kept waiting for her to realize that white people weren't all bad."

Crandall thought Angelou's narrative would be "inflammatory for black kids," because, "if a child didn't have negative feelings about white people, this could sow the seeds." Crandall went so far as to characterize Angelou herself as a racist, concluding that because she "spoke of" the Million Man March, it implied an "alignment" with Louis Farrakhan which therefore "equals hatred of whites and Jews."[131]

As the controversy over *Caged Bird* escalated, superintendent Parham announced that she would ask the schools' curriculum committee to review the book in the spring for possible reinstatement.

On April 29, 1998, a thirteen-member committee of parents, teachers, and two students met at the board of education offices in Annapolis and voted unanimously to return *I Know Why the Caged Bird Sings* to the ninth-grade curriculum in Anne Arundel County. However, the specially convened committee ruled that teachers who intend to assign the book must alert parents to the nature of its content. If a parent objects to the book, a teacher may assign other reading to the student.

Sharon Taylor, who, with her husband Barry, had filed the formal complaint that required the committee's review, supported the committee's parental alert recommendation, but she expressed disappointment at the decision to reinstate the book. "I thought we had gotten our point across well and that at least one of the committee members would have voted against it," she said. She continued to claim that ninth-grade students were "too immature" to appreciate the book as literature.

The most unusual aspect of the Taylors' complaint was the charge that the book's profanity and sexually explicit scenes violated the school system's policy on *student conduct*. "You can't ask a student not to use vulgar language or racial slurs if they are reading about it in class and reading it out loud in class," explained Barry Taylor. "[O]ur kids are not allowed to use profanity or go to movies where there is profanity."[132]

The public and official debate continued as the Taylors decided to appeal the committee decision to the full school board. The August 22 board hearing on whether to remove the book from the ninth-grade curriculum was attended by about thirty people, most of whom supported Taylor's views. The hearing was conducted much like a courtroom proceeding, with a court reporter recording the words of the "prosecution," represented by the Taylors, and the "defense," represented by the attorney for School Superintendent Parham. The school board would act as the jury.

The school board heard an emotional Barry Taylor read a graphic description of the rape of an eight-year-old from *I Know Why the Caged Bird Sings*. Another prosecution witness, Reverend Earl Thompson of the local Community Baptist Church, testified that he and his wife were offended by the book. Reverend Thompson repeated the argument that reading about prohibited conduct was equivalent to performing it. Citing the Code of Student Conduct for county schools, he said it was hypocritical to allow students to read about sexual harassment, racial slurs, and profanity but not be allowed to speak that way.

"The standards in the student handbook ought to be followed," he said. "A student who reads Ms. Angelou's book and reads the profanity ought to be disciplined."

Other witnesses told the board that the book was vulgar and had no literary value, but local teacher Sheila Finlayson said Angelou's book was great literature that was appropriate and beneficial for ninth-grade students. "Reading Maya Angelou is like reading a letter from your mother," she said. "It's something they [students] can immediately relate to. It teaches them tremendous lessons in life. . . . This book shows they can persevere even under the worst circumstances."[133]

When the eight-member school board had heard both the "prosecution" and "defense," it was faced with the task of evaluating the evidence and rendering a verdict on Angelou's book. On October 13, the board released its thirteen page decision, concluding that they "simply disagreed" with Barry and Sharon Taylor's belief that the book is inappropriate for students.

"This board has concluded that the value of *Caged Bird* outweighs the concerns expressed by Mr. and Mrs. Taylor," said the report.

School board member Paul Rudolph admitted that even though he too was bothered by the book's profanity, "the value of the book is that it shows how a person who came from the most socially and economically disenfranchised background can succeed."[134]

NOTES

1. James Moffett, *Storm in the Mountains: A Case Study in Censorship, Conflict, and Consciousness* (Carbondale: Southern Illinois University Press, 1988), p. 15.

2. Ibid., p. 16.

3. Ibid., p. 19.

4. Thelma R. Conley, "Scream Silently: One View of the Kanawha County Textbook Controversy," *Journal of Research and Development in Education*, Spring 1976, p. 95.

5. Moffett, *Storm in the Mountains*, p. 24.

6. George Hillocks, Jr., "Books and Bombs: Ideological Conflict and the Schools," *School Review*, August 1978, pp. 632, 636.

7. Moffett, *Storm in the Mountains*, p. 26.

8. Robert Oscar Goff, *The Washington County Schoolbook Controversy: The Political Implications of a Social and Religious Conflict* (Ph.D. diss., Catholic University, Ann Arbor, University Microfilms, 1976), p. 47.

9. Ibid., p. 241.

10. Ibid., p. 300.

11. Ibid., p. 265.

12. Ibid., p. 82.

13. Frank R. Kemerer and Stephanie Abraham Hirsh, "School Library Censorship Comes Before the Supreme Court," *Phi Delta Kappan*, March 1982, p. 444.

14. Steven Pico, "An Introduction to Censorship," *School Library Media Quarterly*, Winter 1990, p. 84.

15. *Board of Education, Island Trees Union Free School District No. 26 v. Pico*, 102 S. Ct. 2799, 2803 (1982).

16. *Board of Education, Island Trees Union Free School District No. 26 v. Pico*, 474 F. Supp. 387, 390 (EDNY 1979).

17. Pico, "An Introduction to Censorship," p. 85.

18. Ibid., p. 87.

19. "Letters to the Editor: Sex Book Called Source of Immorality," *Prince George's Journal*, March 17, 1978, p. A6. Reprinted with permission of *The Prince George's Journal*.

20. Interoffice memorandum from Stephen C. Orenstein to Arthur A. Marshall, Jr., state's attorney for Prince George's County, Maryland, September 15, 1977.

21. Memorandum from William R. Gordon to library board members, September 21, 1977.

22. Telephone interviews with William Gordon, spring 1992. Unless separately endnoted, all other Gordon quotes are from these interviews.

23. Letter from William Gordon, director, Prince George's County Memorial Library System, to Winfield M. Kelly, Jr., county executive, Prince George's County, December 14, 1977.

24. County Council of Prince George's County, Maryland, Bill No. CB-42-1978, June 27, 1978, "An Act Concerning Obscene Matter."

25. Peter D. Pichaske, "Libraries, Schools Attack Porno Ban," *Prince George's Journal*, September 1, 1978, p. A5.

26. Ibid., p. A1.

27. "A Punch at Playboy May KO," *Prince George's Sentinel*, August 17, 1978, p. A5.

28. "Libraries, Schools Attack Porno Ban," p. A5.

29. Quoted in Joan DelFattore, *What Johnny Shouldn't Read: Textbook Censorship in America* (New Haven: Yale University Press, 1992), p. 20.

30. Beth McLeod, "Are These Textbooks Wrong?" *Johnson City Press Chronicle*, November 27, 1983, p. 41.

31. "Intolerant Zealots Threaten Our Schools," *USA Today*, July 23, 1986, p. A8.

32. Quoted in David W. Dellinger, "My Way or the Highway: The Hawkins County Textbook Controversy" (Ph.D. diss., University of Tennessee, Knoxville, University Microfilms, May 1991), p. 148.

33. David Brooks, "Hawkins School Board, Principals Focus on COBS," *Kingsport Times-News*, December 7, 1983, p. A6.

34. Quoted in Dellinger, "My Way or the Highway," p. 217.

35. Quoted in ibid., p. 224.

36. *Mozert v. Hawkins County Board of Education*, 827 F.2d 1058, 1069 (1987).

37. Quoted in Joan DelFattore, *What Johnny Shouldn't Read: Textbook Censorship in America* (New Haven: Yale University Press, 1992), p. 75.

38. "County Board Bans Faulkner Book," *Mayfield Messenger*, September 5, 1986, p. 1. This censorship incident has been dramatized in detail in William Noble's *Bookbanning in America: Who Bans Books and Why*, Middlebury, Paul S. Erickson, 1990.

39. Noble, *Bookbanning in America*, pp. 10–11.

40. Ibid., pp. 8–9.

41. "County Board Bans Faulkner Book," p. 1.

42. "Book's Loss Doesn't Kill Controversy in Graves," *Louisville Courier-Journal*, September 11, 1986, p. B3.

43. "Graves Board Bans Faulkner Book from School Library," *Paducah Sun*, September 5, 1986, p. A1.

44. "ACLU Letter Addressed to Book-Banning Topic," *Mayfield Messenger*, September 10, 1986, p. 1.

45. "Graves Board Bans Faulkner Book from School Library," *Paducah Sun*, September 5, 1986, p. A1.

46. "Book's Loss Doesn't Kill Controversy in Graves," p. B3.

47. "Graves School Board to Take 'Further Action' in Bookbanning Case," *Paducah Sun*, September 11, 1986, p. A12.

48. Ibid.

49. "Graves Sticks to Ban," *Paducah Sun*, September 12, 1986, p. A18.

50. "Faulkner Wasn't a Pornographer," *Paducah Sun*, September 11, 1986, p. A4.

51. Quoted in Noble, *Bookbanning in America*, p. 29.

52. "Ban-Fighter Says She's Getting Lots of Support," *Paducah Sun*, September 14, 1986, p. A16.

53. "Graves Sticks to Ban," p. A1.

54. Ibid., p. A18.

55. Quoted in Noble, *Bookbanning in America*, pp. 32–33.

56. "Graves Sticks to Ban," p. A18.

57. Ibid., p. A1.

58. "Ban-Fighter Says She's Getting Lots of Support," p. A16.

59. Jim Paxton, "Graves' Theatre of the Absurd," *Paducah Sun*, September 14, 1986, p. C2.

60. "Ban-Fighter Says She's Getting Lots of Support," p. A16.

61. "Graves Ban Makes 'As I Lay Dying' a Hot Item," *Paducah Sun*, September 14, 1986, p. A1.

62. "Ban-Fighter Says She's Getting Lots of Support," p. A1.

63. "Book-Banners Having 2nd Thoughts: Lawyer," *Paducah Sun*, September 17, 1986, p. A1.

64. "Publicity, Legal Questions Reverse Book Ban Decision," *Paducah Sun*, September 19, 1986, p. A18.

65. "Text of Statement by Jeff Howard, Board Chairman," *Paducah Sun*, September 19, 1986, p. A1.

66. "Graves Teachers Praise End of Ban on Faulkner Book," *Louisville Courier-Journal*, September 20, 1986, p. B5.

67. Peter Carlson, "A Chilling Case of Censorship," *Washington Post Magazine*, January 4, 1987, p. 13.

68. ReLeah Hawks, "The Year They Came to Arrest the Books," *Florida English Journal*, Fall 1986, p. 14.

69. Peter Carlson, "A Chilling Case of Censorship," p. 14.

70. "Book Ban Issue: Parents' Rights vs. Censorship," *Panama City News-Herald*, June 1, 1986, p. A2.

71. Ibid.

72. "Everyone Seeks the Last Word in Book Battle," *Miami Herald*, May 26, 1987, p. A6.

73. Ibid.

74. "Book Ban Issue: Parents' Rights vs. Censorship," p. A2.

75. Ibid.

76. Hawks, "The Year They Came to Arrest the Books," p. 14.

77. Peter Carlson, "A Chilling Case of Censorship," p. 16.

78. Ibid., p. 17.

79. "A Tumultuous Chapter in Fla.," *Atlanta Journal and Constitution*, June 7, 1987, p. A21.

80. Peter Carlson, "A Chilling Case of Censorship," p. 40.

81. Ibid., p. 10.

82. Ibid.

83. "Teacher Vows Fight," *Panama City News-Herald*, November 13, 1986, p. B2.

84. Peter Carlson, "A Chilling Case of Censorship," p. 41.

85. Ken Kister, "Censorship in the Sunshine State," *Wilson Library Bulletin*, November 1989, p. 29.

86. "Everyone Seeks the Last Word in Book Battle," p. A6.

87. "Library Takes Stand on Censorship," *Panama City News-Herald*, May 13, 1987, p. A2.

88. DelFattore, *What Johnny Shouldn't Read*, p. 109.

89. *Farrell* v. *Hall*, Order, July 18, 1988, U.S. District Court for the Northern District of Florida.

90. Kister, "Censorship in the Sunshine State," pp. 29, 32.

91. Patrick Dilger, "Author Laments 'Pitiful People' in Book-Ban Flap," *New Haven Register*, November 9, 1991, p. A10.

92. Marianne Cipriano, "Cheshire Parents Want 'Filthy' Books Yanked from Schools," *Meriden Record-Journal*, November 8, 1991, p. A4.

93. "Editorials: Cheshire Books," *Meriden Record-Journal*, November 13, 1991, p. A16.

94. Jacqueline Weaver, "A Mother Calls Two Books Inappropriate for Fifth Grade," *New York Times (Connecticut Weekly)*, January 12, 1992, Section 12, p. CN9.

95. "Parents Ask for Ban on 2 'Obscene' Kids' Books," *New Haven Register*, November 8, 1991, p. A19.

96. Marianne Cipriano, "Couple Battles Books for Being 'Abusive' of Kids," *Meriden Record-Journal*, November 18, 1991, p. A13.

97. "Disputed Books Out of Classes," *Meriden Record-Journal*, November 9, 1991, p. A9.

98. Dilger, "Author Laments 'Pitiful People' in Book-Ban Flap," pp. A1, A10.

99. Marianne Cipriano, "Author Defends Her Book," *Meriden Record-Journal*, November 13, 1991, p. A1.

100. "Efforts Grow to Censor Books," *New Haven Register*, December 1, 1991, p. A17.

101. "Editorials: Cheshire Books," p. A16.

102. Christopher Collier, "Two Objectionable Books Are Not Obscene," *New Haven Register*, December 15, 1991, p. B3.

103. "Board Witholds Comments As More Books Come Under Fire," *New Haven Register*, January 20, 1992, p. 16.

104. Patrick Dilger, "Board Refuses to Ban Two Books from Schools," *New Haven Register*, February 7, 1992, pp. A1, A16.

105. John Boe, "Good Impressions in Winters," unpublished article, 1992 (available from the author).

106. Don Biasotti, Jr., "Forum Discusses 'Nappy Hair,' " *The Orion*, March 17, 1999, p. 2, http://orion.csuchio.edu.

107. Liz Leyden, "Story Hour Didn't Have a Happy Ending," *Washington Post*, December 3, 1998, p. A3.

108. Lynette Clemftson, "Caught in the Cross-Fire," *Newsweek*, December 14, 1998, p. 38.

109. Liz Leyden, "Story Hour Didn't Have a Happy Ending," p. A3.

110. Judy Glave, "Teacher in Book Flap Weighs Return to Class," *Bergen Record*—online, November 27, 1998, p. 2, www.bergen.com/region/nappy.

111. Joanne Wasserman, "Teacher's Painful Test," *New York Daily News*—online edition, December 5, 1998, p. 4, www.nydailynews.com.

112. "Controversy over 'Nappy Hair,' " *Newsletter on Intellectual Freedom*, March 1999, p. 55.

113. Lynette Holloway, "School Officials Support Teacher on Book That Parents Call Racially Insensitive," *New York Times*, November 25, 1998, p. B10.

114. Lynette Holloway, "Crew Defends Teacher in Book Dispute," *New York Times*, December 15, 1998, p. B3.

115. Judie Glave, "Acclaimed Kids' Book Gets Teacher Ousted," *Detroit Free Press*—online, November 25, 1998, pp. 1–2, www.freep.com.

116. Michele Norris, "Nappy Hair Flap," *ABCNEWS*.com, December 4, 1998, pp. 1–2, http://204/202.137.

117. Ibid., p. 3.

118. "Controversy over 'Nappy Hair,'" *Newsletter on Intellectual Freedom*, March 1999, p. 55.

119. Martin Mbugua, "Book-Flap Teach Regroups," *New York Daily News*—online edition, December 8, 1998, pp. 1–2, www.nydailynews.com.

120. Don Biasotti, Jr., "Forum Discusses 'Nappy Hair,'" *The Orion*, March 17, 1999, p. 2, http://orion.csuchio.edu.

121. Annie Gowen, "In 2 Md. Counties, a War over Words," *Washington Post*, January 11, 1998, p. A20.

122. Ibid.

123. Annie Gowen, "St. Mary's Commissioners Back Removing Morrison Novel from Curriculum," *Washington Post*, January 18, 1998, p. B4.

124. Ibid.

125. Dail Willis, "Arundel Removes Angelou Novel," *Baltimore Sun*, January 12, 1998, p. B1.

126. Ibid.

127. Ibid.

128. Gowen, "In 2 Md. Counties, a War over Words," p. A20.

129. Dail Willis, "Arundel Removes Angelou Novel," p. B1.

130. Ibid.

131. Ibid.

132. Kris Antonelli, "School Panel OKs Use of Books," *Baltimore Sun*, April 30, 1998, p. B1.

133. Kris Antonelli, "Parent Testifies against Book," *Baltimore Sun*, August 23, 1998, p. B6.

134. "Arundel School Board Keeps Angelou's Book on Shelves," *Baltimore Sun*, October 14, 1998, p. B4.

| 2 |

The Law on Bookbanning

BACKGROUND

Since the first edition of this book appeared, the core of legal precedent with respect to bookbanning, including the Supreme Court's controlling decision in *Hazelwood* v. *Kuhlmeier* (1988), has remained essentially unchanged. But the body of relevant law has expanded tangentially through legislation and litigation in diverse areas like the Internet and the publishing industry. An examination of the law involving bookbanning in schools and libraries reveals two interesting surprises. First, the major legal precedent relates *exclusively* to public school censorship, rather than public library censorship. Second, most of the case law on such bookbanning does not deal directly with books at all, concentrating more generally on the authority of school officials to control the curriculum and the libraries as part of the process of inculcating and socializing students. School boards are as often the victim as the villain in bookbanning incidents. Sometimes school officials exercise administrative authority to repudiate censorship attempts by religious or political pressure groups. Other times, they invoke seemingly arbitrary authority to impose their own taste or ideology on the local curriculum or school library. We will see that the latter has become more likely since the 1988 *Hazelwood School District* v. *Kuhlmeier* decision, which gave almost unlimited authority to school officials to control curricular expression.

The virtual absence of major litigation concerning censorship in public libraries is probably attributable to their more diverse clientele and the relative ease with which disputes can be resolved in this less sensitive environment. Deanna Duby, an attorney for People for the American Way (PAW), says that some degree of public school censorship for "educational purposes" is tacitly accepted by the law and the community. This is in part due to mandatory school attendance, the homogeneous curriculum, and the absence of parental oversight within the classroom. On the other hand, it is assumed that parents monitor their children's use of the public library. For all these reasons, there is much more law regulating public schools than public libraries; and where there is law, there is litigation.

School censorship cases go to court because the conflicts are sensitive, legalistic, and intractable. But how are teachers and librarians to sort out the legal precedent that protects them from bookbanning? Today, *Hazelwood School District* v. *Kuhlmeier* (1988) is regarded as the benchmark of legal doctrine toward school and library censorship. It appears to have established a greater authority for school officials to control the content of the curriculum, including school libraries, than had been previously accepted. However, from *Meyer* v. *Nebraska* (1923) to *Hazelwood* (1988) and beyond, the body of legal precedent concerning bookbanning in schools and libraries is often contradictory and inconclusive, and the current status of First Amendment protection therein may seem unclear. This chapter analyzes the major legal precedent concerning bookbanning in schools and libraries to reveal its evolution and current status.

APPROPRIATE MEANS AND LEGITIMATE PURPOSES

The earliest cases from which current constitutional guidelines on bookbanning in schools and libraries are derived are *Meyer* v. *Nebraska* (1923) and *Bartels* v. *State of Iowa* (1923).[1] In these two "companion cases," the Supreme Court struck down state laws against teaching subjects in any language other than English prior to the eighth grade. The decision demonstrated that the Supreme Court, when treating an appropriate case, will interfere with a curricular decision made by state or local authorities.

Justice James Clark McReynolds's opinion in *Meyer* suggests a "means test" for judging the constitutionality of state control over schools: "Perhaps it would be highly advantageous if all had ready understanding of our ordinary speech, but this cannot be coerced by methods which conflict with the Constitution—a desirable end cannot be promoted by prohibited means."[2]

Two years later, in *Pierce* v. *Society of Sisters* (1925), an Oregon military academy challenged a state law requiring all children between the ages of eight and sixteen to attend public school in the district where they reside. The lower court ruled that the conduct of schools was a property right and that parents, as a part of their liberty, may direct the education of their children by selecting reputable schools and teachers outside the public schools. Enforcement of the Oregon statute would, therefore, not only deprive parents of their liberty but would destroy the business and property of private school owners. The Supreme Court subsequently affirmed that decision.

In striking down mandatory public school attendance, the Court in *Pierce* stated:

> The fundamental theory of liberty upon which all governments in this Union repose excludes any general power of the state to standardize its children by forcing them to accept instruction from public teachers only. The child is not the mere creature of the state; those who nurture him and direct his destiny have the right, coupled with the high duty, to recognize and prepare him for additional obligations.

This statement has been interpreted as condemning the state's *purpose* in attempting to standardize its children. More particularly, in writing for the Court in *Pierce*, Justice McReynolds declared:

> Under the doctrine of *Meyer v. Nebraska*, 262 U.S. 390, we think it entirely plain that the Act of 1922 unreasonably interferes with the liberty of parents and guardians to direct the upbringing and education of children under their control. As often heretofore pointed out, rights guaranteed by the Constitution may not be abridged by legislation that has no reasonable relation to some purpose within the competency of the State.[3]

This suggests that legislation abridging these guaranteed rights may be found unconstitutional if its *purpose* goes beyond the limited competency of the state or if the state's *means* to accomplish a legitimate purpose is not reasonably related to that purpose. Both *Meyer* and *Pierce* have been interpreted as applying a First Amendment test based on the purpose or motivation behind the disputed actions of school authorities. Justice Oliver Wendell Holmes, dissenting in *Meyer*, clearly favored a means test rather than a motivation test. Indeed, though he was writing in dissent in *Meyer*, Holmes's opinion is still cited by modern writers as support for a constitutional means test. For example, years later in *Board of Education, Island Trees Union Free School District No. 26 v. Pico* (1982), Justice Harry Blackmun invoked *Meyer* in rejecting the view that a state might so conduct its schools as to foster a homogeneous people.

Pierce established the states' authority over the public school curriculum but maintained that such authority is limited by the constitutional protections for individual rights. Neither *Meyer* nor *Pierce* provided grounds for deciding the limits on state power. Not until 1940, in the flag salute case, *Minersville School District v. Gobitis* did the Supreme Court go beyond *Meyer* and *Pierce* in clarifying these limits. Here, the children of a

Jehovah's Witnesses family had refused to join the flag salute ceremonies at their school, claiming that they were following the biblical prohibition against bowing down to graven images. After the Gobitis children were expelled from school, their parents brought the suit decided by the Supreme Court in 1940. The court ruled that the school authorities *did* have the right to require participation in the flag salute, and that the religious beliefs of the Jehovah's Witnesses did *not* represent a First Amendment exemption.

In proclaiming that our flag summarized all the values of our free society, Justice Felix Frankfurter wrote for the Court: "A society which is dedicated to the preservation of these ultimate values of civilization may in self-protection utilize the educational process for inculcating those almost unconscious feelings which bind men together in a comprehending loyalty." Once more addressing the *means* by which the state may control educational expression, Frankfurter claimed that the issue before the Court was "whether the legislatures of the various states and the authorities in a thousand counties and school districts of this country are barred from determining the appropriateness of various means to evoke that unifying sentiment without which there can ultimately be no liberties, civil or religious." Frankfurter concluded that

> the courtroom is not the arena for debating issues of educational policy. It is not our province to choose among competing considerations in the subtle process of securing effective loyalty to the traditional ideals of democracy, while respecting at the same time individual idiosyncracies among a people so diversified in racial origins and religious allegiances. So to hold would in effect make us the school board for the country.[4]

Justice Harlan Stone, dissenting in *Gobitis*, declared:

> The state concededly has the power to require and control the education of its citizens, . . . [but] there are other ways to teach loyalty and patriotism . . . than by compelling the pupil to affirm what he does not believe. . . . Without recourse to such compulsion, the state is free to compel attendance at school and require teaching by instruction and study of all in our history, . . . including the guarantees of civil liberties which tend to inspire patriotism and love of country.[5]

Justice Stone's dissenting opinion in *Gobitis* laid the foundation for the majority in *West Virginia State Board of Education* v. *Barnette* (1943), just three years later, in which *Gobitis* was overruled. The challenge in *Barnette* was again brought by Jehovah's Witnesses, but Justice Robert H. Jackson's statement went beyond any religious claims: "If there is any fixed star in our constitutional constellation, it is that no official, high or petty, can prescribe what shall be orthodox in politics, nationalism, religion, or other matters of opinion or force citizens to confess by word or act their faith therein." Jackson sharply distinguished the bureaucratic authority of school boards from that of, say, a public utility, which has the power to impose legislatively adopted restrictions. He concluded that "freedoms of speech and of press, of assembly, and of worship may not be infringed on such slender grounds."

In overruling *Gobitis*, *Barnette* established a legal restraint on the power of school officials to impose their "socialization" process on students. Justice Jackson's repudiation of Justice Felix Frankfurter's *Gobitis* opinion reinforced the notion of a "means test" for judging the limits of the state's authority: "National unity as an end which officials may foster by persuasion and example is not in question. The problem is whether under our Constitution compulsion as here employed is a permissible means for its achievement." Jackson suggested clear limits upon the authority of school officials to impose their ideas on students. "That they are educating the young for citizenship is reason for scrupulous protection of constitutional freedoms of the individual, if we are not to strangle the free mind at its source and teach youth to discount important principles of our government as mere platitudes."[6]

This doctrinal debate continued in subsequent cases like *Keyishian* v. *Board of Regents*, *Epperson* v. *Arkansas*, and *Tinker* v. *Des Moines Independent Community School District*. In *Keyishian* (1967), the Supreme Court professed broad First Amendment protection for academic freedom, striking down sections of a New York law that disqualified members of "subversive" organizations from teaching. Writing for the majority, Justice William Brennan declared that the First Amendment "does not tolerate laws that cast a pall of orthodoxy over the classroom." Brennan explained:

> The vigilant protection of constitutional freedoms is nowhere more vital than in the community of American schools. The classroom is peculiarly the "marketplace of ideas." The Nation's future depends upon leaders trained through wide exposure to that robust exchange of ideas which discovers truth "out of a multitude of tongues," [rather] than through any kind of authoritative selection.

Brennan concluded: "Our Nation is deeply committed to safeguarding academic freedom, which is of transcendent value to all of us and not merely to the teachers concerned. That freedom is therefore a special concern of the First Amendment."[7] However, because the circumstances in *Keyishian* concerned college faculty, the extension of academic freedom to elementary and secondary education was left to two cases addressed by the Court during the following year.

Epperson v. *Arkansas* (1968) and *Tinker* v. *Des Moines Independent Com-*

munity School District (1969) were argued within four weeks of each other, and none of the justices siding with Frankfurter in *Gobitis* remained on the Court. Though *Epperson* and *Tinker* did not focus on the socializing function of schools that had been emphasized in *Meyer* and *Barnette*, the cases did involve disputes over the appropriate extent of legislative and administrative discretion in controlling school operations, including libraries. *Epperson* threw out an Arkansas law against teaching evolution and indicated that the principles of academic freedom established in *Keyishian* should also apply to precollegiate levels of education. Writing for the court in *Epperson*, Justice Abe Fortas quoted *Keyishian's* rejection of "laws that cast a pall of orthodoxy over the classroom." In dissent, Justice Hugo Black accused Fortas of applying a "motivation test" in *Epperson*, claiming, "[T]his court has consistently held that it is not for us to invalidate a statute because of our views that the 'motives' behind its passage were improper." Black concluded:

> I am not ready to hold that a person hired to teach school children takes with him into the classroom a constitutional right to teach . . . subjects that the school's managers do not want discussed. . . . I question whether it is absolutely certain, as the Court's opinion indicates, that "academic freedom" permits a teacher to breach his contracted agreement to teach only the subjects designated by the school authorities who hired him.[8]

But Justice Potter Stewart, in his concurring opinion, stated:

> It is one thing for a state to determine that the subject of higher mathematics, or astronomy, or biology shall or shall not be included in its public school curriculum. It is quite another thing for a State to make it a criminal offense for a public school teacher so much as to mention the very existence of an entire system of respected human thought.[9]

The decision in *Epperson* was based on the First Amendment prohibition against religious establishment and was not, strictly speaking, a precedent for free speech rights of elementary and secondary school students. But *Keyishian* and *Epperson* prepared the way for the momentous First Amendment decision in *Tinker* v. *Des Moines Independent Community School District* (1969). Like *Epperson*, *Tinker* involved disputes over the limits of legislative and administrative discretion in controlling school operations. Indeed, *Epperson* and *Tinker* were considered almost contemporaneously by the Court. Four weeks after the Court heard arguments in *Epperson*, the decision in that case was announced on the same day that *Tinker* was argued.

Tinker arose when a number of students in Des Moines chose to demonstrate their objection to the Vietnam War by wearing black armbands to school. The principals of the Des Moines schools announced that any student wearing such an armband would be asked to remove it, and if the student refused, he or she would be suspended from school. One group of students, including John and Mary Beth Tinker, wore the armbands to school, where they were told to remove them in accordance with the principals' edict. They refused and were ordered to leave school. The students subsequently returned to school without their armbands, but only after filing suit in federal court.

The Tinkers lost their case at both the district court level and in the U.S. Court of Appeals, but the U.S. Supreme Court reversed these decisions. In the Supreme Court's first affirmation of First Amendment rights for schoolchildren, the majority opinion held that school officials may not place arbitrary restraints on student speech in public schools. In *Tinker*, Justice Fortas wrote: "First Amendment rights, applied in light of the special characteristics of the school environment, are available to teachers and students. It can hardly be argued that either students or teachers shed their constitutional rights to freedom of speech or expression at the schoolhouse gate." Quoting heavily from Brennan's opinion for the court in *Keyishian*, Fortas emphasized the classroom as the "marketplace of ideas" and declared, "In our system, students may not be regarded as closed-circuit recipients of only that which the State chooses to communicate."[10]

Though the courts after *Tinker* continued to examine the state's means and motives for suppressing educational expression, they were soon to test the notion of a student's explicit right to receive ideas.

THE RIGHT TO RECEIVE IDEAS

The courts have long acknowledged a citizen's right to receive information. In *Martin v. City of Struthers* (1943),[11] the Supreme Court gave the first explicit recognition of the right to *receive* information. Justice Hugo Black wrote: "This freedom [of speech and press] embraces the right to distribute literature, and necessarily protects the right to receive it." In Black's view, the right to receive information was "vital to the preservation of a free society." In *Lamont v. U.S. Postmaster General* (1965),[12] the Court gave implicit support for the right to receive information, stating: "The dissemination of ideas can accomplish nothing if otherwise willing addressees are not free to receive and consider them." Justice Brennan noted that it would be a barren marketplace indeed that allowed only sellers and not buyers. The Court's opinion in *Virginia State Board of Pharmacy v. Virginia Citizens Consumer Council* (1976)[13] has become a cornerstone in the protection of the right to receive information. Here the Court extended First Amendment protection to commercial speech, declaring: "Freedom of speech presupposes a willing speaker. But where a speaker exists as in the case here, the protection afforded is to the communication, to its source and to its recipients both."[14] This statement was the Court's first explicit recognition of First Amendment protection for *both* the dissemination and reception of information.

Despite the clarity of these pronouncements, the courts have never unequivocally affirmed such rights within the classroom or school library. In *Wisconsin* v. *Yoder* (1972) and *San Antonio Independent School District* v. *Rodriguez* (1973), it was argued that in order for Americans to exercise their right to participate in a democracy, they must have the right to universal education. The Court majority in both cases dismissed this argument, so it cannot be regarded as precedent for a student's First Amendment right to receive information.

In *Yoder*, Chief Justice Warren Burger wrote for an almost unanimous Court in affirming the right of Amish parents to have their children exempted from compulsory schooling beyond the age of fourteen. Burger claimed that Amish children must acquire "Amish attitudes" and the specific skills to be an Amish farmer or housewife. In clarifying the purposes and powers of public education, Burger concluded: "Indeed it seems clear that if the state is empowered as *parens patriae*, to 'save' a child from himself or his Amish parents by requiring an additional two years of compulsory formal high school education, the State will in large measure influence, if not determine, the religious future of the child." In rejecting Wisconsin's claim that mandatory public education beyond the eighth grade was necessary to protect Amish children from ignorance, Burger rejected the notion that students had a constitutional "right to know."[15]

In dissenting in *Yoder*, Justice William Douglas warned: "It is the student's judgement, not his parents, that is essential if we are to give full meaning to what we have said about the Bill of Rights and of the right of students to be masters of their own destiny." Douglas expressed concern that the child's choices and judgments be respected before allowing the imposition of Amish attitudes:

> Where a child is mature enough to express potentially conflicting desires, it would be an invasion of the child's rights to permit such an imposition without canvassing his view.... And, if an Amish child desires to attend high school, and is mature enough to have that desire respected, the State may well be able to override the parents' religiously motivated objections.[16]

In *Rodriguez* (1973), the Court rejected a claim that the Texas school finance system violated the equal protection clause because of severe inequalities in educational spending. Emphasizing the importance of education to the realization of the right to free speech, the plaintiffs argued that a "strict scrutiny" standard was required to justify state-sponsored inequalities. Writing for the majority, Justice Lewis Powell argued that *if* children have a fundamental right to education, it would not be violated simply by relative differences in spending levels.

Justice Thurgood Marshall's dissenting opinion in *Rodriguez* invoked *Yoder* in arguing, "Education directly affects the ability of a child to exercise his First Amendment rights, both as a source and as a receiver of ideas, whatever interests he may pursue in life." But Marshall's claim that a student's right to education is derived from a First Amendment right to *receive* ideas was again rejected by the majority in *Rodriguez*, for whom Justice Powell wrote:

> The Court has long afforded zealous protection against unjustifiable government interference with an individual's rights to speak and vote. Yet we have never presumed to possess either the ability or the authority to guarantee to the citizenry the most *effective* speech or the most *informed* electoral choice.[17]

When addressing bookbanning in schools, the courts have usually held that a student's right to receive information is subject to a school board's authority to determine the curriculum, including the library's collections. Sometimes this authority may be exercised to deny students' access to information, but it also has been used to deny demands to censor library and curricular materials. Among the earliest major opinions that directly addressed the right of a school board to remove books from a school library was the decision in *Presidents Council District 25* v. *Community School Board No. 25* (1972). After receiving several complaints about offensive language in a junior high school library book, *Down These Mean Streets* by Piri Thomas, a school board acted to prevent access to the book. The board took this action over the objections of parents, teachers, librarians, students, the local PTA, and a junior high school principal. Nonetheless, the U.S. Court of Appeals for the Second Circuit deferred to the school board's judgment, upholding its action in denying access to the Thomas novel.

The court in *Presidents Council* declined to review either the wisdom or the efficacy of the determination of the board, saying that *Epperson* precluded the court's intervention "in the resolution of conflicts which arise in the daily operation of school systems and which do not directly and sharply implicate basic constitutional values." Judge William H. Mulligan, writing for the court, stated:

> Since we are dealing not with the collection of a public book store but with the library of a public junior high school, evidently some authorized person or body has to make determination as to what the library collection will

be. . . . The ensuing shouts of book burning, witch hunting and violation of academic freedom hardly elevate this intramural strife to first amendment constitutional proportions.[18]

The court thus ruled that since school boards are statutorily empowered to operate the schools and prescribe the curriculum, they are the appropriate body to assume responsibility for book selection. Indeed, the court reduced the issue to the level of shelving books:

> The administration of any library, whether it be a university or particularly a public junior high school, involves a constant process of selection and winnowing based not only on educational needs but financial and architectural realities. To suggest that the shelving or unshelving of books presents a constitutional issue, particularly when there is no showing of a curtailment of freedom of speech or thought, is a proposition we cannot accept.[19]

The appeals court in *Presidents Council* did not regard the removal of the book from the library as an effort by the state to aid or oppose religion, as was at issue in *Epperson*, nor did it consider the removal to be a restraint on nondisruptive silent expression, which was prohibited in *Tinker*.[20] But *Presidents Council* did provide some guidelines by which the legitimacy of bookbanning in schools may be judged. For one, school authorities are expected to follow established procedures when removing books. Indeed, the court noted that such procedures did exist and that the school board had followed them properly. School authorities are also required to demonstrate proper motivation in removing books, showing economically justified or politically neutral reasons for such action.

In 1975, the lengthy Kanawha County (West Virginia) textbook dispute, described in Chapter 1, found legal resolution in *Williams* v. *Board of Education of County of Kanawha* (1975). The plaintiffs alleged that the board of education had adopted textbooks containing "both religious and anti-religious materials offensive to Christian morals, matter which defames the Nation and which attacks civic virtue, and matter which suggests and encourages the use of bad English." Plaintiffs sought injunctive relief restraining the board from using the textbooks, which they alleged violated the state's neutrality in religious matters and inhibited the free exercise of their religion as guaranteed by the First Amendment. In rejecting these complaints, the court, quoting heavily from *Epperson*, declared:

> A complete loosening of imagination is necessary to find that placing the books and materials in the schools constitutes an establishment of religion contrary to the rights contained in the Constitution. Further, the Court finds nothing in defendant's conduct or acts which constitutes an inhibition

on or prohibition of the free exercise of religion. These rights are guaranteed by the First Amendment, but the amendment does not guarantee that nothing about religion will be taught in the schools nor that nothing offensive to any religion will be taught in the schools. . . . In the absence of bases for relief in the courts, where no violation of constitutional rights is found, plaintiffs . . . may find administrative remedies through board of education proceedings or ultimately at the polls on election day.[21]

The following year in *Minarcini* v. *Strongsville (Ohio) City School District* an appeals court seemed to reverse the *Presidents Council* opinion by denying a school board's authority to remove books from the curriculum and library. When high school teachers recommended the use of Joseph Heller's *Catch-22* and Kurt Vonnegut's *God Bless You, Mr. Rosewater* in the school curriculum, the Strongsville City Board of Education not only rejected their recommendation but also ordered that those books plus Vonnegut's *Cat's Cradle* be removed from the library. No official reason was given for the removal, but the minutes of a board meeting described the books as "completely sick" and "garbage." Five high school students, through their parents, brought class action against the city school district, members of the board of education, and the school superintendent, claiming violation of their First and Fourteenth Amendment rights. On appeal, the Sixth Circuit ruled against the school board, upholding the First Amendment right of teachers and librarians to disseminate information and the students' right to receive it.

In an affirmation of the students' right to know, the Appeals Court stated:

A public school library is also a valuable adjunct to classroom discussions. If one of the English teachers considered Joseph Heller's *Catch-22* to be one of the more important modern American novels (as, indeed, at least one did), we assume that no one would dispute that the First Amendment's protection of academic freedom would protect both his right to say so in class and his students' right to hear him and to find and read the book. Obviously, the students' success in this last endeavor would be greatly hindered by the fact that the book sought had been removed from a school library.

The court made reference to Justice Harry Blackmun's earlier opinion that "where a speaker exists . . . the protection afforded is to the communication, to its source and to its recipients both."[22]

The court in *Minarcini* said that the school board had removed the books "because it found them objectionable in content and because it felt it had the power, unfettered by the First Amendment, to censor the school library for subject matter which the Board members found distasteful." In rejecting the absolute right of a school board to remove books from the library, even when those materials are available outside the school, the court held that the removal of books from a school library was a much more serious burden upon the freedom of classroom discussion than the action found unconstitutional in *Tinker*. The court concluded:

> A library is a storehouse of knowledge. When created for a public school, it is an important privilege created by the state for the benefit of students in the schools. That privilege is not subject to being withdrawn by succeeding school boards whose members might desire to "winnow" the library for books the contents of which occasioned their displeasure or disapproval.[23]

The opinion in *Minarcini* was soon applied to resolve a Chelsea, Massachusetts, bookbanning. In 1976, the Chelsea School Committee banned the use of poetry anthology *Male and Female under 18*, describing it as "objectionable," "obnoxious," "filthy," and "vile and offensive garbage." The committee's actions were challenged in federal court by the Chelsea school librarian, Sonja Coleman, and a support group, the Right to Read Defense Committee of Chelsea. The complainants contended that the use of *Male and Female under 18* was fully protected under the First Amendment, that students possess a right to have access to such materials, and that the school committee's objections to the book did not constitutionally justify its suppression.

In *Right to Read Defense Committee* v. *School Committee of the City of Chelsea* (1978), the school committee argued that under Massachusetts law it had clear authority to approve or disapprove materials used in the schools, but the U.S District Court relied on *Minarcini* in requiring the school committee to return the anthology to the high school library. The *Chelsea* court found that the book was "tough but not obscene," and "no substantial government interest was served by cutting off student access to 'Male and Female' in the library." School officials were enjoined from removing *Male and Female under 18*, which was to be made available to students "in accordance with standard library procedures." Judge Joseph L. Tauro ruled:

> The library is "a mighty resource in the marketplace of ideas." There a student can literally explore the unknown, and discover areas of interest and thought not covered by the prescribed curriculum. The student who discovers the magic of the library is on the way to a life-long experience of self-education and enrichment. That student learns that a library is a place to test or expand upon ideas presented to him, in or out of the classroom. The most effective antidote to the poison of mindless orthodoxy is ready access to a broad sweep of ideas and philosophies. There is no dan-

ger from such exposure. The danger is mind control. The committee's ban of the anthology *Male and Female* is enjoined.[24]

As in *Minarcini*, the court distinguished between the authority of school boards to control the curriculum as opposed to library collections and also between the board's authority to *select* library books as opposed to *removing* them.

The following year, in *Cary* v. *Board of Education Arapahoe School District* (1979), an appeals court seemed to recognize both a teacher's right to independently select curricular materials and a school board's authority to remove them, even though they were stipulated to be "non-obscene." A Colorado school board banned ten books from use in high school English courses, giving no written reasons for banning the books. The board also declared that no books could be purchased or used for class assignment without board approval, and no student could be given credit for reading such books. The ten banned books were to be given to the department chairman who was to hold them pending further directions. Teachers were subject to dismissal if they violated any of these stipulations. Five teachers brought action against the board, claiming rights under the First and Fourteenth Amendments. The trial court found that the teachers had a First Amendment right to choose the contested books for their high school English courses but said their rights were waived under a collective-bargaining agreement previously reached with the school district.

The teachers appealed, and the U.S. Court of Appeals declared: "Thus we are presented with a conflict between the school board's powers over curriculum and the teachers' rights to classroom expression in a context somewhat different and more sharply drawn than any case which has arisen heretofore." The court claimed that "the board was acting within its rights in omitting the books, even though the decision was a political one influenced by the personal views of the members." Because the board gave no reasons for banning the books, the appeals court considered remanding the case for trial to determine if the board's purpose was constitutionally permissible. But the court chose not to remand for trial after concluding that the board's seemingly indiscriminate censorship showed no systematic effort to exclude any particular kind of thought. In a ruling that seemed to tolerate the banning of individual titles, so long as comparable alternatives were available, the court concluded: "No objection is made by the teachers that the exclusions prevent them from studying an entire representative group of writers. Rather the teachers want to be freed from the 'personal predilections' of the board. We do not see a basis in the Constitution to grant their wish."[25]

In *Salvail* v. *Nashua Board of Education* (1979), the Federal District Court for New Hampshire followed the *Chelsea* analysis, requiring the Nashua

Board of Education to return to the high school library copies of *Ms.* magazine, which had been removed because of alleged advertisements for "vibrators, contraceptives, materials dealing with lesbianism and witchcraft and gay material" as well as procommunist advertising. Here the court found that the board had failed "to demonstrate a substantial and legitimate government interest sufficient to warrant the removal of *Ms.* from the Nashua High School Library."[26]

Another 1979 case, *Ambach* v. *Norwick*,[27] affirmed the role of public schools as socializing agencies and the state's authority in performing that role. Here two teachers challenged the constitutionality of a New York statute that denied teaching certification to aliens not in the process of acquiring citizenship. The teachers cited *Meyer, Pierce, Barnette, Keyishian, Epperson,* and *Tinker,* among other cases, to support their argument that the New York statute should be subject to strict scrutiny on First Amendment grounds because it directly affects academic freedom. The district court agreed in an opinion emphasizing the First Amendment values involved, yet when the U.S. Supreme Court considered the case, it found no First Amendment violation. *Ambach* upheld discrimination in occupations, such as public school teaching, that "go to the heart of representative government," so long as the state could show that it was "reasonably related" to the legitimate public purpose for which it was employed. Although *Ambach,* like *Rodriguez,* was decided on equal protection grounds, it later became a pivotal case for First Amendment doctrine in the schools, cited in cases such as *Board of Education, Island Trees Union Free School District No. 26* v. *Pico* (1982), *Bethel* v. *Fraser* (1986), and *Hazelwood School District* v. *Kuhlmeier* (1988).

In *Zykan* v. *Warsaw (Indiana) Community School Corporation and Warsaw School Board of Trustees* (1980), an appeals court addressed the school board's removal of several books from a high school library, including *Growing Up Female in America, Go Ask Alice, The Bell Jar,* and *The Stepford Wives.* A student brought suit to reverse the school officials' decision to "limit or prohibit the use of certain textbooks, to remove a certain book from the school library, and to delete certain courses from the curriculum." The suit, which charged that school officials had violated constitutional guarantees of academic freedom and the "right to know," was dismissed by the district court. On appeal, the Court of Appeals for the Seventh Circuit upheld the school board's right to establish a curriculum on the basis of its own discretion, so long as it did not impose a "pall of orthodoxy" on the classroom.

In *Zykan,* the court once more refused to acknowledge a student's right to *receive* information, and the shocking court record in *Zykan* revealed that the school board turned the offending books over to complaining citizens who had them publicly burned. The court condemned this ceremony as "contemptible" but nonetheless held that two factors tend to limit the relevance of "academic freedom" at the secondary school level. First, the student's right to and need for such freedom is bounded by the level of his or her intellectual development. . . . Second, the importance of secondary schools in the development of intellectual faculties is only one part of a broad formative role encompassing the encouragement and nurturing of those fundamental social, political, and moral values that will permit a student to take his place in the community.

Following this argument, the court concluded that "complaints filed by secondary school students to contest the educational decisions of local authorities are sometimes cognizable but generally must cross a relatively high threshold before entering upon the field of a constitutional claim suitable for federal court litigation."[28]

At the same time that *Zykan* was being decided, the Second Circuit was reconsidering its 1972 *Presidents Council* opinion through two cases: *Board of Education, Island Trees Union Free School District No. 26 v. Pico* and *Bicknell v. Vergennes Union High School Board of Directors*. The two cases, both of which involved the removal of books from a school library, were decided on the same day and by the same panel, and the opinions invoked both the court's earlier concern with motivation as well as its more recent debate over a "right to know." The dismissal of the complaint in *Bicknell* was affirmed, whereas the dismissal of the complaint in *Pico* was reversed, both by 2–1 majorities. The deciding vote in each case focused on the school board's *motive* in removing books from the library. In *Bicknell*, the deciding judge approved the board's action, saying it had been motivated by the desire to remove vulgar and indecent language from the library, but in *Pico* the deciding judge said the board had removed the books in order to suppress "ideas," not language. The latter was held to be an unconstitutional attempt to purge the library of ideas, whereas the former was considered an appropriate part of the school's process of value inculcation.

In *Bicknell*, U.S. District Judge Albert W. Coffin had dismissed a complaint filed by librarian Elizabeth Phillips and several students to protest the school board's removal of *The Wanderers* and *Dog Day Afternoon* from the library and a freeze on library acquisitions. The district court declared:

Although the Court does not entirely agree with the policies and actions of the defendants we do not find that those policies and actions directly or sharply infringe upon the basic constitutional rights of the students of Vergennes Union High School. . . . [N]either the board's failure to purchase a work nor its decision to remove or restrict access to a work in the school library violate the First Amendment rights of the student plaintiffs before this court. . . . Nor do we believe that school librarians have an independent

First Amendment right to control the collection of the school library under the rubric of academic freedom.[29]

Bicknell relied heavily on the *Presidents Council* decision in rejecting the notion of academic freedom for librarians, suggesting that any claims of academic freedom made in library censorship cases must be linked in some way to the classroom and curriculum. The court ruled that the rights of neither the students nor the teachers had been violated, since the board removed the books because it viewed them as vulgar and in bad taste.

In *Pico* (see Chapter 1 for further discussion of this case), a district court addressed the action of a school board in Long Island, New York, which removed nine books from the school library shelves after three members of the school board saw the titles on a list of "objectionable books" distributed by a conservative educational organization. The board claimed the books were "anti-American, anti-Christian, anti-Semitic, and just plain filthy" and cited its "duty, or moral obligation, to protect the children in our schools from this moral danger as surely as from physical and medical dangers." Five of the books were removed despite a report by the board's own Book Review Committee, which noted the books' educational suitability, good taste, relevance, and appropriateness for age and grade. Five students from the local junior high school and high school brought suit to challenge the school board's action, but the district court initially followed the *Bicknell* approach, granting summary judgment in favor of the board of education. The district court concluded:

> [T]he issue is whether the First Amendment requires a federal court to forbid a school board from removing library books which its members find to be inconsistent with the basic values of the community that elected them. . . . In the absence of a sharp, focused issue of academic freedom, the court concludes that respect for the traditional values of the community and deference to the school board's substantial control over educational content preclude any finding of a First Amendment violation arising out of removal of any of the books from use in the curriculum.[30]

The plaintiffs in *Pico* appealed, and in October 1980, the U.S. Court of Appeals for the Second Circuit reversed the judgment of the district court and remanded the action for trial on the plaintiffs' allegations. The three-judge panel was badly split, but Judge Charles B. Sifton, who wrote the opinion, maintained that although the school board may have broad authority to remove books from the library, their removal cannot be for the purpose of suppressing ideas contained in them. Noting the board's procedural irregularities and absence of specific criteria for removing the books, Judge Sifton concluded that the school officials' concern is less to cleanse the libraries of all books containing material insulting to members of one or another religious group or which evidences an inaccurate view of the nation's history, than it is to express an official policy with regard to God and country of uncertain and indefinite content which is to be ignored by pupils, librarians, and teachers at their peril.[31]

Judge Walter R. Mansfield dissented, arguing that the majority was, in effect, overruling the *Presidents Council* decision. He wrote: "Absent some evidence that speech or ideas by anyone are likely to be suppressed, I believe this court should keep its hands off. The effect of the majority's decision is improperly to substitute a court's view of what student curriculum is appropriate for that of the Board."[32] Mansfield noted that the teachers remained free to discuss the ideas in the books in class and on school grounds. Judge John O. Newman, however, pointed out that removing a book from the library because of its ideas would inevitably have a chilling effect on students' and teachers' rights of expression. He added, "I wonder how willing members of the school community are to discuss the virtues of Malcolm X after the School Board has condemned a book . . . because it equated Malcolm X with the founding fathers of our country."[33]

The school board responded in 1981 by requesting that the Supreme Court review the *Pico* case, and certiorari was granted. By a vote of 5 to 4 the Supreme Court affirmed the Second Circuit's ruling that the board's removal of books from the libraries denied the students their First Amendment rights. Justice William Brennan wrote the plurality opinion, with Thurgood Marshall and John Paul Stevens joining, Byron White concurring, and Harry Blackmun concurring in part. Chief Justice Warren Burger and Justices Lewis Powell, William Rehnquist, and Sandra Day O'Connor dissented in four separate opinions. The argument centered upon the motivation behind the board's actions. If the board *intended* to deny the students access to ideas with which the board disagreed, then the board had violated the Constitution. The plurality said the case should be tried in district court to determine whether the school board had acted to suppress ideas with which it disagreed, or whether it had removed the books simply because they were vulgar. In his concurring opinion, Justice Blackmun, while not sharing the plurality's opinion, agreed that the case should be tried to determine the school board's reason for removing the books. "In my view," wrote Blackmun, "we strike a proper balance here by holding that school officials may not remove books for the *purpose* of restricting access to the political ideas or social perspectives discussed in them, when that action is motivated simply by the officials' disapproval of the ideas involved."[34]

In writing for the plurality in *Pico*, Brennan said that the current action did not require the Court to reenter the difficult terrain that *Myer* and *Epperson* had traversed. Brennan explained:

> For as this case is presented to us, it does not involve textbooks, or indeed any books that Island Trees students would be required to read. [The students] do not seek in this Court to impose limitations upon their school Board's discretion to prescribe the curricula of the Island Trees schools. On the contrary, the only books at issue in this case are *library* books, books that by their nature are optional rather than required reading. Our adjudication of the present case thus does not intrude into the classroom, or into the compulsory courses taught there. Furthermore, even as to library books, the action before us does not involve the *acquisition* of books. Respondents have not sought to compel their school Board to add to the school library shelves any books that students desire to read. Rather, the only action challenged in this case is the *removal* from school libraries of books originally placed there by the school authorities, or without objection from them.[35]

Thus Brennan established a hierarchy of censorship that distinguished between curricular controls, library acquisitions, and the removal of library materials.

Brennan acknowledged that all First Amendment rights accorded to students must be construed in light of the "special characteristics of the school environment," but he said school boards had no authority "to extend their claim of absolute discretion beyond the compulsory environment of the classroom, into the school library and the regime of voluntary inquiry that there holds sway."[36]

The *Pico* plurality attempted to establish that the Constitution protects the right to receive information and ideas, but there were opinions within both the majority and dissenting justices that specifically denied a "right to access." The plurality nonetheless proclaimed that "a right to receive ideas follows ineluctably from the *sender*'s First Amendment right to send them" and "the right to receive ideas is a necessary predicate to the *recipient*'s meaningful exercise of his own rights of speech, press, and political freedom." They concluded:

> In sum, just as access to ideas makes it possible for citizens generally to exercise their rights of free speech and press in a meaningful manner, such access prepares students for active and effective participation in the pluralistic, often contentious society in which they will soon be adult members. . . . The special characteristics of the school *library* make that environment especially appropriate for the recognition of the First Amendment rights of students.[37]

In his *Pico* dissent, Justice Rehnquist was joined by Burger in rejecting such rights within the special circumstances of the school:

> When it acts as an educator, at least at the elementary and secondary school level, the government is engaged in inculcating social values and knowledge in relatively impressionable young people. . . . In short, actions by the government as educator do not raise the same First Amendment concerns as actions by the government as sovereign.[38]

Rehnquist distinguished between the First Amendment rights of high school students as opposed to college students, drawing upon the conclusion in *Zykan* that high school students lack the intellectual skills necessary to take full advantage of the marketplace of ideas. Their need for academic freedom is therefore bounded by their level of intellectual development. Burger, Rehnquist, and Powell rejected any constitutional right to receive information as having no application to the public school, which they regarded as a place for the selective conveyance of ideas.

Rather than go to trial, as the *Pico* plurality ordered, the school board voted to return *all* the banned books to the library shelves, effectively ending the dispute. But the fractured and relatively feeble judgments in *Pico* showed the depth of the Court's philosophical change since 1943, when it held in *Barnette*:

> Probably no deeper division of our people could proceed from any provocation than from finding it necessary to choose what doctrine and whose program public educational officials may compel youth to unite in embracing. . . . The First Amendment to our Constitution was designed to avoid these ends by avoiding these beginnings.[39]

Because the decision in *Pico* was fractured, with seven of the nine justices writing separate decisions, the application of the First Amendment to the schoolbook issue remained ill-defined. However, *Pico* was significant not so much for the precedent established as for the clarity with which it revealed the doctrinal dichotomy within the Burger Court and its predecessors. The opinions in *Pico* documented a fundamental philosophical dispute between two entrenched factions within the Court. The faction led by Justice Brennan regarded education as having an analytic objective that should not be subordinated to indoctrination. Such education would require that teachers and students together examine information and values in a joint search for truth. On the other hand, the faction led by Chief Justice Burger regarded elementary and secondary education to be indoctrinative or prescriptive in purpose. The function of the teacher and the curriculum is thus to convey prescribed truths.

William D. North, former general counsel for the Freedom to Read Foundation, reminds us:

> The concept that secondary schools can, consistent with the First Amendment, be reduced to a purely indoctrinative function serving the will of

any transient political majority which might gain control of the system appears as a repudiation of the very purpose for which this amendment was adopted. That purpose was not to protect the rights of the majority, but rather to protect the rights of the minority *from* the majority.[40]

North notes that the narrow view of the school as an inculcating mechanism will guarantee that secondary schools become political and ideological battlegrounds, allowing the winner of this battle to control the curriculum and purge the library of competing ideas.

Still, the *Pico* plurality saw nothing incompatible between the students' "right to know" and the inculcative function of secondary schools, so long as that function was performed by persuasion and example rather than intellectual force-feeding. Chief Justice Burger's characterization of schools as vehicles for inculcating the fundamental values of our political system caused Brennan to fear that students would become nothing more than "closed circuit recipients of only that which the State chooses to communicate." Burger's primary concern was with the "social interest in order and morality," and he was inclined to grant school authorities broad discretion to fulfil their inculcative function, including the right to make "content based decisions about the appropriateness of retaining school materials in the school library and curriculum." Burger did not share Brennan's fear of a pall of orthodoxy in the classroom, except for the possibility that the orthodoxy imposed might not be representative of community values. As for those in the community who might not be represented in the curricular orthodoxy imposed by school officials, Burger simply advised: "They have alternative sources to the same end. Books may be acquired from book stores, public libraries, or other alternative sources unconnected with the unique environment of the local public schools."[41]

Burger placed his faith in local political control of school boards, whereby "parents influence, if not control, the direction of their children's education." He concluded that "a school board reflects its constituency in a very real sense and thus could not long exercise unchecked discretion in its choice to acquire or remove books." Burger therefore advised, "[I]f parents disagree with the decisions of the school board, they can take steps to remove the board members from office."[42]

This glib assurance has been questioned by attorneys like William D. North, who points out that less than 20 percent of voters are parents of elementary and secondary school children. In addition, the usual six-year term of school board members makes changes in the board's composition and orientation a long and problematic struggle with a bureaucracy whose budget and manpower exceed that of any other government activity. It should also be noted that bookbanning is often initiated without the participation of parents, or indeed, against their wishes. In *Zykan*, the bookbanning was demanded by an organization of senior citizens, who proceeded to burn the books. In *Chelsea*, a book was removed on the demand of one parent over the objections of many parents. In *Pico*, the books were removed from the library, not at the request of local parents but on the basis of an "objectionable book list" prepared in another state and promoted by a national conservative organization.

Following the *Pico* decision, the courts once more considered the notion of a student's right to receive information in *Sheck v. Baileyville School Committee* (1982). *Sheck* addressed the banning of the book *365 Days*, by Ronald Glasser, which had been acquired by the Woodland High School library in 1971 and used frequently for a decade before being banned by the Baileyville School Committee in 1981. The action arose from a complaint by parents whose daughter borrowed the book from the library, after which the school committee voted 5 to 0 to remove *365 Days* from the library. Michael Sheck, a Woodland High School senior, brought a copy of the book to school, where he was informed by the principal that mere possession of the book on school property would result in its confiscation. The plaintiffs asked redress of the First Amendment "rights of freedom of speech [and] freedom of access," and an appeals court declared that "[t]he burden of persuasion that there has been no *unnecessary* abridgement of first amendment rights rests with the defendants."

The court advised:

> The first amendment right of secondary students to be free from governmental restrictions upon nondisruptive, nonintrusive, silent expression in public schools was sustained by the Court in *Tinker* notwithstanding full awareness of the "comprehensive authority" traditionally afforded local officials in the governance of public schools. . . . Book bans do not directly restrict the readers' right to initiate expression but rather their right to receive information and ideas, *the indispensable reciprocal of any meaningful right of expression*. . . . The information and ideas in books placed in a school library by proper authority are protected speech and the first amendment right of students to receive that information and those ideas is entitled to constitutional protection.[43]

The court concluded that the bookban was overly broad, applying to adults as well as well as students and to mature as well as immature students, and the plaintiffs were provided injunctive relief.

The following year, in *Johnson v. Stuart* (1983),[44] public school teachers, students, and parents brought suit against the Oregon State Board of Education, challenging the constitutionality of Oregon's textbook selection statute, which prohibited the use of any textbook that speaks slightingly of America's Founders or of those who preserved the Union or that belittles or undervalues their work. The case was appealed to the U.S.

Court of Appeals, Ninth Circuit, which concluded that the teachers did not have standing to challenge the constitutionality of the statute, because they failed to show that they had suffered some actual or threatened injury. On the other hand, the court accepted the students' claim that the schoolbook screening system restricted their First Amendment right of free access to information. The appeals court affirmed the standing of the students and the ripeness of their claims, applying that conclusion as well to the parents, who may assert claims of constitutional violation affecting their children's education.

SECULARISM AND SEX: THE TWIN THREATS TO AMERICA

In 1985, *Grove* v. *Mead School District No. 354* rejected a parent's claim that a book should be removed from the curriculum because it fostered a belief system called "secular humanism." After Mrs. Grove complained to her daughter's tenth-grade teacher about the use of *The Learning Tree*, by Gordon Parks, the daughter was assigned another book and given permission to leave class during discussions of the book. Still, the mother filed a formal complaint with the school district, claiming that the book embodied the philosophy of secular humanism and thereby violated her religious beliefs. A school textbook evaluation committee subsequently concluded that *The Learning Tree* was an appropriate element of the sophomore English curriculum, and after a hearing, the board of education denied the request to remove the book. Plaintiffs then brought a civil rights suit against the school district, seeking damages and injunctive relief. They contended that use of *The Learning Tree* violated the religion clauses of the First Amendment. After a hearing, the judge granted summary judgment for the defendants.

With respect to the establishment clause, the court in *Grove* stated:

> It is true that *The Learning Tree* poses questions and ponders doubts with which plaintiffs may be uncomfortable. Yet to pose questions is not to impose answers. Since the first amendment is designed as much to protect the former as prevent the latter, I cannot conclude, on the record presented, that the use of *The Learning Tree* inhibits religion.

The court also ruled that the burden on the free exercise of religion was "minimal" because the child was assigned an alternate book. In this regard, the court concluded: "The state interest in providing well-rounded public education would be critically impeded by accommodation of Grove's wishes. . . . In light of the absence of coercion and the critical threat to public education, we conclude that the school board has not violated the free exercise clause."[45]

Two years later, in a similar judgment, *Mozert v. Hawkins County Board of Education* (1987) concluded a lengthy controversy (see Chapter 1) by rejecting parents' demands to remove a textbook series from the curriculum. Tennessee parents were plaintiffs in a civil rights action in district court seeking damages and injunctive relief based on their objections to the requirement that all Hawkins County public school children through the eighth grade must read from the Holt *Basic Readings* textbooks. The plaintiffs alleged that the textbooks taught nine different objectionable things, including witchcraft, magic and the occult, relative values, disrespect and disobedience to parents, idolatry, generalized faith in the supernatural, humanism, and Darwinism. The plaintiffs claimed that the First Amendment freedom to believe as they choose was meaningless if the state could force their children to read books that contain ideas and values to which they did not subscribe. The court decided that only one of the nine complaints (that the texts accept any type of faith as an acceptable method of salvation) might represent a constitutional violation but said that the plaintiffs had not specified which parts of which books substantiated their complaint. The court concluded that no basic constitutional values were implicated in the allegations against the Holt *Basic Readings*, saying: "The First Amendment does not protect the plaintiffs from exposure to morally offensive value systems or from exposure to antithetical religious ideas."[46] The court thereby decided against the plaintiff's request for an injunction to prohibit compulsory use of the Holt *Basic Readings*.

Though the Tennessee fundamentalists were unsuccessful in their lawsuit, the specter of censorship remained. Parents complained that a passage in *The Diary of Anne Frank*, one of the sources included in the Holt *Basic Readings*, suggested the equivalence of all religions, contradicting the notion of one true religion. As a result, school officials chose to cancel the performance of a play based on *The Diary of Anne Frank* rather than face further complaints and litigation.

That same year, another challenge to secular education was rebuffed in *Smith v. Board of School Commissioners of Mobile (Ala.) County* (1987). Here 624 Christian Evangelicals in Mobile, Alabama, brought suit against a school board, charging that the school system was teaching an antireligious religion called "secular humanism." The complainants asked that forty-four different textbooks, from elementary through high school, be removed from the curriculum. They claimed that the texts contained passages about one-parent families and divorce, offending their belief in the sanctity of traditional families. The case grew out of Alabama's earlier adoption of silent prayer in schools, upheld in court by Federal District Judge W. Brevard Hand. When silent prayer was overturned by a higher court and declared unconstitutional by the Supreme Court, Judge Hand responded by approving the ban of the forty-four textbooks. In ruling in favor of the fundamentalist plaintiffs, Judge Hand declared: "If this Court is compelled to purge 'God is great, God is good, We thank him for our daily food' from the classroom, then this Court must also purge from the classroom those things that serve to teach that salvation is through one's self rather than through a deity."[47]

The U.S. Court of Appeals for the Eleventh Circuit reversed Judge Hand, ruling that as long as the school was motivated by a secular purpose, its curriculum and textbooks could present ideas held by one or more religious groups. The appeals court ruled that the textbooks neither endorsed theistic religion as a system of belief, nor discredited it, but rather promoted important secular values, such as tolerance, self-respect, and logical decision making. The answer to the fundamentalists' complaint, said the court, was not less speech, but more.

Cases like *Kanawha*, *Grove*, *Mozert*, and *Smith* reveal the courts' reluctance to endorse fundamentalist attempts to censor school materials, suggesting that vulgarity or indecency remains the most acceptable legal basis on which to ban books in schools. Interestingly, vulgarity and indecency are not constitutionally justifiable reasons for banning books in *public libraries*, where a higher standard, obscenity, must be met. But virtually every act of school censorship upheld by the courts has turned on the sexual content of the material, and the special characteristics of the school environment have allowed the age of the school audience to be a deciding factor. This has been seen in cases like *Presidents Council, Zykan, Bicknell*, and *Seyfried* v. *Walton*.[48] Even Justice Brennan in *Pico* noted: "[R]espondents implicitly concede that an unconstitutional motivation would *not* be demonstrated if it were shown that petitioners had decided to remove the books at issue because those books were pervasively vulgar." Justice Blackmun's concurring opinion in *Pico* stated that "First Amendment principles would allow a school board to refuse to make a book available to students because it contains offensive language."[49]

In *Bethel School District No. 403* v. *Fraser* (1986), a high school student was suspended for making sexually suggestive remarks at a student-government assembly. Here the Supreme Court rejected the student's claim that his First Amendment rights were violated when he was disciplined for an alleged sexual innuendo in his speech nominating another student for school office. *Fraser*, like *Pico*, was decided as a First Amendment case, with Chief Justice Burger invoking *Ambach* for a doctrinal definition of public education as the inculcation of "fundamental values necessary to the maintenance of a democratic political system." In supporting the school board, Burger advised:

> The undoubted freedom to advocate unpopular and controversial views in schools and classrooms must be balanced against the society's counter-

vailing interest in teaching students the boundaries of socially appropriate behavior. . . . It does not follow . . . that simply because the use of an offensive form of expression may not be prohibited to adults making what the speaker considers a political point, that the same latitude must be permitted to children in a public school.

Writing for the majority, Burger concluded:

> Surely it is a highly appropriate function of public school education to prohibit the use of vulgar and offensive terms in public discourse. . . . Nothing in the Constitution prohibits the states from insisting that certain modes of expression are inappropriate and subject to sanctions. . . . The determination of what manner of speech in the classroom or in school assembly is inappropriate properly rests with the school board.[50]

Cases like *Fraser* suggest that if there is a legal and societal consensus on any free speech issues, it is that children should not be exposed to sexual content. This would mean that children's rights to free expression in this area are clearly less than for adults, an approach seemingly endorsed by the benchmark *Hazelwood* decision.

HAZELWOOD: A CHILL WIND FOR THE 1990s

In the 1988 *Hazelwood School District* v. *Kuhlmeier* decision, the Supreme Court affirmed the principle of judicial restraint in educational affairs by stating that "the education of the Nation's youth is primarily the responsibility of parents, teachers, and state and local school officials, and not of federal judges." Here the Court saw no constitutional restraint on a Missouri school principal who removed portions of a student newspaper produced as part of a high school journalism class. When the principal removed pages containing articles on pregnancy and divorce from the high school newspaper, the student staff filed suit, claiming violation of their First Amendment rights. The school principal claimed he was properly protecting the privacy of pregnant students described, but not named, in the articles and also protecting younger students from inappropriate references to sexual activity and birth control. The principal also claimed that because a school-sponsored newspaper could be perceived as an expression of official school opinion, censorship was justified to protect the school from possible libel action. The Supreme Court held that the principal acted reasonably and did not violate the students' First Amendment rights. The Court declared that a school need not tolerate student speech "that is inconsistent with its 'basic educational mission,' even though the government could not censor similar speech outside the school."[51]

Because the newspaper was part of the journalism curriculum, it was held to be subject to control by a faculty member. The newspaper was thus regarded not as a forum for the free expression of ideas but "as supervised learning experience for journalism students." The Court ruled that "educators do not offend the First Amendment by exercising editorial control over the style and content of student speech in school-sponsored expressive activities so long as their actions are reasonably related to legitimate pedagogical concerns." The Court did caution, however, that this authority does not justify school action

> to silence a student's personal expression that happens to occur on the school premises. . . . It is only when the decision to censor a school-sponsored publication, theatrical production, or other vehicle of student expression has no valid educational purpose that the First Amendment is so "directly and sharply implicate[d]" as to require judicial intervention to protect students' constitutional rights.

Hazelwood therefore established that teachers, principals, and school boards may take action within the school's educational mission that might otherwise be unconstitutional.[52]

Though *Hazelwood* addressed the limits of official control over the student press, the decision was broadly interpreted and had an immediate and profound effect on book censorship. *Hazelwood*, like virtually all the relevant cases that preceded it, attempted to define the mission of the public education system and the authority vested in its officials. In many ways it contradicted the Court's declaration in *Tinker* that students do not shed their constitutional rights at the schoolhouse gate. But there is a strong suggestion in *Hazelwood* that postsecondary educational institutions or libraries outside the school system (e.g., public libraries) would receive greater First Amendment protection than do the elementary and secondary school curriculum and libraries. In fact, the courts following *Hazelwood* appear to have established different levels of constitutional protection for books and other publications, depending on whether they are removed from a classroom, a school library, or a public library.

Within a year of *Hazelwood*, the fears that it would lead the courts to place school censorship outside of First Amendment protections seemed realized. In *Virgil* v. *School Board of Columbia County* (1989), the Eleventh Circuit applied the Supreme Court's approach in *Hazelwood*, upholding a school board's removal of a previously approved textbook because of alleged vulgarity and sexual explicitness. For a decade, the Columbia County High School had been offering an elective course using the state-approved text *The Humanities: Cultural Roots and Continuities*. In addition to the optional status of the course itself, parents were allowed to request alternative readings if they found any of the assignments objectionable.

During the 1985–1986 school year, the daughter of a fundamentalist minister took the course and objected to two selections in the text: "The Miller's Tale," by Chaucer, and *Lysistrata*, by Aristophanes. Neither selection was assigned reading, though portions of *Lysistrata* were read aloud in class.

The complaint form filled out by the minister cited vulgar language and "promotion of women's lib," and the complaint was pursued even after his daughter had completed the humanities course. An advisory committee made up of Columbia County teachers read the two challenged selections in *The Humanities* and recommended retaining the text but not assigning either of the challenged works. The superintendent of schools rejected the recommendation, saying that "any literature in which God's name is used in vain is not appropriate for use in the classroom."[53] The school board then felt obliged to vote unanimously to ban the book from the curriculum.

The parents of some Columbia High School students objected to the fact that the views of a small number of people, led by the minister, had determined what could be read by all of the students in the school. Under threat of a lawsuit, the school board voted 4–1 to put one copy of *The Humanities* in the school library, although the book remained banned from the curriculum. Nonetheless, on November 24, 1986, the ACLU brought suit against the board on behalf of a parent named Moyna Virgil. The case, *Virgil* v. *School Board of Columbia County*, argued that the removal of the textbook suppressed free speech and free thought while advancing religion through the public schools. The defense claimed that, despite the superintendent's comments, the board had rejected the book solely because it contained sexually explicit scenes and inappropriate language. The defense relied on *Hazelwood*, whereas the ACLU relied on *Pico*, arguing that if the Supreme Court had intended to supercede *Pico* with *Hazelwood*, it would have said so.

U.S. District Judge Susan Black concluded that *Hazelwood* was the relevant Supreme Court precedent, saying:

> In light of the recent decision of the United States Supreme Court in *Hazelwood* . . . , this Court need not decide whether the plurality decision in *Pico* may logically be extended to optional curriculum materials. *Kuhlmeier* resolves any doubts as to the appropriate standards to be applied whenever a curriculum decision is subject to first amendment review. . . . Although it did not specifically refer to textbooks, the Court [in *Hazelwood*] evidently sought to address a wide realm of "curriculum decisions," including those affecting textbooks.

Judge Black admitted, "The Court finds it difficult to apprehend the harm which could conceivably be caused to a group of eleventh- and twelth-grade students by exposure to Aristophanes and Chaucer,"[54] yet she concluded that the *Hazelwood* interpretation of the limited scope of students' First Amendment rights compelled her to decide in favor of the school board.

The ACLU appealed, arguing that *Hazelwood* applied to student writing, not literary classics, and that the board's action was "rooted, indeed steeped, in philosophic valuing rather than pedagogical concern." The ACLU brief argued, "There must be some First Amendment recourse against the tyranny of bad taste. Literary classics generally considered part and parcel of a liberal arts education cannot be constitutionally bannable because a board doesn't 'like' them."[55] The Florida Department of Education, along with many national educational organizations, filed amici curiae briefs supporting the ACLU position, but the U.S. Court of Appeals for the Eleventh Circuit upheld Black's decision, stating:

> Of course, we do not endorse the Board's decision. Like the district court, we seriously question how young persons just below the age of majority can be harmed by these masterpieces of Western literature. However, having concluded that there is no constitutional violation, our role is not to second guess the wisdom of the Board's action.[56]

The decision in *Virgil*, as in *Hazelwood*, had repercussions in lower court decisions around the country. We saw in Chapter 1 that a Florida bookbanning incident produced litigation (*Farrell* v. *Hall*, Order, July 18, 1988, U.S. District Court for the Northern District of Florida)[57] and subsequent compromise contemporaneously with the deliberations in *Virgil*. During the course of negotiations overseen by the court in *Farrell*, the announcement that *Virgil* was lost despite what appeared to be a strong First Amendment case had a sobering effect on the *Farrell* plaintiffs. The secondary school teacher who was prominent among the plaintiffs admitted that their willingness to settle out of court was heavily influenced by the outcome of *Virgil*.

Though the trend since *Hazelwood* has been for lower state and federal courts to reject claims of First Amendment protection against official censorship of the curriculum, this view has been contested in cases like *McCarthy* v. *Fletcher* (1989). There, a teacher, a student, a parent, and a taxpayer brought suit against the administrators and trustees of the Wasco Union High School District after school officials banned the use of two novels, *Grendel*, by John Gardner, and *One Hundred Years of Solitude*, by Gabriel García Márquez, from use in a twelfth-grade English class. In response to an initial complaint about the books, the school superintendent and the principal had restricted their use to only those students whose parents gave written permission. But when *all* students produced signed permission slips, the school board decided to ban the books formally.

The school officials filed suit for summary judgment, claiming that their action was "cloaked with a legislative immunity preventing judicial inquiry into the board members' motives or intent in excluding the books."[58] The trial court granted summary judgment in favor of the school officials, ruling that the plaintiffs had not shown sufficient cause to even hold a trial. The court ruled that even if all the allegations of bookbanning by school officials were proved, those officials were still permitted to take such actions without violating the First Amendment. The teacher appealed to the California Court of Appeals, which reversed the lower court's judgment, interpreting *Hazelwood* in a way that recognized the possible violation of First Amendment rights for teachers and students, depending on the outcome of a trial clarifying the board's motivation in banning the books.

In *McCarthy*, the court found that the school officials' evaluations of the banned books included statements suggesting that the books were removed for religious reasons. For example, the superintendent's evaluation of *Grendel* said it "was designed to break down a student's belief in God," and the vice-principal's evaluation charged that *Grendel* "contains many anti-government, anti-God, and anti-religion statements." Similar comments were made by the superintendent at a public school board meeting. Based upon such information, the court concluded that religious motives were behind the deletion of the two books. The court therefore remanded the case for a trial to determine whether "the administrators were acting to protect and advance the Christian ideology on behalf of the Wasco religious community—a patently illegitimate educational purpose."

In remanding the case for trial, the court said that even under the broad *Hazelwood* standard, school officials may not be motivated by an intent to "prescribe what shall be orthodox in politics, nationalism, religion, or other matters of opinion." The court in *McCarthy* revealed its skepticism about the school board's real reason for banning the books when it stated that "the educational unsuitability of the books ... must be the true reason for the books' exclusion and not just a pretextual expression for exclusion because the board disagrees with the religious or philosophical ideas expressed in the books." *McCarthy* thus made clear that *Hazelwood* did not authorize school officials to ban books on the mere *claim* of a valid educational purpose. Allowing such an interpretation, said the court, would enable school officials to "camouflage religious 'viewpoint discrimination' ... which we do not believe *Hazelwood* intended."[59]

The decision in *McCarthy* suggests that even *Hazelwood* can be read as providing First Amendment limitations on official power to interfere with intellectual freedom in the public schools. The ruling depended on the judge's argument that the legal doctrines in *Hazelwood* still allow the courts a substantial role in reviewing the constitutionality of actions by local school officials, beyond the limited role recognized in *Virgil*. Still, the First Amendment seemed threatened in schools around the country in the wake of *Hazelwood*.

There have even been ominous signs that the *Hazelwood* guidelines will be extended to postsecondary education. "Although *Hazelwood* did not include post-secondary institutions in its decision, it is clear that many cases involving colleges are relying upon it," wrote Andrew Luna, assistant director for Research and Public Relations at the University of Alabama. "Through these decisions, an ideology emerges which supports the inculcation of society's values on college students and affirms administrative controls over student expression as a means of articulating those values."[60]

Indeed, on November 14, 1997, the U.S. District Court for the Eastern District of Kentucky ruled that college students were subject to the same restrictions that *Hazelwood* placed on high school students. It was the first time that a court had applied *Hazelwood* to postsecondary education. In *Kincaid* v. *Gibson*, the court addressed the claims of two students at Kentucky State University that school officials had violated their First Amendment rights by confiscating the student yearbook and controlling the content of the student newspaper.

Judge Joseph M. Hood ruled that the university "was entitled to exercise reasonable control over the yearbook" because *Hazelwood* had established that a yearbook is not a "public forum" under the First Amendment. On the students' claim that the university had censored the newspaper, Judge Hood said they had failed to show "any type of injury."[61]

On September 8, 1999, a three-member panel of the U.S. Court of Appeals for the Third Circuit voted 2–1 to uphold the confiscation of the yearbook and censorship of the school newspaper. Writing for the majority, Judge Alan E. Norris cited *Hazelwood*'s ruling that if a school did not intentionally create a publication as a "public forum," then school officials may impose "any reasonable, non-viewpoint-based restriction on student speech exhibited therein."

In his dissent, Judge R. Guy Cole criticized the majority for failing to distinguish between high school and college students. "A yearbook is a student publication constructed by students, intended for students," he wrote. "I believe that the university's proffered reasons for withholding distribution of the yearbook . . . are content-based restrictions that do not serve any compelling governmental interest."

Mark Goodman, director of the Student Press Law Center, warned, "Make no mistake, if allowed to stand, the decision today will gut student journalism programs at some colleges and universities. We've seen that happen at a number of high schools in the eleven years since *Hazelwood* was handed down."[62]

The plaintiffs promptly requested that the full panel of judges sitting on the Sixth Circuit reconsider the decision. Lawyers for the students argued that the Third Circuit had ignored thirty years of legal precedent providing strong First Amendment protection to college students. On January 5, 2001, the Sixth Circuit voted 10–3 to reverse the lower court decision that upheld the confiscation of the student yearbook, rejecting the application of *Hazelwood* to college students. The court concluded that "the KSU officials' confiscation of the yearbook violates the First Amendment, and the university has no constitutionally valid reason to withhold distribution of the 1992–94 Thorobred from KSU students."[63]

On February 28, 2001, the two students who had brought the suit agreed to settle their case against the university in exchange for $5,000 each and $60,000 in attorneys fees. In addition, the university agreed to distribute the 717 remaining copies of the 1994 yearbook, which had been locked in a storage room since their confiscation. If the two sides had not agreed to a settlement, the case would have been sent to a district court judge to determine damages and fees, or the university could have appealed to the U.S. Supreme Court.

IMPROVING ON THE FIRST AMENDMENT: STATES SEEK REMEDIES TO *HAZELWOOD* RESTRAINTS

One of the ironic consequences of the 1988 *Hazelwood* decision was that it led states to conclude that because the First Amendment was no longer adequate to protect free expression in schools, they would have to provide local protection. Individual states have attempted to surmount the Supreme Court's *Hazelwood* guidelines through both judicial and legislative means. A judicial solution has been sought through narrow interpretations of the censorship authority granted to school officials by *Hazelwood* and through the recognition that state constitutions often provide greater protection for student expression than does the post-*Hazelwood* federal Constitution. On the legislative front, many states have passed laws protecting student expression.

It should be noted that, though most state courts and legislatures are attempting to protect the rights of student journalists, the court rulings and associated legislation have addressed a more general notion of student expression that goes beyond journalism. As we have seen, bookbanning is often directed against classroom activities, including reading aloud from challenged books, blurring the distinction between expression and reading. Indeed, many parents who challenge books have taken the position that merely reading profanity or vulgarity is equivalent to speaking it and should therefore be prohibited under the various formal codes controlling student conduct. Seen in this context, protecting student expression from *Hazelwood*'s restraints is essential in the battle against bookbanning.

The first lower court rebuke to a broad reading of *Hazelwood* came in *Romano* v. *Harrington* (1989), where the U.S. District Court for the Eastern District of New York refused to give school officials carte blanche in controlling student newspapers. The case arose after Michael Romano, a tenured English teacher at Port Richmond High School, was fired from his position as faculty adviser to the school's extracurricular newspaper after the publication of a student-written article opposing a federal holiday in honor of Martin Luther King, Jr. The teacher brought a civil rights action against the principal and the board of education, claiming that his First Amendment rights had been violated.

The school district asked the court for summary judgment dismissing the complaint, arguing that *Hazelwood* gave them virtually unlimited control over the content of student newspapers. They argued that the newspaper was part of the curriculum in the broadest sense of the word and that firing the paper's faculty adviser was reasonably related to the legitimate pedagogical goal of minimizing racial tensions at the school.

District Judge Raymond Dearie ruled that *Hazelwood* does not give school officials editorial control over a school newspaper that is produced as an extracurricular activity for which students do not receive course credit. The newspaper in *Hazelwood* was both school-sponsored and a part of the course curriculum. The court therefore distinguished *Hazelwood* from *Romano* and relied heavily on the earlier Supreme Court decision in *Island Trees* v. *Pico*. In *Pico*, the Court had ruled that the removal of nine books from a school library denied students their First Amendment rights.

In equating the school newspaper in *Romano* with the school library in *Pico*, the court held that "inroads on the First Amendment in the name of education are less warranted outside the confines of the classroom and its assignments." Judge Dearie emphasized that "because *Hazelwood* opens the door to significant curtailment of cherished First Amendment rights" and "[b]ecause educators may limit student expression in the name of pedagogy, courts must avoid enlarging the venues within which that rationale may legitimately obtain without a clear and precise directive."[64] In short, extending the *Hazelwood* guidelines to extracurricular student activities was an unwarranted expansion of school authority over student expression.

Another prominent victory over *Hazelwood*-inspired censorship occurred in 1992 at Clearview Regional High School in New Jersey, where school officials had censored two movie reviews that a student, Brien Desilets, wrote for the school newspaper. When Desilets sued the school for banning the reviews, school officials asserted that they withheld the reviews under the authority granted in the *Hazelwood* decision.

The trial court ruled that the school's censorship of the reviews did *not* violate Desilets' First Amendment rights under the federal Constitution, because the action met the *Hazelwood* requirement that it be reasonably related to "legitimate pedagogical concerns." Nevertheless, the court found that the student's rights *had* been violated under the state constitution, which the court said provided broader protection for free expression. Clearview then appealed to the New Jersey Appellate Division, which affirmed the trial court's decision, but on different grounds. It ruled that the school had indeed violated the student's First Amendment rights, because, even under the *Hazelwood* standards, school officials had not shown that their censorship was "reasonably related to legitimate pedagogical concerns." Thus, said the court, there was no need to consider the state constitution.

"When censorship of a school-sponsored publication has no valid educational purpose, the First Amendment is directly implicated and requires judicial intervention," said the appeals court. "Substantial deference to educational decisions does not require a wholesale abandonment of First Amendment principles simply because the medium for the student's expression is funded by a school board. . . . The significant distinction between *Hazelwood* and this case is that the matter in *Hazelwood* was censored because of its content and journalistic style. In [this] matter, it is conceded that the censorship had nothing to do with the style of the review. Nor was the content of the review a basis for the censorship, only its subject matter."[65]

When Clearview appealed once more, the stage was set for a final determination before the New Jersey Supreme Court. In arguing before that Court, the school board's attorney, Robert Muccilli, urged the justices to grant wide discretion to school officials in meeting the *Hazelwood* standards. Allowing school newspapers to publish reviews of R-rated movies, he said, would interfere with parental decision-making. The justices were not convinced.

Justice Gary Stern said, "The substantive speech regulated in *Hazelwood* was much more provocative" than Desilets' reviews. He said Muccilli was asking the Court to grant "extraordinary discretion to school officials," and, indeed, if Desilets' reviews met the *Hazelwood* test, "then there isn't much speech that couldn't be regulated."[66]

In affirming the appeals court ruling, the New Jersey Supreme Court said that the school had violated the student's First Amendment rights. It said Desilets' reviews did not present the kinds of pedagogical problems specified in *Hazelwood*, namely, articles that were poorly written, ungrammatical, inadequately researched, biased, prejudiced, vulgar, profane, or unsuitable for immature readers. Because the case could be decided on federal constitutional grounds, the Court did not consider the State constitutional claims.

Though other lower court cases have suggested that states may be able to provide greater freedom for student expression than was anticipated after *Hazelwood*, the most reliable method of protection has been new state legislation. At the time of *Hazelwood*, only one state—California— had a statute protecting student expression. Within a few years of *Hazelwood*, twenty-eight state legislatures had proposed such laws. Massachusetts became the first state to respond to the *Hazelwood* decision when Governor Michael Dukakis signed legislation in August 1988 stating: "The rights of students to freedom of expression in the public schools of the commonwealth shall not be abridged, provided that such rights shall not cause any disruption or disorder within the school."

When school officials in Massachusetts went to court to test their power to censor "vulgar" speech in "underground" school newspapers, an appeals court upheld the student press statute by declaring that "high school students in public schools have the freedom . . . to engage in non-school-sponsored expression that may reasonably be considered vulgar, but causes no disruption or disorder." The court added:

> The statute is unambiguous and must be construed as written. . . . The parties agree that the authors of the bill intended to codify the First Amendment protection discussed in *Tinker v. Des Moines Independent School District*. The defendants, however, argue that more recent Supreme Court decisions in the area of students' First Amendment rights . . . have narrowed and redefined the holding of *Tinker* to allow school administrators to regulate vulgar or indecent speech in school-sponsored expressive activities. This may be true, but there is no reason to believe that these cases . . . in any way limit the protection granted under the statute. Our legislature is free to grant greater rights to the citizens of this commonwealth than would otherwise be protected under the United States Constitution.[67]

In July 1989, Iowa became the second state to improve on *Hazelwood* when it passed a law stating that "students of public schools have the right to exercise freedom of speech, including the right of expression in official school publications," provided that the expression is not "obscene, libelous or slanderous" and does not "incite students to commit unlawful acts on school property or break school rules." Under the Iowa law, the material censored by the Hazelwood principal would, in all likelihood, have been protected.[68]

Colorado quickly followed with its own student freedom of expression law. The new law, signed by the governor on June 7, 1990, protects student expression unless it is considered libelous, obscene, incites students to break the law, or creates a substantial threat of disruption to the educational process. Fran Henry, a high school teacher who began the campaign for the Colorado law, explained, "Under *Hazelwood*, students and advisers often had to guess about what a particular administrator might find objectionable. Under Colorado law, now the rules are clear."[69]

A 1994 censorship incident at Little Rock Central High School in Arkansas produced a state law designed to extend protection for student expression beyond the *Hazelwood* guidelines. The controversy arose when editors of the school's newspaper were threatened with suspension if they printed stories about gang fights and vandalism. They responded by producing their own underground newspaper, but were warned that disciplinary action would be taken if they distributed the paper near the high school. The embarrassing controversy was widely covered in the press, leading local politicians to seek a legislative solution. The result was Act 1109 of 1995, which provides qualified protection to high school journalists and their advisers with respect to all school publications, including newspapers and yearbooks.

Of all the states with laws protecting the student press, only Arkansas allows administrators and student advisers in each school district to develop their own written policies. "Twenty-eight states have tried to pass student publication acts since 1988," said Bruce Plopper, a journalism instructor at the University of Arkansas. "I think what makes the Arkansas act such a plausible model is that it recognizes the need for flexibility in individual school districts."[70]

Another recent state attempt to improve upon First Amendment protection for student expression was the Illinois Student Publications Act. The 1997 law provides safeguards against arbitrary censorship of students working on school-sponsored publications, the very kind of publication that lost full constitutional protection in the *Hazelwood* decision.

Even Missouri, the home of the *Hazelwood* case, has attempted to surmount that decision through state legislation. In 1993, Joe Jolly and Amy Zeman, two teenagers from Brentwood High School, went to the state capital to argue for legislation protecting student journalists. Zeman said the bill "would grant students freedom, not license without limits." She told the legislators that the *Hazelwood* decision "was a mighty blow to the Bill of Rights" and asked, "If the state is allowed to restrict our freedoms, how will we ever come to know what freedom is, what our rights truly are, or when they finally are granted? Denying rights in the classroom begins the process of denying the rights of every American citizen."

Also testifying in support of the legislation was Mary Beth Tinker, who had earned celebrity status in the landmark 1969 Supreme Court Case, *Tinker* v. *Des Moines Independent Community School District*, which upheld a student's right to wear a black armband to protest the Vietnam War. Indeed, *Tinker* had been the controlling legal precedent on all school censorship until the *Hazelwood* decision. In support of the Missouri bill, Mary Beth Tinker said, "For 19 years, high schools across the country operated very effectively under the *Tinker* standard. All we are asking is to go back to that standard."[71]

Despite the support of advocates like Mary Beth Tinker, the Missouri bill has failed to gain the necessary votes each year that it has been proposed.

POSITIVE IMPRESSIONS: COURTS AND SCHOOLS FIND COMMON GROUND

Two very recent cases concerning the most frequently banned book of the early 1990s—the *Impressions* textbook series from Holt, Rinehart and Winston—suggest the best defense against bookbanning in post-*Hazelwood* schools and libraries: enlightened school boards and supportive courts. In *Fleischfresser* v. *Directors of School District 200* (1994) and *Brown* v. *Woodland Unified Joint School District* (1994), district and appellate courts in Illinois and California sided with school boards that rejected attempts by religious groups to ban *Impressions*.

In *Fleischfresser*, parents in Wheaton, Illinois, filed suit claiming that their school district's use of the *Impressions* text violated the establishment clause of the First Amendment by fostering "a religious belief in the existence of superior beings exercising power over human beings by imposing rules of conduct, with promise and threat of future rewards and punishments" and by focusing on supernatural beings such as "wizards, sorcerers, giants and unspecified creatures with supernatural powers." The parents also claimed that the use of *Impressions* violated their right to free exercise of religion by indoctrinating children in "values directly opposed to their Christian beliefs by teaching tricks, despair, deceit, parental disrespect and by denigrating Christian symbols and holidays."[72]

District Judge James B. Moran dismissed the action, writing:

> The *Impressions* series has, apparently, generated a certain amount of controversy around the country, with parents having views similar to the plaintiffs complaining to other school boards about the contents. . . . It is not the province of this court, however, to sit as some sort of reviewer of the decisions of local school boards. Plaintiffs must be able to establish that the series fosters a particular religious belief, and a review of the series establishes that it cannot be reasonably concluded that it does so. . . . Whether or not it [*Impressions*] is the best available educational medium is up to defendant to decide. It certainly passes constitutional muster.[73]

The parents appealed to the Seventh Circuit, which on February 2, 1994, ruled in favor of the school board, declaring:

While the parents and their children may be sincerely offended by some passages in the reading series, they raise a constitutional claim only if the use of the series establishes a *religion*. The parents insist that the reading series presents religious concepts, found in paganism and branches of witchcraft and satanism; this hardly sounds like the establishment of a coherent religion.... [T]his 'religion' that is allegedly being established seems for all the world like a collection of exercises in 'make-believe' designed to develop and encourage the use of imagination and reading skills in children that are the staple of traditional public elementary school education.... The parents would have us believe that the inclusion of these works in an elementary school curriculum represents the impermissible establishment of pagan religion. We do not agree. After all, what would become of elementary education, public or private, without works such as these and scores of others that serve to expand the minds of young children and develop their sense of creativity?[74]

In reaching its decision, the court applied what is called the *Lemon* test for an establishment clause challenge. Under that test, first employed in *Lemon v. Kurtzman* (1971),[75] state action with respect to religion must (1) have a secular purpose; (2) have a primary effect that neither advances nor inhibits religion; and (3) not foster excessive state entanglement with religion. As for the first prong in the *Lemon* test, the *Fleischfresser* court noted that even the complaining parents had not claimed that the purpose of using *Impressions* was exclusively religious. It pointed out that public schools traditionally rely on fantasy and make-believe in their curricula and concluded, "As a result, we hold that the directors' use of the series had a secular purpose."

With respect to the second prong of the *Lemon* test, the court said that in order for the use of *Impressions* to constitute an impermissible advancement of religion, that action must amount to an endorsement of religion. "In this case," wrote the court, "the primary or principle effect of the use of the reading series at issue is not to endorse these religions, but simply to educate the children by improving their reading skills and to develop imagination and creativity. Any religious references are secondary, if not trivial. Therefore, the use of the series withstands scrutiny under this prong of the test."

Finally, the court rejected the claim that the school failed the third requirement of the *Lemon* test because it appointed a curriculum review committee to examine the series before it was purchased. "This claim is without merit," declared the court. "School boards have broad discretion in determining curricula in their schools. Surely, the mere exercise of this discretion cannot constitute excessive entanglement with religion."[76]

As for the parents' charge that they were being denied the right to freely exercise their religious beliefs, the court declared: "The directors are not precluding the parents from meeting their religious obligation to instruct their children. Nor does the use of the series compel the parents or children to do or refrain from doing anything of a religious nature. Thus, no coercion exists, and the parents' free exercise of their religion is not substantially burdened."[77]

Just four months after the decision in *Fleischfresser*, the Ninth Circuit addressed an almost identical challenge to *Impressions* in Woodland, California. The California suit against *Impressions* had followed a legal path similar to that in *Fleischfresser*. During the 1989–1990 school year, several parents of school children in the Woodland Joint Unified School District filed a formal written request to remove the *Impressions* series from their school's curriculum, contending that the Canadian publisher had included too many references to Canadian culture in the text, that it intruded upon the privacy of children and their families, that it contained excessive violence and morbidity, and that it emphasized the occult. The School District had earlier conducted a lengthy piloting and review process, including field testing and public comment, from which *Impressions* emerged as the overwhelming favorite of teachers and students. At the conclusion of the process, nine of the twelve elementary schools in the district had selected *Impressions* as part of their curriculum. When some parents continued to complain about *Impressions*, the Woodland school superintendent appointed a review committee consisting of a school administrator, two teachers, the librarian of the Woodland Public Library, a parent, and a local fundamentalist minister. The committee concluded that the parents' complaints were unwarranted and recommended retention of *Impressions* in its entirety.

On January 8, 1991, the complaining parents initiated legal action in U.S. District Court. In *Brown* v. *Woodland Unified Joint School District*, plaintiffs requested injunctive and declaratory relief, now alleging that the school district's acquisition and use of portions of the *Impressions* series endorsed and sponsored the religions of "Witchcraft" and "Neo-Paganism," in violation of federal and state constitutional requirements of separation of church and state. The school district contended that the case was controlled by *Grove* v. *Mead School District No 354* (1985), which upheld a school board's refusal to remove a book, *The Learning Tree*, from the curriculum because it allegedly advanced the religion of "secular humanism." U.S. District Judge William B. Schubb wrote:

> Factually, this case bears a strong similarity to *Grove*. Here, plaintiffs, Evangenlical Christians, bring a religiously based challenge to a public school's use of a reading series. Here, as in *Grove*, plaintiffs argue that the religion at issue denigrates or inhibits their own religion and establishes a somewhat novel religion. As in *Grove*, the challenged material serves secular goals. Similar to *Grove*, plaintiffs object to isolated and small portions of all the activities in the *Impressions* series. . . . The *Impressions* series, like *The*

Learning Tree, is only one part of the two part language arts curriculum utilized in the School District.[78]

The plaintiffs claimed that *Grove* only addressed the relatively passive act of reading a book, whereas *Brown v. Woodland* also involved exercises that convert neutral reading into sponsorship of witchcraft and neo-Paganism. Judge Schubb rejected this claim, stating:

> A school district may incorporate folk traditions into learning exercises. The convergence of a School District and religious organization on the same exercise or practice does not necessarily suggest that the former is conveying a message of government endorsement of the religious aspects of the practice. The School District's purchase and use of certain prescribed exercises within the *Impressions* series does not suggest a religious preference for Witchcraft or Neo-Paganism.[79]

In ruling that the school district was entitled to summary judgment, Judge Schubb concluded:

> While the court is not unsympathetic to plaintiffs' concerns, there is no constitutional basis [for] the court to order that the activities in question be excluded from the classroom simply because isolated instances of those activities may happen to coincide or harmonize with the tenets of two relatively obscure religions. . . . Finally, there is no evidence that *Impressions* was initially selected or retained by the School District out of hostility toward Christianity or fealty to any Wiccan or Neo-Paganist credo. . . . [F]ar from preferring one religion over another, *Impressions* materials were chosen in part to reflect the cultural diversity of North American society.[80]

The Woodland parents appealed Judge Schubb's ruling to the U.S. Court of Appeals for the Ninth Circuit, and, as in *Fleischfresser*, the court applied the *Lemon* test to determine if the establishment clause had been violated. The first part of the *Lemon* test requires the state to have a secular purpose in its activities. On this matter, the court noted that the parents themselves conceded that the authors-editors of *Impressions* had a secular purpose, as did the school district that adopted the text.

The parents claimed that the use of *Impressions* violated the second part of the *Lemon* test because by engaging the children in make-believe witchcraft, a message of endorsement is communicated. Following an argument similar to that of the district court, the appeals court rejected that allegation, citing *Grove v. Mead School District* (1985): "As in *Grove*, the Challenged Selections are only a very small part of an otherwise clearly nonreligious program. It thus is unlikely that . . . an objective observer would perceive the inclusion of the selections in *Impressions* as an endorsement of or disapproval of religion."

Citing *Fleischfresser*, which had upheld an Illinois district's use of *Impressions* just four months earlier, the *Brown* court concluded: "The Browns have not persuaded us that the second, 'effects,' prong of *Lemon* has been violated here."

The Browns argued that the use of *Impressions* violated the third prong of *Lemon* because it involved the state in excessive administrative surveillance to ensure that witchcraft is not endorsed in the curriculum. But the court rejected this claim, saying that because the use of *Impressions* does not endorse or approve of religion, no future monitoring would be necessary.

In rejecting all the allegations against *Impressions*, the court concluded: "The Browns have failed to persuade us that any of the three prongs of the *Lemon* test has been breached here. We conclude, therefore, that the School District has not violated the federal Establishment Clause in its use of the *Impressions* series."[81]

LEGISLATIVE ATTACKS ON THE INTERNET: IMPLICATIONS FOR BOOKBANNING IN SCHOOLS AND LIBRARIES

When the system of linked computer networks called the Internet leapt onto the public stage from its cradle in the U.S. Defense Department in the late 1970s, it offered the intimacy of the telephone, the immediacy of the newspaper, and the drama and entertainment of television. Libraries quickly recognized the almost limitless research possibilities in the Internet's constantly proliferating linked databases, but only recently has the electronic book or "e-book" become a fundamental part of library collections, with all the attendant censorship problems. Typical of the current library approach is the policy in Chicago's suburban public libraries, where patrons are able to search for, borrow, read, and return e-books through the Internet twenty-four hours a day. The checkout period for e-books is three days, and once the time is up, the book is automatically retrieved and electronically checked back into the netLibrary collection.

"It worked out that we spent about $1 per book, which was pretty good," said Ann Stoval, head of technical and computer services in the library system. "Electronic books are edging into the mainstream now."[82]

As the distinction between printed books and e-books has blurred, the legislative campaign to censor the Internet has had profound implications on bookbanning in schools and libraries. Recent laws and court decisions affecting the content of and access to the Internet have broad implications for censorship of both print and electronic material in the school and library setting.

Early Internet advocates believed that this unique new medium was censor-proof, and many assumed that bookbanning would inevitably de-cline as the influence of cyber-freedom spread throughout society. It now appears that teachers and librarians who provide Internet content are vulnerable to the same kinds of censorship that they have suffered with traditional print collections. Of particular concern is the current attempt to impose Internet censorship on schools and public libraries through federal legislation. The implications for bookbanning are clear.

The details of early congressional attempts to censor the Internet are documented in my book *From Watergate to Monicagate* (Greenwood, 2001), but a quick review of the major legislation and resultant court cases during the 1990s will serve as an introduction to the current state of affairs. The first congressional hearing on Internet pornography was convened on July 24, 1995, by the Senate Judiciary Committee to consider a bill sponsored by Senator Charles Grassley (R-Iowa) that criminalized online "indecency," a constitutionally protected category. Some on the committee warned of the potential for bookbanning in cyberspace. Sen-ator Russ Feingold (D-Wis.) asked, "Where should we draw the line? Should we prohibit *Playboy*? Swearing? *The Catcher in the Rye*? What about a discussion forum about how to avoid getting AIDS?"[83]

Michael Hart, whose Project Gutenberg places electronic texts of classic literature on the Internet, told the committee that legislative restrictions on indecency could prevent people from enjoying serious works of lit-erature. With great emotion, Hart warned that Grassley's bill would force him to remove some of Shakespeare's plays and books like *Catcher in the Rye*, *Lady Chatterley's Lover*, and *Alice in Wonderland*, all of which have been classified as indecent in various parts of the country.[84]

Immediately upon the conclusion of the Senate's cyberporn hearing, the House held a hearing on the use of software to "filter" such material from the Internet.

The two congressional hearings produced a flurry of bills designed to censor the Internet. The most prominent of these initiatives was the Com-munications Decency Act (CDA), introduced by Senator James Exon (R-Nebr.). The CDA criminalized any "comment, request, suggestion, pro-posal, image or other communication" on a "telecommunications de-vice," even messages between adults that are found by a court to be "obscene, lascivious, filthy or indecent." The penalties for such expres-sion included fines of up to $100,000 and two years in jail.

The CDA was passed on February 1, 1996, and was promptly signed into law by President Bill Clinton. The American Civil Liberties Union (ACLU), joined by several public service organizations, brought suit challenging the constitutionality of the CDA. On February 15, 1996, *ACLU* v. *Reno* was heard by District Judge Ronald Buckwalter, who blocked enforcement of the CDA until a three-judge panel could rule on it. On February 26, 1996, the American Library Association led another group of organizations, including the major online companies and professional associations of newspaper publishers, editors, and reporters, in a suit that was combined with the ACLU suit. On June 12, 1996, the three-judge panel ruled that the CDA violated the First Amendment.

Chief Judge Dolores Sloviter wrote: "Whether Congress's decision was a wise one is not at issue here. It was unquestionably a decision that placed the CDA in serious conflict with our most cherished protection— the right to choose the material to which we would have access."

The Justice Department appealed the decision to the Supreme Court which, on June 26, 1997, ruled the CDA to be an unconstitutional abridgement of " 'the freedom of speech' protected by the First Amendment." Even the two minority opinions written by Justice Sandra Day O'Connor and Chief Justice William Rehnquist supported the majority on the question of constitutionality.

Justice John Paul Stevens, writing for the majority, was unequivocal in rejecting the CDA. "[T]he CDA lacks the precision that the First Amendment requires when a statute regulates the content of speech," wrote Stevens. "In order to deny minors access to potentially harmful speech, the CDA effectively suppresses a large amount of speech that adults have a constitutional right to receive and to address to one another. . . . The general undefined terms 'indecent' and 'patently offensive' cover large amounts of nonpornographic material with serious educational or other value."

Stevens concluded: "The interest in encouraging freedom of expression in a democratic society outweighs any theoretical but unproven benefit of censorship."[85]

Having been rebuffed in their attempt to directly censor the Internet, several lawmakers prepared new, more carefully drawn laws that they hoped would pass constitutional muster. Among these initiatives were "filtering" bills like Representative Ernest Istook's (R-Okla.) Child Protection Act of 1998, which denied federal funds for computer equipment in schools and libraries that do not filter "content inappropriate for minors." The Safe Schools Internet Act (H.R.368) similarly required schools and libraries to filter "inappropriate" material on the Internet. The Neighborhood Children's Internet Protection Act (S.1545) required schools and libraries to install systems for "blocking or filtering Internet access to matter inappropriate for minors."

Senator John McCain (R-Ariz.) introduced two important filtering bills. The Internet School Filtering Act, introduced in February 1998, would forbid schools that did not have blocking software in place from receiving government subsidies for Internet access, and the Children's Internet Protection Act (H.R.543, S.97), introduced in the Senate in January 1999, made schools and libraries ineligible for federal funding if they did not install "a technology for computers with Internet access which filters or blocks material deemed harmful to minors."

The rash of Internet filtering bills alarmed librarians, who saw themselves and their profession being targeted along with the First Amendment. A group of librarians published The Internet Filter Assessment Project (TIFAP) challenging the effectiveness of filters in a library setting. Keyword blocking was shown to exclude everything from nursery rhymes to government physics archives.

As librarians spoke out publicly against mandatory filtering, Congress turned once more to direct censorship of Internet content, drafting a modified version of the CDA designed to pass constitutional muster. The Child Online Protection Act (COPA), introduced in April 1998 by Representative Michael Oxley (R-Ohio), was quickly characterized as the "Son of CDA." It specified: "Whoever knowingly and with knowledge of the character of the material, in interstate or foreign commerce by means of the World Wide Web, makes any communication for commercial purposes that is available to any minor and that includes any material that is harmful to minors shall be fined not more than $50,000, imprisoned not more than 6 months, or both."

Librarians were prominent among those opposing the COPA. The Internet Free Expression Alliance, a twenty-three-group coalition including the American Library Association and the ACLU, expressed its opposition in a letter to the subcommittee considering the bill: "H.R. 3783 should be rejected because it contains many of the unconstitutional provisions of the Communications Decency Act. . . . Like the CDA, the bill would have the effect of criminalizing protected speech among adults. Whatever governmental interest may exist to protect children from harmful materials, that interest does not justify the broad suppression of adult speech."[86]

Despite such public criticism, the Child Online Protection Act was passed by Congress and signed into law by President Clinton in October 1998. A coalition of seventeen plaintiffs, including the ACLU, immediately challenged the law in a Philadelphia court, arguing that serious medical and educational Internet sites could be closed down under the COPA. The first legal judgment in *ACLU* v. *Reno II* came in Philadelphia on November 20, 1998, when U.S. District Judge Lowell Reed Jr. granted a temporary restraining order and a preliminary injunction against enforcement of the COPA. Judge Reed said:

> The plaintiffs have uniformly testified or declared that their fears of prosecution under COPA will result in the self-censorship of their online materials in an effort to avoid prosecution, and this Court has concluded . . . that such fears are reasonable given the breadth of the statute. Such a chilling effect could result in the censoring of constitutionally protected

speech, which constitutes an irreparable harm to the plaintiffs.... For plaintiffs who choose not to self-censor their speech, they face criminal prosecution and penalties for communicating speech that is protected for adults under the First Amendment, which also constitutes irreparable harm.[87]

The Department of Justice appealed Judge Reed's decision, and on June 22, 2000, the U.S. Court of Appeals for the Third Circuit struck down the COPA, saying it imposed an impermissible burden on constitutionally protected First Amendment speech. Judge Leonard I. Garth wrote for the three-judge panel, which focused chiefly on the impossibility of establishing one "community standard" to govern the nationwide scope of Internet expression. The court found that the over breadth of the COPA in this regard "must lead inexorably to a holding of a likelihood of unconstitutionality of the entire COPA statute." In affirming the district court's preliminary injunction, the appeals court concluded, "Due to current technological limitations, COPA ... is more likely than not to be found unconstitutional on the merits."[88]

The Justice Department disagreed, and once more appealed, this time to the highest court in the land, placing the Son of CDA on the same path that its parent legislation followed. The petition to the Supreme Court for a Writ of Certiorari was submitted in February 2001 by John Ashcroft, the new Attorney General under President George W. Bush, changing the name of the case to *Ashcroft* v. *ACLU*.

The petition argued that COPA differs from the CDA in important ways that support the congressional judgment that COPA is the least restrictive way to further the government's compelling interest in protecting children from materials that are harmful to minors.

First, said the petition, the CDA applied to all forms of communication on the Internet, whereas "COPA applies only to material posted on the World Wide Web."

Second, the CDA prohibited the transmittal of materials that were "indecent" or "patently offensive," without indicating whether those determinations should be made with respect to minors or the population as a whole. By contrast, argued the petition, COPA "is specifically limited to material that is patently offensive to minors," and it identifies the particular types of sexual activities that may not be described or depicted.

Third, the CDA applied to large amounts of nonpornographic material with serious educational value, whereas "COPA contains all three prongs of the Ginsberg test, and thus ... applies only to material that is designed to appeal to the 'prurient interest' of minors and that, taken as a whole, lacks serious literary, artistic, political or scientific value for minors."

Fourth, the CDA defined a minor as any person under the age of 18, whereas "COPA, like the state law in *Ginsberg*, defines minor to mean 'any person under 17 years of age.' "

Fifth, the CDA applied to both commercial and noncommercial entities or transactions, whereas "COPA applies only to those Web communications that are made 'for commercial purposes.' "

Sixth, the CDA made it unlawful for parents to permit their children to view indecent or offensive material on the home computer, whereas COPA contains no such provision.

In rejecting the appellate decision, the petition concluded: "The decision prevents the government from enforcing a recent Act of Congress against anyone under any circumstances, and it suggests that there may be no constitutional means to protect children from the harmful effects of the voluminous amount of pornographic material on the World Wide Web. The court of appeals' decision therefore clearly warrants this Court's review."

On May 21, 2001, the Supreme Court granted certiorari and agreed to review *Ashcroft* v. *ACLU* during the term beginning in October. The ACLU remained confident that the Court would find the COPA unconstitutional. "Although Congress claims to have narrowed the law to address only material that is 'harmful to minors,' in our challenges to state versions of this law not one federal judge has ruled in favor of this unworkable approach," said Chris Hansen, ACLU senior attorney and a member of the legal team challenging COPA.[89] Nevertheless, in oral arguments before the Supreme Court during November 2001, questions from several justices suggested a reluctance to strike down the entire COPA. They asked Ann Beeson, lawyer for the ACLU, whether the case could be resolved by defining "community standards," the basis on which the COPA determined whether Internet material was harmful to minors, as a kind of average national opinion. Beeson responded, "National standards would be an exercise in futility."[90] A decision in *Ashcroft* v. *ACLU* is expected some time before July 2002.

As the school and library community awaited the Supreme Court's momentous decision on COPA, Congress and the lower courts continued on a collision course with respect to the growing phenomenon of Internet filtering. A district court in Virginia had seemed to deal a severe blow to congressional plans to impose filtering in public libraries. In *Mainstream Loudoun* v. *Board of Trustees* (1998), Loudoun County residents and the local ACLU chapter brought civil suit against the Loudoun County Public Libraries, charging them with violating their First Amendment rights by requiring filtering software on all library computers. At issue was the libraries' "Policy on Internet Sexual Harassment," passed on October 20, 1997, which stated that the libraries would use filtering software to block any Internet site containing obscenity, child pornography, or material deemed harmful to juveniles. The policy specified that the police may be called to intervene if patrons used terminals to access such sites.

In its complaint, the ACLU charged that by using blocking software to implement its policy, the library board was "removing books from the shelves" of the Internet, in violation of the Constitution. "Blocking software is nothing more than CDA in a box," said Ann Beeson, an ACLU staff attorney who appeared before the court.[91]

On April 7, 1998, the U.S. District Court for the Eastern District of Virginia addressed the issue of "whether a public library may, without violating the First Amendment, enforce content-based restrictions on access to Internet speech." The defendants, the Loudoun County Public Library Board of Trustees, requested summary judgment, arguing that the "First Amendment does not in any way limit the decisions of a public library on whether to provide access to information on the Internet." Indeed, defendants went so far as to claim that a public library could constitutionally prohibit access to speech simply because it was authored by African-Americans or because it espoused a particular political viewpoint.

In analyzing the First Amendment issues, Judge Leonie Brinkema, herself a former librarian, relied almost exclusively on *Board of Education* v. *Pico* (1986), the Supreme Court's landmark bookbanning case described in detail earlier in this chapter and in Chapter 1. The defendants in *Mainstream Loudoun* v. *Board of Trustees* contended that *Pico* had no application to their actions, because *Pico* addressed the arbitrary *removal* of books from a high school library, whereas Loudoun's restriction on Internet access was equivalent to a decision not to *acquire* materials. Plaintiffs, on the other hand, analogized the Internet to a set of encyclopedias from which the library had decided to "black out" articles considered inappropriate for adult and juvenile patrons.

Judge Brinkema ruled that Loudoun's Internet restrictions were indeed equivalent to removing library materials. "By purchasing Internet access, each Loudoun library has made all Internet publications instantly accessible to its patrons," she wrote.

> The Internet therefore more closely resembles plaintiff's analogy of a collection of encyclopedias from which defendants have laboriously redacted portions deemed unfit for library patrons. As such, the Library Board's action is more appropriately characterized as a removal decision. . . . In sum, there is 'no basis for qualifying the level of First Amendment scrutiny' that must be applied to a public library's decision to restrict access to Internet publications.[92]

Brinkema concluded, "[I]n this case, the Library Board need not offer Internet access, but having chosen to provide it, must operate the service within the confines of the First Amendment."[93]

Brinkema denied Loudoun's motion for summary judgment, requiring a trial to examine material factual issues. At trial, Brinkema once more relied heavily on *Pico* as well as *Reno* v. *ACLU* (1997), the Supreme Court case that found the CDA to be unconstitutional.

On November 23, 1998, Brinkema ruled that Loudoun's Internet policy "constitutes an unconstitutional prior restraint on speech." The opinion concluded:

> Defendant has asserted a broad right to censor the expressive activity of the receipt and communication of information through the Internet with a Policy that (1) is not necessary to further any compelling government interest; (2) is not narrowly tailored; (3) restricts the access of adult patrons to protected material just because the material is unfit for minors; (4) provides inadequate standards for restricting access; and (5) provides inadequate procedural safeguards to ensure prompt judicial review. Such a policy offends the guarantee of free speech in the First Amendment and is, therefore, unconstitutional. . . . Defendant will be permanently enjoined from enforcing its Policy on Internet Sexual Harassment.[94]

On April 13, 1999, Judge Brinkema awarded the ACLU and People for the American Way $106,918.25 in attorney fees and costs associated with their suit against Loudoun County. A week later, the Loudoun library board voted not to appeal, leaving the decision against the use of library filters standing. But Ken Bass, the attorney for Loudoun County, predicted that there would soon be other cases addressing the constitutionality of Internet filtering. "I can't imagine there isn't going to be a suit in some other jurisdiction, where the state statutes are now requiring libraries to put in filtering software, or the McCain bill if it passes," he said.[95]

Bass was prescient in anticipating the legislative and legal battle ahead. Senator McCain's Children's Internet Protection Act (CIPA) and a companion filtering bill, the Neighborhood Internet Protection Act (NIPA), were attached to a rider on an education appropriations bill and passed by Congress on December 15, 2000. President Clinton signed the bills into law just a week later. Both bills withhold federal funding from schools and libraries that do not filter Internet content from their computers.

Perhaps more disturbing was the accompanying rush by state legislatures to prepare similar bills. During 2000, eighteen states followed Congress's lead, introducing legislation mandating the use of filters in schools and libraries. The legislative bodies in Colorado, Michigan, Minnesota, and Utah succeeded in passing such bills. The trend continued during early 2001, as state representatives in Arkansas, Maine, Mississippi, Missouri, Oklahoma, Texas, and Virginia filed bills requiring the use of filters in public schools and libraries.

The Texas bill, introduced on March 12, contained provisions similar to those in Senator McCain's federal bill, making Texas schools ineligible for state funding unless they use filters on all school computers. Public libraries could retain their eligibility by opting to write their own policies banning the display of obscene materials. On March 16, 2001, the Oklahoma House passed a similar bill by a landslide 92–2 vote. The viability of these state laws will undoubtedly be tested in state courts, but the legal judgment eventually rendered on Senator McCain's CIPA will undoubtedly determine their fate as well.

On March 20, 2001, the American Library Association (ALA) filed a lawsuit in U.S. District Court for the Eastern District of Pennsylvania seeking to overturn the CIPA. The complaint in *ALA* v. *United States*, filed by the ALA and supporting organizations, charged that the CIPA "imposes unprecedented, sweeping federal speech restrictions on public libraries nationwide . . . invading and distorting the traditional functions of public libraries by requiring them to violate patrons' constitutional right to receive information."

The complaint predicted:

> Any attempt to meet the Act's requirements inevitably will lead to suppression of vast amounts of protected Internet speech that would otherwise be available to public library patrons. Through the Act, Congress has used its spending power to conscript public libraries into its censorship program. The federal filtering mandate requires that libraries do what Congress plainly could not: directly restrict access to information in a traditional sphere of free expression.[96]

In making a pointed reference to *Mainstream Loudoun* v. *Board of Trustees*, the complaint noted that in the rare instances where public libraries have imposed mandatory filtering, it has produced serious constitutional concerns and legal challenges.

At the ALA's March 20 press conference, Theresa Chmara, counsel for the plaintiffs in *ALA* v. *United States*, explained:

> Under well-established First Amendment principles, the government may not subsidize a forum or medium for private expression, such as the Internet in a public library, and then attempt to suppress a category of protected speech based on its disfavored content. . . . The courts have recognized the critical role that libraries play in maintaining the fabric of our society and promoting freedom of expression. This law tears at that fabric.[97]

ALA President Nancy Kranich said, "This legislation imposes a one-size-fits-all mechanical solution on libraries that are as diverse as our families and takes away local and parental control, ceding it to unaccountable filtering companies."[98]

John Berry, ALA President-elect, said,

> Filters are contrary to the mission of the public library which is to provide access to the broadest range of information for a community of diverse individuals. Filters block access to critical, constitutionally protected speech related to many subject areas. . . . The American Library Association believes strongly that the Children's Internet Protection Act is unconstitutional. The filtering mandate imposed by Congress is unworkable in the context of a public institution because it restricts access to constitutionally protected speech on the users served by libraries.[99]

William Gordon, ALA Executive Director, noted, "If the same standards used in online blocking technologies were applied to a library's books the way that they are applied to the Internet, our shelves would be practically empty."[100]

Gordon pointed out that the ALA lawsuit challenges only the CIPA's application to public libraries, not school libraries. "Although ALA believes strongly that CIPA is unconstitutional in both the context of the school library as well as the public library, ALA lacks the legal standing to bring a lawsuit on behalf of the schools that are the fund recipients under the statute." This is because school libraries are not the direct recipients of federal funds under the CIPA, but rather receive funding through their individual schools. Nonetheless, Gordon said the ALA pledged to support any legal effort by school groups to challenge the CIPA in the school context.[101]

The ACLU and People for the American Way also indicated their intention to challenge the CIPA in court. Charles Hansen, ACLU Senior Staff Attorney, said:

> This is the first time since the development of the local, free public library in the 19th century that the federal government has sought to require censorship in every single town and hamlet in America. More than a hundred years of local control of libraries and the strong tradition of allowing adults to decide for themselves what they want to read is being casually set aside."[102]

Supporters of the CIPA, including the conservative Family Research Council, have vowed to defend the law in court. "Because of the policies of the American Library Association, public libraries with unrestricted Internet access are virtual peep shows open to kids and funded by taxpayers," said Jan LaRue, the Council's director of legal studies. "No one has ever claimed that a library has First Amendment duty to provide every book or video or magazine the public wants."[103]

In the wake of the suits, a congressional subcommittee held hearings on the CIPA. On April 4, Marvin Johnson, an ACLU legislative counsel, testified, "Emasculating the First Amendment under the banner of protecting our children teaches children our principles are a hollow shell, to be cast aside when they seem inconvenient.... We fully expect the courts to overturn this constitutional briar-patch of a law."[104]

The CIPA's judicial review provisions specify that a three-judge panel appointed by the U.S. Court of Appeals for the Third Circuit will hear both the ALA and ACLU cases, which have been consolidated and will be heard together. On July 26, 2001, in a one-paragraph decision, the panel denied the government's motion to dismiss the case. The decision came just three days after the Philadelphia court heard oral arguments on the government's motion. The trial is set for February 14, 2002, and any appeal of the panel's decision must go directly to the U.S. Supreme Court.

HIT MAN: THE COURTS SAY THE BOOK MADE HIM DO IT

As we have seen, court decisions from disparate circumstances can have implications for bookbanning in schools and libraries. One of those unusual cases is *Rice* v. *Paladin* (1999). In May 1999, Paladin Press, the publisher of the book *Hit Man*, agreed to pay $5 million to the relatives of three individuals killed by a real "hit man" who had allegedly followed the book's detailed description of murder for hire. Paladin Press was also required to turn over all copies of *Hit Man* and to cease publishing the book. The unprecedented settlement was reached after the U.S. Supreme Court let stand an appellate court ruling that the First Amendment did not protect the publisher.

This was the first time in the history of American jurisprudence that a lawsuit blaming an act of violence on a book had succeeded. Legal precedent in this regard had heretofore been guided by *Branzberg* v. *Ohio* (1969),[105] which established that only speech that is directed to producing or inciting "imminent lawless action" and that is likely to produce such action is beyond First Amendment protection. How could *Hit Man*, which had been published in 1983 and sold over 13,000 copies without incident, have produced "imminent" lawless action a decade later? What unique aspects of this book, its author, and publisher led Rodney Smolla, a prominent First Amendment scholar and attorney, to "transform" himself—as he put it—into a bookbanning prosecutor? What are the implications for bookbanning in schools and libraries?

Paladin Press is a small publishing house located in Boulder, Colorado, that publishes a wide variety of books and relies primarily on catalog sales. The portion of its catalog that contains *Hit Man* is what some have called its "macho" line, books presumably marketed to gun fanciers, survivalists, militia members, and soldiers of fortune.

And what of the tough and malevolent author of *Hit Man*, who wrote under the absurd pseudonym of Rex Feral? (The dictionary synonyms for feral are barbarous, beastly, brutish, primitive, and savage.) Throughout the trials associated with *Hit Man*, the author's true identity was protected by Paladin Press, but a reporter eventually discovered that the author was, of all things, a divorced mother of two who does not even own a gun. She had originally written *Hit Man* as a novel, but was asked by Paladin to rework the manuscript to fit Paladin's catalog of "how-to" books. The result had the artificial structure of an assassin's manual while retaining the melodramatic prose of an adventure novel.

Paladin's catalog description of *Hit Man* had the tongue-in-cheek swagger of a Mickey Spillane novel, but the catalog entry concluded with the warning: *"For academic study only."*[106]

The process leading to *Rice* v. *Paladin* was set in motion on March 3, 1993, when a Maryland woman, her disabled son, and his nurse were brutally murdered in their home. The woman's ex-husband, Lawrence Horn, was subsequently arrested and accused of hiring a hit man named James Perry to kill the son in order to inherit his disability award. At Perry's trial, the police introduced into evidence several books found in Perry's home, including two Paladin titles: *How to Make Disposable Silencers* and *Hit Man*.

On October 12, 1995, after five hours of deliberation, the jury found Perry guilty of murder, and the same jury subsequently agreed on the death sentence. Lawrence Horn's trial followed soon thereafter, and he was found guilty of three counts of murder, for which he was sentenced to life imprisonment.

The guilty had been punished. Now it was time to punish society for enabling Horn and Perry to perpetrate their violence. The families of the murder victims filed a civil damages lawsuit in a Maryland district court charging wrongful death, an action similar to the successful suit against O. J. Simpson. But here the target of the suit was not the alleged murderer, but Paladin Press and its publisher, Peter Lund, who were charged with "aiding and abetting" the murders committed by Horn and Perry. The legal team that would argue the case against Paladin consisted of Rodney Smolla, Howard Siegel, and John Marshall.

Paladin's defense team, knowing that no book had ever been held responsible for a reader's violent actions, chose to rely entirely on the First Amendment. In an effort to focus the proceeding exclusively on the publisher's First Amendment rights, Paladin's attorneys, Tom Kelley and Lee Levine, agreed to a Joint Statement of Fact for the court. Prepared during a surprisingly easy week of negotiations between the two sides, the Joint Statement of Fact included Paladin's catalog advertising for *Hit*

Man and the disclaimer that appears on the page preceding the book's title page. It stipulated that Perry had acquired *Hit Man* and *Silencers* from Paladin about ten days before the murders, and it listed excerpts from *Hit Man* that matched the steps followed by Perry in committing the murders.

The Joint Statement of Fact concluded:

> In publishing, marketing, advertising and distributing *Hit Man* and *Silencers*, Paladin intended and had knowledge that their publications would be used, upon receipt, by criminals and would-be criminals to plan and execute the crime of murder for hire, in the manner set forth in the publications. . . . All the parties agree that Paladin's marketing strategy is intended to maximize sales to the public, including authors who desire information for the purpose of writing books about crime and criminals, law enforcement officers and agencies who desire information concerning the means and methods of committing crimes, persons who enjoy reading accounts of crimes and the means of committing them for purposes of entertainment, persons who fantasize about committing crimes but do not thereafter commit them, and criminologists and others who study criminal methods and mentality.[107]

The outcome of the case would ultimately turn on the damaging defense stipulations in the Joint Statement of Fact, because those stipulations suggested "intent" on the part of Paladin to aid and abet a crime. District Court Judge J. Williams did not see it that way. In his opinion, he noted:

> Defendants conceded that they intended that their publications would be used by criminals to plan and execute murder as instructed in the manual. However, Defendants clarify their concession by explaining that when they published, advertised and distributed both *Hit Man* and *Silencers*, they knew, and in that sense 'intended,' that the books would be purchased by all of the categories of readers previously described and used by them for the broad range of purposes previously described.[108]

Judge Williams thereby dismissed the case against Paladin Press, and in May 1998 the case proceeded to the U.S. Court of Appeals. The three judges on the appeals panel were William W. Wilkins, Jr., Karen J. Williams, and J. Michael Luttig, three conservatives appointed by Presidents Reagan and Bush.

The appeals court reversed the district court's ruling in an unusually emotional opinion written by Judge Luttig. Following their defeat at the hands of Judge Luttig, Paladin's lawyers petitioned the entire Fourth Circuit to rehear the case "en banc," before all fourteen Fourth Circuit judges, but the petition was swiftly denied. As expected, Paladin then petitioned the U.S. Supreme Court to review Judge Luttig's decision. In its petition, Paladin characterized Luttig's decision as emotional, extremist, and contrary to mainstream First Amendment analysis. In particular, Paladin warned that Luttig's opinion would open the floodgates for suits against a wide variety of legitimate expression.

The Supreme Court denied Paladin's petition, leaving Luttig's opinion undisturbed. The case would now be remanded for trial before Judge Williams and a district court jury. The outcome of the trial remained in doubt, but national events outside the legalities of *Rice* v. *Paladin* suddenly took control of the case. One month before the trial was to begin, a national calamity occurred that would strongly prejudice the outcome. Two students at Columbine High School in Littleton, Colorado, massacred fellow students using guns and homemade bombs. Fifteen people were dead and twenty-three wounded. Paladin's lawyers filed a motion to postpone the trial, arguing that media coverage of the Columbine killings would prevent a fair trial.

Judge Williams denied Paladin's motion to postpone. The very next day, newspaper headlines told of another shocking school killing, this one in Conyers, Georgia, where six students were wounded. Pressure was building for Paladin to settle the case before trial. On the last business day before the trial was to begin, Paladin threw in the towel, agreeing to a multimillion dollar payment to the families as well as yearly contributions to two charities of their choice. Most significant, Paladin agreed to cease selling *Hit Man* and provide all remaining copies to the plaintiffs.

Just six months after *Paladin* was decided, another spectacular case fulfilled the worst fears of First Amendment advocates and the most dire predictions of Paladin's attorneys. The Court of Appeals for the First Circuit ruled in *Byers* v. *Edmondson* (1998) that Warner Brothers and Oliver Stone, director of the film *Natural Born Killers*, could be found liable at trial "as the result of their misfeasance in that they produced and released a film containing violent imagery that was intended to cause its viewers to imitate the violent imagery."[109] The opinion relied heavily on *Paladin*, concluding that because Byers's allegations were analogous to the stipulations in *Paladin*, the First Amendment did not require dismissal of the action. Though the subsequent trial concluded on February 12, 2001, that the film was entitled to First Amendment protection, the plaintiffs vowed to appeal once more, and the issue remains in doubt.

At a recent roundtable discussion sponsored by the American Library Association, Peter Irons, a professor of politics and director of the Warren Bill of Rights Project at the University of California, and Rodney Smolla, the victorious attorney in *Rice* v. *Paladin*, had the opportunity to examine the implications of that case. Irons, in particular, was concerned about the vulnerability of libraries and librarians now that the distributor of a book could be held liable for the actions of its readers.

When the moderator of the panel asked Irons to describe the potential liability of librarians in cases like *Paladin*, Irons answered, "Actually, I think there is a stronger legal argument to hold the seller or distributor liable. Librarians don't sell publications, but they distribute them."[110]

Irons pointed out that the controlling precedent on such matters before *Paladin* was *New York Times* v. *Sullivan* (1964),[111] in which the allegedly libelous material was not created by the *Times*. The Supreme Court said the *Times* could not be sued for distributing the material, establishing protection for the media in general. But all that seems to have been reversed in *Paladin*.

Irons concluded, "My point here is that the distributors of material are often more or equally liable than the creators."

Smolla insisted that in prosecuting the publisher of *Hit Man*, he never intended to threaten the ability of publishers or libraries to distribute controversial books. "If you believe that . . . the precedent of something like the *Hit Man* case is going to be . . . the foot in the door that will slide open a great swath of liability against movie producers, librarians, everybody involved in the creative process, then I deserve to lose."[112]

When it was pointed out to Smolla that a major libel case against the movie *Natural Born Killers* was being prosecuted on the basis of the *Hit Man* precedent, he said he personally would never have involved himself in such a suit.

NOTES

1. *Bartels* v. *State of Iowa*, 43 S.Ct. 628 (1923).

2. *Meyer* v. *Nebraska*, 262 U.S. 390, 401 (1923).

3. *Pierce* v. *Society of Sisters*, 286 U.S. 510, 535 (1925).

4. *Minersville School District* v. *Gobitis*, 310 U.S. 586, 598 (1940).

5. *Minersville School District* v. *Gobitis*, 310 U.S. 586, 604 (1940).

6. *West Virginia State Board of Education* v. *Barnette*, 319 U.S. 624, 637, 640 (1943).

7. *Keyishian* v. *Board of Regents*, 385 U.S. 589, 603 (1967).

8. *Epperson* v. *Arkansas*, 393 U.S. 97, 105, 113, 114 (1968).

9. *Epperson* v. *Arkansas*, 393 U.S. 97, 105, 115–116 (1968).

10. *Tinker* v. *Des Moines Independent Community School District*, 395 U.S. 503, 506, 511 (1969).

11. *Martin* v. *City of Struthers*, 319 U.S. 141 (1943).

12. *Lamont* v. *U.S. Postmaster General*, 381 U.S. 301 (1965).

13. *Virginia State Board of Pharmacy* v. *Virginia Citizens Consumer Council*, 425 U.S. 748 (1976).

14. Mary Elizabeth Bezanson, "The Right to Receive through the School Library," *Communication Education*, October 1987, pp. 340–41.

15. *Wisconsin* v. *Yoder*, 406 U.S. 205, 234, 240 (1972).

16. *Wisconsin* v. *Yoder*, 406 U.S. 205, 242, 245 (1972).

17. *San Antonio Independent School District* v. *Rodriguez*, 411 U.S. 1, 36 (1973).

18. *President's Council District 25* v. *Community School Board No. 25*, 457 F.2d 289, 291–92 (1972).

19. *President's Council District 25* v. *Community School Board No. 25*, 457 F.2d 289, 293 (1972).

20. *President's Council District 25* v. *Community School Board No. 25*, 457 F.2d 289, 291 (1972).

21. *Williams* v. *Board of Education of County of Kanawha*, 388 F. Supp 93, 96 (1975).

22. *Minarcini* v. *Strongsville (Ohio) City School District*, 541 F.2d 577, 582, 583 (6th Cir. 1976).

23. *Minarcini* v. *Strongsville (Ohio) City School District*, 541 F.2d 577, 581 (6th Cir. 1976).

24. *Right to Read Defense Committee* v. *School Committee of the City of Chelsea*, 454 F. Supp. 703, 707, 713 (1978).

25. *Cary* v. *Board of Education Arapahoe School District*, 598 F.2d 535, 542, 544 (1979).

26. *Salvail* v. *Nashua Board of Education*, 469 F. Supp. 1269, 1272, 1275 (1979).

27. *Ambach* v. *Norwick*, 441 U.S. 68 (1979).

28. *Zykan* v. *Warsaw Community School Corporation and Warsaw School Board of Trustees*, 631 F.2d. 1300, 1304, 1306 (1980).

29. *Bicknell* v. *Vergennes Union High School Board of Directors*, 475 F. Supp 615 (1979).

30. *Board of Education, Island Trees Union Free School District No. 26* v. *Pico*, 474 F. Supp 387, 396–97 (1982).

31. *Board of Education, Island Trees Union Free School District No. 26* v. *Pico*, 638 F.2d. 404, 416 (1982).

32. *Board of Education, Island Trees Union Free School District No. 26* v. *Pico*, 638 F.2d. 404, 419 (1982).

33. *Board of Education, Island Trees Union Free School District No. 26* v. *Pico*, 638 F.2d 404, 437 (1982).

34. *Board of Education, Island Trees Union Free School District No. 26* v. *Pico*, 457 U.S. 853, 879–80 (1982).

35. *Board of Education, Island Trees Union Free School District No. 26* v. *Pico*, 102 S. Ct. 2799, 2805–6 (1982).

36. Ibid., at 2809 (1982).

37. *Board of Education, Island Trees Union Free School District No. 26* v. *Pico*, 457 U.S. 853, at 867–68 (1982).

38. *Board of Education, Island Trees Union Free School District No. 26* v. *Pico*, 102 S. Ct. 2799, 2829–30 (1982).

39. *West Virginia State Board of Education* v. *Barnette*, 319 U.S. 624, 641 (1943).

40. American Library Association, Office for Intellectual Freedom, *Intellectual Freedom Manual*, 4th ed. (Chicago: ALA, 1992), pp. 182–83.

41. *Board of Education, Island Trees Union Free School District No. 26* v. *Pico*, 102 S. Ct. 2799, 2808, 2821 (1982).

42. *Board of Education, Island Trees School District No. 26* v. *Pico*, 102 S. Ct. 2799, 2821 (1982).

43. *Sheck* v. *Baileyville School Committee*, 530 F. Supp. 679, 684–85, 689 (1982).

44. *Johnson* v. *Stuart*, 702 F.2d 193 (1983).

45. *Grove* v. *Mead School District No. 354*, 753 F.2d 1528, 1534, 1541 (1985).

46. *Mozert* v. *Hawkins County Board of Education*, 579 F. Supp. 1051, 1053 (1987).

47. *Smith* v. *Board of School Commissioners of Mobile (Ala.) County*, 827 F.2d 684, 688 (1987).

48. *Seyfried* v. *Walton*, 572 F. Supp. 235 (D. Del. 1981).

49. *Board of Education, Island Trees Union Free School District No. 26* v. *Pico*, 457 U.S. 853, 870, 871, 880 (1982).

50. *Bethel School District No. 403* v. *Fraser*, 478 U.S. 675, 681, 682 (1986).

51. *Hazelwood School District* v. *Kuhlmeier*, 108 S. Ct. 562, 571 (1988).

52. Ibid.

53. *Virgil* v. *School Board of Columbia County*, 862 F.2d 1517, 1522 (11th Cir. 1989).

54. *Virgil* v. *School Board of Columbia County*, 677 F. Supp. 1547, 1551–52 (M. D. Fla.1988).

55. *Virgil* v. *School Board of Columbia County*, Appellants' Initial Brief, submitted by the American Civil Liberties Union on April 29, 1988, pp. 13, 25.

56. *Virgil* v. *School Board of Columbia County*, 862 F.2d 1517, 1525 (11th Cir. 1989).

57. *Farrell* v. *Hall*, Order, July 18, 1988, U.S. District Court for the Northern District of Florida.

58. *McCarthy* v. *Fletcher*, 254 Cal. Rptr. 714, 718 (1989).

59. *McCarthy* v. *Fletcher*, 254 Cal. Rptr. 714, 720, 724 (1989).

60. Andrew Luna, "*Hazelwood* v. *Kuhlmeier*. Supreme Court Decision Does Affect College and University First Amendment Rights," *NASPA Journal*, v. 33, no. 4, Summer 1996, pp. 314–15.

61. "Student Press," *Newsletter on Intellectual Freedom*, January 1998, p. 20.

62. "Student Press," *Newsletter on Intellectual Freedom*, January 2000, pp. 21–22.

63. *Kincaid* v. *Gibson*, 236 F.3d 342 (6th Cir. Jan. 5, 2001).

64. *Romano* v. *Harrington*, 725 F. Supp 687 (E.D. N.Y. 1989).

65. *Desilets* v. *Clearview Regional Board of Education*, 266 N.J. Super. 531 (App. Div. 1993).

66. "Student Press Freedom Debated Before Court," *New Jersey Law Journal*, May 9, 1994, p. 4.

67. "Public High School Students—Vulgarity—State Law," *Massachusetts Lawyers Weekly*, August 5, 1996, p. 9.

68. "About Education," *New York Times*, July 5, 1989, B7.

69. "Colorado Passes Free Press Law," *SPLC Report*, Fall 1990, p. 4.

70. "Bill Gives High School Journalists Limited Protection," *Arkansas Democrat-Gazette*, April 23, 1995, 5B.

71. "Students Seek Control Over School Papers," *St. Louis Post-Dispatch*, February 14, 1993, 1C.

72. *Fleischfresser* v. *Directors of School District No. 200*, 15 F.3d 680, 683 (7th Cir. 1994).

73. *Fleischfresser* v. *Directors of School District No. 200*, 805 F. Supp 584 (1992).

74. *Fleischfresser* v. *Directors of School District No. 200*, 15 F.3d 680, 687–88 (7th Cir. 1994).

75. *Lemon* v. *Kurtzman*, 403 U.S. 602 (1971).

76. *Fleischfresser* v. *Directors of School District No. 200*, 15 F.3d 680, 688–89 (7th Cir. 1994).

77. *Fleischfresser* v. *Directors of School District No. 200*, 15 F.3d 680, 690 (7th Cir. 1994).

78. *Brown* v. *Woodland Joint Unified School District*, E.D. Cal. Case No. Civ. 5-91-0032 (April 2, 1992).

79. Ibid.

80. Ibid.

81. *Brown* v. *Woodland Joint Unified School District*, 27 F.3d 1373, at 1381, 1383–84 (9th Cir. 1994).

82. Lynn Van Mastre, "Libraries Will Expand Collections with eBooks," *chicagotribune.com*, July 13, 2001, p. 1.

83. Center for Democracy and Technology, *Policy Post*, July 26, 1995, p. 3, www.cdt.org/publications.

84. Ibid.

85. *American Civil Liberties Union* v. *Reno*, in *United States Law Week*, 65 LW 4715, at 4723–27.

86. Internet Free Expression Alliance, Joint Statement Submitted to the Subcommittee on Telecommunications, Trade and Consumer Protection, Committee on Commerce, U.S. House of Representatives, September 11, 1998, p. 3, www.aclu.org.

87. *American Civil Liberties Union* v. *Reno*, Civil Action No. 98–5591, U.S. District Court for the Eastern District of Pennsylvania, February 1, 1999.

88. U.S. Court of Appeals for the Third Circuit, No. 99–1324, June 22, 2000, www.coplaw.com/laws.

89. "Supreme Court Will Review COPA This Fall," *Online Newsletter*, June 2001, www.infointelligence.com.

90. Charles Lane, "ACLU Assails Internet Anti-Smut Law," *Washington Post*, November 29, 2001, p. A3.

91. "Judge Sets Highest Hurdle for Using Blocking Software in Libraries," *American Civil Liberties Union Freedom Network*, April 7, 1998, pp. 1–2, www.aclu.org/news.

92. "Memorandum Order and Opinion, *Mainstream Loudoun* v. *Loudoun County Libraries*, April 7, 1998, *Tech Law Journal*, pp. 7–10, www.techlawjournal.com/courts/loudoun.

93. Ibid.

94. "Memorandum Opinion and Order in Loudoun Co. Library Case (November 23, 1998), Electronic Frontier Foundation, p. 16, www.eff.org/Legal/Cases/Loudoun_library.

95. "Loudoun Library Board Decides Not to Appeal Filtering Decision," *Tech Law Journal*, April 21, 1999, p. 1, www.techlawjournal.com/censor.

96. "Complaint for Declaratory and Injunctive Relief," *ALA* v. *United States*, pp. 1, 3, www.ala.org/cipa/cipacomplaint.

97. "Remarks on CIPA Suit: Theresa Chmara," Press Conference, March 20, 2001, www.ala.org/cipa/chmararemarks.

98. "Remarks on CIPA Suit: Nancy Kranich," Press Conference, March 20, 2001, www.ala.org/cipa/kranichremarks.

99. "Remarks on CIPA Suit: John W. Berry," Press Conference, March 20, 2001, www.ala.org/cipa/berryremarks.

100. "Remarks on CIPA Suit: William Gordon," Press Conference, March 20, 2001, www.ala.org/cipa/gordonremarks.

101. "School Libraries Not Covered by ALA Suit," *Newsletter on Intellectual Freedom*, May 2001, p. 89.

102. "ALA to Challenge CIPA," *Newsletter on Intellectual Freedom*, March 2001, p. 80.

103. "ALA Files Suit against CIPA," *Newsletter on Intellectual Freedom*, May 2001, p. 126.

104. Ibid, p. 127.

105. *Branzburg* v. *Hayes*, 408 U.S. 665 (1972).

106. *Rice* v. *Paladin Enterprises, Inc.*, 940 F. Supp 836 (D. Md 1996), at 838.

107. *Rice* v. *Paladin Enterprises, Inc.*, 940 F. Supp 836 (D. Md 1996), at 839–40.

108. *Rice* v. *Paladin Enterprises, Inc.*, 940 F. Supp 836, 846 (D. Md 1996).

109. *Byers* v. *Edmondson*, 712 So. 2d 681, 687 (La.App. 1 Cir. 1998).

110. "The Book Made Me Do It," *Newsletter on Intellectual Freedom*, September 1999, pp. 144, 148.

111. *New York Times Co.* v. *Sullivan*, 376 U.S. 254 (1964).

112. "The Book Made Me Do It," *Newsletter on Intellectual Freedom*, September 1999, pp. 144, 148.

| 3 |

Voices of Banned Authors

This chapter of interviews with banned authors has been expanded and updated since the first edition of *Banned in the U.S.A.* Interviews with two new authors, David Guterson and Lesléa Newman, have been added, and the earlier conversations with Judy Blume, Daniel Cohen, Robert Cormier, Katherine Paterson, and Jan Slepian have been updated. Because of his untimely death on November 2, 2000, Cormier's interview stands as it originally appeared in the first edition, amended only by remarks and recollections from some of his colleagues. All other interviews from the first edition have been supplemented by conversations conducted with the authors in summer and fall 2001.

All the authors represented here share a strong commitment to free expression, but they differ on how to confront the censors. Some have become personally involved in defending their books in schools and libraries across the nation. Others feel that their job is to write books, not to defend them. In any case, the following seven interviews, alphabetically arranged, reveal the hopes, fears, and frustrations of important voices targeted by the censors.

Judy Blume

The American Library Association's list of the 100 most banned books from 1990 to 1999 includes five of Judy Blume's novels, more than any other author. My own list of the fifty most banned books from 1996 to 2000 includes two of Blume's books, *Forever* and *Blubber*. Unlike the

Harry Potter books, which are targeted by the censors because of their magical fantasies, Blume's books have been vulnerable because of their true-to-life descriptions of the common fears and modest triumphs of adolescent girls.

Several years ago, the head librarian of the New York Public Library's Children's Room said she had never seen a children's author as popular as Judy Blume. Indeed, Blume's novels are so popular with adolescents that one critic claimed "there is, indeed, scarcely a literate girl of novel-reading age who has not read one or more of Blume's books."[1]

Judy Blume has written twenty-five books, including *Deenie*; *Blubber*; and *Here's to You, Rachel Robinson*. Among her books for younger readers is the popular "Fudge" series: *Tales of a Fourth Grade Nothing*; *Otherwise Known as Sheila the Great*; *Superfudge*; and *Fudge-a-mania*. She has also written books for young adults (e.g., *Forever* and *Tiger Eyes*) and for adults (e.g., *Wifey*, *Smart Women*, and *Summer Sisters*). With this broad readership it is not surprising that over 50 million copies of her books are in print, and her work translated into fourteen languages.

Blume has received numerous awards for her books, including Children's Choice Awards in thirty states, Australia, England, and Germany. She is a board member of the Society of Children's Book Writers and a member of PEN American Center, and she serves on the Council of the Authors Guild, Planned Parenthood Advocates, and the Council of Advisors of the National Coalition against Censorship. She has received the Carl Sandburg Freedom to Read Award, the Civil Liberties Award, and the John Rock Award, and has been routinely chosen as a "Hero of Young America" in the annual World Almanac poll award.

Blume's two most recent works, *Summer Sisters* (1998) and *Places I Never Meant to Be: Original Stories by Censored Writers* (1999), are something of a departure for her. *Summer Sisters* is an adult book, her third. It is the story of a friendship between two girls and the problems they face as they grow up and grow apart. Blume follows the two girls for twenty years, through young love, college, and eventual marriage.

In a recent conversation, Blume told me of her doubts and misgivings about writing such a book.

"Just before the book came out I became so insecure, as writers often do, I begged my husband George to give back my advance and burn the manuscript," she said only half in jest. "I thought, this is going to be so awful, I don't want to go down this way. I'd rather never write another book. And George said to me in a very matter-of-fact way, as he has in the past, 'There's nothing we can do about this now. The book is going to be published, so why don't you go on a trip to Europe or somewhere. When you come back, this will be all over.' But, of course, I couldn't leave, because my publisher had lined up a tour for me."[2]

Hearing this tale of anxiety from such a prominent and successful writer led me to ask for more details.

"Only another writer would enjoy hearing about such problems," she said with a laugh. "If you want to read more about my turmoil, go to my Web site, judyblume.com, and click on 'Judy's Anxiety Diary.' I read it over the other day and it really tickled me. It chronicles how anxious I was when *Summer Sisters* came out and how horribly things went in the beginning. Ironically, despite all my fears and setbacks, the book turned out to be my biggest success. On my tour, it was wonderful to go around the country and meet these incredible young people in their twenties and thirties who had grown up on my books. It was very emotional."

Given the very positive outcome of *Summer Sisters*, I said, "I guess the way things turned out, you've learned never to indulge that kind of anxiety again."

"Oh really?" Blume responded. "I wouldn't say so."

But Blume had no such misgivings about her most recent book, *Places I Never Meant to Be: Original Stories by Censored Writers*. Here Blume edits a provocative collection of previously unpublished stories for young adults by important authors like Norma Klein, Katherine Paterson, Jacqueline Woodson, Harry Mazer, Chris Lynch, Rachel Vail, Julius Lester, Walter Dean Myers, Susan Beth Pfeffer, Norma Fox Mazer, Paul Zindel, and David Klass, writers who, like Blume, have frequently suffered at the hands of the censors. The stories are accompanied by insightful and instructive comments from the contributors and from Blume herself.

"There's a lovely story behind this book," Blume told me. "A lot of us wanted to do something to honor Leanne Katz, the head of the National Coalition against Censorship (NCAC), who was seriously ill. David Gale at Simon and Schuster suggested that I edit a collection of original pieces by banned authors. The idea was appealing—it would be a way to raise some much needed funds for NCAC and it would also serve as a tribute to Leanne. Even Simon and Schuster offered to make a donation.

"I talked to Leanne just two days before her death. She knew she was dying, yet she was fund-raising to the end. She said, 'Use me, tell everybody, write letters, do whatever you can to keep NCAC going.' She never lost her sense of humor. I spoke at her memorial service, but I'm so hopelessly emotional that I had difficulty maintaining my composure."

Blume said that author Norma Klein, another recently deceased friend, was an important part of *Places I Never Meant to Be*. "Though she was with us in spirit only, I couldn't have done the book without her," said Blume. "Her husband Erwin was kind enough, generous enough to take the time to find one of Norma's stories that had been written back in 1959 when she was in college. I added a little remembrance of Norma in lieu of her own comments. I've never done a book of this sort before, and I may never do such a book again, but it's important to hear the personal stories of these wonderful writers who express their feelings about having their books banned or challenged."

In the 1993 interview for the first edition of *Banned in the U.S.A.*, Blume spoke of her own problems with the censors. The first act of censorship that she could recall against one of her books was initiated by her own children's elementary school principal. Blume had given the school some copies of *Are You There God? It's Me, Margaret* when it first came out, but the principal refused to allow the books in the school's library. Blume thought the principal was "a nut," and it never occurred to her that this sort of thing would happen again. In the beginning, her publishers tried to protect her from controversy, and as a result she never saw the letters or heard about the phone calls. Today she realizes that was wrong.[3]

When I asked Blume if she was offended or angered when one of her books was banned, she responded: "Years ago a woman called me on the phone and asked me if I had written *Are You There God? It's Me, Margaret*. When I said yes, she called me a communist and hung up. But this was a long time ago, perhaps twenty years ago. I was bewildered and perplexed in the beginning, and I was personally hurt. Now I understand that this is something much bigger than any kind of personal attack on any one of us. It's like a grieving process. One goes through different stages. Of course, all of those angry feelings cross your mind. What is wrong with these people? How can they possibly think this is something to be afraid of? But I don't feel that way any more, because I'm too familiar with it. I'm glad I'm beyond that.

"This kind of bookbanning has been going on for a long time, but in 1980, after the election of Ronald Reagan, it really took off. I was very lucky because I wrote all of these books that are now under fire before any of the broader controversy arose. Aside from the phone call I mentioned, I really had no early contact with any of the bookbanners. They weren't yet organized the way they are now. The major censorship groups that now exist didn't exist then. There were the occasional frightened parents who came into the library, waving a book that they didn't want their children to read, but today it is organized in a way that is much more dangerous. I feel badly for the children because it sends a message to them that there is something wrong with reading, that we don't want them to read this book because there's something in it that we don't want them to know."

I asked Blume if her parents had attempted to control or censor her reading habits. She quickly answered, "No, they didn't. I was very lucky. My father had a fairly extensive library, and no one ever told me what

I could read or what I couldn't read. Not that my mother discussed the subjects in those books, but I never felt that I couldn't read them. My mother was very shy, but she was a reader, and reading was always considered a good thing in my house."

Blume's first two books bore little resemblance to the controversial works that followed. When she wrote *The One in the Middle Is the Green Kangaroo* and *Iggie's House* she was learning her trade, but after they were done, she said to herself, "Now that I've figured out how to write books I'm going to write what I know to be true." At that point, she began *Are You There God? It's Me, Margaret*. During this period, she was taking a writing course with Lee Wyndham, a children's writer during the late 1940s and 1950s, who gave Blume her first professional encouragement. Wyndham had absolute rules and regulations for writing children's books, but Blume recalls saying to herself, "Never mind these rules. This isn't what it's really like."[4] She says she was not breaking rules in a hostile or rebellious way. She was simply determined to write about what she remembered. When Wyndham saw the manuscript to *Margaret*, she wrote Blume a long letter about it, questioning some of the sensitive or intimate subjects. But Wyndham was also the first to write to congratulate her when the *New York Times* gave *Margaret* a good review.

While Blume was writing *Iggie's House*, she came across an announcement in a magazine that a new publishing company was interested in realistic books about childhood and adolescence. Through this ad, she contacted Bradbury Press and met Dick Jackson and Bob Verrone, who agreed to publish *Iggie's House* and, after that, *Margaret*. Blume says she always had the happiest publishing experiences with Bradbury Press, where Dick Jackson taught her how to revise and rewrite her books on her own.

Did it take courage for Blume to write candidly about topics like menstruation, not previously covered in young adult books? She says, "It was not courage. It was naivete. I had absolutely no idea I was writing a controversial book. There was nothing in it that wasn't a part of my sixth grade experience."[5] She recalls that she and her friends talked endlessly about menstruation and breast development, just as Margaret and her friends do in the book.

Blume was surprised when I told her that public libraries were increasingly banning her books. She had assumed bookbanning was primarily confined to school libraries. She added, "It's difficult keeping track of these events, because the authors don't find out unless someone else notifies them. More recently, thanks to the National Coalition against Censorship, we are hearing more promptly about when and where our books are being banned. I don't think any school board or school library or teacher has ever tried to contact me directly. In the past, that information has usually been communicated to me through the newspapers, but today it is more effectively documented in publications by the American Library Association, People for the American Way, and the organization I'm most involved with, the National Coalition against Censorship. As soon as they hear of any book that's been challenged, they will contact the author and try to work with everyone involved. They're a small but wonderfully effective organization, located in New York. ALA is terrific on censorship issues, and People for the American Way is too, but they are involved in many other activities. The National Coalition deals only with censorship."

When Blume talked to the National Council of Teachers at their 1991 annual meeting in Seattle, she discovered that the classroom teachers and school librarians knew surprisingly little about how to respond to censorship, how to prepare for it, and the need to have policies in place. She says, "When I gave them the names and phone numbers of the organizations available to help them, most of them didn't seem to know how to proceed, how to get help. I told them that the National Coalition against Censorship was just a phone call or fax away, and the sooner they were informed of a challenged book, the better they would be able to help. I'm not aware of what may be going on in public libraries, but the school librarians, teachers, and principals who are under fire should know that they are not alone, that there is a support group. That is very important. A lot of the censors out there claim that a challenged book can be harmlessly removed from a classroom or school library, because a reader can always go to a public library to find it. That's one way the censor is able to get a book out of a school."

Like most writers for young people, Judy Blume receives a good deal of mail from her readers. She says: "About 99.9 percent of the letters I receive from children are positive. The negative ones will list the curse words and the pages where they appeared. Such letters are curiously similar, though they come from different parts of the country. I have no doubt that they are written by children, but one can't be sure whether an adult requests that they be written. You never know how some of these censorship groups operate. I had my secretary subscribe to the newsletter of one of these organizations, and they were advertising a pamphlet titled, *How to Rid Your Library of Books by Judy Blume.*"

The most painful letter she ever received from a child was addressed to "Jewdy Blume." It was from a nine-year-old child who referred to her as "Jewdy" throughout the letter, underlining the letters *JEW* in crayon. The letter attacked the book, *Starring Sally J. Freedman as Herself*, complaining of its reference to Jewish angels. Blume says that although she is used to objections about sex and language in her books, that kind of hate from a young child was particularly disturbing.

Blume believes that because many adults are uncomfortable with their own sexuality, they can't begin to deal with their children's sexuality.

They are embarrassed and uneasy when their children ask them questions about sex, and they are often unable to answer those questions. She says the letters she receives indicate that most parents grew up without ever talking about sex. The message they got from their parents was that sex was neither good nor enjoyable, and that pattern may continue generation after generation. Blume notes that some adults are suspicious of any books that kids like, and even some children's librarians tend to tell kids which books they *should* read, rather than encouraging them to read what they enjoy.

Blume says censorship grows out of fear, and there is a tremendous amount of fear on the part of parents who wish to control their young children and shield them from the world. She points out that children are inexperienced, but not innocent, and their pain and unhappiness do not come from books. They come from *life*. She says parents should ask themselves what harm is likely to occur if their child browses through the books at the library and happens to pick up a book for older children or even adults. The child may ask the parents a question, and if the child does, the parents should answer it. Blume says children have problems not just with sex but with death, with money, with feelings and emotions—everything that is most important in life. Like all age-groups, children simply want people to be honest with them. Children learn from adults, yet many adults do not know how to talk to kids about anything personal. Blume grew up hating secrets, and she still hate secrets.

I asked Blume what it was that the censors found so objectionable in her books. She said, "I think in the old days the complaints concerned language and sexuality, but perhaps the censors have become more sophisticated. With respect to *Blubber*, which I think may be my best book for younger kids, the complaints focused on something called 'lack of moral tone,' which I now understand to mean that the bad guys go unpunished, or as the bookbanners put it, evil goes unpunished. In other words, I don't beat the kids over the head with the 'message.' When I lecture and refer to 'lack of moral tone,' I always add, 'whatever that means,' and the audience laughs. There is also the claim that my books do not show sufficient respect for authority. But the letters of complaint that I have received are much more specific about offensive language, often specifying a particular curse word."

A school librarian once told Blume that the principal of her school would not allow her book *Deenie* to be put in the library because Deenie masturbated. He said it would be different if the character were a boy. Interestingly, the only time Blume's editors tried to soften her work, the sensitive passages involved masturbation. "I have a story that I tell on my favorite editor," she said. "It pains me to tell it and it pains him to hear it. But it happened. *Tiger Eyes* was published shortly after the 1980 elections, and the censors were all over the place. My editor said to me,

'We want this book to be read by as many young people as possible, don't we?' And I said yes. He said, 'Well, then we don't want to make this a target for the censors, do we? Is it really necessary to include this one passage?' He agreed that the passage was psychologically appropriate to the character, but asked whether it was necessary.

"I took it out, and I have regretted it ever since. Was the passage essential to the book? Well, every appropriate passage helps you to know the character. This character was a girl who turned herself off, didn't allow herself to feel emotion after her father was killed. She was beginning to get her feelings back as she explored her body. She masturbated. That's the passage that I was asked to take out, because masturbation is far more threatening than intercourse in a book about young people. I'm sorry that I took it out, and I have done nothing of the sort since then. The last time that I was asked to delete material from one of my books, the publisher's concern was with specific language rather than sexuality. There were just three words involved, but the publisher felt that their inclusion would reduce the paperback book club sales. I thought about it long and hard, but I concluded that the characters would not be read with sanitized speech. The book was eventually published without change."

Blume, like some of the other authors interviewed for this book, is uncomfortable with the attempts to narrowly define her audience: "I hate to categorize books. . . . I wish that older readers would read my books about young people, and I hope that younger readers will grow up to read what I have to say about adult life."[6] She is concerned that, increasingly, children's books that deal realistically with life are being published as adult books or young adult books. She is still angry with Bradbury Press for advertising *Forever* as her first book for adults. She says *Forever* was not intended for adults, but the publishers hoped to protect themselves and her from controversy by suggesting that younger people were not the primary audience.

Blume says some teachers have told their students that if they use her books for a book report, they will automatically have points taken off their grade. She says, "When I began writing, I never thought of my books as classroom materials. I've always hoped that my books would be read the way I read books, which is to become involved in a story that I can't put down, to be swept away by a character, to be entertained and shown how other people live and solve their problems. All the reasons that I read fiction are the very reasons that I write fiction and hope what I write will be read. None of that involves the classroom. Over time, I've become used to the fact that teachers read my books aloud. But in the beginning it bothered me, because I thought of reading as a personal experience between the reader and the book, the kind of thing that you go away in the corner to do. You don't have to talk about it, you don't have to do a book report on it, you're never going to be graded on it, and you don't have to share it if you don't want to. On the other hand, if handled sensitively, my books can be useful classroom tools. I know of one teacher who begins his course each year by reading *Blubber* aloud. He then proceeds to a careful, often intense, discussion of the book and the issues it addresses. Of course, my 'Fudge' books are probably the most commonly used in class because they are fun."

The controversy surrounding her books has also discouraged their inclusion in textbooks and anthologies. She notes, "I've turned down a lot of book club editions, and the like, because they asked me to remove this, this, and this. Some of my material for younger kids has been excerpted, for example, *Tales of a Fourth Grade Nothing*, but not much of my work has been included in anthologies. Frankly, I would rather have a child read an entire book rather than excerpts. Most schools today are moving away from traditional anthologies and texts, toward the creation of genuine classroom libraries. That's very positive." When asked to analyze the First Amendment implications of school and library censorship, Blume commented: "Obviously, school officials, teachers, and librarians engage in a selection process. But do they select under fear and intimidation or under professional guidelines? Do they select books that the students really want to read and need to read? There is a good deal of censorship by selection, by 'avoidance/selection,' one might say. But once the book has been selected for sound reasons, once it's there, then there are First Amendment rights to protect its availability. Children have rights, too, and in some places, children are beginning to understand that they have a right to choose what they want to read. I think it's very positive that they become involved in these struggles within their community. I encourage young people to become involved."

Blume says her books have been defended by teachers, librarians, concerned citizens, and the kids themselves, the people she believes must be encouraged to take a stand to protect the books that they want to read. She told me: "I frankly feel that my job is to write the books, not to defend them. It is always the reader's job to defend the books, to ensure that they are available. What I try to do now is offer all the support I can to those who are under fire by the bookbanners, whether it is the teachers, librarians, parents, or students. I feel that I should help by making available any information I can, so I send them letters from readers, letters from teachers, letters from parents. In the case of *Forever*, I sent my personal letter describing how I came to write the book and why it is dedicated to my daughter. But I don't travel to the scene of the conflict in an attempt to defend my books."

Like fellow banned author Robert Cormier, Judy Blume feels that the more time she spends defending her books, the less time she has to write. Back in 1993, Blume was prescient when she commented, "Cormier and

I are of an age where suddenly we realize there isn't all that much time remaining.[7] I don't really see the point of entering the fray, interceding in conflicts over my books. I think that should be done without the author present. I don't believe the issue should be personalized. It's not about the author—it's about the book. I cannot defend my books. I wouldn't even know how to do it. How do you explain why you wrote what you wrote when you wrote it. I just don't think that's part of the job. I love to read letters from kids, because it always seems to me that they make the point so much better than I could. I remember when *Deenie* was under fire, and a seventh-grade girl went before the school board and read a letter she had prepared, explaining why the book was important to her and how it had helped her and her friends to talk about scoliosis [curvature of the spine]. She said that if there was something bad in this book, she didn't know what it was—and maybe they could explain it to her. Such comments are far more persuasive and more important than anything Judy Blume could say before a school board.

"I'm not saying that no writer should go before a school board and put himself or herself on the line. I just don't feel it's right for me. I once put myself in the position of having to debate the Moral Majority on television, and I came away saying I'm never going to do that again. It's not what I want to do. On the other hand, I can think of many wonderful experiences, like the group of people in Gwinnnett County, Georgia, who came together when a group of my books was banned. They came together without me, because they cared about reading and about choosing. Even people who had no children in the school became involved because they were readers. They became strong, and even though they lost their case and *Deenie* was banned, it will never happen there again. Not to those people. I came to talk to them after the event, and, even now it makes me cry because it was so moving an experience to meet them and talk with them.

"The point I would like to make is that it is the kids who are the losers in all these battles. We're really talking about what they have a right to know, what they have a right to read. The adults' fears prevent them from talking to their children about subjects that all kids have a right to discuss and learn about. You know, puberty is not a dirty subject, but the censors seem to feel that it is, and that message is sent to the kids. When books are taken away from them because the natural events of puberty are discussed, the message is that these biological processes must not be anticipated or discussed, even though they are going to occur. This is bowing to fear. This is giving the censors power. That bothers me more than anything."

In a recent interview conducted just two days after the September 11, 2001, terrorist bombings, Blume told me of her current literary project, another in the popular series of "Fudge" books for children, and how her work on the book had been affected by the tragedies in New York and Washington.

"My ten-year-old grandson had been asking me when I was going to finish the new 'Fudge' book," said Blume. "I plan to dedicate the book to him, but my work on it has pretty much come to a halt. I had been working for about six weeks on three chapters based on a trip that he and I took to Washington, D.C., and suddenly those chapters weren't funny. I can't use them. I know my grandson is going to be disappointed, but there's no way I can include a chapter called 'The Most Wanted' about Fudge's tour of the FBI. When we went there, we acquired a copy of the Bureau's Most Wanted List, and do you know who was number one on the list?"[8]

"Bin Laden," I guessed.

"Right," said Blume. "With a $5 million reward for his capture. In the book, Fudge is obsessed with money, and when he sees the $5 million reward he says, 'Wow, I'm going to find this guy.' I don't see how I can use that part."

I suggested that Blume might want to set the material aside for a few weeks and look at it with fresh eyes. Under present circumstances, nothing would seem humorous to her.

"We'll see," she said. "The book doesn't depend on the visit to Washington, but there are some delightful scenes that I'd hate to lose. I have a little chapter called 'The Panda Poop Club' in which Fudge visits the Washington Zoo and becomes enraptured with the pandas. My grandson and I actually joined that club when we visited the zoo, although I think the panda keeper made it up on the spot. In any case, despite my agonizing, I still hope to have the book published next fall."

Blume noted that, coincidentally, there had been a recent spate of unusual censorship incidents associated with the already published Fudge books.

"I find it amazing that since I last talked to you we've received more and more letters about a chapter in *Superfudge* called 'Santa Who?' I'll tell you how crazy this is. There were two children's musicals this year, theatrical pieces based on the Fudge books. One was adapted from *Superfudge* and one from *Otherwise Known as Sheila the Great*. During the tour of *Superfudge*, Theaterworks, a major New York producer of theater for children, began receiving letters and phone calls from schools saying the musical would not be welcome so long as the production retained a few lines from 'Santa Who?' in which Fudge admits to his older brother, Peter, that he knows about Santa. Fudge says he pretends because it will make Mom and Dad happy. 'Aren't I a good pretender?' he asks Peter. And Peter says, 'Yeah, you're the best.' Theaterworks told me they would lose bookings and children around the country would be denied the opportunity to see the play if we didn't change these lines. I'm sure there are five year olds who believe in Santa, but I think those lines would have gone right over their heads."

I asked how she handled such a dilemma.

"I suppose I could have told them they absolutely couldn't change those lines (I had script approval) and maybe I should have. I'd certainly never let anyone alter a book once it's been published. But this wasn't my adaptation. Many things about it were different from the book. Kids who know the book are quick to point out those differences. Do I wish Theaterworks had had the courage to stand up for their production? Yes, absolutely. Would I work with them again? Probably not. But I have to hope the play will lead children to the book where they'll discover the real Fudge on the pages."

Blume, a New York City resident, was reluctant to speculate on the current political climate for censorship, choosing to withhold judgment in the wake of the terrorist tragedy in New York.

"Right now I can't address any of that, because I'm seeing people every day on television whose censorship policies I oppose, but whose immediate responsibilities I must respect. I think Mayor Giuliani has been brilliant and statesmanlike throughout all of this. You know, there's good and bad in all of us. I feel so strongly against his free expression views that I always boycott the annual 'New York Is Book Country' party at the Mayor's Gracie Mansion.[9] That's my way of saying I won't celebrate at this house as long as you occupy it. I even spoke at the rally opposing his policies. But I have to admit that from the first moment that I saw him talking about the disaster in New York I've been proud of him."

Despite being clearly shaken by the catastrophe in New York, Blume ended our conversation with a positive thought. "Perhaps I'm being unduly hopeful," she said, "but I feel that, because this attack was committed by religious fanatics, perhaps our own society will stop conceding so much to such people on matters of free expression. Perhaps we will no longer give in to them so easily in our schools and libraries."

I said that sounded like wishful thinking to me.

"That's the optimist in me," said Blume.

Daniel Cohen

Books about the supernatural are probably the most common target of the censors, as the rhetoric of religious leaders and politicians makes clear. Fundamentalist Pat Robertson, former Republican presidential candidate, issued a fund-raising letter linking radical feminism and witchcraft. "The feminist agenda," wrote Robertson, "is not about equal rights for women. It is about a socialist, anti-family political movement that encourages women to leave their husbands, kill their children, practice witchcraft and become lesbians."[10] Author Daniel Cohen, who has written extensively about myths and superstition, has seen his books censored on the basis of such outrageous claims.

Cohen draws heavily upon folk tales about superstition and fantasy in his writing. He began his career as an editor and journalist, serving as managing editor of *Science Digest* from 1960 to 1969. He is an amazingly prolific writer, having published about 150 books covering everything from computers to biorhythms to *The Monsters of Star Trek*. No sex, no profanity here. The trouble is, many of Cohen's books have titles like *Masters of the Occult, Superstition, In Search of Ghosts, Magicians, Wizards and Sorcerers,* and *Curses, Hexes, and Spells.* He lends no credence to occult beliefs, writing only to inform and entertain. In fact, a common theme in his books is that superstition is nonsense. Still, his books are frequently banned because they address such topics at all.

The following discussion with Cohen consists of our original interview for the first edition of this book, as well as a recent conversation in which he provided an update on his latest work and plans for the future. In the spring of 1992 I asked Cohen if he knew that one of his books had appeared on People for the American Way's ten most frequently banned books. He answered: "Yes, I indeed am aware of it. Apparently it was on the AP wire, because I received a call from my local newspaper asking me if I was aware of this. I was surprised to hear it. The same book was also on a *New York Times* list a year or two ago, a list of the most frequently stolen books. The book ranked just beneath *The Joy of Sex.*" When I pointed out that another Cohen book, *The Restless Dead: Ghostly Tales,* was on the American Library Association's most banned list, he responded with surprise. "Really? I didn't know about that at all. I had not heard about that, but I guess it shouldn't surprise me anymore."[11]

Did Cohen feel that this kind of censorship entered First Amendment territory? "My gut reaction is that they are certainly getting into First Amendment territory, but not being a lawyer, I simply do not know. What disturbs me about this far more than the occasional school board that wants to pull a book off of the shelves is the chilling effect that this has on authors. The effect is particularly insidious on childrens' books which appear primarily in libraries. Once a book or an author or a subject acquires the reputation of being controversial, you don't have to worry about pulling it off the shelves, because it's not going to appear on the shelves in the first place. The library is not going to buy it, and that effect moves up the chain. The publishers are less likely to accept manuscripts by that author or about that subject. I can give you an example from my own experience. For years I have been writing a series of books on folk lore and ghost tales that has been very, very well received. *The Restless Dead* was one of them. Right now I'm doing a book for Putnam and it's going to be called *The Demon Lover*. There is a whole series of folk tales warning that if you grieve too much, you will call down the evil spirit in the form of the deceased, and the spirit will take you away. There is a cycle of legends and tales on that theme, particularly in Central Europe. The 'Demon Lover' is a well-known phrase. I was going to include such tales in my book and call it *The Demon Lover*. It sounded like a great idea, but when the book salesmen heard about it, they all said, 'Oh, my God, you can't call this book *The Demon Lover*. That will not only get you thrown out of the Bible Belt, but it'll get you thrown out of Oregon as well.' So we changed the title of the book. The upshot is, the book is now called, *Ghostly Tales of Love and Revenge*. Same book.

"I'll give you another example, again from something I'm working on now. Milbrook Press, a new publisher that handles a lot of school books, is publishing a series for school libraries. They handle reasonably controversial topics, and, given their audience, that takes a certain amount of guts. The editor there is one of the best in the business, a woman I've known for many, many years. I said, 'Look, how about a book on the alleged influence of satanism? That's something that kids talk about all the time, and it has aroused fears in the media.' She thought that was a terrific idea. But when she brought it up before her editorial board, they practically fell over dead. They said, 'My God, you can't do that. It'll get you thrown out of all the libraries in the country.' So, in the end we actually changed the entire concept of the book. It will focus on cults. It will cover the subject, but it will be a different book and not as strong a book. It represents a compromise, and that's what I mean by the chilling effect."

Cohen explained that though he has done a good deal of writing on the supernatural and the occult, he is not an occultist. "I think it's a bunch of crap, and I say so in my books. In the book that got in all the trouble, I say this kind of superstition is nonsense. But the people who challenge my books—*they actually believe it*! They believe in it, and they think that if you say anything about it, other than their particular line, you are somehow opening the door to hell, and all these spirits are going to rush out and suck the brains out of the kids. You know this is a great fund-raiser for the fundamentalist religious groups. I gather that books on satanism and the occult are the best sellers in Christian bookstores. I've heard the subject labeled 'Christian pornography.' I think there is a certain manipulation that's going on here, and it does present real problems for a writer."

When I told Cohen that the director of the Prince George's County Public Library had said the hot censorship topic this year was the devil, Cohen recalled that one of his books had been challenged in that county. "You know, they get tired of one hot topic and they go on to another. What bothers me is that I often don't know when a book is being challenged. I'm never told. I pick it up in the newspapers, or someone sends me a clipping, or a newspaper reporter will call me up, or I'll hear about it years later when someone publishes a list. But when my books are challenged, no one from any school or library board has ever contacted me and asked for a reaction. Never."

Did that mean he was usually outside the fray? "I'm not usually outside the fray—I'm *always* outside the fray," said Cohen. "I just don't know anything about it. For example, the People for the American Way list came out in September and was played up in our local newspaper, because I've been here for a long time. I'm very well known. People came up to me on the street and said, 'Oh God, isn't this nonsense? We don't take this sort of thing seriously.' But usually around Halloween I get a dozen or more calls from schools, asking me to tell ghost stories to the kids. I keep the kids amused for an hour and, as a favor to the community, I don't charge anything. This year, perhaps because of the bookbanning publicity, I did not receive a single call. Do you think that's coincidence? The people here know better, but they're frightened."

I asked whether Cohen regarded all this fuss about witches and goblins as more of a farce than a conspiracy. He answered: "It's certainly not a sinister conspiracy, but it has not been a laughable farce either. When people truly believe in this sort of thing, for or against, it can be dangerous. In a society where people deeply believe in magic, magic will work. Not because there is any power emanating from a spell but because a person who believes that he can be killed by magic will sicken and die. It's not something that you can take lightly. But in modern America, to think that some kid is going to sprinkle salt around a candle and reverse the course of nature is absolute nonsense. My books explain this kind of thinking and reveal it as primitive. Yet they are banned from schools, while children can go to the drug store and pick up books that pander to these beliefs. The kids are given no choice. They either get books that pander to occultism or they get nothing. Any attempt to present these matters responsibly for kids is shut out of the schools. The fundamentalists are against it, and the school boards and librarians are simply afraid to confront this. They have enough problems with the budget and community support, and they figure, 'We don't need this. Just take it off the shelf.' Look, *Curses, Hexes, and Spells* is not one of the world's great contributions to literature. It was a relatively lighthearted, simple, easy-to-read book which created no problems at all when it first came out. Over the years, as this fear of satanism has grown among certain groups, this book has loomed larger. Why this book, and not any one of a hundred other books? I really do not know why this rather nondescript book has gained this kind of notoriety."

Has Cohen ever had the opportunity to intercede on behalf of his challenged books? "Never," he said. "Not once. No one who has ever challenged the books, no school board that ever faced such a challenge has ever had the decency to call me up and ask what I think. We had an incident in this area a few years back when one of my books was challenged. These people knew who I was. They knew my phone number, yet they never called me. It wasn't until I called them and really yelled at them that I received any response from them at all. If you call yelling at the school principal interacting, then I suppose I did interact. I'm not the kind of person who takes these things quietly. The response of the principal was, 'I guess I ought to look at the book. Besides, I'm only here temporarily.' So I sent him a copy of the book, and in the end, I think the problem just sort of faded away. After the controversy erupted, the teenager who had complained about the book didn't bother to fill out the form necessary to initiate a formal challenge, so the controversy just sort of petered out. But I would not be willing to bet that if you went to that school you would still find that book on the shelf."

When asked if he felt common cause with the other banned authors interviewed for this book, Cohen said: "I wish I felt common cause with their sales. I'm by far the most obscure member of that group, let me tell you. But I do invoke this commonality. I'm just sorry that authors do not always express themselves aggressively on the issue of censorship. Judy Blume does, but the publishers don't. They are too frightened. It's a bottom-line situation for them. They don't want trouble. You can have two or three people in a school, a small handful of people in an area, and their effect goes right to the editorial offices in New York where books get killed before they're born. That's where the real chilling effect is felt, not in libraries."

In July 2001, Cohen spoke with me once more and provided a glimpse of his recent activity. "Over the last few years I've done a number of books on the supernatural, which are the ones that got me into trouble with the censors," he said. "I've just finished a big one for Dutton. My wife Susan and I did it together. It's a sort of guidebook to legendary spooky places, haunted houses. For example, the Bell Witch House concerns a haunting that allegedly drove John Bell, the patriarch of the family, to his death. This was back in Andrew Jackson's time. The Bell Witch House is down in Tennessee, Bible Belt country, and while some people didn't want to talk about the subject, Susan found one fellow who did—and he talked a lot. It turns out the Bell Witch is actually promoted as a tourist attraction in Adams, Tennessee, and there is an annual Bell Witch Bluegrass Competition. Susan gathered the photos, which is a pretty hard job. The book doesn't have a title yet, but it will be out on Halloween 2002."[12]

I asked whether the publisher planned it that way.

"Absolutely," said Cohen. "They rushed it because they want to get it on their fall list next year. It will probably be appropriate for bookstores as well as libraries because of its guidebook quality: Here's the haunted house, here's how you get to it, here's the story behind it. Given the supernatural topic, we may come a cropper on it with some schools and libraries, but Dutton doesn't seem worried about it."

I wondered if he was worried about the censors.

"With kids' books, it can be a problem," he said. "For example, some of the history books that I have done can be hurt by the censors because those are books that sell primarily to school libraries. That's your market, and if they can keep you out of the school market or discourage whole areas from even looking at the book, you can be badly hurt. Recently I have done more kids' books about history and politics. For example, I did one on the Manhattan Project that was very well received and one on 'yellow journalism' that was similarly praised. It covers some of the more sensational stories and trials. But the trickiest project I've done in the last few years was a kids' book on the Clinton impeachment. How do you cover the Clinton impeachment without talking about oral sex? It's like doing Hamlet without the Prince of Denmark. The reviewer said it was delicately handled."

Given such delicate topics, did Cohen ever tend to self-censor or tone down his books?

"Yes, sure," he admitted. "Sometimes you think it's a matter of good taste. Sometimes it's concern over the age of the target audience. There are certain areas you don't want to spend a lot of time on, although I suspect those are the very areas that kids would find most interesting. That was really obvious in the Clinton impeachment book, where I tried to concentrate on the constitutional and political issues while staying away from the gossip."

When I told Cohen that his earlier book, *Curses, Hexes, and Spells*, was still number 71 on the American Library Association's list of most banned books for 1990 to 1999, he laughed and said, "That has been out of print for I don't know how many years. I don't know where they're finding those copies." He was more interested in talking about his recent books, such as his biography of Governor Jesse Ventura and a children's book on economics. "I'm trying to do a kids' book on the boom and bust economic cycles, particularly the collapse of the 'dot.coms' and the other economic bubbles that have burst. My thinking is that you've probably got two generations that have grown up not knowing that economic hard times come. The book is something of a cautionary tale. I try to make it interesting for kids, but that's a hard project. It's a real challenge."

Cohen said he had a "gut feeling" that censorship might be worse under the Bush administration, but he had no evidence to support such an assumption. "You know their point of view, their core constituency, their claim to speak for family values, so my feeling is that censorship will be encouraged. How much influence the national administration has on the activities of local school boards I couldn't begin to gauge."

Robert Cormier

The death of Robert Cormier on November 2, 2000, removed a powerful voice from the literary world, but it was also a tragic misfortune for teachers and librarians, who lost a faithful ally in the continuing struggle against censorship. Gloria Pipkin, the Florida school teacher whose problems with the censors are detailed in Chapter 1, recalls his support for her during that difficult time. "He was so unassuming, warm, gentle, and totally without malice that even our worst critic came up to shake his hand afterwards."[13]

Judy Blume, whose problems with the censors were revealed in the first interview of this chapter, felt a close kinship with Cormier. "In the early 1980s, Bob and I were thrown together when we became targets of the censors," she said recently. "Like the best writers, audience wasn't on his mind. Like the best of writers, he wrote from deep inside. He knew instinctively that if you tell a story well, respecting your characters, there is no topic that is off limits."[14]

Jean Craighead George, whose book *Julie of the Wolves* was number 32 on the ALA's most banned list during the 1990s, called Cormier "one of the greatest storytellers of all time." He began his career as a radio writer, newspaper reporter, wire editor, and associate editor, before becoming a successful author. While still a journalist, he earned prizes for the best human interest stories of the year (Associated Press) and best newspaper column. But his literary career began with a bang in 1974 when *The Chocolate War* won the *New York Times* "Outstanding Book of the Year" award. Cormier won the same award in 1977 for *I Am the Cheese* and in 1979 for *After the First Death*. He has also won a host of other awards, including several of ALA's Best Book for Young Adults citations. His most recent book, *We All Fall Down*, has been lauded by reviewers.

Although Cormier claimed that he wrote *about* adolescents, not for them, his books have come to be characterized as young adult literature, a category within which *Newsweek* called him a "best-selling heavyweight writer, an equivalent to Saul Bellow or William Styron." Because any writing aimed at America's youth arouses fear and anxiety in our *adult* population, Cormier's work was criticized and often banned because of its uncompromisingly realistic portrayal of life. Yet Cormier said his young readers were not troubled by the messages in his novels. "They're not upset about the world I portray because they're in that world every day and they know it's war, psychological war," Cormier insisted, "I'm not worrying about corrupting youth. I'm worrying about writing realistically and truthfully to affect the reader."[15]

Cormier was about a third into his first important book, *The Chocolate War*, when his agent called and asked what he was working on. When Cormier said he was writing a book about kids selling chocolates in a high school, the agent said it sounded like a young adult book, a term Cormier had not heard before. Four major publishers refused the book, one complaining that it was neither a children's book nor an adult book. The other three publishers wanted Cormier to change the ending, and he was tempted to oblige them. He was offered a $5,000 advance and major promotion of the book if he would give it a more upbeat ending, but he couldn't bring himself to make the change. His agent sent the book to Fabio Coen at Pantheon, who agreed to publish it without change.

Cormier's books appear to have aroused controversy, not just on matters of sexuality or vulgarity, but on his depiction of human nature. His novels underscore the fact that good guys do not always win, and, as a result, his work has sometimes been criticized for an absence of hope. He has also been accused of being critical of authority and presenting subject matter that could upset children. In short, he tends to write realistically. Perhaps this stems from the fact that Cormier spent much of his life as a journalist.

During the spring of 1992, Cormier discussed his background and his writing with me. "I was a reporter, editor, columnist," he said. "I started from a police beat and went right up to associate editor over a period of about thirty years. I left in 1978 when things reached the point that I could support my family and send my kids to college on my writing."[16]

Cormier was initially quite surprised to discover that much of his audience was made up of young adults. "I was flabbergasted. When I wrote *The Chocolate War*, about a high school chocolate sale, I regarded the high school as a metaphor for the world. It could just as easily have been set in, say, the business world. When it came out and the *New York Times* had it as the lead review in the children's book review section, I was immediately hailed as a brilliant 'young adult' author writing a landmark book. And I wasn't. I had just written this book and wondered who would ever read it. Ostensibly it was about high school kids, but I thought it had a deeper meaning. It was immediately controversial. I don't write for the kids, but I know they're my audience, although in recent years I've had an increasingly adult audience. Today, when I go out to speak, there are sometimes more adults than children in the audience. It's great. I can write to the full extent of my ability. I believe that I'm accepted by young people because they are a very tough audience. They know when you're pandering or writing down to them or patronizing them. And I don't do that. My books are complex and hard-hitting and they're fully characterized. The kids know that I'm not just patting them on the back. They are tough books, and I think the kids respect me for that."

Cormier chose to characterize his novels not as young adult fiction but as books with young adults in them. His early novels were about adults, but since the 1970s he wrote mostly about adolescents. A few years ago he decided to write a novel in which the main character was a middle-aged man, but he says he soon became bored with the character, with his personality, and his reactions to things. He put the book aside and went back to writing about adolescents.

When *The Chocolate War* came out, the critics seemed to think that Cormier had set out to write an unhappy ending in order to break some taboo. He said he was just writing a novel about the adolescent experience. *Booklist* presented a prepublication review of *The Chocolate War*, criticizing the book for being cynical and undermining moral values. Soon after the book came out in paperback, there were censorship attempts, such as the request in Groton, Massachusetts, that the book be removed from a school reading list. A compromise was reached, placing warning labels on the book. Cormier concluded, "That's why I say that in censorship cases, even when you win you lose."[17]

When nervous school officials across the country made early attempts to ban *The Chocolate War*, Cormier was not reassured that the book survived. "The book always triumphed, but even when you won, you lost," he told *Publishers Weekly*. "They'd say, 'Well, okay, but we'll put a mark on it indicating there's special permission needed to read it, or we'll put it in a special section.' And the narrowness of the victories always bothers me—a three-to-two committee vote isn't any resounding triumph. And I'm just a minor part of it all, when you consider the great books that are being attacked."[18]

Cormier said he spent a good deal of his time answering the hundreds of letters he received from young readers. "They are supportive, because they say I tell it like it is. This is the way life is, and they are tired of books where everyone walks off into the sunset together. My books don't always have happy endings. There is a lot of psychological violence, more psychological violence than physical violence." Cormier was not sure where this preoccupation with happy endings comes from. Perhaps from fairy tales, though he pointed out that many tales and nursery rhymes have disasterous endings. He believed that happy endings should not be one of the requirements of children's books. He said, "*The Chocolate War* was a big battle over selling chocolates in school. I have received letters from students saying, 'Hey, chocolates are mild. You ought to see what's going on in my school.' So you're not shocking the students, because the kids live with this. You're shocking the parents."

Until 1986, *The Chocolate War* was the only one of Cormier's books that attracted the censors, but then *I Am the Cheese* came under attack. It had gone unchallenged for almost ten years, but suddenly it was criticized for being too complex and too critical of government. In 1986 there were at least three attempts to censor it—two in Massachusetts and one in Florida—and all three attempts succeeded.

Cormier was amazed that people believe they can obliterate certain words from their children's lives by banning books. He said such people would be in for a shock if they rode a school bus or walked down a corridor in any junior high school. It is in these locations, not in books, that children learn the words that offend their parents. He warned that when writing dialogue, an author's personal taste can easily conflict with the speech patterns of real children. In such an event, the author should not impose his personal standards onto his characters.

I asked Cormier what it was that the self-appointed censors found so objectionable in his books. Was it vulgarity? "That's the least of it," he said. "What they don't like about my books is the absence of role models, the fact that the bad guy often wins in the end, that the heroine may be killed. But this is the way life is. Sometimes it's almost absurd. You'd laugh if it weren't so serious. One fundamentalist objected to *I Am the Cheese* because the parents in the book would not tell their child that they were in the federal government's witness protection program. That was the last thing I would have thought would upset anyone. The man complained that the book was virtually an essay on lying to one's children. He could never allow his son to read the book because he might conclude that parents lie to their children. The parent wasn't concerned about the language, or that the book was antigovernment or antiauthority. It was a bad book to read because his son would get the message that parents lie to their kids. Well, it happens that parents do lie to their kids. Lying is part of our daily life. If we all told the truth, people would stop talking to each other. We lie to them to protect them."

Cormier said some critics characterized his books as antigovernment and antibusiness. "*I Am the Cheese* is looked upon as critical of the United States government. *The Chocolate War* is considered critical of authority. The strange thing is, teachers aren't painted in a very positive light in this book, yet the books are requested by teachers around the country because there are teachable values in it. The book is selling more today than it ever has, and it came out it 1974. That's astonishing to me. Recently, a teacher in Connecticut wrote a defense of *The Chocolate War* for use as a teaching tool. He submitted this document to the school board and convinced them that the book had value for the curriculum."

When asked if there were any benefits from being a banned author, Cormier answered: "Just one, and that's that you find yourself in pretty good company."[19] He recalled reading a list of books that had recently been banned, and *The Chocolate War* was in the middle of many classics.

Robert Cormier and Katherine Paterson, another frequently banned author, were old friends who have appeared on many anticensorship programs together. When I told Cormier that Paterson had been unable to recall a single example of a school administrator contacting her directly after one of her books had been banned, Cormier said that, on the contrary, it happened to him frequently.

"In fact, that's how I usually learn about one of my books being banned. For instance, just outside of Hartford, Connecticut, recently, the head of the Curriculum Department at the high school called to notify me of a school board hearing the following week. He wanted to know if I had any 'supportive materials.' So I sent some materials immediately, by overnight mail, and the school board voted 8 to 1 to keep *The Chocolate War* in the classroom. We don't always win. Sometimes I'm contacted by a journalist who gets wind of it while doing a story, and he wants my side of it. You see, when bookbanning occurs in a small town, it's not just a one-shot thing. It goes on and on and on. There are hearings and new hearings, there are decisions and appeals."

Cormier had mixed feelings about his personal involvement in anticensorship work. He said it was important to resist censorship pressures, and he spoke out on numerous occasions, lending his support to the people who were defending his books. But, in a way, he resented having to do it, because he believed that anything that diverts an author from writing is a victory for the censors. Cormier said his biggest frustration in fighting censorship was that the cards were stacked in favor of the censors. He described a man in Florida who took out a newspaper ad in which he reprinted lines from *The Chocolate War* and *I Am the Cheese* with the so-called dirty words left blank. Cormier said he felt like taking out an ad urging people to read the whole book, but he knew it wouldn't work.

When his books came under fire, Cormier tended not to focus on the broader First Amendment implications. He told me: "I concern myself with the individual case that we're battling at the time. I seldom worry about the broader legality or ethics of it. I can't afford to do that much worrying, you know? Here's what I *can* do. I flew down to Panama City a few months after the violence surrounding the bookbanning had receded somewhat. [See Chapter 1.] They sequestered me in a hotel way out in nowhere. But we had a good talk with all of the concerned parties down there. So I do this sort of thing, but then I think, this is exactly what the would-be censors want me to do. That is, stay away from the typewriter. I mean, the last place they want me to be is at the typewriter. So if I spend a lot of time and energy away from writing, that plays right into their hands."

When I commented that he appeared, nonetheless, to play an active role in fighting censorship, Cormier responded, "Frankly, that's why I'm a little weary, because just a few months ago there was another battle, also in Connecticut. I've gone to the fray so many times, and I've been interviewed so many times that . . . , you know. First of all, I'm irritated and upset when the censorship problem does come up, so I'm not in the best of moods when I'm called and asked to defend my books. I always feel that the books speak for themselves. I wrote them. Why should I have to defend them? Of course, the proper thing to do is to try to defend the book, to help these poor teachers who sometimes put their jobs on the line. How can I be indifferent? But I do resent it. I could tell you some horror tales that are documented down in Florida. I don't know if you are familiar with the debacle down there, right outside of Panama City. There were death threats and firebombings. It was so inflammatory that Gloria Pipkin, the teacher who led the battle, was honored in Washington, D.C., last year by the Courage Foundation. The *Washington Post* did a major cover story in their feature magazine, and *60 Minutes* even went down to investigate it. The battle was over *I Am the Cheese*, but it concerned a lot of other books as well. There were numerous death threats to the teachers. One teacher, Gloria Pipkin, went to her locker one afternoon and found one of those ransom-type notes, with words cut out of newspapers to avoid detection. In addition, a young female reporter who had gone on TV to challenge the bookbanning petition had her car firebombed. You know, this is America. I received a recent letter from Gloria Pipkin in which she said that all of the challenged books have been restored to the school except *I Am the Cheese*. But they're teaching another one of my books that the censors haven't caught up with yet."[20]

Why was *I Am the Cheese* the only one of the challenged books that was not returned to the school? Cormier told me: "I suppose the original objection is still maintained. Mr. Collins, who led the opposition to the book, ran a large ad in the newspaper, listing selections from the book, with the objectionable words excised, of course. For example, in one selection a girl complains that her breasts are too large. The word *breast* is blacked out. In reality, that selection was not written in a titilating way. The girl was simply complaining that she had to lug her large breasts all over town. *I Am the Cheese* has very little in it that anyone could object to. Perhaps it remains out of the school because the curriculum was built around it, and it was the first book that was challenged."

Cormier described the typical pattern of censorship that he had experienced. "Here's the way it usually happens. One of my books is assigned to a student. The student brings the book home. The parent picks it up, doesn't read it, but looks through it and finds bad words or a sexual scene. Though it's quite mild compared to what's really out there, the parent complains to the school. Most times, when the school deals alone with a parent, they come to some accord. Frequently, if the child doesn't want to read the book, another book may be assigned to that child. Or, once the book and its purpose in the curriculum is explained and discussed, the parent will sometimes agree that there are teachable aspects to, say, *The Chocolate War*." I asked Cormier if he considered the assignment of a different book to the children of complaining parents to be "caving in." He responded: "It's not caving in, because there are so many, many books out there that may be as good as *The Chocolate War*. The main thing is to get the child reading. If a different book from mine is chosen for a particular child, fine. The teachers are just trying to get the kids interested in reading. Censorship just gets in the way of teaching, and that's the tragedy of it all."

Cormier said he often had trouble with fundamentalist groups. "When a fundamentalist organization enters the picture, that's where the issue becomes intractable and reasonable negotiation becomes impossible. For me and a lot of other authors, the fundamentalists have become the major problem. Yet I really sympathize with these people because of their complete sense of righteousness." The fundamentalists remind Cormier of the young terrorist he wrote about in *After the First Death*. Like that character, they are so convinced of the righteousness of their cause that they don't consider what they are doing to other people when they ban a book. Cormier said, "They really believe that they're protecting their children from the world, though that's an impossible thing. That's why they're so hard to fight, because they are so sincere and well-meaning."

Was Cormier ever able to convince fundamentalist critics that they were wrong about a challenged book?, "No," he said. "The most I can do is what I did when I went to Panama City to speak to these people. Charles Collins, the man who led the forces against me, a born-again Christian and wealthy businessman, was in the audience. I spoke for about forty-five minutes and received a standing ovation, even from the fundamentalists. My only reason for going down there was to show them that I wasn't a monster from New England trying to corrupt their children. And that what I was writing, whether they objected to it or not, was sincere and to the best of my ability. I was not trying to corrupt their children, but to open their eyes to certain things. I'm a human being, I'm a father, I'm a husband. Right now I'm a grandfather, too. After my talk, Charles Collins came up to me and shook my hand. He said, 'I can't agree with what you write, but I can see where you're coming from. I can admire what you're doing by your own standards.' That's the closest I ever came to a meeting of the minds with such people, but then, I haven't met many of them. I only know them through their petitions and the material I receive in the mail."

Cormier sympathized with a parent's impulse to shelter children. He admitted that as a father he tried to keep his children from being hurt or from being exposed to disturbing sights. But he said this impulse often leads parents to attempt to control the entirety of their children's lives, an impossible task. He said children begin thinking on their own while they are still in the sandbox, and if we try to control their fantasies, thoughts, and emotions, we will only drive them away from us. He argued that children have already heard of corruption, terrorism, and sexuality, and he saw no reason to expunge those subjects from children's books. Yet he pointed out that he did not consciously consider these issues when writing a book, concentrating instead on realistically developing his characters and their situations. Cormier said he didn't write his books worrying about what a fourteen- or fifteen-year-old can absorb. He believed his readers deserved an honest story that is neither exploitative nor sensational, and if some kid finds that upsetting, that's just too bad.

Cormier told me of an incident in the Cape Cod schools, where a child brought home *The Chocolate War* and her parents objected to it. "It became a big brouhaha out there. As you may know, when a book is challenged and a hearing scheduled, the book is sometimes kept in the curriculum until the hearing. In other cases, the book is removed until the hearing. In this particular case, the book was maintained in the classroom, so the complaining parents insisted that when the book was being discussed, their daughter must go to the library to avoid being affected. Well, I received a letter from the daughter's classmate who said that by being removed from the classroom in this way, the girl was being ostracized and poked fun at. Now, as an adolescent, at a time of life when you want to belong, this isolation from her classmates was more harmful to her than reading the book. In a postscript to her letter, the classmate confided that her ostracized friend had read *The Chocolate War* the previous year anyway. She had already read the book. So you see, there are kids being hurt by a kind of ricochet effect of censorship. The parents who thought they were protecting their child were separating her from her peers, perhaps exposing her to ridicule."

Textbook publishers, always a hypersensitive lot, have borrowed sparingly from Cormier's work. "A lot of my short stories have been in textbooks," he said, "but my short stories are very innocent. Nothing inflammatory. The only excerpt from my novels that I can recall was part of a Russian exchange project, where they excerpted a chapter from *The Chocolate War*."

Aside from some mutually agreed editing on *The Chocolate War*, Cormier said he felt no pressure from his publisher to avoid controversy. Had his publisher ever asked him to tone things down a bit? "Never," he said. "Never with me. They wouldn't dare. My last book begins with a terrible act of violence, and I wrote it in language designed to shock the reader. I didn't use polite words, because I wanted the reader to feel it. You can see that I'm not bending over backwards to soften my work."

Indeed, that book, *We All Fall Down*, received a starred review from *School Library Journal* and a glowing review from *Hornbook*, a major children's review journal. It received similar commendation from *Kirkus*, and *Publishers Weekly*, which said it was one of the seven best young adult books of the year.

In March 1992, Robert Cormier sent me a small package of materials containing a letter from an angry parent, some letters of support from teachers, some newspaper clippings on censorship, and a sheet of paper signed by Cormier and titled, "Some Thoughts on Censorship." Among those thoughts were expressions of sympathy for parents who sought control over what their children should do, see, and read, and objections to such control over other people's children. Cormier noted: "The irony of book-banning attempts is that the publicity often causes people to read the books for the wrong reasons. If a book is controversial, perhaps the best place for it is the classroom where, under the guidance of a teacher, the book can be discussed and evaluated, where each student will be free to proclaim how he or she feels about the book and, in fact, can even refuse to read the book. The point is that free choice must be involved."

Cormier concluded: "I try to write realistic stories about believable people, reflecting the world as it is, not as we wish it to be. I think there is room in the great halls of reading for this kind of book. The hundreds of letters I receive each year from both teachers and young people are what sustain me at moments when censorship threatens my work. I owe a great debt to the many teachers, librarians and parents who support my work. The blessing is that in doing so they also strike blows for freedom."[21]

David Guterson

David Guterson's first novel, *Snow Falling on Cedars*, won the PEN/ Faulkner award for fiction, the largest annual juried prize in the United States. He thereby joined the ranks of notable previous winners such as Phillip Roth, E. Annie Proulx, and E.L. Doctorow. Predictably, he quickly joined the prestigious club of America's banned authors, with *Snow Falling on Cedars* ranked as the seventeenth most banned book in our current list (see Chapter 4). Like most of the books on our list, *Snow Falling on Cedars* demonstrates that curious tendency of the censors to target success. Literary awards and public acclaim are no defense. They seem to attract the vultures.

Snow Falling on Cedars won the Barnes and Noble Discover Great New Writers Award, the Pacific Northwest Booksellers Association Award, and the American Booksellers Book of the Year award. It spent a year on national best-seller lists and has been translated into twenty-five languages around the world. The film version of the book was released by Universal Pictures in 1999.

Guterson's next novel, *East of the Mountains*, was also well-received, demonstrating a maturing talent and continuing popular appeal. Though he never had the proverbial "second-book jitters," Guterson says, "it's always hard to write another book, whether it's your second or your twelfth." "It doesn't matter who you are, how many awards you've won, how popular you are, or how much critical acclaim you've had. When it comes time to sit down and write the next book, you're deathly afraid that you're not up to the task. That was certainly the case with me after *Snow Falling on Cedars*."[22]

In addition to his literary accomplishments, Guterson has a strong background in journalism, writing for magazines like *Harper's*, where he is now a contributing editor. Teaching is another of his loves. He taught English at the local high school in Bainbridge Island in Puget Sound, and he homeschooled his own kids. His 1992 book, *Family Matters: Why Home Schooling Makes Sense*, demonstrates that homeschooling is just one way of reaffirming the bond between parents and children.

"Writing is only a part of my life," says Guterson. "Every writer must find a way to contend with the rest of life and still get the writing done. . . . There are no tricks, no secrets, or words of wisdom. There is only hard work and talent."[23]

Guterson says that *Snow Falling on Cedars* is utterly misread if it is construed as a historical novel, or even as the story of a romance. "It was written primarily to explore and consider a basic philosophical question about the human condition," he says. "In a universe so indifferent to our fate, how best to endure, to go on?"Guterson says he is interested in themes that endure from generation to generation. "Fiction is socially meaningful," he says. "Every culture is sustained by certain central myths. At its heart, fiction's role is to see these myths are sustained. . . . My work comes from inner disturbances, from seeing injustices and accidents and how they affect people's lives in a tragic way."[24]

Though he denies that *Snow Falling on Cedars* has a political message, Guterson notes with interest the feedback he has received with respect to his portrayal of the internment of Japanese-Americans during World War II. "Most readers seem glad to have come across a book that prompts a reconsideration of that era and asks us to reflect on its meanings, on what it tells us about our own society. In that regard, the novel seems to have made a social contribution that I did not expect, corollary to my main concerns, but nevertheless a good thing."[25]

Guterson often reflects on the moral function of literature. "Fiction writers shouldn't dictate to people what their morality should be," he says. "Yet not enough writers are presenting moral questions for reflection, which I think is a very important obligation."[26]

Guterson's father, Murray Guterson, is a distinguished criminal defense lawyer. "I often heard about his cases and sat in on his trials," recalls Guterson. "In the late 1960s when I was growing up, I wanted to be a crusader like him but I didn't want to wear a suit and commute. When I went to college, I took a creative writing class and decided in a week to be a writer."[27]

Guterson says he owes much of the success of *Snow Falling on Cedars* to Harper Lee's *To Kill a Mockingbird*, which, ironically, is also represented on our most-banned list (number 40). "I owe a lot to *To Kill a Mockingbird*," says Guterson. "I followed very much the same structure and addressed the same concerns. I'm glad that book was part of my life."

As a high school English teacher, Guterson adopted *To Kill a Mockingbird* as his favorite book. "No other book had such an enormous impact," he said. "I read it 20 times in 10 years and it never got old, only richer, deeper and more interesting."[28]

During January 2001, I had an opportunity to ask David Guterson about his attitudes toward censorship and whether he had anticipated that *Snow Falling on Cedars* would be the target of censors.

"It never entered my mind while writing *Snow Falling on Cedars* that it could possibly be controversial in any way," said Guterson. "I have not paid much attention to the specific objections raised about the book, but I do know that in one school district those in objection to it culled out a list of its various depravities to put before their local school board—sex, violence and foul language. This mystifies me. There are respectful descriptions of marital sex in the book of the sort no reasonable person could object to, and there are descriptions of young people engaging in something even more fleeting than coitus interruptus and agonizing about the emotional implications of so doing. The depictions of violence are there to communicate the horror of war, and the occasional foul language is never gratuitous. So the objections flabbergast me.

"Here is a book that is about as moral and ethical as you can get, a book examining questions of the human heart in conflict with itself, and somehow people want to censor it. It makes me think that something must be wrong with the universe. It makes me feel like Piggy in *Lord of the Flies*, not able to get a word in edgewise while terrorists take control of things and finally smash him to smithereens."[29]

Given the fact that authors like Mark Twain and John Steinbeck are prominently represented on my most-banned list, I suggested to Guterson that his inclusion on the list might be viewed as a kind of badge of honor. He disagreed.

"Banned books are, of course, ubiquitous," he said. "There is no honor for an author in being banned, in part because it isn't rare or special— the banned author can no longer feel that he or she is joining a select group. Besides, why take pride in the fact that someone out there finds you offensive? It isn't something to be proud of, really. To feel pride about being banned suggests, to me, a kind of arrogance. You shouldn't be smug about the fact that someone out there dislikes your book enough to want to keep others from reading it. What good would that do? In this case I prefer sadness to pride. Being banned, I feel misunderstood, frustrated. I want to explain myself to those who've banned me, but this is an impulse I strictly curtail. I don't argue back. I don't make a defense. I don't mean to be above the fray, and I think the debate is enormously important, but to rail about regarding one's own book is an empty exercise in self-justification. I'd rather argue about someone else's book when it comes time to argue with book-banners."

I told Guterson that a censored author like Robert Cormier, interviewed for this book, felt compelled to support the teachers and librarians who defend his books against the censors, but he resented being diverted from his real task, writing books. Guterson's response is more temperate.

"I have always felt a certain detachment regarding the censorship of my own work," he says. "I watch from a distance. Consider that I wrote *Snow Falling on Cedars* between 1984 and 1994. By the time anyone thought to censor it, it was 1998. By then *Snow Falling on Cedars* was long gone from my consciousness. I had replaced it with other books. I was thinking about other things, interested in other things. I read about *Snow Falling on Cedars* and censorship in the papers. It wasn't something that was happening to me, and it isn't something that is happening to me. What's happening to me is that every morning I get up, sit down at my desk, and write. The rest of it is all external to me and feels unreal."

Guterson is reluctant to judge school officials harshly simply because they remove a book from the curriculum.

"I'm not sure that 'censorship' is the right term to use regarding the efforts of school and library officials to make wise judgements regarding what gets included in curricula and what gets put on library shelves," he said. "Review boards have to take seriously their mandates to assess the suitability of books and sooner or later must make decisions that are inherently difficult. What do we require 9th graders to read? What do we put on a recommended reading list for seniors? What do we leave out of the high school curriculum but place in the high school library? I don't think that answering these questions by excluding certain books very often involves 'censorship.' Certainly excluding certain books is always going to be necessary."

Despite his understanding attitude, Guterson recognizes that arbitrary action against books, often under political pressure, can have damaging effects on the educational process.

"There is an issue of censorship involved when a book has been entered into the curriculum and then is withdrawn because of complaints about it," admits Guterson. "The withdrawal is meant to keep the book away from the eyes of students after the point at which a review board has decided to include it. Politics and coercion take over from sound judgement and deliberation. This sort of thing has happened with *Snow Falling on Cedars*, which I have always felt is a wonderful book to include in a high school curriculum. It yields itself comprehensibly to literary analysis by students and provides them with cross-curricular opportunities. It provides for meaningful discussion and debate about historical, cultural and moral issues. It engages students with a compelling story and brings their attention to important matters.

"I was a high school teacher when I wrote the book, and while I wrote it with an adult audience in mind, I couldn't help but hope that students would read it, too. The fact that they do and respond strongly to it is enormously rewarding to me. I have never felt for one minute that the book in any way does them a disservice or harms them in some fashion. On the contrary, I feel that the novel does exactly what a novel should do—provoke in readers young and old a confrontation with the human condition that ultimately leads to deeper reflection on what it means to be human. And who would want to censor that?"

I asked Guterson what I asked the other authors interviewed for this book, whether his publisher had ever put pressure on him to censor certain material, moderate the language, or in any way make his writing "safer."

"No publisher has ever asked me to alter something to avoid controversy and I can't imagine that happening for a couple of reasons," responded Guterson. "The first is that publishers like controversy because it sells books. They would rather see you be outlandish and objectionable than staid and dull any day. Don't censored books sell more copies? Isn't it true that censoring a book often means more curiousity about its contents? In one school district where *Snow Falling on Cedars* was removed from the curriculum, a liberal law firm bought 20 or more copies for the school library as an act of protest. They were all eagerly checked out by students as soon as they were put on the shelves. So it's more censorship and controversy, *please*, as far as publishers are concerned.

"Second, asking an author to change something in order to avoid controversy is risky for a publisher. Authors are a cranky and persnickety lot, easily alienated, sensitive to slights, unwilling to compromise, neurotic about the integrity of their work—you get the picture. So publishers tread warily around authors, for the most part. As well they should. Recall Jack Nicholson in the motion picture *As Good as It Gets*. Jack Nicholson in *The Shining*."

When I asked Guterson for some general reflections on censorship, he seemed more bemused than angered by the phenomenon.

"I don't understand censorship," he declared candidly. "I have always felt that if you object to something the best thing to do is look at it closely, discuss it, analyze it, criticize it, ponder it. I think students are well-served, for example, by an open discussion of Hitler's *Mein Kampf*, and that it is a bad idea to try to hide it from them. On the other hand, I value the right of parents to make decisions about what their children read and see, even if I might disagree with those decisions.

"Free expression is vital to the sustenance of all human freedoms. There is nothing more terrifying than the silencing of voices. The repression of free expression is generally born of either fear or self-righteousness or of the two in combination. The kind of fervor and zeal that throttles its opponents is always worth fighting. Censorship can be insidious. It sometimes takes careful observation to note its presence. When this happens you know that the fascists are winning. They're even inside your brain."

Lesléa Newman

Lesléa Newman is a poet and fiction writer known for her many books dealing with lesbian identity, Jewish identity, and the intersection of the two. She has also written on subjects such as AIDS, eating disorders, and sexual abuse. Ms. Newman, born in Brooklyn, New York, is the author of more than thirty books for which she has received many literary awards: Poetry Fellowships from the Massachusetts Artists Fellowship Foundation and the National Endowment for the Arts, the Highlights for Children Fiction Writing Award, the James Baldwin Award for Cultural Achievement, and two Pushcart Prize nominations. Six of her books have been Lambda Literary Award Finalists.

Despite her bold examination of controversial issues, only her children's books seem to have roused the censors against her. Those books include *Belinda's Bouquet*, *Gloria Goes to Gay Pride*, *Runaway Dreidel*, *Heather Has Two Mommies*, and *Cats, Cats, Cats!* Of them all, *Heather Has Two Mommies* (number 37 on our most banned book list) has been the primary focus of controversy. In a recent article, Newman described some of the uproar over this seemingly harmless book about a little girl with two female parents.

"There was the time Representative Robert Smith read portions of the book to the entire United States Senate, though no milk and cookies were served. There was the time a man took the book off a public library shelf, went into the bathroom and defecated on it. There were many instances when I was accused of writing a book that taught first graders the ins and outs of sodomy, no pun intended. And there was that nasty 'no promo homo' bill which, if approved, would make reading *Heather Has Two Mommies* to a child without parental permission a felony. (Luckily the bill never passed)."[30]

Newman says the idea of writing *Heather* actually came from an acquaintance who approached her on the street and said, "Listen, somebody needs to write a book I can read to my kid about a family like ours: a family with two moms and a daughter."

Newman recalls, "I went home, started writing and came up with little Heather, who has two elbows, two earlobes, two kneecaps, and two mommies."[31]

When the book was finished, Newman sent it to a number of publishers, none of whom would touch it. Finally, Newman approached a friend who had started a small desktop publishing business. They sent out fund-raising letters, raised $4,000 in small donations, and found a printer and distributer. Soon a truck pulled into Newman's driveway and forty cartons of 100 books each were unloaded into her living room. In this modest way, *Heather* was introduced to the public. Six months later, publication rights to the book were acquired by Sasha Alyson, the publisher of *Daddy's Roommate*, a book about a child whose father is gay.

In a recent interview, I asked Newman about her battles with the censors. Because her writing covers a broad range, from poetry to adult fiction to children's books, much of it containing lesbian themes, I wondered whether the threat of censorship extended far beyond *Heather Has Two Mommies.*

"Not that I'm aware of," she said, "except for some of the other children's books, like *Gloria Goes to Gay Pride* and *Belinda's Bouquet*, which are now out of print. So it's a moot point. Those were also Alyson titles. I'm not aware of censorship problems with any of my books intended for an adult readership."[32]

Her lone young adult or "middle grade" book, *Fat Chance*, has also been free of the censors. "*Fat Chance* was written for young teens, and it has been very, very popular," she said. "I've never heard of any kind of controversy around it. It's presented as the fictitious diary of a girl with an eating disorder."

The most common rationalizations for censorship (vulgar or profane language, lack of respect for authority, mysticism, etc.) are never brought to bear on Newman's work. "In my case, it really seems to be nothing more than homophobia," she said. "Apparently, the subject of gay or lesbian parenting is very distasteful to a segment of the population. I haven't had complaints about language, witchcraft or any of that thrown at me."

I suggested to Newman that the rampant censorship of *Heather Has Two Mommies* shows that many people believe it is inappropriate for children to read about homosexuality. Her response was, "First, I don't know that one can say that children who read *Heather Has Two Mommies* are reading about homosexuality," she said. "They're reading about a family with a child who has two moms. It's about a little girl who goes on a picnic with her moms and then goes to day care and meets kids with all kinds of families. That's really it. If you're going to say reading *Heather* is teaching a child about homosexuality—emphasis on the "sexuality"—you would have to say reading a book about a mom and a dad is teaching a child about heterosexuality—emphasis on the "sexuality"— I think we have to avoid having double standards here. People have said they're afraid that reading this book will make a child grow up gay. This is a book about family life, not about sexuality. In any case, I don't think a book is powerful enough to determine one's sexuality. I always cite the fact that I read thousands of books about heterosexual people and their families when I was growing up, and none of that changed my sexuality."

Strange as it seems, Newman never anticipated that *Heather Has Two Mommies* would be a prime target of the censors. "I didn't think about it at all," she says. "This was very early on in my career, and I had a lot of trouble getting the book published. A friend and I published it ourselves before Alyson Publications bought the book from us. After that, it seems as if word got out because Alyson is a more prominent publisher and was doing *Daddy's Roommate* at the same time. Suddenly, we began hearing of all these incidents relating to the book. In the beginning, I guess I was very naive, but because I had trouble getting the book published, I assumed no one would pay any attention to it."

Because *Daddy's Roommate* and *Heather Has Two Mommies* have very similar themes and were published at about the same time, they are frequently linked together by the censors. In reality, Newman did not meet Michael Willhoite, author of *Daddy's Roommate*, until after both books had been published, though they subsequently worked jointly on the book *Belinda's Bouquet*. "I had no idea that someone else had been doing something similar to *Heather Has Two Mommies*," recalls Newman.

Newman seldom seeks out information about the banning of *Heather Has Two Mommies*. She recalls initially receiving an article about it from her publisher or from friends. "It was a long time ago," she says. "Once I heard about it, I kept my ear to the ground. Once I started looking for it, it was pretty easy to find. When the Rainbow Curriculum was introduced in New York, that's when things really heated up. *Heather Has Two Mommies* and *Daddy's Roommate* were included in the Rainbow Curriculum, and there were large protests and a lot of public debate in the

New York media, including newspaper editorials and editorial cartoons. It was pretty easy to follow."

I wondered how Newman felt about the public attacks on her book. "I think it baffled me," she said. "It amazed me. I was completely unprepared. Maybe I became a little angry, but I'm not really an angry person. People who meet me are often surprised. They ask, 'Are you really the person who wrote *Heather Has Two Mommies*?' I don't know what they're expecting. I don't enjoy confrontation. I went on a talk show that was a very unpleasant experience and I decided not to do that any more. I do go around the country and give the talk, 'Heather's Mommy Speaks Out: Homophobia, Censorship and Family Values.' I talk mostly at colleges or to library associations. But I find I don't do well in a confrontational situation where the person I'm talking to doesn't have an open mind. I'm not often asked to defend *Heather* in the midst of an actual censorship incident. When *Heather* was banned in Wichita Falls, Texas, a civil suit was brought against the censors, and I was invited to be a plaintiff. I declined, but I did write an affidavit for them which the judge did consider.

"I don't often intervene in such controversies. I feel that if the conflict is taking place in your community, then it's your job to defend your rights. I don't believe that, as an outsider, I need to step in and tell people what to do. But if I'm asked for an affidavit, a letter to the editor, something like that, I'm usually happy to provide it. As I said earlier, I do quite a bit of traveling, giving talks like Heather's Mommy Speaks Out. That's the sort of thing I can do to educate people about what happens when a book is challenged and what you can do about it in your community. I try to make the point that freedom of expression is a vital right that must be defended."

Newman has simple advice for librarians and teachers who are confronted by censors. "I think it's important to stay calm, to know what support systems are in place. If someone says, 'I don't want this book taught at this school' or 'I don't want this book in the library,' the librarian or teacher needs to know how to respond. They need to know the procedure for dealing with such challenges. They need to know where they can find support, whether from supervisors or from the broader community. They can turn to local library associations, their intellectual freedom committees, the American Library Association or the National Coalition Against Censorship. It's important to have a team together so that they are not facing this alone. Sometimes good things can come out of such confrontations. You certainly learn who your friends and enemies are, and you build coalitions. If you take a stand, you might find courage in yourself that you didn't know you had."

Because much of the opposition to *Heather Has Two Mommies* comes from religious organizations, I asked Newman how she could argue rationally with someone who simply says, "God says it's wrong."

"I would ask such a person if they have had a personal conversation with God," she said. "I don't know anyone who has. Also, if we read the Bible literally, there would be countless kinds of legal behavior that we would prohibit or punish. There would be a lot of people stoned for their beliefs or behavior. There would be a lot of people walking around with one arm or one leg. So I am disturbed when people take one sentence of the Bible literally while ignoring all the rest."

Like most banned authors, Newman feels that every reader has a right to reject her books, but not to impose prohibitions on others. "I have a very hard time with censorship in any form," she said. "I believe if you don't want your child to take the book out of the library, if you don't want to buy the book in a bookstore, that's fine. It's your right to make that decision. But I don't think anyone should have the right to tell other people what their choices in literature should be. If you don't like what somebody is saying or writing, you can say or write your own opinions. But I don't think the answer is to silence the other person."

Newman cannot recall much in the way of restrictions placed on her own reading when she was a child. "We couldn't watch the Three Stooges on television, I remember that," she said. "But as far as I can remember, I pretty much read what I wanted to read. I just loved to read, and I virtually lived at the library. I don't remember my parents ever saying that I couldn't read something."

And what of the future for Lesléa Newman? Her newest children's book, *Cats, Cats, Cats!*, was published March 1, 2001, by Simon and Schuster. Soon to come are *Dogs, Dogs, Dogs!*, scheduled for 2002, and *Runaway Dreidel*, due in 2002. Also planned for 2002 is *Felicia's Favorite Story*, a book that Newman believes has special importance. "*Felicia's Favorite Story* is about a little girl from Guatemala who is adopted by a lesbian couple," she says. "The book has added significance because it is being handled by a new publisher, Two Lives Publishing, that will exclusively publish books for kids with gay parents."

My immediate response was, "Uh oh, sounds like more trouble."

"Right," said Newman. "More trouble."

Katherine Paterson

Katherine Paterson is as unlikely a banned author as one can imagine. Her parents were missionaries in China and she herself became a missionary in Japan. She attended Union Theological Seminary in 1962, where she met and married John Paterson, a young Presbyterian pastor.

In 1966, the United States Presbyterian Board of Education asked her to write a church schoolbook from a child's point of view. The text she produced, *Who Am I?*, was widely used by the church, and its success encouraged Paterson to try her hand at professional writing. She decided that she wanted to write what she loved to read—fiction.

Paterson enrolled in a course geared specifically to writing for children, and by the end of the course, she had written her first novel, *The Sign of the Chrysanthemum*, the first of her three children's historical novels set in Japan. Next came *Bridge to Terabithia*, her first book set in contemporary America, and then *The Great Gilly Hopkins*. Both books have been major targets of censorship, but Paterson is unwavering in her commitment to writing.

"[T]he joy of writing far outweighs the struggle," she says, "and I know beyond any doubt that I am the most fortunate person in the world to have been given such work to do."[33]

Since my 1992 interview with Paterson for the first edition of this book, she has completed several children's novels, including *Parzifal*, a retelling of the romantic poem about the quest of the Grail Knight. Another recent work is *Images of God*, a book for all ages that she wrote with her husband. *The Field of the Dogs*, also recently published, is a suspenseful book that first appeared in more than a hundred newspapers. Coming soon are *Marvin One Too Many* and *The Invisible Child*.

Who would have thought that this dedicated author and Christian educator could possibly write books that spark controversy around the country? Yet her books are sometimes banned in schools and libraries on the grounds that her stories contain "unhappy" endings and realistic language that might be damaging to children. She responds, "The books ended the way I thought the books had to end. That's not satisfying to everybody, but it seems to me that if you're really 'in' a story then the story seems to have a life of its own. The story seems to have necessities and its own ending. . . . If you try to change what is the inevitable ending of that story, you violate the story and the reader will recognize that."[34]

Among the many honors that have been accorded to Katherine Paterson's books are ALA's Notable Children's Book award, the National Book Award for Children's Literature, and the John Newbery Medal. She has received the Irvin Kerlan Award "in recognition of singular attainments in the creation of children's literature" and the Catholic Library Association's Regina Medal Award for demonstrating "the timeless standards and ideals for the writing of good literature for children." In 1998 she won the prestigious Hans Christian Anderson award for children's literature, which she discusses in the following interview.

These conversations include the original 1992 interview as well as an update Paterson gave me in August 2001. I asked Paterson about the attempt to ban *The Great Gilly Hopkins* in Cheshire, Connecticut, during

1991–1992 (see Chapter 1). She said, "I just received a letter indicating that they voted in Cheshire to keep the book in the curriculum. Have you seen the letters that the children wrote in support of the book? The *Hartford Courant* Sunday Magazine recently published the children's letters describing their own experience with the book. They are the most eloquent defense of literature that you would ever hope to see, on First Amendment grounds, on the need to read a book before judging it, and much more."[35]

Given the extreme sensitivity of publishers to these censorship controversies, has Paterson been pressured to alter her writing? "Certainly not by my editor. Never. I have received no pressure at all from my publishers or editors. I'm totally free to write exactly the way I want to write. I put the book out, and when the challenge to it arises, it's the teachers and librarians who have to put their jobs and reputations on the line to defend what I've done. I had a teacher who, after seeing an early draft of one of my books, suggested that I reconsider using the word *Jesus* in the mouth of a black child. I reconsidered it and decided that it was so inconsequential that it was not worth causing a problem over. So I dropped it. But I would not consider changing the words in the mouth of Jesse Aarons or Gilly Hopkins [in *The Great Gilly Hopkins*]. That would be quite a different proposition."

When I suggested that it was part of the professional obligation of librarians and teachers to defend against bookbanning, Paterson said, "Sure, in theory. It's easy for all of us to say, but not so easy when you're the one who has to do it. Years ago there was a challenge against *Gilly Hopkins* in Salinas, Kansas. I can't remember exactly what year, but I know my kids were still in high school. They had a swimming meet the day the school board was going to vote. I was sitting there at that swimming meet wondering what was going on in Salinas. I wrote about that two or three years ago in an article on censorship in the *New Advocate*. I called the librarian who had stood up to keep the book available. I had never met her, but she was one of my heros because she was alone in the whole school. There were some teachers who suggested that the book be hidden under the desk, or perhaps sequestered so that only the teachers could read it. But this librarian took the lead in convincing her supervisor and the other librarians to pursue the issue with the school board or carry it to the courts if necessary. They were terrific. The librarian wrote me to say how grateful she was for the article. She said I might not have regarded her as a hero if I had known how frightened she was. She said she was the only black on the staff, and had gotten along very happily until that moment. Then suddenly things became very difficult. Even though the book was reinstated by the school board, she couldn't go back to work the next year. Things were so uncomfortable for her that she moved on to another job. She's now a university librarian at Lincoln University. My heart goes out to such people in these bookbanning situations."

I asked Paterson if she had difficulty getting her works included in textbooks. She said, "Textbooks are a different world. They are notorious for sanitizing literature, which is why you will seldom ever find anything written by me in a textbook. Because the minute they get hold of my material, they try to cleanse it of all personality. When a textbook publisher wants to publish excerpts from one of my books, they try to take out the words they don't like. I just tell them, 'I'm sorry, you can't use this.' Now I simply have a blanket policy that I do not write for textbooks. I have had a complete chapter put in a textbook, but even there they wanted to remove the word *damn*. It was not even used as an oath. It was used as a verb. I said, 'If you can't publish the chapter without that word, then you can't use it at all.' They decided to go ahead and use the word. Another time, a popular school magazine wanted to use a short story of mine in which a mother is nursing a baby. That wanted to eliminate that. I said, 'I'm sorry, I don't care if you use the story or not, but if you do, the mother will nurse the baby.' I want children to know that women's breasts are used for something besides pornography. For them to call nursing a baby dirty was beyond my belief. They ended up using the story with the mother nursing the baby."

When asked whether school and public library censorship was a First Amendment issue or simply a problem of administrative authority, Paterson answered: "It's both. I think it's a First Amendment problem, because I don't think children should have fewer rights than other human beings." But what about the right of parents in a community to determine what their children read? "In every case that I know of," Paterson said, "when a parent objects to a book used in the classroom, there is no problem in assigning a different book for that child. But the parent often claims that the child would feel strange reading a different book. In other words, the parent obtains control over the entire classroom because one child would feel uncomfortable. It's like saying my child is uncomfortable with mathematics, so there should be no math in the classroom. Perhaps, though I might argue otherwise, a parent has the right to tell his or her child what to read, but that parent may not prevent my child from reading the book. A parent has the right to object to a book, but not the authority to prevent anyone in the school from reading it.

"I was raised by very conservative parents who were very careful about what movies we saw. There was no television, so that was not a problem. But they never censored our reading. I considered that a great vote of trust and confidence in me, and it encouraged a sense of responsibility in me. Every time my parents trusted me, and I could see that many other parents were not trusting their children, it made me feel more responsible. We cannot protect our children from this world, which is a scary place. The only thing we can do is to help them develop an inner strength to meet the inevitable challenges they will face."

I mentioned that one of the hot topics among the bookbanners today was satanism. "I've been accused of that, too," said Paterson. "In *Bridge to Terabithia*, the children play an imaginative game where they enter the 'Sacred Grove' and invoke the spirits of the Grove. Some critics have charged that this is an example of 'New Age Religion.' When I was told that, I said, "Please don't accuse me of New Age religion when I haven't even figured out what secular humanism is. In addition, *Bridge to Terabithia* was published in 1977, before the notion of New Age religion was conceived. I guess I'm so avant-garde that I knew about it before anyone else did."

I asked Paterson if she had any advice for teachers and librarians when dealing with censorship. "Schools and libraries need to have a procedure in place to deal with book challenges, so that one parent's objection is not going to result in a book immediately being removed from the library shelf. At the same time, full respect must be shown to those people who object to books. Frequently, these are people who are desperate to be heard. If they know that their objections are given a full hearing, the problem can often be defused. We should be less defensive and more sympathetic to these people, because all of us want to protect our children, don't we? We may not agree on how that is best done, but to despise someone for trying to protect his children is wrongheaded."

But Paterson was quick to add, "I think eternal vigilance is the price of liberty. If you think it won't happen here, you may be sadly surprised. It can happen anywhere, and it won't always be the fundamentalist lunatic fringe that you expect. It may be the doctor's wife who dresses impeccably. It may be the wealthy or the well-educated. The challenges may come from unexpected sources and may be directed against unlikely books. You have to be ready. Get in touch with the American Library Association, the Freedom to Read Foundation, and the National Council of Teachers of English for advice and up-to-date information on what is happening throughout the country. The Cooperative Children's Book Center at the University of Wisconsin has a wonderful system for helping people all over the country involved in bookbanning incidents. They are concerned that as these incidents proliferate, authors are going to begin to exercise self-censorship. They may be afraid to write what they really want and need to write. That certainly is a real danger, because it's easy to begin weighing every word to avoid offending anyone. This can cripple an author's work.

"I can't imagine Gilly Hopkins being Gilly Hopkins without the language she uses. You don't have a child who is so angry at the world, and who lies and steals and bullies, whose mouth doesn't somehow reflect that anger. She would not be a believable character otherwise. In the case of Jesse Aarons, that's the way those people talk. If you want him to be a country boy from the rural part of northern Virginia, that's part of the package. On the other hand, some amount of discretion is not altogether a bad thing. If a word or phrase is not fundamental to the book, and if it is going to be a gratuitous offense, then I might question it."

I asked Paterson if the various acts of censorship against her books had been brought to her attention by school officials. "No, no, never," she said. "I've never had a call directly from a school board. It's usually a teacher or a librarian or a reporter. It's haphazard notification. Somebody may call me up and ask if I know what's going on in our school systems. I say no, and they tell me. Apparently, the school officials think that authors are the last people on earth who could shed light on a conflict over their books. When it reaches that point, there is such heated feeling about the author that the author becomes a dangerous commodity. For example, the protester in Connecticut was calling Jan Slepian and me 'perverts.' "

What is the basis for most objections to Paterson's books? "It used to be language entirely," said Paterson. "Now it's become more broadly rationalized. I've been accused of anti-Christian bias. Actually, I'm very pro-Christian. In fact, it would be much more reasonable to accuse me of a pro-Christian bias. I regard *Gilly Hopkins*, the book that was challenged in Cheshire for being anti-Christian, as my rewriting of the parable of the prodigal son. I thought it was so Christian that a secular publisher might not want to publish it."

In August 2001, Paterson spoke with me once more and provided a glimpse of her recent activity. "What's coming out next is a new collection of essays," she said. "It contains some of the essays from previous collections, but there are about eight new ones in it. It's going to be called *The Invisible Child* and should be out in November 2001."[36]

I asked Paterson if any important events had occurred in her life since we last spoke. "Do you know that I won the Hans Christian Anderson award in 1998?" she asked. "That's probably the biggest thing that's happened to me. The award is for the body of my work. It's given every two years to a writer anywhere in the world who is considered to have [made]—and I'm reading from the plaque here—'a distinguished contribution to children's literature.' It's presented by the International Board of Books for Young People. I was thrilled."

I asked if any of Paterson's more recent books had run afoul of the censors. "Not really," she said. "*Bridge to Terabithia* is still the main target of the censors, and occasionally *Jacob Have I Loved*. I think that's because these are the books that appear most frequently in schools. It's the books that are in the public eye, that are prominently represented in schools and libraries that get you in trouble. School curricula are slow to change, so if they find a book they like, they don't go looking for a new one."

When I asked Paterson if she was working on a new project, she said, "Yes, I'm in the middle of a book, but I'm one of those people who can't talk about what I'm working on. I never share anything about a book that's in the process of creation. I hear my friends going on and on about their current projects and I wonder, maybe they're more grown up than I am. But I just can't do it."

On the subject of the current climate of censorship, Paterson was not sure that the Bush administration would diminish free expression more than the Clinton administration had. "I think the same groups and individuals who are unhappy with American literature are going to continue to exercise their concern in ways that you and I find very disturbing," she said. "I doubt that the administration will get into it. I imagine Attorney General Ashcroft will be careful for the first year or so, because he's aware of the controversy surrounding his nomination. Sometime that keeps people from applying a heavy hand to literary expression. But we would do well to keep an eye on the man."

Like all those familiar with Paterson's life and work, I expressed astonishment that the religious right could target a person with such a strong and impeccable religious background. Paterson responded, "It's ironic. I'm happy to call them my Christian brothers and sisters, but they're not happy to call me their Christian sister. Still, I like to remind myself from time to time, not every Conservative is a censor. One would do well not to be too self-righteous when accusing others of being self-righteous."

Jan Slepian

Jan Slepian is a straight-talking political liberal with a wry sense of humor and a broad range of interests. She says, "I'm a writer by chance. I didn't go from the cradle to the typewriter. I set out to be a clinical psychologist, turned to speech therapy and because of that work began writing picture books when my own children were young."[37]

Slepian soon joined the ranks of the premier writers for young adults. *The Alfred Summer* was selected as one of *School Library Journal's* Best Books of the Year for 1980, and it was a finalist for the American Book Award. It won the *Boston Globe/Horn Book* Award Honor Book for Fiction in 1981. *Lester's Turn* was selected as one of the *New York Times'* Best Books for Children, one of *School Library Journal's* Notable Children's Books, and one of *Social Education's* Notable Children's Trade Books in Social Studies. *The Night of the Bozos* was selected as one of the American Library Association's Best Books for Young Adults, one of the Child

Study Association of America's Children's Books of the Year, and one of Library of Congress' Books of the Year.

Slepian's more recent works have also been well received. They include *Back to Before* (1993), *Lost Moose* (1995), *Pinocchio's Sister* (1995), *The Mind Reader* (1997), and *Emily Just in Time* (1998).

During 1992, I interviewed Slepian for the first edition of this book, and the current edition supplements those conversations with an interview conducted in August 2001. In the original interview, Slepian identified language as the focus of most of the objections to her books, but she said there were more subtle social irritants as well. "I think Lester, the handicapped boy in *The Alfred Summer*, may be seen by some of the censors as having a bad attitude, of being irreverent, saying things like, 'I don't appreciate God's sense of humor,' " she said. "Lester, a fourteen-year-old cerebral palsy victim, has the same kinds of private sexual fantasies that any fourteen-year-old would have. I tried to make clear that these unfortunate people have the same dreams and the same hormones as any other boy or girl."[38]

Like most "banned" authors, Slepian has never been contacted by school or library officials when her books were banned. She says, "In Cheshire, Connecticut, I wasn't contacted at all by the officials involved. A newspaper reporter called me and said he had heard that there was a complaint about one of my books. He wanted to know what I thought about the incident, and I told him. I asked him to send me a copy of the article, but I never received it. Perhaps it was never published. That's the only time anyone has contacted me about the censorship of my books. No one else ever tried. Actually, there was a very nice outcome in Cheshire, and I was quite pleased with the board. There was a wonderful meeting at which the parents demonstrated that they were too knowledgeable and sophisticated to allow this sort of censorship to occur.

"The Cheshire incident was very interesting, because the censors focused their anger on two important books that are acknowledged as illustrious in children's literature. Katherine Paterson's *The Great Gilly Hopkins* won the Newbery Award, and my book, *The Alfred Summer*, was a nominee for the American Book Award. These are not like most of the 'hazerei' [junk] that parents might think is alright for their children. Ultimately, Cheshire parents recognized these books as the kind of literature that they should be proud to have their children read.

"Parents and librarians really have to stand fast. Librarians should not buckle under to fear and intimidation. There are organizations that are willing to come to our help, organizations like the American Civil Liberties Union, the American Library Association, People for the American Way. Librarians are our conduit. They are our best friends. They're the channel through which our books are funneled. We depend on them to help us tell the truth as we know it."

Like Judy Blume, Slepian seldom participates directly in the local censorship battles involving her books. "I've followed Judy Blume's advice. I believe she recommended that rather than trying to fight the critics personally, authors should refer challenges or complaints about their work to those organizations designed to deal with such matters, organizations like the American Library Association or the National Coalition Against Censorship."

However, Slepian has occasionally written letters to those who attempt to ban her books. In 1983 she was informed by Scholastic Press, the publishers of the paperback edition of *The Alfred Summer*, that the book might be removed from the school library shelves in Charlotte, Virginia. In a letter to Otis Lovelace, library supervisor in the Charlotte County Public Schools, Slepian spoke of the book, its purpose, and point of view. "The book largely deals with the growing friendship between two afflicted young people, Alfred and Lester," she wrote. "My intention was to get to know the person behind the damaged body. I wanted to show that such a person shares the same fears, the same need for love and friendship, that he yearns for and responds to much the same things as we all do. . . . In *The Alfred Summer*, my spokesman for these sentiments is Lester, a 14 year old cerebral palsy victim. . . . It was important to the book that Lester be shown as having natural internal language, one that any other kid that age would have. To have left this point out, to not allow him to express himself naturally would not have been true or faithful to what he is. Actually, only once does he openly use what could be thought of as an objectionable word, but that once was necessary to make the point. . . . The book affirms the wonder and the joy of life despite affliction. It seems to me that this is a timeless message that I sincerely hope will remain open to the children of Charlotte. . . . The Alfred in this book is based on my own brother Alfred, and the observations based on my experience with growing up with a damaged boy. . . . Finally, I feel the book is its own best spokesman and will speak for itself in the hearing."[39]

Did the letter convince the school officials in Charlotte? "I don't think so," said Slepian. "If all it took were letters, we probably would have convinced all these people long ago. Perhaps if I could speak one-on-one with a complaining parent, I might be able to reach some understanding. But the motivation behind these well-organized censorship campaigns is beyond my ken and beyond my control."

I asked Slepian if she had received many letters from her readers. "I've heard from a lot of kids," she said, "and most of the letters are very positive. Their letters are enough to bring tears to your eyes. Even when a child's letter is critical of my books, it never expresses shock at the language. I may have bored a child, but I don't seem to have offended them. I have never heard anything from a child suggesting that my readership has been affronted in any way. It would be a weird child who would write me and complain that I had said a bad word. I've never received such comments from children, yet some parents seem compelled to protect their children from such harmless language."

"In my generation my parents hardly knew what I was doing in school. This may be in part because I was a good girl, but they were also busy making a living. I was reading all the time, and they wouldn't question what I was reading. I never thought much about my parents' influence on my reading habits, or about censorship generally. My parents never attempted to tell me what I should or shouldn't read. There were always lots of books around the house, and reading and learning were always encouraged. I remember reading Voltaire's *Candide* when I was twelve years old, and there were things in it that I had never thought about. Of course, I didn't understand the book's irony, but I've always been entranced by the music of words, and I remember thinking that some of those words were dancing around the page."

Was she embarrassed or offended by the "adult" portions of *Candide*? "Offended?" she exclaimed. "I would have been thrilled to think I was old enough to be offended by something. I was too innocent to be offended."

When I asked if she thought the attempts to ban her books were First Amendment violations, Slepian responded: "It depends on the individual case. For instance, in Charlotte, Virginia, there were just a few vocal Moral Majority people who wanted the book removed from the library shelf, and they intimidated the school principal and the librarians. I have the impression that it's not the teachers, educators, or even the school officials or board members who initiate these censorship incidents. It's usually a group of citizens within the community who exploit local politics to impose their taste upon others. There is a disturbing climate in this country which allows a few noisy people to frighten school officials into removing books. These officials simply want to avoid trouble, and they will do anything to make it go away. In the case of Cheshire, where the book was being read in the classroom, the school board apparently decided that they would raise the grade level for the book from fourth grade to fifth grade. If parents feel that their children would benefit more by reading the book next year rather than this year, that seems perfectly alright to me. But when a book is removed from a library shelf, denying all children the right to read it, that is certainly interfering with First Amendment freedom. What we're awakening to is the threat of book burning. It has echoes for us all, because the looney few are able to put their imprint on the rest of us by making enough of a stir. This problem has a different face each generation. The religious groups today are much more aggressive, and the fundamentalists are gaining ground, forcing many publishers to withdraw certain textbooks."

Has Slepian ever felt pressure from her publisher to soften her writing? "Never," she answered. "Never have I felt the hint of pressure from my publishers or editors. I've been very lucky. No one has told me not to use certain words or not to address certain topics to avoid trouble. It was always up to me. I don't think about the effect of what I say, or what my characters say, on my audience. That's not the way to write a true book. Rather, one inhabits the skin of a character, say an eleven-year-old girl, ensuring that she is saying something true and in character. Would this character say that? Regardless of what it is, whether she's saying a string of curses or a string of novenas. I don't think about whether this would offend someone. I simply consider whether it's true. If it isn't, I would take it out. But the recent furor has made me more conscious of what I put on paper.

"My friend Barbara Cohen had an interesting run-in with her editor. Barbara wrote *Molly's Pilgrim*, which was made into an Academy Award-winning short subject. *Molly's Pilgrim* is a storybook for six-, seven-, eight-year olds. When the book was about to be reprinted in a textbook, Barbara was called by the textbook editor who wanted her to delete a section about God. She simply mentions God. There was nothing blasphemous about it, but the publisher was frightened. Barbara considered that section to be critical to the book, and she absolutely refused to remove it. The section remained in the book, but the incident demonstrates how frightened, how sensitive, publishers have become. They respond to any hint that a book might offend someone on the right, on the left, in the middle, someone up, someone down."

Have any of her works been excerpted in textbooks or anthologies? "I know my picture books have been reprinted here and there. Many of my books have been reprinted in braille for the blind. By the way, I've never had a blind person say he was offended by my books."

I told Slepian of the travails of one of the most censored book series in the country, the *Impressions* textbook set by Holt, Rinehart and Winston. Interestingly, three of the seven authors interviewed in this chapter were excerpted in *Impressions*. Jan Slepian's *The Hungry Thing*, a harmless rhymed tale for small children, was among the selections, and I asked Slepian if she could imagine any basis on which it could be considered offensive. She was incredulous, but I pointed out that excerpts from *Winnie the Pooh* and the *Wizard of Oz* had already been attacked by critics of *Impressions*. Why not *The Hungry Thing*? "If they are banning that," she said, "it's pathetic. That's scraping the bottom of the barrel."

I asked Slepian if she was currently working on a new book. "Of course," she answered. "That's like asking if I'm breathing. I'm working on a book for eleven- or twelve-year-olds, a book about beginning again, about renewal. It's called *Back to Before*. It's about children who go back in time, giving them a second chance at things, a chance to make them right."

Was there anything in this new book that could conceivably offend the censors? Slepian's first response, as always, was to call that an absurd impossibility, but she told me, "There is a section of the book that puritans might object to. The father in the book is going out with a woman, whom he describes as an 'associate,' but the reader knows the father is really fooling around. It's conceivable that someone might be offended, but there is more to object to in Grimm's fairy tales than there is here."

When I spoke once more with Slepian in August 2001, she confirmed that there had been no discernable censorship of *Back to Before* since its publication in 1993. She also described some of her other recent publications, including *The Mind Reader* and *Pinocchio's Sister*, published in 1995. "One reviewer said *Pinocchio's Sister* was a 'dark book,' meaning it didn't have a happy ending," she said.[40]

When I noted that critics had applied the same term to Robert Cormier's books, Slepian said, "Exactly. They seem to like sugar-coating. But *Pinocchio's Sister* had an interesting premise. You're old enough to remember the ventriloquist Edgar Bergen and his dummy Charlie McCarthy. Well, I had read somewhere that Candice Bergen, his daughter, had been terribly jealous of Charlie McCarthy. You can understand, it was Charlie McCarthy who occupied her father's lap, who was the focus of the father's attention, who played an important role in the family as a star and breadwinner. In fact, Charlie was always introduced as her brother. Candice couldn't match him and couldn't do anything about it. Well, I developed that same theme in *Pinocchio's Sister*, where a ten-year-old girl travels with her father, a ventriloquist, on the vaudeville circuit. During each performance she is dressed in rags and upstaged by the pretty blonde, blue-eyed dummy. Fearing that the dummy is replacing her in her father's life, she plots to kidnap the dummy."

Slepian also told me of her latest project. "I've returned to working with my partner and colleague, Dr. Ann Seidler, on a series of picture books, all of which have to do with some aspect of language. It's an ongoing project that may not sound too exciting, but it is to us. It concerns what is called 'phonemic awareness.' We're calling the series *Funny Talk*. There are four already done, and we'd like to do a fifth. We're also working on another sequel to *The Hungry Thing*. It's called *The Hungry Thing and the Gobbler*. We've just about finished it, and we'll send it to Scholastic, the publisher who did the original book in the series. Dr. Seidler and I have collaborated on these books for many years."

When I asked about any significant recent events, Slepian asked, "Did you know that *The Alfred Summer* was on *School Library Journal*'s Millennium List of the most significant books of the century? *SLJ* had four experts in the field—Zena Sutherland was one of them—to select the 100 most significant books of the century, and not only was *The Alfred Summer* included, but the works of some of the other authors you have interviewed were there. I know Katherine Paterson and Robert Cormier were represented on the list."[41]

At the conclusion of our conversation, I asked Slepian what she thought the climate of censorship would be under the new Bush administration. "I think the ascendency of the right wing in this administration may have an adverse effect on free expression," she said. "Even if there is no direct interference, authors will be influenced, consciously or unconsciously, to self-censor or tone down their work."

I wondered how she had been able to avoid such influence herself. "I can't think of any particular instance where I self-censored my writing," she said, "but I'm sure I felt the same pressure that all authors of children's books do."

NOTES

1. *Contemporary Authors. New Revision Series,* vol. 13 (Detroit, Mich.: Gale Research Co., 1984), p. 60. (Hereafter references to various volumes of *Contemporary Authors* are cited by title and volume.)

2. Telephone interview with Judy Blume, September 13, 2001. Unless separately noted, all subsequent Blume quotes are from this interview.

3. Telephone interviews with Judy Blume during Spring 1992. Unless separately noted, all subsequent Blume quotes are from these interviews.

4. Mark I. West, *Trust Your Children: Voices against Censorship in Children's Literature,* (New York: Neal-Schuman, 1988), pp. 4–5.

5. Ibid., p. 4.

6. *Contemporary Authors. New Revision Series,* vol. 13, p. 60.

7. Robert Cormier died on November 2, 2000.

8. Telephone interview with Judy Blume, September 13, 2001. All subsequent Blume quotes are from this interview.

9. The "New York Is Book Country" (NYIBC) literary festival was founded in 1979 to celebrate books and communicate the joy of reading to children and adults in New York City. In addition to a reception held at the mayor's mansion, the festival includes author talks, readings, work shops, and performances.

10. Judy Mann, "The Witching Hour," *Washington Post,* September 16, 1992, p. E19.

11. Telephone interviews with Daniel Cohen during spring 1992. Unless separately noted, all subsequent Cohen quotes are from these interviews.

12. Telephone interview with Daniel Cohen on July 16, 2001. All subsequent Cohen quotes are from this interview.

13. "Robert Cormier," *Newsletter on Intellectual Freedom,* January 2001, p. 7.

14. Ibid.

15. *Contemporary Authors. New Revision Series,* vol. 23, p. 88.

16. Telephone interview with Robert Cormier, February 1992. Unless separately noted, all other Cormier quotes are from this interview.

17. West, *Trust Your Children*, p. 33.

18. *Contemporary Authors. New Revision Series*, vol. 23, p. 89.

19. West, *Trust Your Children*, p. 37.

20. Cormier later sent me a note indicating that *I Am the Cheese* had finally been returned to the library.

21. "Some Thoughts on Censorship," a page of comments prepared by Robert Cormier and distributed to authors, journalists, and other interested parties.

22. Alden Mudge, "First Person," *Bookpage*, April 1999, p. 1, www.bookpage.com/9904bp.

23. "David Guterson: Rewriting History," *iVillage.com*, December 30, 2000, pp. 1–3, www.ivillage.com.

24. Ellen Kanner, "Snow Falling on Cedars," *Bookpage*, 1996, pp. 1–2, www.bookpage.com/9601.

25. "David Guterson: Rewriting History," *iVillage.com*, December 30, 2000, pp. 1–3, www.ivillage.com.

26. "David Guterson," *Reading Group Center: Vintage Books*, www.randomhouse.com/vintage.

27. Elisabeth Sherwin, "New Writer Thanks Harper Lee for Leading Way," *Printed Matter*, November 12, 1995, p. 1, www.den.davis.ca.us/go/gizmo/cedars.

28. Ibid.

29. E-mail interview with David Guterson during January 2001. All subsequent Guterson quotes are from this interview.

30. Lesléa Newman, "Happy Birthday, Heather!" www.lesleanewman.com/articles.htm. *See also* www.lesleakids.com.

31. Ibid.

32. Telephone interview with Lesléa Newman on March 13, 2001. All subsequent Newman quotes are from that interview.

33. "Katherine Paterson," Web page, www.terabithia.com/bio.

34. *Contemporary Authors. New Revision Series*, vol. 28, p. 363.

35. Telephone interviews with Katherine Paterson during spring 1992. Unless separately noted, all subsequent Paterson quotes are from these interviews.

36. Telephone interview with Katherine Paterson on August 20, 2001. All subsequent Paterson quotes are from this interview.

37. *Something about the Author: Facts and Pictures about Authors and Illustrators of Books for Young People*, vol. 51 (Detroit, Mich.: Gale Research Co., 1988), p. 156.

38. Telephone interview with Jan Slepian in spring 1992. Unless separately noted, all subsequent Slepian quotes are from this interview.

39. Letter from Jan Slepian to Otis Lovelace, library supervisor, Charlotte County Public Schools, May 11, 1983.

40. Telephone interview with Jan Slepian in August 2001. All subsequent Slepian quotes are from this interview.

41. Four of our seven interviewees (Judy Blume, Robert Cormier, Katherine Paterson, and Jan Slepian) are represented on SLJ's list of One Hundred Books That Shaped the Century.

| 4 |

The Most Frequently Banned or
Challenged Books, 1996–2000

Ranking the most banned or challenged books is an inexact and often arbitrary process. Many books that are challenged or banned in schools and libraries are never reported to the media or the library associations that document them. We can therefore rank only the known, overt examples of book banning. The most consistent and extensive documentation of book banning is done by the American Library Association's Office for Intellectual Freedom, though other lists and rankings are occasionally prepared by organizations like the American Civil Liberties Union (ACLU) and People for the American Way (PAW). Until 1996, PAW produced an annual report on book banning that included rankings and important analysis. That report has ceased publication, replaced by a newsletter documenting selected instances of censorship.

The list of most frequently banned books in the first edition of *Banned in the U.S.A.* was compiled from 1990 through 1993; the second edition's list, covering 1996 through 2000, was compiled almost entirely from information provided by the ALA Office of Intellectual Freedom and its newsletter. In both editions, only a representative number of censorship incidents could be included, with the number of incidents described under each title roughly proportional to the number of challenges reported. The purpose of documenting these incidents is to describe the nature of the controversy surrounding each book. Often there is no final resolution, with the original parental complaint replaced by a succession of new ones.

As one might expect, there is a substantial overlap of titles between the two lists, but more than half the titles on the current list did not appear in the first edition's ranking. Nonetheless, many of the classic targets of the censors remain on the current list, demonstrating once more that book banning knows no historical bounds. Only four of the fifty most-banned books were published in the year 2000 or later, and they were the most recent titles in continuing series: the *Harry Potter* books, the *Goosebumps* books, the *Alice* books, and the *Captain Underpants* books. The 1990s have twelve titles on our list, the 1980s have eleven, and the 1970s have twelve. The list contains just five titles from the 1960s, one from the 1950s, two each from the 1940s and 1930s, and one from the nineteenth century.

1. **The *Harry Potter* Books**, by J.K. Rowling. Arthur A. Levine Books, 1998–2000.

Synopsis and Background: Why is it that the most popular books are usually the most censored as well? In less than three years of publication life, the Harry Potter books have suffered enough censorship incidents to place the series in the top position on our banned book list. During this period, the first three Harry Potter books (*Harry Potter and the Sorcerer's Stone* [1998], *Harry Potter and the Chamber of Secrets* [1999], *Harry Potter and the Prisoner of Azkaban* [1999]) had the enviable honor of simultaneously holding the number 1, 2, and 3 slots on the *New York Times* best-seller list. The fourth book, *Harry Potter and the Goblet of Fire*, published in June 2000, quickly became number 1 on the *Times* list of best-selling children's books. (The other three Potter books were, of course, numbers 2 through 4.) Though *Goblet of Fire* has not been available long enough to be heavily represented among the censorship incidents described in our survey, reports of challenges are rapidly accumulating.

The Harry Potter books are substantial works (the most recent spanning 752 pages), and all have received considerable critical acclaim. *Goblet of Fire's* American publisher, Scholastic Press, printed 3.8 million copies, probably the biggest initial print run in history. Scholastic had already sold more than 20 million copies of the first three books, and the British editions had sold 7.3 million copies. In addition, the merchandising of Harry Potter paraphernalia was estimated in excess of $1 billion by the time the Harry Potter movie came out in November 2001. The movie broke all box office records: the biggest first day, second day, third day, biggest November opening, etc.

What can explain the spectacular popularity of the Harry Potter books? Lee Siegel, writing for *The New Republic*, said, "The rapturous reception of the Harry Potter books is heartening, because J. K. Rowling is a literary artist, and these . . . books possess more imaginative life than the majority of novels that are published in this country in any given year. They are full of marvelous invention and humor and fun, but they have more than that. . . . With Harry Potter, Rowling has brought reality back into the literature of escape, and back into our fantasy-culture. What a rarity, a literary imagination that is not self-conscious, and studied, and up-tight."[1]

"It's great storytelling, that's what it is," says John Sterling, president of rival publisher Henry Holt. "It's the biggest phenomenon in publishing anywhere." Colette Whitehouse, who works for Rowling's British publisher, Bloomsbury, says, "The merits of the book are what has shone through—the structure, complexity, language and characters—rather than the marketing."[2] Indeed, the most interesting aspect of the Harry Potter craze is that it wasn't created by an ad blitz, but by kids who told their friends about the books.

The reason that *Harry Potter and the Sorcerer's Stone* is the most banned of the Harry Potter books is simply that it was the first written and has therefore been in the sights of the censors for a longer time. *The Sorcerer's Stone* introduces us to Harry Potter, an eleven-year-old orphan as the series begins. As an infant, Harry had been left on the doorstep of his Uncle Vernon and Aunt Petunia Dursley, who tell him that his parents died in a car crash. Harry spends ten years with the Dursleys and their bullying son Dudley, during which time they treat him cruelly. But on his eleventh birthday Harry discovers a secret about his parents: They had been powerful members of England's wizard community. They had not died in a car crash as he had been told, but were killed by the evil wizard Voldemort, who had tried to kill Harry as well, but failed. Harry himself is destined to become a great wizard. The wizard friends of his parents free Harry from the cruel treatment of his aunt and uncle, and a giant named Hagrid takes him to a secret street in London known as Diagon Alley, where Harry purchases all the tools of an aspiring sorcerer: wand, robe, cauldron, broomstick, and owl. Hagrid then escorts him to King's Cross Station where he boards a train at Platform 9 ¾ for the trip to Hogwarts, a famous private school for wizard children.

At Hogwarts Harry learns that nonwizard people are called Muggles. He also becomes a star at playing Quidditch, a game whose players must knock about three different balls while flying through the air on broomsticks. His best friends turn out to be a young Mudblood (half-wizard) girl and a boy from an impoverished wizard family. Harry goes through exciting adventures, including a battle with a mountain troll and a friendship with an orange-eyed creature called a hippogriff, all on the path to his destiny and the secret of the sorcerer's stone.

J.K. Rowling has told her readers that she will add one year to Harry Potter's age in each successive volume of the series. He was eleven in the first book, and he is twelve in the second, *Harry Potter and the Chamber of Secrets*, whose story opens as a house-elf named Dobby comes to Harry's room and warns him not to return to the Hogwarts school where danger awaits him. Harry doesn't believe him and goes off in a flying car to Hogwarts to begin his second year. There he learns that the Muggle-blooded (nonwizard) students are being threatened by a mysterious new force. Salazar Slytherin, one of the great wizards who founded Hogwarts 1,000 years ago, had sought to restrict student admission to purebred magic families, keeping out Muggles or Mudbloods. According to Hogwarts legend, the true Heir of Slytherin will resurface at Hogwarts, open his dreaded Chamber of Secrets, and release the monster within in order to purge the school of those unworthy to study magic. Who is the evil heir? Suspicion first falls on Harry himself, who risks his life to solve the mystery.

In *Chamber of Secrets*, Rowling uses Harry's magical adventures to demonstrate the real social problems of origin and class. The dangers of racism and xenophobia are implicit in the anti-Muggles hysteria at Hogwarts. The moral of the book is that people are defined by their choices, not their origins. We see apparently good people who are villains and apparently guilty people who turn out to be innocent.

The third book, *Harry Potter and the Prisoner of Azkaban*, continues Harry's fantastic adventures at Hogwarts School of Witchcraft and Wizardry. At the end of his third year at the school, Harry is forced to endure the summer holidays with the dreaded Aunt and Uncle Dursley. Harry runs away after casting a spell on his aunt, causing her to blow up like a balloon. His subsequent meetings with the mysterious Knight Bus and Cornelius Fudge, the Minister of Magic, result in a pleasureful vacation in the wonderful surroundings of the Leaky Cauldron. When Sirius Black, who had caused the death of Harry's parents, escapes from Azkaban, the tension rises. Back at school, Harry's actions are circumscribed by the presence of the Dementors—guards from Azkaban who are the lookout for Sirius Black—but Harry has no trouble throwing himself into the new Quidditch season. Still, he is determined to discover why Sirius Black, formerly a close friend of his parents, would have wanted to harm them. The surprising answer to that mystery forms the conclusion of *The Prisoner of Azkaban*.

In the fourth book, *Harry Potter and the Goblet of Fire*, Harry is 14 years old. He has a crush on a classmate at Hogwarts and goes to his first dance, but danger lurks as Lord Voldemort and his murderous Death Eaters plan to regain the power lost in the ill-fated attempt to kill Harry. As always, Harry is diverted from such peril by his anticipation of the Quidditch matches. Particular excitement is generated with the announcement of the first Triwizard Tournament in years, during which students from three rival schools of magic are tested by means of three ordeals. The students are to be selected by a goblet of fire, and although the rules say that Harry is not old enough to be a candidate, he is named a participant by the goblet. The first ordeal pits the students against dragons, the second against water, and the third against a maze that is rigged to lead Harry into the hands of his enemy, Lord Voldemort. The book ends with horror, hilarity, and enough uncertainty to bring readers back for the fifth book.

The popularity of the series seems unending, with adults and children alike captivated, yet the Harry Potter books have been number one on the American Library Association's most banned list for both 1999 and 2000. What is the basis for the broad campaign of censorship against the books? The primary complaints have been that the stories are too violent and glorify witchcraft, but they are no more violent than most fairy tales. As to the charges of support for witchcraft, it should be noted that the Hogwarts school that Harry attends celebrates Christmas, Easter, and Halloween, the kind of cross-pollination of Christianity and paganism that is typical of fairy tales.

Paul Hetrick, speaking for the conservative Christian organization Focus on the Family, admits that the Harry Potter books contain valuable lessons about love, courage, and the victory of good over evil. "But these positive elements are packaged in a medium—witchcraft—that is specifically denounced in Scripture," he adds.[3]

The most highly publicized early protest against the books came in South Carolina during October 1999, where a group of parents persuaded the board of education to reconsider whether the books should be allowed in the schools. The board was told that they "have a serious tone of death, hate, lack of respect and sheer evil." Elizabeth Mounce, a mother of two from Columbia, South Carolina, became a nationally known critic of the Harry Potter books when she spoke against them at a school board meeting in October 1999. "They're trying to disguise things as fun and easy that are really evil," she said.[4]

Other prominent protests soon occurred in Marietta, Georgia; Simi Valley, California; Douglas County, Colorado; and Lakeville, Minnesota. In Moorpark, California, parents Teresa and Dominic Schmidt removed their son from school because *Harry Potter and the Sorcerer's Stone* was being read. "It was a horrible book," said Teresa Schmidt. "It talked about death and killing. It talks about drinking animal blood. That is witchcraft, and as a religion it doesn't belong in school."[5]

Similarly, some parents in Mount Vernon, Washington, removed their children from school rather than have them hear Harry Potter books read. One of the parents, Joe Nichols, told a special book review committee, "Harry Potter is not the hero we should want for our children. These books could be an introduction to sorcery for some of our children. Our children could be led to where we do not want them to go."[6]

Young adult author Judy Blume commented on the Harry Potter controversy in the *New York Times*.

I knew this was coming. The only surprise is that it took so long—as long as it took the zealots who claim they're protecting children from evil (and evil can be found lurking everywhere these days) to discover that children actually like these books. If children are excited about a book, it must be suspect.

I'm not exactly unfamiliar with this line of thinking, having had various books of mine banned from schools over the last twenty years. In my books, it's reality that's seen as corrupting. With Harry Potter, the perceived danger is fantasy. . . . According to certain adults these stories teach witchcraft, sorcery and satanism.

Blume concludes, "The real danger is not in the books, but in laughing off those who would ban them. The protests against Harry Potter follow a tradition that has been growing since the early 1980s and often leaves school principals trembling with fear that is then passed down to teachers and librarians."[7]

The fact that the Harry Potter books are atop our most-banned list confirms Blume's analysis. We could have ranked and analyzed the books title by title, but their consistent themes and characters make them more appropriately treated under a single series entry. Typical of censored series, they tend to be banned as a series.

Selected Challenges, 1996–2000: In November 1999, Simi Valley (California) school officials said that a seven-member committee of parents, teachers, and administrators had read *Harry Potter and the Sorcerer's Stone* and decided to continue to allow it to be read aloud in district classrooms. However, it will not be required reading, and parents will be allowed to take their children out of class when it is read aloud. An elementary school parent had complained that the book was violent, antifamily, had a religious theme, and lacked educational value. Rebecca Wetzel, director of elementary education for the district, said, "When we finished it, we made the recommendation that none of the concerns were so great we would prohibit a child from reading it for recreation." Cynthia Kersey, the complaining parent, said she was disappointed with the committee's decision. "I think it's pathetic that the school district is afraid to make a moral decision," she said.[8]

A similar process was played out in the Frankfort (Illinois) School District during the same month. That district chose not to censor the Harry Potter books, but will allow parents to remove their children from any reading sessions that they consider inappropriate. That decision was made after a group of people asked Superintendent Pamela Witt to prohibit the reading of the Potter books to any students in the district. The parents had complained that the Potter books contained lying and smart-aleck retorts to adults. "We're not going to censor; that's the parents' responsibility," explained Witt.[9]

In December 1999, the Bruckner Elementary School in Saginaw, Michigan, became the first school in the county to remove the Harry Potter books from the classroom. In response to a parent's religious objection to the books, Principal Myra Fall decided to prohibit the reading of the books in class in order to avoid controversy. The students in that class will be assigned a different book series. After reading portions of *Harry Potter and the Sorcerer's Stone*, parent Kathryn MacGown decided to challenge all three of the Potter books. "The books are based on sorcery, which is an abomination to the Lord," said MacGown. "I read a couple of chapters and felt like God didn't want me reading it."[10]

In January 2000, a couple in Bend, Oregon, asked school officials to ban the Harry Potter books from the district's twenty schools, charging that the books would lead children to hatred and rebellion. Greg and Arlena Wilson, parents of a fourth-grader, filed the request after a teacher read from one of the Potter books. Arlena Wilson complained that the books include witchcraft and divination. "It's the fact that the evil wizard inhabits another man's body, and in order for him to stay at half power he has to drink the blood of a unicorn," she explained. Interim Superintendent Gary Bruner felt that banning the book was going too far. "They want it withdrawn not only for their own child, but for all children," he said.[11]

During the same month, administrators at Florida's Carrollwood Elementary School decided to prohibit any future purchases of the Harry Potter books for the school library, fearing that parents might object to the wizardry and witchcraft themes in the series. The school decided to retain the first book in the series, which had been purchased earlier, and to allow children to bring their own books to school. Principal Joan Bookman admitted that there had been no complaints about the books, but said, "We just knew that we had some parents who wouldn't want their children to read these books."[12]

In March 2000, a couple in Cedar Rapids, Iowa, asked the school district to remove *Harry Potter and the Sorcerer's Stone* from school libraries. Brad and Brenda Birdnow objected to the book's romantic characterization of witches, warlocks, wizards, goblins, and sorcerers. "I appeal to you to avoid presenting material that in any way glorifies or romanticizes witchcraft, Satanism, spiritism or any occult ideas," said Brad Birdnow. "These things by their very nature erode the morality of our children, and therefore ultimately our society."[13]

In April 2000, a request to have all Harry Potter books banned from schools in Whittier, California, was rejected by a district committee. Parent Ann Lopez had submitted a petition signed by fifty-three parents at Orange Grove Elementary School charging that the Harry Potter series "exposes our young children's minds to black magic and . . . horrible experiences that our children don't need to hear or read about." In its decision to retain the books, the district committee concluded, "If books were to be banned from schools due to violence depicted, then stories such as Hansel and Gretel, Little Red Riding Hood and the Three Little Pigs would need to be added to the list."[14]

On April 12, 2000, the Board of Education of Salamanca, New York, decided to leave the Harry Potter books in the elementary school libraries. A family had complained about the dark themes in the books, and in response a teacher at Seneca Elementary School was told to cease reading the books to her fourth-grade class. A review committee at the school was subsequently told to examine the Potter books and make a recommendation. It advised the board that the books should not be required reading, but should remain available for use by teachers and students. The board approved the recommendation by a vote of 4–1.

In Zeeland, Michigan, Superintendent of Schools Gary Feenstra first banned the Harry Potter books and then removed most of the restrictions. Initially, the Potter titles were removed from library shelves and made available only with parental restrictions. Feenstra had also stated that no future titles in the series would be purchased. But on May 11, 2000, ten days after a committee of parents and school district employees recommended that the restrictions be reduced, Feenstra announced that the Harry Potter titles would be available in elementary and middle school libraries without restrictions and that future titles would be evaluated for purchase according to standard selection procedures. Students will no longer need written parental permission to use the titles for book reports. The only remaining restriction is that there will be no reading aloud from the Potter books in kindergarten through fifth grades.

In July 2000, the Jacksonville (Florida) Public Library was forced to cease a promotion campaign for the Harry Potter books after some parents and a national religious organization complained. The library had passed out a Hogwarts' Certificate of Accomplishment to children, which related to the Hogwarts School of Witchcraft and Wizardry in the books. "We don't want our children to be exposed to witchcraft," said parent John Miesburg. "If they are going to pass out witchcraft certificates, they should promote the Bible and pass out certificates of righteousness."[15] Miesburg was supported by the Liberty Counsel, a religious rights organization in Orlando, whose president, Matthew Staver, threatened the library with a lawsuit.

Also in July, a man in Pace, Florida, insisted that the Harry Potter books be removed from all local school libraries. Mike Wilson, who leads a ministry for boys at the Pace Assembly of God Church, complained that the books glorify witchcraft and the occult and opposed Biblical teachings. "I know a lot of parents and teachers love it because the kids are excited about reading," he said. "But there's excitement in drugs, there's excitement in fornication, there's excitement in crime, but that doesn't mean they're good for a person."[16]

In Dallas, Texas, the school board upheld the decision of a review committee to allow the Harry Potter books to continue being read aloud to children. The books were challenged by a group of parents who complained that the plots emphasized violence and deception. The initial challenge had been directed at the first book in the series, *Harry Potter and the Sorcerer's Stone*, but the complaints were broadened to include the subsequent volumes as well. After the board voted in September 2000 to retain the books, Michelle Cox, one of the complaining parents, said, "Unfortunately, the board's main concern seemed to be with what the teachers thought instead of what parents' concerns were for their children."[17]

In Fresno, California, parent Larry Finch said his daughter, a fifth-grader at Bullard Talent Elementary School, was told by her teacher that the *Harry Potter* books could not be read in class. Finch said school officials told him in October 2000 that a religious group had expressed concerns about sorcery and witchcraft in the series, leading to a district prohibition on use of the books in class. "This is censorship and it's wrong," said Finch. Carol Bloesser, the district's deputy superintendent, acknowledged the religious complaints, but said teachers had simply been told to be careful about the use of the books. "There is no ban on poor Harry," said Bloesser. "We just asked teachers to be cautious. If you're using Harry Potter, think about its instructional value and be cautious that some parents may not want their kids to read it." Finch disputed Bloesser's account, saying Bloesser, two assistant superintendents, and the principal had told him that teachers "cannot read [Potter] aloud. I heard that from everybody. . . . If we're going to step into the area of censorship, let's put it on the front burner and in a spot where we all can discuss it."[18]

On October 26, 2000, Janet Weaver, a parent in Arab, Alabama, asked the board of education to remove the Harry Potter books from school libraries and accelerated reading programs. Weaver said she was speaking on behalf of other Christians when she charged that author J.K. Rowling was a member of the occult and her books encourage children to practice witchcraft. "It was a mistake years ago to take prayer out of the schools because it left Satan in," Weaver told the board. "We need to put God back in the schools and throw the Harry Potter books out." School Superintendent Edwin Cooley explained that there were no Harry Potter books at Arab Primary School and only two or three at the elementary, junior high, and high school libraries. Elementary teacher Cynthia Green said most of the Harry Potter books read in school were purchased by parents. "You don't want to start banning books like the

Harry Potter books because you don't know where it will lead," Green said. "Next, someone will want to ban *The Wizard of Oz* because it has a wizard in it."[19] Three different review committees were created to examine the books, and all three recommended that the books remain in the school, though the books would not be required reading. This would leave the books in basically the same circumstances that existed before the complaint. On December 18, the school board approved the recommendation.

In November 2000, Julie Barker, a parent with three children in the Bristol, New Hampshire, elementary school, appealed a district decision to allow the reading of Harry Potter books in class. Claiming that the books contained occult teachings and were scaring her daughter, Barker asked the school board to ban the classroom readings. Superintendent David Corey said he had reviewed information provided by the elementary school principal and decided that the Potter books fell within school board policy on class readings. "These books are fiction," said Principal George Kelley. "They don't teach witchcraft or wizardry." Barker disagreed. "Parents don't know what kind of books these are," she told the board. "I'm pleading with you to put the power back in parents' hands."[20] On December 11, the board decided against Barker's proposal that parents be informed in advance of books read in class, saying parents have always had the right to request an alternative assignment for their children when an objectionable book is read in class.

Santa Fe, Texas, school principals are requiring written consent before allowing students to check out any of the Harry Potter books. The policy, established in fall 2000, singles out the Potter books as the only ones requiring such parental approval. "Some parents just don't want their kids reading that," said Superintendent Richard Ownby. "If they want to read it, we'll have it. But we'll need parental permission. We don't want to ban it." Ownby said he probably would allow his own children to read the books. Jay Clements, a local bookseller, said targeting the Potter books sets a dangerous precedent. "That's my concern, that this book is being singled out," he said. "When you start setting up obstacles to certain works, you're starting down that road to censorship."[21]

2. **The Adventures of Huckleberry Finn**, by Mark Twain (Samuel Clemens). Harper and Row, Centennial Edition, 1978, © 1885.

Synopsis and Background: The Adventures of Huckleberry Finn, a narrative written in the idiom of a shiftless, unlettered boy from the lowest class of the antebellum South, was considered objectionable by America's genteel society almost immediately after its publication in 1885. Huck, the outcast son of the town drunkard, was the hero and narrator of a tale that ridiculed America's work ethic, polite manners, prayer, and piety.

Before its publication as a book, *Huckleberry Finn* was excerpted in a magazine, but only after references to such things as nakedness and dead cats were deleted. In order to have the book published in unexpurgated form, Mark Twain was forced to set up his own publishing house. Immediately upon its publication, it was banned by the Concord Public Library in Massachusetts, which described the book as follows:

It deals with a series of adventures of a very low grade of morality; it is couched in the language of a rough dialect, and all through its pages there is a systematic use of bad grammar and an employment of rough, coarse, inelegant expressions. It is also very irreverent. To sum up, the book is flippant and irreverent in its style. It deals with a series of experiences that are certainly not elevating. The whole book is of a class that is more profitable for the slums than it is for respectable people, and it is trash of the veriest sort.

Twain's response was:

That will sell 25,000 copies for sure. For instance, it will deter other libraries from buying the book and you are doubtless aware that one book in a public library prevents the sale of a sure ten and a possible hundred of its mates. And secondly it will cause the purchasers of the book to read it, out of curiosity, instead of merely intending to do so after the usual way of the world and library committees; and then they will discover, to my great advantage and their own indignant disappointment, that there is nothing objectionable in the book, after all.[22]

During Twain's lifetime, *Huckleberry Finn* was banned from numerous other libraries, including the Denver Public Library, the Omaha Public Library, the Brooklyn Public Library, and even the New York State Reformatory. Upon hearing that his books had been banned in Brooklyn, Twain provided the library with the following straight-faced defense:

I wrote *Tom Sawyer* and *Huck Finn* for adults exclusively, & it always distresses me when I find that boys & girls have been allowed access to them. The mind that becomes soiled in youth can never again be washed clean. I know this by my own experience, & to this day I cherish an unappeasable bitterness against the unfaithful guardians of my young life, who not only permitted but compelled me to read an unexpurgated Bible through before I was 15 years old. None can do that and draw a clean, sweet breath again this side of the grave.... Most honestly do I wish that I could say a softening word or two in defense of Huck's character since you wish it, but really, in my opinion, it is no better than those of Solomon, David, and the rest of the sacred brotherhood. If there is an unexpurgated [Bible] in the Children's Department, won't you please ... remove Tom & Huck from that questionable companionship?[23]

In 1907, *Library Journal* printed an article entitled "The Children's Librarian versus *Huckleberry Finn*" in which it was claimed that Twain's book had been banned somewhere in the United States each year since its publication. Yet the book has been translated into virtually every language spoken on earth and is widely regarded as America's greatest novel. Ernest Hemingway proclaimed, "All modern American literature comes from one book by Mark Twain called *Huckleberry Finn* . . . the best book we've had." H.L. Mencken said his discovery of *Huckleberry Finn* in 1889, when he was nine years old and the book only four, was "probably the most stupendous event of my whole life. . . . If I undertook to tell you the effect it had upon me my whole talk would sound frantic, and even delirious." He proclaimed Mark Twain as "the true father of our national literature, the first genuinely American artist of the royal blood." T.S. Eliot said that in *Huckleberry Finn* Twain had proved himself to be one of those few writers "who have brought their language up to date" and "who have discovered a new way of writing, valid not only for themselves, but for others."[24]

In the face of such universal acclaim, how could schools and libraries entering the new millennium make this the second most banned book in the nation? Lionel Trilling has characterized *Huckleberry Finn* as a subversive book. Huck's agonizing struggles with right and wrong, freedom and slavery, humanity and racism suggest that society's moral pronouncements are often nothing more than the ingrained customary beliefs of a particular time and place. Together, Huck and Jim ruthlessly examine the social contract upon which the stability of modern society rests, and in the process, they reject public opinion as a basis for human conduct. Huck's heart and conscience showed him the evil of slavery and led him to help Jim run away from his legal owner, an act that society regarded as both a sin and a crime. Huck was happy to live as a pariah, rejecting what he considered unjust and immoral laws. Even today, Huck and Jim are an affront to polite society. In *Born to Trouble*, Justin Kaplan wrote, "They are simply too good for us, too truthful, too loyal, too passionate, and, in a profounder sense than the one we feel easy with, too moral."[25]

A more recent twist in the continuing controversy over *Huckleberry Finn* is the allegation that it is racist. The major basis for such charges is that some of the book's characters use the racial epithets common to the Mississippi Valley thirty years before Emancipation. But Mark Twain and Herman Melville may have been the least "racist" of all the major writers of their time. In particular, *Huckleberry Finn* is a devastating satire on racism, bigotry, and property rights in American society. Huck and Jim seek escape on their raft from a nightmare society torn by bigotry, violence, exploitation, greed, ignorance, and depravity.

Selected Challenges, 1996–2000: On July 8, 1996, the school board in Lindale, Texas, voted to ban thirty-two books on an advanced placement (AP) reading list because a trustee said the books conflicted with the values of the community. Prominent among the titles banned by the Lindale board was *Huckleberry Finn*. The decision followed recommendations from a book committee of parents and teachers. Trustee Gary Camp said the books were especially unsuitable for boys fifteen and sixteen years of age. "We're turning our young men into ticking time bombs," he said.[26]

In July 1996, Superintendent Dr. Claire Brown, Jr., told eighty people at a school board meeting that *Huckleberry Finn* would be dropped from the required reading list at Upper Dublin (Pennsylvania) High School. Brown said the removal was an administrative action rather than a board decision. Black parents and students had protested the book because the frequent use of the word "nigger" made black children uncomfortable. In June, the board's curriculum committee had recommended retaining the book as required reading, but moving it to eleventh grade and reassessing how it could be sensitively presented in class.

In September 1996, Shalon Bradford, a student in Federal Way, Washington, complained about the use of the word "nigger" in *Huckleberry Finn*, saying the word made her uncomfortable and sad. "It's a horrible word," she said. Her aunt and legal guardian, Tamara Cobb, challenged the district to remove the novel from its approved reading list. English teacher Dave Matthews, who had assigned the book to students for twenty-eight years, acknowledged that some of the novel's language is offensive, but he said the book "raises our consciousness because it shows how terribly blacks were treated back then. We need to know who we are and what we come from. That's how society can change for the better." District representative Karen Stevens noted that a committee of parents, teachers, and administrators chooses all books in the curriculum. "We don't just drop a book because one person says they don't like it," she said. "That's censorship."[27]

In February 1997, the Reverend Charles Sims and about twenty members of the African American community in Columbus, Indiana, attended a school board meeting to protest the use of *Huckleberry Finn* and *Tom Sawyer* in the local high school's classrooms. Sims said exposing African American children to the books was "degrading, insensitive, and oppressive." The following month, the board was given a letter in support of the books written by Shirley Lester, English Department chair, and signed by all seventeen of the school's English teachers. Assistant Superintendent Linda McClure assured Lester, "Nobody is taking *Huck Finn* off the shelves."[28]

In March 1997, the parents of an eleventh-grade girl in Lyndhurst, Ohio, objected to the classroom use of *Huckleberry Finn* in the South Euclid–Lyndhurst City Schools. The student had complained that some classmates giggled as the word "nigger" was read aloud in class. The girl was given an alternative assignment, but her parents and the parents of eight other students asked school officials to remove the book.

On July 14, 1997, the Fairfax County (Virginia) School Board denied a request to remove *Huckleberry Finn* from McLean High School's required reading list, despite an angry, boisterous demand from a local family. Student Halima Alkisswani argued that the book is racist and offensive to African Americans. Her father then stormed out of the meeting, shouting at board chair Kristen Amundson. The board voted 8–0 not to remove the book from the English curriculum, arguing that *Huckleberry Finn* was a classic with significant literary and social value. The book is required reading in eleventh-grade English classes at fourteen of the county's twenty-three high schools.

On December 8, 1997, the Cherry Hill (New Jersey) School Board approved a new curriculum that teaches *Huckleberry Finn* in the context of nineteenth century race relations. Mark Twain's work is presented along with other African-American writers such as Maya Angelou and Langston Hughes. The new approach reinstated *Huckleberry Finn* almost a year after the book was removed from classrooms in response to parental complaints that the book's racial epithets made African American students uncomfortable. Teachers opting to teach the new curriculum unit are required to attend a half-day training session conducted by the Villanova University professors who helped develop it.

In January 1998, the Pennsylvania NAACP added its voice to the debate over *Huckleberry Finn* by passing a resolution calling on school districts to remove the book from required reading lists, but not school or public libraries, because of its offensive racial language. The resolution, which was sent to Governor Tom Ridge and school districts across the state, noted the psychologically damaging effect that the book's use of the term "nigger" could have on African American children. The NAACP said it would target school districts that insist on having the book read aloud to students. Richard P. Burton, Sr., president of the state NCAAP, said, "We don't believe in censorship. But as far as curriculum is concerned, it should not be taught."[29]

A father in Dalton, Georgia, led a campaign to ban *Huckleberry Finn* from local classrooms, claiming the book was offensive. Ron Clark said the constant use of the word "nigger" tears down self-esteem and teaches racial slurs. In his effort to prohibit schools from using the book as required or even recommended reading, Clark collected several hundred signatures on a petition and spoke with city and county school leaders. In fall 1998 a review committee of high school leaders, teachers, and parents convened by Superintendent Billy Bice denied Clark's request. Bice said, "I understand the concern surrounding the book, but if you're going to start taking books away because someone finds them offensive, where do you stop? Everyone can probably find something offensive in every book."[30]

On October 19, 1998, the U.S. Court of Appeals in San Francisco rejected a black woman's request to remove *Huckleberry Finn* from the required reading list at her daughter's Tempe, Arizona, high school. Kathy Monteiro, a teacher at McClintock High School in Tempe, Arizona, had been arrested and led away in handcuffs after a series of confrontations with district officials over her charges that *Huckleberry Finn* was a racist book and that the school district was racially insensitive for not removing it. She then sued the school district for failing to respond to complaints that the book was encouraging white students to harass blacks with racial slurs. Monteiro attracted support from the Phoenix Urban League, the NAACP, and the Nation of Islam, which held demonstrations outside the high school. Monteiro filed a civil rights complaint against the district, but the U.S. District Court dismissed the complaint, saying it had insufficient evidence that the book was racially discriminatory. The appeals court agreed saying the school could not be required to remove the books as a way to reduce harassment. Courts cannot "ban books or other literary works from school curricula on the basis of their content . . . even when the works are accused of being racist," the three judge panel unanimously agreed.[31]

On April 24, 2000, the Enid (Oklahoma) School Board voted 7–0 to maintain *Huckleberry Finn* as required reading for sophomores in American literature classes at Enid High School. The book had been challenged by a group of African American ministers, who complained that the novel used language that was offensive to black students, and a textbook review committee had recommended that the book be restricted to students taking advanced literature classes. Jocelyn Chadwick, an African American Twain scholar from Harvard, addressed the school board and encouraged it to keep the book in the current curriculum. She did recommend, however, that students be taught the book's background, and the board passed a resolution calling for Chadwick to lead teacher training in the book's use.

In May 1999, the Fairbanks (Alaska) North Star School District's ethnic committee prepared a resolution to remove *Huckleberry Finn* from high school required reading lists. Bill Burrows, the school board representative on the committee, said the book should be removed from the list because of its use of the word "nigger." Superintendent Stewart Weinberg was skeptical about the removal of the book from the list, saying that it was "important to expose students to Twain's classic. "He thought the district might consider maintaining *Huckleberry Finn* on the list but supplementing it with literature by minority authors from the same period." Not reading this work is really unfair to the students who are trying to understand that period in American history," he said.[32]

3. **I Know Why the Caged Bird Sings**, by Maya Angelou. Random House, 1969.

Synopsis and Background: In the first of her four-volume autobiographical series, Maya Angelou, the famous black writer, dancer, singer, director, and civil rights activist, recounts her childhood and adolescence. The book describes the divorce of her parents and her subsequent difficulties as she moves about the country, living with various relatives and bearing an illegitimate son when she was just sixteen years of age. The censors have complained of sexually explicit scenes, foul language, and irreverent religious descriptions. Some have accused Angelou of blasphemy simply because she rejects the fatalism that religion brought to many southern blacks who gave all credit to God for whatever meager pleasures they enjoyed but did not blame God for their many misfortunes.

Poet James Bertolino says that a reading of *I Know Why the Caged Bird Sings* led him to see Maya Angelou as three different writers. "The first is a writer of extraordinary imagination and verbal originality, well worth reading for her artistic effects, her style," says Bertolino. "The second writer is one who bears honest witness to her own development as a sensitive, highly intelligent human being, probing deeply into powerful childhood experiences, examining how wounds can bring the gift of awareness. The third is a socially conscious writer whose portrayal of the pain, frustration and waste caused by racial prejudice is stunning and persuasive."

Bertolino concludes, "I believe *I Know Why the Caged Bird Sings* is one of the essential books produced by our culture, and we should all read it, especially our children."[33]

Author Opal Moore describes *Caged Bird* as a "literary masterpiece" that can benefit junior high and high school students. "It is an affirmation; it promises that life, if we have the courage to live it, will be worth the struggle," says Moore.[34]

How then do we explain the torrent of censorship of *Caged Bird* in schools around the country. "*Caged Bird* elicits criticism for its honest depiction of rape, its exploration of the ugly specter of racism in America, its recounting of the circumstances of Angelou's own out-of-wedlock teen pregnancy, and its humorous poking at the foibles of the institutional church," explains Moore. "Arguments advocating that *Caged Bird* be banned from school reading lists reveal that the complainants, often parents, tend to regard any treatment of these kinds of subject matter in schools as inappropriate—despite the fact that the realities and issues of sexuality and violence, in particular, are commonplace in contemporary teenage intercourse and discourse. . . . *Caged Bird*'s critics imply an immorality in the work based on the book's images. However, it is through Angelou's vivid depictions of human spiritual triumph set against a backdrop of human weakness and failing that the autobiography speaks dramatically about moral choice."[35]

Moore notes that though *Caged Bird* is easily read, it is not an "easy read." This may partly explain the objections of parents who feel that the book is too sophisticated for children. But Moore notes that what is easier for a student or teacher is not necessarily good. "We should be careful, as teachers, designers of curriculum, and concerned parents, not to fall into the false opposition of good vs. easy. . . . A book that has the potential to liberate the reader into life is one that deserves our intelligent consideration, not rash judgements made from narrow fearfulness."[36]

I Know Why the Caged Bird Sings offers a message of survival and hope. The author is a real-life role model who overcame low self-esteem, economic deprivation, and societal barriers to reach artistic success. Reading of Angelou's troubled beginnings and knowing of her later triumphs instill confidence and motivation in adolescent students. After Maya Angelou wrote and delivered the inaugural poem for President Bill Clinton, *I Know Why the Caged Bird Sings* reached number eight on the Ingram's paperback best-seller list.

Selected Challenges, 1996–2000: On January 19, 1996, the Round Rock (Texas) Independent School District board endured seven hours of emotional debate over a proposal to ban a dozen books, including *I Know Why the Caged Bird Sings*, from high school reading lists. Some parents and school officials had charged that the books were too violent. The proposal had been initiated by board member Nelda Click, who wanted the books, all of which were used in honors or advanced placement classes, removed from the reading lists at Westwood and McNeil high schools. Click's proposal would have circumvented a review system put in place after a previous uproar over *I Know Why the Caged Bird Sings*. In the early hours of the morning, the board voted 4 to 2 to maintain the books on the reading lists.

At an emotional hearing on March 12, 1996, the East Lawrence High School media committee in Moulton, Alabama, turned down parent George Thomas's request to ban *I Know Why the Caged Bird Sings*. The twelve-member committee decided that the book should be required reading for all high school honors classes, advanced placement seniors, and pre-advanced placement junior English classes. Students in other English classes can use the book as supplementary reading, though an alternative must be available to students whose parents object. School superintendent Patrick Graham had become part of the controversy when he entered teacher Ernestine Robinson's English class and told her that she must cease using the book immediately because of its sexually explicit passages. Robinson asked for a public apology from Graham for questioning her ethics and violating board policy.

On January 30, 1997, the board of education in Union Township, Ohio, banned *I Know Why the Caged Bird Sings* from the district's high school reading list, citing the book's sexual content. By a 3 to 2 vote, the board prohibited teachers from assigning the book or from leading class discussions of it. "There is no question in my mind this book pushes the limits of decency," said board member Roger Jeter, who had pushed for removal of the book. "If we cannot take a stand against the most challenged book in America, what can we take a stand against?" Sixteen-year-old Katie Owen, a self-proclaimed Christian who read the book in a sophomore honors class, said she opposed banning the book. "Yes, it was graphic, but it made the message that much stronger," she said. "Seeing what Maya Angelou went through, it helped me to be a stronger person as well."[37]

When parents in Richfield, Minnesota, complained that *I Know Why the Caged Bird Sings* is too explicit to be on the ninth-grade reading list at Richfield High School, it was reassigned in July 1997 to the eleventh- and twelfth-grade reading lists with a written parental advisory. Some parents had complained about the book's molestation and rape scenes and other sections where the author questions her sexual orientation. Richfield teachers, on the other hand, objected to the school's action, saying it amounted to censorship. Dennis Laingen, district director of curriculum and instruction, defended the reassignment of the novel, saying, "We're certainly not banning the book. Everybody got some of what they wanted."[38]

In September 1997, the principal and teachers at Turrentine Middle School in Burlington, North Carolina, decided to remove *I Know Why the Caged Bird Sings* from the required reading list after receiving complaints from parents about the profanity and sexual references in the book. School officials said they would stop teaching from the book, but would not remove it from library shelves. The school board also proposed to formalize their action under a new policy which would allow school officials to remove questionable books from the school before deciding on whether or not to use them. Local teachers spoke out against this. "Such a policy would allow individuals or groups with an agenda of their own to empty library shelves or disrupt classroom instruction," said media specialist Libby Lasley. "Such a policy goes against one of the fundamental tenets of a democratic society: innocence until guilt is proven."[39]

In November 1997, Debbie Klymshyn asked the Jessup, Georgia, board of education to remove *I Know Why the Caged Bird Sings* from the advanced placement program at Wayne County High School. She told the board that the language and sexual descriptions in the book were inappropriate for high school students. "It's not only our child that we're concerned about," said Klymshyn. "It's all the other children in the AP program. And if we allow this now, what will there be when my youngest child gets up there?"[40] But instructor Jamie Denton explained that the AP program was designed to prepare students for college, and that books like *Caged Bird* were appropriate for such advanced classes. A seven-person committee unanimously found that the book had merit as a class text and that it enhanced the study of other important books.

On February 5, 1998, Marvin Gordon, principal of the Dolores Parrott Middle School in Brooksville, Florida, decided to follow the recommendation of a parent-teacher committee and ban *I Know Why the Caged Bird Sings* from the school's library and classrooms. The school's media advisory committee had voted 5 to 2 to remove the book, with both votes in favor of the book coming from the teachers on the committee. Gordon wrote, "Our students, like other students assigned to this level, already have to deal with a tremendous amount of internal and external changes. We don't need to compound the problems that confront them."[41] The two parents who had filed written complaints about the book said the rape scene was particularly objectionable.

On October 13, 1998, the Anne Arundel County (Maryland) school board released a thirteen-page decision in which the eight board members said they "simply disagree" with Barry and Sharon Taylor, a couple who complained that profanity and sex make *I Know Why the Caged Bird Sings* unfit reading for freshman English classes. The report said, "This board has concluded that the value of *Caged Bird* outweighs the concerns expressed by Mr. and Mrs. Taylor." A curriculum committee had voted unanimously to keep the book in the classroom. The Taylors, who had complained of sexually explicit passages, said, "We are not surprised; we thought this was going to happen. If they had done anything different, they would not be supporting their teachers."[42]

In April 1999, the school board in Unity, New Hampshire, voted to remove *I Know Why the Caged Bird Sings* from the seventh- and eighth-grade reading lists at the Unity Elementary School in response to complaints from parents. The following month, the board met once more to consider a petition asking for the removal of the book from the school library. Board members were unable to reach agreement and took no action at the meeting, which, in effect, allowed the book to remain in the library. This turned out to be a hollow victory, because it was soon discovered that the book was not in the library at all. Sheila Purington, one of the parents who lodged complaints against the book and organized the petition drive, said she was under the impression that the library owned the book, but Principal Robin Grumman said that as far as she knew, the book was never in the library.

4. **Of Mice and Men**, by John Steinbeck. Viking Penguin, 1937.

Synopsis and Background: *Of Mice and Men*, published in 1937, has earned a host of awards while leaving a trail of controversy within the public school curriculum. In making it the fourth-most banned book on our current list, the censors claim to be protecting the young and impressionable from this tragic tale of crude heroes speaking vulgar language within a setting that implies criticism of our social system. The story focuses on two vagrant workers, Lennie, big and simpleminded, and George, small and clever, who take jobs at a large ranch. The childishly naive Lennie is tormented by the boss's arrogant son Curley. Simultaneously, Lennie forms a friendship with Curley's young wife, which eventually leads to her accidental death at his hands. George's act of self-sacrifice to protect Lennie from a vengeful mob forms the tragic conclusion to the story.

Despite the controversy surrounding its use in the classroom, *Of Mice and Men* remains an extremely popular choice of teachers and educators. Thomas Scarseth, of the University of Wisconsin at LaCrosse, says, "There is one good reason for reading John Steinbeck's short novel *Of Mice and Men*—it is a very good book. There is one good reason for teaching it—it is a teachable good book: simple and clear, yet profound and beautiful." Scarseth says that *Of Mice and Men* treats the great themes of dreams and death and love with simple power and clarity. "It does so with a classically elegant structure—another reason for using the book as a teaching tool: it allows a reader—especially an untrained or beginning reader of literature—to see (or be shown) how structure supports and presents content."[43] *Of Mice and Men* has plot structure uncluttered by diversions, distractions, or subplots, and its stark inevitability makes the point of the story unavoidable. The style is simple, using clear, direct sentences of description and action and the unadorned speech of simple people.

Scarseth describes *Of Mice and Men* as a book to show beginning readers the paths to great books that might initially be too difficult for them. It is a tragedy in the classic Aristotelian/Shakespearean sense, showing humanity's ability to achieve nobility through and in spite of defeat. Steinbeck democratizes the tragic world, extending the realm of tragedy beyond the royal or God-like figures to the lowly of the earth. In the modern tradition of *The Hairy Ape* and *Death of a Salesman*, *Of Mice and Men* shows that even the least of us has the human potential for tragic nobility.

Scarseth says,

Some people seem to believe that the function of literature is to provide vicarious "happy endings," to provide in words a sugary sweetness we would like to have but cannot always get in real life. To such people, true literary tragedy is distasteful. But the greatest writers and the best readers know that literature is not always only mere sugar candy; it can sometimes be a strong medicine: sour perhaps—at least to the untrained taste—but necessary for continued health.[44]

There are no purely good or purely bad people in *Of Mice and Men*. The characters are a complex mixture of good and bad, of bad results from good intentions. They occupy subordinate positions in a gross and dirty world in which they do the best they can. But, as the poet Robert Burns wrote long ago, "The best laid schemes o' mice and men gang aft a-gley." Lennie and George are good friends who share a good dream. They are too inarticulate to express their love for each other, but it is revealed through Steinbeck's moving narrative. The simple desire of Lennie and George to have a small place of their own is doomed by their own limitations and the tragic chain of circumstance and coincidence that destroys them.

Selected Challenges, 1996–2000: The Louisville (Ohio) board of education voted at a special meeting on January 28, 1997, to retain *Of Mice and Men* as an optional book in high school English classes. The board's 3 to 2 vote finalized months of heated debate over the book. Board member Andy Aljancic and parent Chuck Lang had proposed the ban on the book, alleging 196 examples of profanity. Twenty people, including students, parents, teachers, and clergy, addressed the board, with thirteen defending the book as a valuable classic and seven objecting to its profanity.

In February 1997, the Peru (Indiana) school board barred an eighth-grade teacher from using *Of Mice and Men*. The following month, when a group of teachers, students, and community members asked the board to reconsider its decision, the board took no action, leaving the book in limbo. Teacher Dan Brooks can no longer teach it as he has for many years because it has been judged "age inappropriate." A petition signed by more than a hundred of Brooks's former students stated: "We feel that the banning of this novel will be detrimental to all future eighth-grade students." Superintendent John Jacobson responded, "Students are not mature enough to handle the work."[45]

On September 8, 1997, the Sauk Rapids (Minnesota) school board voted 7 to 0 to keep *Of Mice and Men* in its curriculum despite a parent's charge that the book was racist. Parent Marilyn Rabsatt had charged that the book's use of racial epithets had led to harassment of her daughter by other students. The board voted to keep the book on the reading list of a freshman literature class at the district high school. Superintendent Greg Vandel explained, "Where better than a classroom to talk about issues of race and culture and the power of language? That's what this is all about, the power of hurtful language."[46]

On October 20, 1997, the Bay County school superintendent in Panama City, Florida, rejected a request to remove *Of Mice and Men* from high school classrooms because its characters use a racial slur. Superintendent Larry Bolinger said that teachers could continue to assign what he called "a classic of literature," but students could request alternative assignments. Bolinger concluded that the novel was appropriate for high school use after he received recommendations from two review committees and Mosley High School Principal Bill Husfelt. A district review panel said that teachers "cannot shield students from emotionally-charged language and sensitive issues, but we can give them a context in which to understand their use in a work of literature."[47] A couple, the Reverends W.E. and B.J. Richardson, had asked that the book be banned after it was assigned to their daughter.

On April 14, 1998, James and Kathy Berkshire told the Bryant (Arkansas) school board that they objected to their child reading *Of Mice and Men*. They said that the book took God's name in vain fifteen times and used Jesus's name lightly. The Berkshires asked the board to remove the book from school library shelves. "As a Christian it offends me that we use this book as a teaching tool," said James Berkshire. School board member Jim Lagrone said he also found the book offensive, but did not support banning it. "I can appreciate your right as a Christian and as an American to air your grievances, but I have to object to taking the book out of the library," he said.[48] The board voted unanimously not to remove the book, but to offer alternative titles when it was assigned to be read in class.

In April 1998, parents in Oakley, California, demanded that *Of Mice and Men* and another book be removed from O'Hara Park Middle School classrooms because they contained racial epithets that upset their children. "This is not a racial thing," parent Harold Turner said. "This a matter of morals and common decency." Turner said Assistant Superintendent Carol Boyd had suspended two students for using such words. "But when teachers are using it in the classroom, what does that tell our students?" he asked.[49]

In October 1998, the Barron (Wisconsin) school district placed *Of Mice and Men* and three other books under review for possible removal from library circulation in the Barron district. Complaints were filed by Karen Williams, whose earlier complaints led to the banning of four books on homosexuality. A twenty-four member committee was appointed to study the issue and report back to the board. Pat Solheid, a parent member of the Book Reconsideration Committee, said, "What troubles me is that I think this puts vast amounts of literature at risk of removal."[50]

On April 19, 1999, the West Middlesex (Pennsylvania) school board voted unanimously to keep *Of Mice and Men* in the high school's sophomore curriculum. A parent, Philip Ames, had appealed to the board to remove the book, citing 173 instances of profanity. "I'm disappointed when people in authority have a chance to make a decision to do something good for our children, but for the sake of literature, etc., they choose not to ruffle any feathers," he said. Board President Donald P. Wilson said this was not an easy decision for board members. "We try to recognize that there is disturbing language, but we affirm the students' right to read or not to read the assignment, knowing that another book would be provided that was acceptable," he explained.[51]

On November 27, 1999, the Tomah (Wisconsin) school board's Reconsideration Committee met to consider a request by Robert Frost that *Of Mice and Men* be dropped from the School's English curriculum. Frost, who said he had read about 85 percent of the book, told the committee, "We're wondering why children are killing each other. We're telling our kids that language in this book is fine for them to use."[52] Frost said that a petition with between 130 and 140 signatures opposing the book would be submitted at a later date.

5. **The Chocolate War**, by Robert Cormier. Pantheon, 1974.

Synopsis and Background: In *The Chocolate War*, the leader of a secret society, the Vigils, in a Catholic high school manipulates and intimidates most students to follow the gang's dictates. One student, Jerry Renault, tries to stand up to the gang when it bullies the students into selling chocolates at the school, but he finds that the struggle against conformity has unfortunate consequences. He shows courage in facing the combined forces of the secret society and school officials, some of whom act in complicity with the gang. Like so many of the heroes of banned young adult novels, Jerry Renault bucks the system, making decisions for himself in an attempt to gain control over his life. Jerry did not set out to be rebellious, but the repressive control of the school over the students' lives causes him to refuse to participate in the annual chocolate sale. For this act of rebellion, he receives personal punishment on the football field, telephone threats, the silent treatment from the student body, and a final brutal beating on stage before the entire school. This assault by the Vigils is perpetrated with the encouragement of the assistant headmaster, who supports "school spirit" over individuality.

The *New York Times* called *The Chocolate War* "masterfully structured and rich in theme." Kenneth Donelson and Alleen Pace Nilsen's *Literature for Today's Young Adults* proclaims: "The book that we have chosen as an example of the best of modern realism for young adults is Robert Cormier's *The Chocolate War*."[53] Why would this textbook example of literary excellence be the source of repeated controversy and censorship? All of Cormier's young adult novels focus on the struggle between individuals and dehumanizing institutions, and in *The Chocolate War*, the institution is a combination of church and school. W. Geiger Ellis of the University of Georgia tells us:

School, church, hospital, government—surely these are people-serving, individual-enhancing institutions. Look more closely, as Cormier guides us, for unsettling views are waiting. Such a negative portrayal of established institutions is bound to be unpopular in some circles and will make some individuals uncomfortable, especially when they themselves are a part of and subject to such an institution. Specifically, many teachers feel that they dare not disturb the universe, and as Cormier has made perfectly clear, there is danger in doing so.[54]

Selected Challenges, 1996–2000: On March 4, 1996, a seven-member Reconsideration Committee voted 4 to 3 to remove *The Chocolate War* from the six middle schools in the Riverside (California) Unified School District. Marcia Weaver, a teacher, and parent Sue Neal argued that students who read the book would not have the opportunity to discuss the serious issues raised by the novel. Copies of the books were to be transferred to the district's high school libraries and the title deleted from an electronic list of books suggested for middle school projects and reports.

On July 15, 1996, the East Stroudsburg (Pennsylvania) school board voted 8 to 0 to remove *The Chocolate War* from the ninth-grade reading list at the local high school. Rachel Heath, assistant superintendent for curriculum, said the book was eliminated because of scheduling conflicting and not because of the uproar it had caused the previous year. At that time, the board voted to keep the book, despite complaints about the novel's language and content, but then reversed its decision on a 5 to 4 vote. The book nonetheless remained in the curriculum, because a two-thirds vote was needed to override Superintendent John Grogan's recommendation to keep the book. The latest vote left no doubt about the fate of *The Chocolate War*.

The Broken Arrow (Oklahoma) board of education voted June 1, 1997, to remove *The Chocolate War* from media centers serving grades six through ten. The book had been used in Broken Arrow schools for more than twenty years without incident, and the vote to ban it touched off a debate on school censorship throughout the Tulsa area. Parent Steve Wolfe, who led the fight to remove the book, called it the antithesis of the district's character development curriculum. Wolfe went beyond his attack on *The Chocolate War* to propose a ratings system for the more than 400 books listed on the district's electronic bookshelf. Broken Arrow High School media specialist Barbara Detmer said the board's action removed choice from the professional educators who are trained for such judgments. "I felt it was worthwhile literature," she said. "It has received a lot of criticism because it didn't paint a rosy picture. But it's a good dose of reality."[55]

On March 12, 1998, the Greenville (Texas) board of trustees announced that a review committee had removed *The Chocolate War* from the Greenville Intermediate School library and from the accelerated reading list for fifth- and sixth-graders. Former board member Ron Rogers said he had challenged the book because it contained blasphemy, profanity, and graphic sexual passages. Mike Cardwell, assistant superintendent for instruction and curriculum, said, "This incident is an indication that the system works."[56]

In June 1999, Dale Robar, a parent of a ninth-grade student in Colton, New York, filed an official grievance complaining about the use of *The Chocolate War* in his son's class. A petition containing more than fifty names was also submitted to the board of education, requesting that the book be removed from the required reading list for the ninth grade. Robar said the book contained profanity, sexual innuendo, disrespect for women, and references to masturbation. "Years ago we used to rely on teachers to provide good wholesome curriculum," said Robar. "Now I think parents need to get involved."

In October 1999, a parent in York County, Virginia, made her first complaint about *The Chocolate War* at a school board meeting. Rita Malpass said her fourteen-year-old son, a student at Grafton High School, told her about the book's profanity and references to masturbation. At least 225 people signed a petition circulated by Malpass supporting her complaint. Since then, two school committees upheld the use of the book in the curriculum, one of them a nine-member committee of school administrators, parents, students, and local professors. Nonetheless, more than 200 members of the Bethel Baptist Church signed a petition supporting Malpass's efforts against the book. Few of the church members signing the petition had ever seen, much less read, the book, but pastor emeritus Reverend Franklin Hall said, "I don't have to dig down into a trash can to know it's garbage."[57]

In November 1999, parents in South Park, Colorado, circulated a petition to remove *The Chocolate War* from the supplemental reading list at Silverheels Middle School. They also voiced their complaints at a school board meeting. Jean Anduri, who wrote the petition, said that she doesn't want the book banned, just kept out of the hands of sixth-graders. Other parents said that they wanted the book out of the library altogether. Most of the complaining parents expressed concerns about the sexually suggestive language in the book. "In my opinion as a parent," said Robert Benjamin, "that language is totally unnecessary. We just don't think that is appropriate."[58] Seventh-grade teacher Jean Jones said that the book had been in the curriculum for twelve years and never generated a complaint.

The Maple Heights (Ohio) school superintendent first learned that there was a parental objection to the use of *The Chocolate War* when Leroy and Sharolyn Colley appeared on a local television news report complaining of sexually explicit passages in the book. "This book teaches immorality," said Sharolyn Colley. "There is no educational purpose you can say you can use this book for. When it gets to be sexually explicit, when every other word is a curse word, I don't see the point." Superintendent Rish said the Colleys' ninth-grade daughter could have been excused from reading the book, but they had not submitted a written complaint nor spoken to the teacher, the curriculum director, or the superintendent. Instead, they simply called the television station.[59]

In June 2000, Robert Cormier once more found himself defending his book *The Chocolate War* from the censors. Parents in Lancaster, Massachusetts, just next door to Cormier's native Leominster, demanded that the book be removed from eighth-grade reading lists at Lancaster Middle School. "I feel, at the earliest, it should be read by juniors and seniors," said Susan Loring, who originated the complaint. Cormier sympathized with the parents' concerns, saying, "I know there are sensitive kids and sensitive parents. My problem is when they want to prevent other people from reading it." Maura O'Connor, the English teacher in whose class the book was used, said *The Chocolate War* fits well into her curriculum, which uses literature to examine what happens when people abuse power. She said it was also relevant to the school's efforts to solve the problem of bullying.

6. It's Perfectly Normal: A Book about Changing Bodies, Growing Up, Sex, and Sexual Health, by Robie H. Harris. Candlewick Press, 1994.

Synopsis and Background: It's Perfectly Normal is a sensitive contribution to the sex-education curriculum for middle schools. The controversy over its inclusion in libraries and schools centers largely on its illustrations by Michael Emberly. The candid, color cartoon drawings include a double-page spread of nudes, demonstrating the varieties of human physiology, and a picture of a couple making love. Emberly also accompanies the text with cartoon characters (a curious bird and an embarrassed bee) that provide relevant and engaging commentary. The text itself addresses all the appropriate issues for middle school children, including the structure of the reproductive system, puberty, and the need for sexual responsibility and respect. Terms such as intercourse, birth, abortion, sexual health, and abuse are examined in detail. The candor and openness of the text and illustrations are intended to help children view sex as a natural part of life. The message to children is that sex comprises many things, not just one. Despite its reasoned, matter-of-fact approach, the book's candor has forced those librarians who acquire it to face frequent challenges. Nonetheless, the review in *Booklist* concludes: "[L]ibrarians will find it well worth fighting for if, by some chance, the need arises."[60]

Selected Challenges, 1996–2000: On May 8, 1996, a committee of teachers, parents, and administrators voted 8–1 to remove *It's Perfectly Normal* from Clover Park (Washington) school district library shelves. Parents had charged that the sex education book was too graphic and could foster more questions than it answers. "I think we always have to make sure that we look at age-appropriateness of materials," said Kathy Lemmer, the district's curriculum director and facilitator for the Instructional Review Committee. "What's available in public libraries is not necessarily the same as in school libraries."[61]

In June 1996, John Chamberlain, a member of the Provo (Utah) library board, was so offended by *It's Perfectly Normal* that he threatened to resign. He said the book should be banned from the children's section because of its graphic illustrations of male and female anatomy, including sex organs, and its discussion of intercourse, masturbation, and homosexuality. Chamberlain was dismayed when library director Julie Farnsworth told him that removal of the book for political, social, or moral reasons was legally prohibited.

At the October 15, 1996, board meeting of the Chester County (Pennsylvania) Library, a group of county residents led by Joan Scalia asked that *It's Perfectly Normal* be removed from the children's section of the library. "The book is an act of encouragement for children to begin desiring sexual gratification, and that's what's causing the degradation of women and men, too," she said. "My own observation is that the book is a clear example of child pornography."[62] Scalia's request followed an earlier demand by Jerry Moore for the removal of *It's Perfectly Normal* and several other titles. Both requests were taken under consideration by the board. At its November meeting, the board heard testimony from county residents who demanded that sexually explicit materials, including *It's Perfectly Normal*, be removed from library shelves or kept in a special adults-only section. Library board chair Judith Shuler concluded, "We will not censor any books or remove any books that are currently in our collection." She cited the library's policy of "independence from undue political intrusion and from any threat of censorship from any source."[63]

On August 20, 1997, the board of trustees of Missouri's Mexico-Audrain County Library voted unanimously to keep *It's Perfectly Normal* in the library's children's section. The Reverend Kevin Weber had asked that the book be removed, but librarian Kurt Lamb said it was written and illustrated for children and was thus appropriately shelved. Weber said he objected not only to *It's Perfectly Normal* but to other books concerning family-sensitive issues such as sexuality, the death of a loved one, or the birth process.

On October 21, 1997, the Fargo (North Dakota) public library board met to consider complaints about *It's Perfectly Normal*. Several parents expressed support for the book, but none of those challenging it spoke at the meeting. The board voted to keep *It's Perfectly Normal* in the library's children's room, but subsequently eight opponents of the book filed statements of concern, saying that the book was sexually explicit, pornographic, and too easily accessible to children.

In May 1999, Carrie Gibson, a parent in Auburn, California, appeared before the county library board to complain about *It's Perfectly Normal* and two other books. In addition to opposing the three particular books, Gibson and other speakers proposed that all books that are "sexually explicit or contain sexual education content" be placed behind the counter for adults only. "We must uphold community standards and make the libraries safe once again for children," said Gibson. The following month, the board voted 5–0 against restricted access to such materials. "The overwhelming majority of the community wants to maintain our library policies of open access," said Director of Library Services Elaine Reed.[64]

In June 2000, the board of trustees of the Holland Public Library in Massachusetts voted to remove *It's Perfectly Normal* from the general collection and relocate it to an adult area. The action followed a meeting at which Reverend Tom Crouse of the Holland Congregational Church charged that the book contained "pictures that are clearly pornographic" and demanded that it be removed from the library. Crouse would later criticize the board's decision to relocate the book, saying, "I wish it were out of the library. I'm definitely not pleased with the town's acceptance of the book. I'm not going to go away on this."[65]

7. **The Color Purple**, by Alice Walker. Harcourt Brace Jovanovich, 1982.

Synopsis and Background: In a story told almost exclusively through the letters of the main character, Celie, and her sister Nettie, *The Color Purple* documents the agonizing struggle and triumph of a black woman over sexist abuse and racist oppression in the Deep South of the 1930s. Fourteen-year-old Celie is raped and twice made pregnant by her stepfather, who warns her to tell no one except God. This begins a series of letters from Celie to God, documenting her pain and struggle. The two sisters, Celie and Nettie, are separated when Nettie is taken from their small southern town to serve as a missionary in Africa. Celie then becomes the child bride of a local widower, beginning a harsh and poverty-stricken marriage. She is sustained only by her continuing letters to God and to her sister Nettie who, in turn, writes back of the brutal colonialism she finds in Africa. Nettie's letters provide the reader with another perspective on the racism and violence Celie endures in the American South. Despite the dreadful circumstances of their youth, Celie and Nettie find joy and beauty that sustain them until their emotional reunion.

Selected Challenges, 1996–2000: At a boisterous meeting held on January

19, 1996, the Round Rock (Texas) Independent School District debated a proposal to remove a dozen books, including *The Color Purple*, from the reading lists at two local high schools. The proposal, made by board member Nelda Click, challenged books that were used in honors or advanced placement courses. Some parents protested the failure of the school system to notify them in advance of offensive material in the books. Other speakers noted that nine of the twelve books challenged by Click were written by minority authors, suggesting a broader agenda to stamp out multicultural curricula. After seven hours of argument, the board voted 4 to 2 against removing the books.

A standing-room-only meeting of the Guilford County (North Carolina) school board decided on February 4, 1997 not to ban *The Color Purple* and *Native Son* from the Advanced Placement English class at Northwest High School. The board also declined to adopt a rating system for school books comparable to that used for motion pictures. Parents Richard and Kathy Penschell said a rating system was necessary to protect their children from books like *The Color Purple*. "You don't have academic freedom with our children," said Richard Penschell. "We never gave it to you."[66] Teacher Sherry Little said she was pleased with the decision to keep the books on her reading list, saying both titles have appeared numerous times on the Advanced Placement Test used for college admission boards.

In November 1997, the Jackson County school board in Ripley, West Virginia, decided to remove seventeen books, including *The Color Purple*, from school libraries. "I do what's best for the kids, not the parents, not the teachers," said board member Happy Joe Parsons, who supported the removal. A few weeks later, the board heard impassioned pleas from students, parents, and teachers to put the books back. The board then voted 3–2 to keep them out of circulation until they could be reviewed. Susan Bowyer, a senior at Ripley High, told board members, "I am appalled by the board's blatant disregard for both county protocol and the law. You simply sat passively allowing one parent to dictate your actions."[67]

On May 18, 1999, the school board in Lima, Ohio, voted unanimously to keep *The Color Purple* in the Shawnee High School English curriculum. Several parents had complained that the book was vulgar and should be removed from the supplemental reading list. A large number of supporters of the book, including parents and current and former students, extolled the book's educational value. Martha Roberts, a 1998 graduate, praised the education she had received and said reading books like *The Color Purple* was an important part of it. "It's not pornographic," she said. "My mind did not go into places of pornography. I was enlightened." After the board's vote, English teacher Kathie Naab said, "I couldn't be happier. We've gone through an awful lot this year from a minute group of parents in comparison to the number of kids we educate."[68]

In July 1999, *The Color Purple* was removed from the library shelves at Ferguson High School in Newport News, Virginia, because of its explicit language. The book, which had been included in the student library collection, was moved to a repository for teachers' textbooks. "I thought because of the sexually explicit language that it would be unsuitable to certain of our students, particularly pre-adolescent or early adolescent students," said principal John Kilpatrick.[69] Students are now required to obtain parental approval before borrowing the book. Kilpatrick said a book review panel had supported his decision to place the book on a restricted list.

On September 29, 2000, an assistant principal at the Mechanicsburg (Pennsylvania) High School stopped students from reading excerpts from banned books during an event celebrating Banned Books Week. Alan Kennedy-Shaffer, a high school junior, complained to the school board that the readings were going smoothly until sophomore Claire Smith read sections from *The Color Purple*. About halfway through the first page, Assistant Principal Dennis Baker stopped the readings. Principal Rick Bollinger said the Pennsylvania School Code allows the district to regulate information distributed to students on school property. He said reading excerpts aloud may infringe on the rights of other students.

8. **My Brother Sam Is Dead**, by James Lincoln Collier and Christopher Collier. Scholastic, 1974.

Synopsis and Background: James Collier is a professional writer with many juvenile titles to his credit; his brother Christopher is a professor of history specializing in the American Revolution. The authors state that the Meeker family depicted in the book is fictitious, but most of the other events and characters are real. The setting for this Newbery Honor Award–winning novel is Redding, Connecticut, during the tense period preceding the bloody American Revolution. Eleven-year-old Tim Meeker has confused loyalties. Although his parents feel no strong loyalty to England's King George III, they are strongly opposed to revolutionary violence. On the other hand, Tim's sixteen-year-old brother Sam is caught up in the clamor for liberation and independence, and he joins the rebel army to serve under Captain Benedict Arnold. Sam later returns to the Meeker home to steal his father's musket, and Tim tries unsuccessfully to talk him out of it. As the violence of the war grows, Tim's father is taken prisoner, and he subsequently dies on a prison ship. Tim becomes sickened by the wanton destruction and death of war. In late 1778, Sam's regiment encamps near Redding, and he steals away from his post to visit his family. Sam is subsequently court-martialed and sentenced to death, and despite pleas for leniency from Tim and his mother, Sam is executed by firing squad. Years later, Tim looks back on the revolution and the way it destroyed his family. We share his doubts about whether the same ends could have been achieved without war.

Selected Challenges, 1996–2000: In April 1996, Marcia Super filed a challenge against *My Brother Sam Is Dead* with the Jefferson County (Colorado) Public Schools, citing twenty-five uses of profanity in the novel. "Students don't have to read stuff like that," said Super. "Don't tell me I'm doing censorship. I'm just asking that what they're doing in the public realm be acceptable to everyone." She said she noticed the language in the book during a visit to her granddaughter's classroom at Stein Elementary School, where fifth-grade students were taking turns reading excerpts from the book to the rest of the class. "Kids probably think it's cool that they get to read swear words in school," said Super.[70]

On September 11, 1996, the Antioch (California) School Board voted to keep *My Brother Sam Is Dead* in its elementary school libraries despite the complaints of parent Judy Nelson about profanity and violence in the Newbery Award–winning novel. Nelson objected to the book after her son, then in the fifth grade, read it in social studies class. In response to the complaint, the school district formed a committee, which subsequently recommended that if the book is read aloud in class, the bad words and the graphic details of two characters' deaths should be left out. Nelson said she wanted the board to go further and remove the book altogether. "I'd never vote to take a book off the shelf," said trustee Rebecca Williams Knapp. "This is the United States. I'm not going to let that happen."[71]

In March 1998, two parents in Staunton, Virginia, objected to the use of *My Brother Sam Is Dead* in fifth-grade classrooms at McSwain Elementary School. Linda Bailey said the book has "a lot of bad language," and she expressed concern that she had not been sent written notice that the book was being used. "I don't think it's appropriate for fifth grade," she said. Beverly Dudley, whose daughter attends McSwain, also found the book's language to be offensive. "I don't think it should be in the schools at all, especially not in elementary schools," she said. "The violence bothers me, but not as much as the language does."[72]

In December 1998, the Hampton (Virginia) school system removed *My Brother Sam Is Dead* from the fifth-grade curriculum after two parents told the school board that "the book uses vulgar and profane language and contains scenes of graphic violence." Parents Michael Harris and Richard Antcliff said the use of words such as "damn," "bastard," and "hell" send a bad message to children. "We obviously have a concern about the decay in the way we speak to one another and express ourselves," said Antcliff. "What we're trying to say is that it's not OK."[73]

In November 1999, concerned parents in Oak Brook, Illinois, asked school board members to remove two books by James and Christopher Collier from the fifth-grade curriculum. Laura Keller told the board that *My Brother Sam Is Dead* is filled with violence and contains too much foul language. Another parent, Debby Stangaroni, said her sixth-grade son was disturbed by the violence in the book. "I don't think it's necessary or appropriate for that grade level," she said.[74]

In June 2000, a parent in the Southern Columbia school district of Pennsylvania complained about "a couple of phrases" in *My Brother Sam Is Dead*. Superintendent Steve Wilcox explained that the district had decided to simply black out those words in most copies of the book. A few copies were not censored in this way and were made available to students whose parents did not object to the language. Curriculum Director Roy Clippinger said that words such as "dammit," "damn you," and "bastard" were crossed out in the books after he and a committee of parents and teachers reviewed the book. "We decided that the swear words really added nothing to the book and really took nothing away from it," said Clippinger.[75]

9. **Kaffir Boy: The True Story of a Black Youth's Coming of Age in Apartheid South Africa,** by Mark Mathabane. Macmillan, 1986.

Synopsis and Background: Mark Mathabane's autobiography *Kaffir Boy* describes his early life in a black ghetto in South Africa during the 1960s and 1970s. Living in a two-room shack without running water, heat, or electricity, Mathabane's family struggles to survive under South Africa's racist apartheid system. The police frequently raid their home, and Mathabane's father is arrested and subjected to forced labor on a white-owned farm. The mother and children are eventually reduced to scavenging for food in garbage dumps. Despite such circumstances, Mathabane's mother is determined that her son should gain an education and have a better life. Mathebane excels in his studies, and, inspired by African American tennis player Arthur Ashe, he also becomes an exceptional tennis player. He participates in protests against apartheid, but he hopes to escape from South Africa entirely by winning a tennis scholarship to an American university. His hopes are fulfilled with the help of American tennis player Stan Smith, whom he meets at a tournament. This inspiring memoir reveals the terrible toll that apartheid wreaked on the lives of South Africa's black majority, but it also celebrates the power of the human spirit to overcome adversity. *Kaffir Boy* has sold over one million copies worldwide, has been translated into twelve languages, and is widely used in high school and university curricula. The American Library Association has chosen it as one of the most important and influential books of its time.

Selected Challenges, 1996–2000: Monique Moore, a sophomore at Smith

High School in Greensboro, North Carolina, was surprised on March 21, 1996, when her teacher told her to turn in one of her favorite books to the school library. Someone had complained about *Kaffir Boy*, and librarians were told to recall all copies and remove them from the shelves pending a review. A school official said the book was pulled after a resident complained that it could encourage young people to assault children. "I was upset," said Monique. "I didn't say anything at the time, but I was upset that they were taking off the shelves such a good book."[76] Other students, parents, and teachers complained as well, and on March 25, a review committee ruled that the book should be returned.

On January 13, 1997, the board of education in Burlington, Connecticut, appeared to violate its own policy when it moved *Kaffir Boy* from the sophomore curriculum to restricted senior use at the Lewis S. Mills High School. The board made the change without having the book reviewed by the curriculum committee as required by board policy. The decision amounted to a ban on the book, which could now be used only if the district created a senior seminar that dealt with sensitive issues. In pointing out the violation of policy, former school board chair Warren Baird said, "The process has been subverted. I ask you to reverse your decision." Students and parents who attended the January board meeting overwhelmingly opposed the board's action. "I think it's censorship and I think it's a way to start abolishing our First Amendment rights to free speech," said sophomore Sarah Hein.[77] At its next meeting, the board agreed to submit the book for review by the curriculum committee.

On March 12, 1997, school trustees in Stockton, California, decided to retain *Kaffir Boy* on a high school sophomore reading list, despite the claims by some parents that the book was pornographic and racially insensitive. The 4–1 vote supported a recommendation by the district's library review board. William Childress had filed a complaint about the book after his daughter brought it home from her tenth-grade English class. "Let us not hold up *Kaffir Boy* as *The Grapes of Wrath*," said Childress. "It is not a classic; it is pornography." Library board members called the book "extremely powerful" and said its "graphic and sensitive nature . . . reflect the gravity and reality of apartheid."[78]

In March 1999, the school board in Athens, Ohio, removed *Kaffir Boy* from class use until a district committee could review its content. District resident Mark Dunfee, a former teacher with no children in district schools, had objected to the book. Board president John Young said that two parents had also requested that their children not read the book, and the school gave those students alternative assignments.

Kearsley (Michigan) High School officials deleted six sentences concerning a homosexual molestation in *Kaffir Boy* after about a half-dozen parents had complained that it was offensive. Parent Lisa Hanson said that the book was more appropriate for an adult book store than a school. In October 1999, a review committee decided to permanently edit out the offending sentences. Kari Molter, chair of the English Department, said, "As an English teacher, I don't like the idea of censorship. I don't like it at all. . . . If we ignore difficult issues, then when [students] do encounter these things in real life, how do they know how to handle it?"[79]

In September 2000, school trustees in Fairfield, California, responded to complaints about two books by proposing a book-rating system similar to that used on motion pictures. The books that caused the commotion were *Kaffir Boy* by Mark Mathabane and *The House of Spirits* by Isabel Allende. Calling the books "immoral and sexually depraved," Cherei Mopas, mother of a fifteen-year-old student, asked that they be removed. "I don't think our students should have to be witness to this type of material," she told the board. The school principal pulled both books from the reading list, in violation of a district policy that requires a special committee to review challenges to the reading curriculum. On December 14, the board voted unanimously to retain the books, but voted 5 to 1 to solicit community input on establishing a book-rating system. "Censorship is a very, very fine line," said board president Gary Falati. "This is America. It's not my position to act as God and tell your children what they should be reading."[80]

10. **The Catcher in the Rye**, by J.D. Salinger. Little, Brown, 1951.

Synopsis and Backgound: When *The Catcher in the Rye* was first published in July 1951, it was simultaneously made available as a Book-of-the-Month Club selection. The book quickly reached number four on the *New York Times* list of best-sellers, and when subsequently released in paperback, it reappeared on the best-sellers list in fifth place among all paperback books. *The Catcher in the Rye* aroused controversy from the beginning, but its sales and curricular appeal continued to climb. The earliest recorded attempts at censorship were in 1954 in Marin County and Los Angeles County, California. In 1955–1956, eight more attempts to ban the book occurred nationwide. A 1961–1962 survey of New York high school librarians and 1963 and 1965 surveys of English teachers in Utah and Arizona found *The Catcher in the Rye* to be their most frequently censored title. Yet a 1962 survey of California English professors showed the book to be their number-one choice to teach to college students.

By 1981 the original edition of the book had been reprinted thirty-five times and the paperback edition fifty-two times, with a total number of copies in excess of 10 million. Indeed, during 1981, *The Catcher in the Rye* had the unusual distinction of being the nation's most frequently censored book and, at the same time, the second-most frequently taught novel in the public schools. What is it about *The Catcher in the Rye* that makes schools and libraries so ambivalent about it? Most of the objections to the book have centered on its profane or vulgar language. A complaining parent in California counted 295 occasions in which God's name was taken in vain; another complainant in Kansas noted 860 obscenities. A parent in Washington counted 785 profanities, including 22 *hells*, 27 *Chrissakes*, 7 *hornys*, as well as numerous *bastards*, *damns*, *craps*, and so on. All this language comes from the adolescent hero of the book, Holden Caulfield. Yet Holden spends much of his time at school trying to wash obscene graffiti off the walls, because he feels younger children should not be exposed to such language.

The book's theme is the difficulty and ambiguity of transition from the world of childhood to adult society. In Holden Caulfield's eyes, childhood is idealistic and innocent, whereas adult society is "phony" and perverted. Holden is a prep school kid who leaves school in anticipation of expulsion, explaining that his nerves were shot. He then takes a train to New York City, where he spends the next forty-eight hours. The book chronicles his aimless activity as he kills time at some local bars, encounters a prostitute, visits his sister, and contacts his favorite teacher from earlier school days. Throughout his meanderings there is a lot of anxious adolescent musing on sex and society, and a lot of doubt expressed about American values. This troubled teenager has grand dreams and idealistic values that overwhelm him. The reader sees Holden as a crazy, mixed-up kid (indeed, the book suggests that he ends up in a mental institution), but we respond favorably to him, perhaps seeing ourselves in him.

The comparison of Holden Caulfield to Huckleberry Finn is inescapable. Both characters hope to escape from a venal and hypocritical society. Holden dreams of hitchhiking west; Huck plans to light out for the "territories." Huck is an alienated fourteen-year-old, and that characterization is surely true of Holden. Both are in idealistic rebellion against and flight from mature society. Huck is thrust into the expansionist nineteenth century; Holden is the prisoner of a contracting twentieth century.

Selected Challenges, 1996–2000: On September 16, 1996, the board of education in Paris, Maine, approved the continued teaching of *The Catcher in the Rye* at Oxford Hills High School, but created procedures to inform parents of the books their children will read. The vote came after an emotional debate over values and censorship among the more than sixty people who turned out for the board's decision. Parent Gary Frechette, who had challenged the book, reiterated his objection to the use of "the 'F' word" in *The Catcher in the Rye*. He said, "Ninety percent of the people I spoke to can't believe these books are being used."[81]

On February 10, 1997, the Glynn County Board of Education in Brunswick, Georgia, decided against removing *The Catcher in the Rye* from required and optional reading lists at the county's two public high schools. The board was considering a protest by eleventh-grader Kimberly Gordon, who objected to the book's profanity and sexual references. She asked that the book be removed from her school's reading list, charging that it lacked literary merit. Board member Chester Taylor, Jr., supported Gordon's complaint and further proposed a ban on classroom discussion of any book deemed offensive by a student. Taylor's motion to remove *The Catcher in the Rye* failed by a 6 to 4 vote.

On April 30, 1997, School Superintendent Peter Pillsbury removed *The Catcher in the Rye* from the required reading curriculum of the Marysville (California) school district. The action was taken despite the recommendation of a review committee that the book be retained in the junior level curriculum. In a press release, Pillsbury explained, "This is not an issue of book banning. Rather, it is an opportunity for parents with varied viewpoints to come together, listen to each other, and define common values." Pillsbury said he had removed *The Catcher in the Rye* to avoid "polarization over a book."[82] The action came after Steve Souza complained of the book's profanity and sexual situations. The school board was planning to hear arguments on whether or not to keep the book, but Pillsbury said the issue would not be put on the agenda.

On March, 13, 2000, *The Catcher in the Rye* narrowly escaped being banned from the Limestone County School District in Alabama. Elkmont High School parent Mike Taylor had told the board that the Lord's name was taken in vain throughout the book, but the school board voted 4 to 3 to retain the book in high school library collections after a committee of parents, students, and teachers judged the book acceptable for students in grades 10 through 12. Elkmont Principal Steve Pettus said, "The parent of one student met with me and met with the teacher with objections to the language used in the book. The child went back and chose to read *To Kill a Mockingbird*. All others in the class read *Catcher in the Rye*."[83]

In November 2000, the Savannah (Georgia) board of education voted initially to block the use of five novels, including *The Catcher in the Rye*, in advanced placement English courses at Windsor Forest High School. Then, just moments later, the board voted 6 to 1 to pass another motion to keep the same books in the curriculum, but to ensure that summer reading lists include at least ten choices and are distributed at least a month before school ends. In this unusual fashion, the books remained available to students.

11. **Daddy's Roommate**, by Michael Willhoite. Alyson Publications, 1990.

Synopsis and Background: One of the earliest books aimed at children with homosexual parents, *Daddy's Roommate* addresses the subject in a straightforward manner. It tells the story of a young son who must adjust to his parents' divorce and to his gay father's new male companion. The boy describes his father's relationship with his roommate, Frank, and his own relationship with the two men. We are told of the normal family activities, shopping, gardening, trips to the zoo, the ball game, the beach, movies, and the like, and the healthy, affectionate bonds that develop between the boy and the adults in his life. The boy concludes that being gay is just one more kind of love. The book delivers the message that alternative lifestyles can be as nurturing as traditional ones. Watercolor illustrations provide a light and attractive tone.

Selected Challenges, 1996–2000: On January 20, 1998, the Hays (Kansas) public library board chose not to remove *Daddy's Roommate*, which had been challenged by Hays resident Denise Chaffin. Chaffin said she objects to the book's representation of the homosexual lifestyle as just another way to show love. But Library Director Melanie Miller said the book met all three of the library's selection criteria: quality, public need, and philosophical balance. "I do not believe in restricting access to those child library patrons who would benefit from the book because there are parents who do not believe that their children should have access to the material," said Miller.[84]

When the Brevard County (Florida) Library Board refused to accede to the demands of a local resident that it remove *Daddy's Roommate* from public library shelves, Coral Lee Craig took matters into her own hands. Throughout 1997 and early 1998, Craig, a member of the Christian Coalition, worked with some of her friends to keep the book in constant circulation and therefore out of hands of those who really wanted it. Craig said she took the action because she felt the book's homosexual themes were inappropriate for children. After Craig's tactics were publicized, the library received a stream of letters protesting the de facto censorship. At least eight copies of the book were subsequently donated to the library.

On July 8, 1999, the Nampa (Idaho) Library Board affirmed the decision of the library staff to keep *Daddy's Roommate* and *Heather Has Two Mommies* in the juvenile nonfiction section. "There are a good number of people who feel the books will be put to good use for children," said Katy Curl, youth services supervisor. "There is no way we can choose a set of books whose content will be accepted by every parent." Nampa resident Joe Gardner, who had submitted a petition asking the library to remove the books from the children's section, expressed disappointment with the board's decision. "In choosing not to act, they've shown they're not open to reasonable debate because the other side screamed censorship and it's clear we're not out for censorship."[85]

On November 17, 2000, the Ada (Idaho) Community Library Board of Trustees refused a patron's request to move *Daddy's Roommate* to the adult section of the library. The board voted 3 to 1 to keep the book in the section on children's social issues. Stephanie Howard of Boise had asked that the book be moved to the adult section or removed from the library altogether. "I didn't want my child to stumble across it like I did," she said. "I'd like it to be in another section where parents have to request it."[86] But the trustees said they wanted to be sure that children who wanted to read the book could find it without asking for help.

On September 26, 2000, a federal judge struck down a Wichita Falls, Texas, "gay books" prohibition stemming from a two-year controversy over *Daddy's Roommate* and *Heather Has Two Mommies*. The books depict children being raised by gay and lesbian parents. City council members had passed a resolution in 1999 setting up a petition system to allow library patrons to remove books from the children's section. Council members said they were offering parents a way to protect their children from written material they might consider unsuitable or inappropriate. But Judge Jerry Buchmeyer said the petition system would allow a few hundred library-card holders to remove a book if they don't like its contents, a clear violation of the First Amendment. The main intent of the petition system was to suppress the two books at the center of the controversy, said Buchmeyer.

12. The House of Spirits, by Isabel Allende. Knopf, 1985.

Synopsis and Background: The House of Spirits is an epic novel spanning most of the twentieth century in an unnamed South American country. It chronicles several generations of the Trueba and del Valle families, focusing on the lives of Clara del Valle and Esteban Trueba, wife and husband. The family saga is narrated through Clara's journals, as presented by her granddaughter Alba. The story is told against the background of political repression and torture, clearly reminiscent of the Pinochet dictatorship in Chile during the 1970s. In the course of the novel, Esteban progresses from conservative landowner to powerful senator, driven by a compulsive desire for wealth and control over others. His success is accomplished at the cost of his relationship with family and tenants. His brutality eventually returns to haunt him as his illegitimate grandson, Esteban Garcia, the product of one of his rapes, becomes a leader in the military regime and arrests his beloved granddaughter Alba, who is then subjected to rape and torture. Alba is the heroic archetype. She has participated in student protests, given food to the poor, and risked her life to secure asylum for refugees fleeing oppression. By the end of the novel, Alba's generosity of spirit has led even her conservative grandfather to reconsider his support for the military dictatorship. The author employs the literary style of "magical realism" to present fantastic events through objective and realistic narration. For example, the deceased Clara visits Alba in the solitary confinement of the concentration camp, inspiring her to transcend hunger and pain by writing stories in her mind. Alba's narration exposes horror and brutality while suggesting hope for the future.

Selected Challenges, 1996–2000: On January 14, 1998, the school board in Prince William County, Virginia voted to keep *The House of Spirits* in the county's high school curriculum. The book had been attacked by some parents for its sexually explicit and violent passages. The board's vote completed a four-step process that began in September 1997 when high school student Amy Smelser and her parents objected to the book. Jeff Smelser, Amy's father and a local minister, went to the high school parking lot and distributed a packet of excerpts from *The House of Spirits* with the heading: "Would you allow your 16-year-old daughter to read this material? And if not, why should the public school be allowed to *require* my 16-year-old daughter to read this material?"[87]

When Christine Schwalm, a parent in Montgomery County, Maryland, filed charges with county police against the school superintendent because he allowed student access to *The House of Spirits* and four other books, the board of education promptly met to consider removing the books. Board president Nancy King said she was disturbed by excerpts from *The House of Spirits* and another book, *One Hundred Years of Solitude*. At the February 10, 1998, board meeting, Mrs. Schwalm read excerpts from the five books, including a passage from *The House of Spirits* in which a young medical student kisses a female corpse. Schwalm criticized the character of school officials for allowing such books in the schools. "How can this body propose teaching character education to students when the educators are morally challenged, lack character and act in an irresponsible manner?" she asked.[88]

In August 1999, parents at La Costa Canyon High School in Encinatas, California, requested that the school board remove *The House of Spirits* from the English curriculum, claiming that the novel contains pornographic passages. Ann and Tom McGinnis said the sexually explicit passages and profanity degraded women, offended Christians, and promoted intolerance. "I don't want the book censored and I do not question the literary value of the book or the author," said Ann McGinnis. "But there are other books out there that are more age appropriate and do not defame the faith."[89] A review committee recommended that the book be retained with certain restrictions applied.

In September 2000, the principal of a high school in Fairfield, California, pulled two books, *The House of Spirits* and *Kaffir Boy*, from the school's required reading list after parents protested passages depicting violence and sexual abuse. The principal's action violated district policy, which requires a review committee to decide on challenges. School board members Ivan Meadows and Robert Patillo supported the principal's decision and suggested a ratings system for books similar to that used for movies. "We need to do a better job of making sure parents are aware of the contents," said Meadows. "We really are trying to be more parent-friendly."[90] Though Meadows and Patillo said that *The House of Spirits* was inappropriate for high school sophomores, they insisted that this was not censorship or bookbanning. They said it was just part of giving parents a say in what their children read. On December 14, the board voted unanimously to retain both books, but also voted to solicit community input in establishing a rating system.

13. **Native Son**, by Richard Wright. Harper, 1940.

Synopsis and Background: Native Son, which appeared in 1940, immediately established Richard Wright as an important literary figure and as a commentator on the social and political problems of African Americans. Wright was born on a Mississippi plantation and grew up in poverty. He attended school sporadically, but was an avid reader and was given an opportunity to write by the New Deal's Federal Writers' Project. He wrote leftist poetry for a number of journals, and in 1937 became editor of the *Daily Worker*. *Native Son* became an explosive best-seller in 1940, selling 215,000 copies in the first three weeks. A stage adaptation of the novel, directed by Orson Welles, ran on Broadway from 1941 to 1943. During the 1950s, Cold War hysteria and McCarthyism diminished the popularity of *Native Son*, but the novel has surmounted politics to gain a place among America's most esteemed literary works.

Many readers saw Bigger Thomas, the central character in *Native Son*, as a symbol of the entire black community. Bigger is a young black man who is hired by a wealthy Chicago family as their chauffeur. One night, the family's daughter, Mary, has too much to drink, and Bigger carries her back to her room. While he is putting her to bed, Mary's mother unexpectedly calls to her, and the frightened Bigger puts a pillow over her head to keep her quiet, accidentally smothering her. In a panic, he attempts to implicate Mary's communist boyfriend and then flees. While hiding from the police, Bigger's paranoia leads him to kill his own girlfriend. He is eventually convicted of murder and sentenced to death. While in prison, he realizes the need for a common brotherhood. The final section of the book features a speech by Boris Max, a communist party attorney defending Bigger. The speech, derived in part from Clarence Darrow's defense of Leopold and Loeb, conveys a Marxist assessment of racism in the United States.

Selected Challenges, 1996–2000: On January 19, 1996, the Round Rock (Texas) Independent School District board argued until 2:30 A.M. over a proposal to remove a dozen books, including *Native Son*, from reading lists at Westwood and McNeil high schools. The proposal had been introduced by board member Nelda Click, who claimed that the books contained too much violence. Other parents complained that the system fails to warn them in advance of books containing offensive material. After seven hours of debate, the board voted 4 to 2 against banning the books.

On February 4, 1997, the Guilford County (North Carolina) School Board decided not to ban *Native Son* and another book from an advanced placement English class at Northwest High School. Parents Richard and Kathy Penschell not only wanted the books banned, but asked for a book rating system to guarantee that such books would not be acquired in the future. Though some board members found parts of the books offensive, they decided that neither a ban nor a ratings system was justified. English teacher Sherry Little, who had assigned the books in her class, said, "I chose these books because they speak to the students in a powerful way."[91]

In May 1998, school officials in Fremont, California, removed 150 copies of *Native Son* from Irvington High School after a few parents complained that the novel was unnecessarily violent and sexually explicit. Beverly Shaw, Fremont's coordinator for instructional materials, said she pulled the books to avoid controversy. The district planned to replace the copies with an abridged version that eliminates most of the graphic passages. "Taking away the unabridged version was wrong," said senior Michelle Jackson. "The parts they want to take away are the parts that opened my eyes most." Another senior, Kristen Evans, complained, "It seems to me that the district is trying to make life sugary sweet by taking out the sex and violence. But life is harder than it's ever been for us teenagers. We see violence every day."[92]

High school students in Fort Wayne, Indiana, had been reading *Native Son* for several years without complaint until November 23, 1998, when attorney Danny Williams brought photocopied excerpts of two passages to a school board meeting. Williams complained about graphic language and sexual content, citing descriptions of masturbation and the dismemberment of a body. Williams also spoke to his daughter's teacher, who agreed to allow her to read another book.

14. **Fallen Angels**, by Walter Myers. Scholastic, 1988.
Synopsis and Background: In one of the few teenage novels about the Vietnam War, Walter Myers tells the painful story of seventeen-year-old Richie Perry. Though the newspapers are filled with stories on the peace talks, Richie, like many others around him, decides to enlist in the army, not so much to defend his country as to escape the Harlem ghetto. He has no idea of what awaits him overseas, where the war will quickly dissolve his youth and test his sanity. Later, he will write from Vietnam, "We're all dead over here. . . . We're all dead and just hoping we come

back to life." The novel shows how the tension and tedium of war breed violence even among comrades, black against white, black against black, white against white. The eventual terror of battle reveals heroism and cowardice, causing young soldiers to question their ideals, their religious beliefs, and their morality. The descriptions of the action are shocking and explicit, and the language is realistic. The social issues of the day— antiwar sentiment, draft dodgers, drug abuse—are also woven into the plot.

Selected Challenges, 1996–2000: In June 1996, review committees in Lakewood, Ohio, upheld the use of *Fallen Angels* and another book at Lakewood High School. The books, which are used in tenth-grade English classes, were challenged by parents who objected to what they called violence and vulgar language.

In May 1999, the Laton (California) school board banned the award-winning book *Fallen Angels* and another book from high school English classes. The book, which won the 1989 Coretta Scott King award, was removed from eleventh- and twelfth-grade English classes. Expressing concern about profanity in *Fallen Angels* and other titles used by the school, the board also formed a review committee to examine all books on the district's core curriculum list to make sure they met standards acceptable to the community.

Fallen Angels was removed from the curriculum in Livonia (Michigan) public schools in August 1999 after parents complained that it contained too many swear words. The book will remain on the school library shelves, but may no longer be taught in the classroom. The original parental complaint cited more than 300 vulgarities in the 261-page book. "I've read it. It's a filthy book," said trustee Daniel Lessard. "I think the language portrays what went on in Vietnam very accurately. But I don't think we should require a 14-year-old to read it."[93]

In April 2000, a parent in Arlington, Texas, complained that the content of *Fallen Angels* was too strong for students at Boles Junior High School. After a review committee recommended retaining the book in local school libraries, a special school board meeting was called to make a final judgment. Most board members said they understood parental concerns about the novel, but concluded that a recent district court ruling prevented them from removing the book. They voted unanimously to keep the book on the shelves of the district's junior high school libraries. Trustee Jim Ash explained, "There is no wiggle room. We are created to uphold the law."[94]

15. Beloved, by Toni Morrison. Knopf, 1987.

Synopsis and Background: When Toni Morrison wrote her fifth novel, *Beloved*, a disturbing tale of the horrors of slavery in America, she was sure it would be the least read of her books. To her surprise, *Beloved* became a best-seller, earning her critical acclaim and a wide readership. The book is dedicated to "sixty million and more," the estimated number of Africans who died on or en route to slave slips. The story is set in the years surrounding the Civil War. Its central character, Sethe, was inspired by a real fugitive slave, Margaret Garner, whose tragic story was discovered by Morrison while she edited *The Black Book* for Random House. When pursued and faced with re-enslavement, the fugitive Garner killed one of her own children, rather than have the child forced back into slavery. Though Morrison includes this act of brutal desperation in telling Sethe's tale, she avoids reliance on further historical details, explaining, "I wanted to invent her life."[95] The novel begins several years after Sethe killed her daughter. Sethe has been ostracized, forced to live an isolated existence shared only by her remaining daughter and a ghost that haunts the house they live in. A character named Paul D., who had toiled with Sethe at the "Sweet Home" plantation, enters her life and drives out the ghost that haunts her house. But another spirit, named Beloved, soon comes to possess the house and its inhabitants, who conclude that it is the ghost of the murdered child. The ghostly Beloved is a mysterious, childlike young woman who also seems to be the embodiment of a slave ship survivor. Morrison says Beloved bridges "the gap between Africa and Afro-America and the gap between the living and the dead and the gap between the past and the present."[96] The novel argues that only by sharing their dreadful experiences will the characters be able to purge their guilt and discover their personal worth.

Selected Challenges, 1996–2000: On January 19, 1996, the Round Rock (Texas) Independent School District board began a debate over banning a dozen books, including *Beloved*. The emotional debate, which would last until the early morning hours, was the result of a proposal by board member Nelda Click, which would remove the books from the advanced placement reading lists at Westwood and McNeil high schools. Some parents complained of excessive violence in the books. Others noted that nine of the twelve challenged books had minority authors, suggesting a broader attack on multiculturalism. "It's a concerted attempt to eliminate studies of communities or ethnicities that are different than what they grew up with," said Cecile Richards, president of the Texas Freedom Network, a statewide group formed to counter religious fundamentalism in public education. After seven hours of debate, the board voted 4 to 2 to keep the books in the curriculum.[97]

At a September 1997 school committee meeting in Madawaska, Maine, *Beloved* was officially challenged by committee member Bert LaChance, who read a passage from the book containing language that he said local students would be punished for using. "We don't need books like this in our school," he said. LaChance acknowledged that he had not read the whole book, but said the selected passage was enough for him to know that it should be removed from the high school's advanced placement English class. Superintendent Tom Scott responded, "This is a college level course, and [the students] should be expected to read college level materials. There is no doubt Toni Morrison is one of America's premier writers."[98]

On March 3, 1998, the Sarasota (Florida) County School Board reiterated its decision to restrict but not ban the controversial novel *Beloved*. County resident David Farabee, complaining of the sexual content of the novel, had asked the board to reconsider its earlier decision allowing parents to select an alternative assignment if they object to the book. Farabee said such an arrangement did not resolve the problem, and he urged the board to ban the book altogether.

In May 1998, the Anaheim (California) Union High School rejected adding the Pulitzer Prize–winning novel *Beloved* to the core reading list for twelfth-grade English classes. Despite positive recommendations from a committee of parents and teachers, the trustees voted 4 to 1 against adopting the novel, citing violent and graphic passages. "I cannot, as a parent and former educator, approve adopting this book," said trustee Molly McGee. "This is not in the best interest of the students."[99] The book had been tested in one classroom during the year and was recommended for adoption by the teachers.

16. *Goosebumps* Series, by R.L. Stine. London, Hippo, 1994–

Synopsis and Background: Author R.L. Stine produces a new *Goosebumps* title every few weeks, and the consistent format followed by the series makes virtually any title as likely to be censored as any other title. Stine, whose full name is Robert Lawrence Stine, began *Goosebumps* as a children's sequel to his already popular young adult horror series *Fear Street*. Stine says it takes him about ten days to write a *Fear Street* book and just eight days for a *Goosebumps* title. The first *Goosebumps* title, *Welcome to Dead House*, written in a little over ten days, was an immediate success, and *Goosebumps* subsequently became the best-selling book series of all time. Its success has spawned a TV series, home videos, T-shirts, games, puzzles, and numerous other spinoff products. Perhaps the most famous *Goosebumps* book was *The Haunted Mask*, the first title in the series to be made into a TV show. In that show a young girl wears a haunted mask when she goes trick-or-treating. She soon discovers that she cannot remove the mask, and it begins to control her behavior. Another popular title within the series is the *Night of the Living Dummy* set, consisting of three books about ventriloquist dummies that come to life. Stine characterizes the *Goosebumps* series as "scary books that are also funny." He says, "I wanted *Goosebumps* to have the same kind of feeling you get on a roller-coaster ride. Lots of thrills. Lots of wild twists and turns. And a feeling of being safe the whole time."[100]

Selected Challenges, 1996–2000: In March 1996, Kip and Lisa Clinton requested that all *Goosebumps* books be banned from Bay County (Florida) elementary schools after a teacher at Highland Park Elementary School read one of them to their daughter's third-grade class. The Clintons cited numerous complaints with the books, including satanic symbolism, spells, chants, and demonic possession. A review committee was formed to examine all forty-three titles then in the series. Loretta Hughhins, who chaired the committee, admitted that the *Goosebumps* books were not high-quality literature, but said they inspired many students to read regularly. On May 2, the school board unanimously adopted the committee's recommendation that the books be retained in the school's media centers and that teachers retain the right to read from them in their classes.

At the December 1996 school board meeting in Parks, Arizona, former board member Zane Morris protested the banning of the *Goosebumps* books and another series by R.L. Stine. When Morris referred to a board policy specifying opposition to censorship, President Clara Pirtle said she was not aware that the policy existed. The parents of a fourth-grader had complained that he had a nightmare as the result of reading one of the books, and the superintendent promptly removed the books from the library shelves. When a parent-teacher organization expressed concern about censorship of the books, the board announced a restriction whereby only third- through sixth-grade students could charge the books out of the school library.

After meeting for almost six hours on February 3, 1997, the Anoka-Hennepin (Minnesota) school district rejected a mother's request that some of the *Goosebumps* books be banned from the district. A district committee unanimously decided that the books offer too many educational benefits to justify removing them from library shelves. Margaret Byron, who complained that the books were too frightening for children and inappropriate for school libraries, said she was disappointed at the committee's decision. "I wish they had at least put parental restrictions on them," she said. The report of the eight-member committee, which included parents and school employees, said the books are age-appropriate, "providing chills which are manageable; they allow a child to work out his or her own strategy for dealing with the possibility of real threat."[101] The panel said the series builds fluency in reading with simple vocabulary, repetitive plot patterns, imaginative content, and satisfactory conclusions.

The *Goosebumps* series was submitted to a review committee by the school board in Hernando, Mississippi, on January 15, 1997, after board member Darrell Hopper questioned their use in an accelerated reading program at a local elementary school. Hopper said the *Goosebumps* books desensitize students to violence. At the February board meeting, a large group of parents and students opposed the board's action. Parent Kelly Jacobs said the board did not follow its own procedure, because no parent had complained about the book. Jacobs said the board was acting as a censor by telling the school that it would only receive money for its accelerated reading program if it removed *Goosebumps*.

17. **Snow Falling on Cedars**, by David Guterson. Harcourt Brace, 1994.

Synopsis and Background: Snow Falling on Cedars was named 1995 book of the year by the American Booksellers Association and won the PEN/Faulkner award. The plot of the book revolves around a murder trial, but the testimony of each witness is transformed by intricate flashbacks into complex historical narrative. In 1954, a fisherman named Carl Heine is found drowned in the waters off San Piedro Island in Puget Sound, his body entangled in his boat's fishing net. A fisherman of Japanese descent, Kabuo Miyomoto, is subsequently put on trial for murder. Miyomoto's apparent motive dates back to 1942, when he and the rest of San Piedro's Japanese population were herded off to a California internment camp. At that time, Miyomoto's parents had almost paid off their mortgage on a strawberry farm bought from Heine's parents, but due to Miyomoto's internment, the farm reverts to Heine. Miyomoto's obsession with regaining his farm combines with a network of circumstances to tie him to the murder, but the reader has a strong impression that he is on trial because he is Japanese. Reporter Ishmael Chambers, a former marine who lost his arm fighting the Japanese in Tarawa, covers the trial for San Piedro's newspaper. Through a series of flashbacks, the reader discovers that Ishmael and Miyomoto's wife, Hatsue, were high school sweethearts back in 1941. Their bitter separation by war and internment turned Ishmael's love into hate. Against this backdrop, Guterson leads us through the mystery and its eventual resolution. In the process, Guterson asks: How can apparently good people in a tightly knit community be torn apart by racism? That question remains unanswered even after the murder mystery is solved.

Selected Challenges, 1996–2000: On June 11, 1997, the Snohomish (Washington) school board heard a spirited debate over *Snow Falling on Cedars*. A group of local parents urged the board to keep the novel on the high school required reading list, saying it was a powerful contemporary work with wonderful insights into Pacific Northwest history. A school committee had earlier recommended that the book be maintained on reading lists for English and American literature honor students, but a group of parents appealed the committee's decision. The complaining parents argued that the book's description of sexual intercourse and its use of obscene language made it inappropriate for high school students. Philip Bastian, who originally raised the issue, said, "While the book may have certain literary qualities, we believe those qualities are outweighed by the repeated references to graphic sex, human genitals and obscenities, which we find to be offensive, objectionable and inappropriate for students."[102]

In September 1999, *Snow Falling on Cedars* was banned from the Boerne (Texas) High School library. School Superintendent John Kelly said passages from the book were "highly offensive" and ordered the novel pulled from the shelves. Principal Sam Champion said that teacher Frances Riley had shown "poor judgement" in assigning the book to her senior English class. After the censorship incident attracted national media attention, school trustees voted 5 to 2 to return the book to the library, though its use was prohibited in the classroom. School board president DeeAnn Wilson emphasized "the difference between mandatory reading, as curriculum, versus the choice to check the book out of the library." School Superintendent John Kelly said, "The board felt that absent a formal protest against the book that is successful, that the book should remain in the library."[103] The Texas Federation of Teachers said it would challenge the reprimand issued to Riley, who had permission to use the book.

In May 2000, the school board in Orchard, Washington, restricted access to *Snow Falling on Cedars* after critics complained about sexual content and profanity. "The book is extremely vulgar," said parent Doug Bean, who addressed the board. "This book doesn't teach respect, it teaches self-indulgence." Supporters of the book told the board of its historic and moral lessons, and warned against banning it. "This shows that the district is not serious about teaching racial tolerance," said Sheldon Levin.[104] The board heard testimony for and against the book from nearly fifty people, and then voted 3 to 2 not to include the book on the district's approved reading list for high school students. In taking its action, the board ignored the advice of committees at the high school and district levels, all of which recommended including the novel on the reading list.

18. **We All Fall Down**, by Robert Cormier. Dell, 1991.

Synopsis and Background: In *We All Fall Down*, Robert Cormier once more presents a dark tale in which failure and defeat are more common than victory. Jane Jerome and her family come home to discover that vandals have destroyed their possessions, urinated on the walls, and left fourteen-year-old Karen in a coma. A deranged neighbor who calls himself "The Avenger" witnessed the break-in by four teenagers and secretly vows to track down them down. Meanwhile, Jane slowly overcomes the fears that descended upon her after the break-in. She meets and falls in love with Buddy Walker. What she doesn't know is that he was one of the group that trashed her home. The Avenger sees the two of them together, recognizes Buddy as one of the trashers, and devises a bizarre plan. He lures Jane into an empty building, ties her up, tells her about Buddy, and then commits suicide at her feet. In the aftermath of the horrible experience, Jane retreats into emotional numbness, her love for Buddy transformed into pity and contempt. Despite the violent theme, the novel is essentially moral, leaving the reader to reflect on issues like broken families, personal responsibility, violence, and guilt.

Selected Challenges, 1996–2000: In March 2000, *We All Fall Down* was removed from the Carver Middle School in Leesburg, Florida, after Lynne and David Kern, parents of a sixth-grader, complained about its language. Lynne Kern said her daughter showed her the novel and said, "Mommy, this book has cuss words in it." David Kern said, "It's not a book for school. It's everything negative about society, like rape, vulgarity, alcohol abuse, murder and how to cover it up." Principal Charles McDaniel agreed and ordered the book removed from the school library. "It's something I wouldn't want my children to read," he said. "I held a faculty meeting and advised them to look carefully at our books. I have also e-mailed the other middle schools concerning the book. . . . We are not going into the book-burning business, but if a book is challenged, we may pull it off the shelves."[105]

On March 17, 2000, Arlington (Texas) Independent School District Superintendent Mac Bernd ordered the library circulation of *We All Fall Down* to be restricted to students who have their parents' written permission to borrow it. His action came in response to a complaint from parent Donna Harkreader and in spite of a decision by a panel of school librarians to retain it in middle and high schools. Harkreader's objection centered on violence in the book. Bernd explained, "It came down to a decision of age-appropriateness." Author Robert Cormier defended his book, saying that controversial materials belong in the classroom so that teachers can "guide [students] in their understanding of the issues."[106]

When parents in the Tamaqua (Pennsylvania) school district complained to the school board in November 2000 about *We All Fall Down* and two other books, school officials agreed to create a new book-selection policy. The parents objected to several violent scenes and a description of a suicide in *We All Fall Down*. School director Robert Betz said, "We're walking a fine line here between appropriateness and censorship. I'm not sure there is an easy answer."[107]

19. Go Ask Alice, by Anonymous. Prentice-Hall, 1971.

Synopsis and Background: Go Ask Alice is a novel said to be based on the actual diary of a fifteen-year-old drug user who is identified only as

"Anonymous" by the publisher. The author/narrator, the daughter of a college professor, is quickly seen to have low self-esteem. She is dissatisfied with her appearance, feels she is fat, dislikes her hair and the condition of her skin, and has just broken up with her boyfriend. During a boring summer, she attends a party at which her cola is spiked with LSD. This first experience with drugs leads her to marijuana, amphetamines, and even her grandmother's sleeping pills. She eventually becomes involved with a college student who convinces her to sell pot, LSD, and barbiturates to not only high school students but grade school students as well. After she breaks up with her boyfriend, she runs away to San Francisco where she becomes addicted to heroin. After being brutally sexually abused, she returns to her parents' home. She is eventually sent to a psychiatrist to help her deal with drug abuse, but she soon runs away once more. The sordid circumstances there lead her to return once more to her parents, and this time she makes a valiant effort to end her addiction, though her former friends do everything they can to prevent her success. While babysitting, she unknowingly consumes some candy that has been laced with LSD, and her reaction results in her placement in a mental institution. Upon her release, she seems confident that she has finally overcome her drug habit, and the final entries in her diary are optimistic. However, an afterword to the book states that just three weeks later she is found dead of a drug overdose.

Selected Challenges, 1996–2000: When principal Raymond Cabral received a parent's oral complaint about *Go Ask Alice* on June 3, 1998, he immediately confiscated all copies of the book from the class that was using them at Tiverton (Rhode Island) Middle School. The book was being used as part of the eighth-grade curriculum when the parent complained about language in the book that referred to the male anatomy. Principal Cabral failed to follow school policy, which requires a parent to file a written complaint and meet with the principal, school librarian, and teacher. The material must then be reviewed by a committee, which sends a recommendation for its approval or rejection to the superintendent. None of these procedures was followed, causing School Superintendent Robert Terrill to return the book to the school.

On June 14, 1999, the Aledo (Texas) School Board voted 3 to 1 to remove *Go Ask Alice* from the middle school library. The board agreed to keep the book in the high school library, but even there students must have parental permission to check it out. The vote was the result of an anonymous parental complaint. Board president Steve Reid, who advocates removing *Go Ask Alice* from the high school library as well, said the parent complained that her daughter had been upset about the book's vulgar language, descriptions of sex, and references to drug use. "What purpose does this book serve in a learning environment?" said Reid. "I'm going to have a hard time being sold that this is a book for learning."[108] Like most of the trustees who voted against the book, Reid had not read it and said he had no intention of doing so.

In February 2000, Diana Cousins, a grandmother of an eighth-grader in Girard, Pennsylvania, complained to the local school board about five books and expressed particular concern about *Go Ask Alice*. She learned about the books after her granddaughter opted to read *Go Ask Alice* for her class. Cousins objected to the book's treatment of sex, drugs, and masturbation. In a March 3 response to Cousins, Girard Schools superintendent Walter Blucas noted that *Go Ask Alice* was one title among many that students could choose from in a reading class. Blucas said, "The board did not wish to employ censorship on these materials." Still, Cousins insisted that "it shouldn't be offered to kids at that age."[109]

20. **Bless Me, Ultima**, by Rudolfo Anaya. Quinto Sol Publications, 1972.

Synopsis and Background: Author Rudolfo Anaya grew up in a small town in New Mexico, where he listened to the magical stories ("cuentos") that the old people told, leading him to a love of books. In *Bless Me, Ultima*, Anaya's first novel, his main character and narrator is Antonio, a young boy who calls books the "magic of words." Antonio tells of his experiences with his family and friends, his schooling, and his special relationship with Ultima, a *curandera* (curer) who comes to live with his family. Anaya weaves myth and legend into his tale of family life and follows Antonio's spiritual quest to reconcile the existence of evil with God. In this process, Antonio learns of the existence of other gods and forces such as sorcery. The book is a candid portrayal of small town Chicano life. As such, it contains some expletives (mostly in Spanish), but it reflects the pride and dignity of Chicano life. Anaya has been a prominent spokesperson for Chicano literature for years. He says, "Even my 'non-political' novel, *Bless Me, Ultima*, has moved people to explore the roots of their agrarian, Mexicano way of life. And the healing work of Ultima, a curandera, illustrated to my generation some of our wholistic, Native American inheritance."[110]

Selected Challenges, 1996–2000: On January 19, 1996, the Round Rock (Texas) Independent School District board heard seven hours of boisterous debate over a proposal to remove a dozen books, including *Bless Me, Ultima*, from local high school reading lists. The proposal, introduced by board member Nelda Click, would drop the books from the advanced placement reading lists at Westwood and McNeil high schools. Some parents and school officials had charged that the books contained excessive violence. The board eventually voted 4 to 2 against the book ban, but did accept a proposal by Superintendent Tom Norris to create a curriculum council to prepare a new policy for selecting reading material.

In May 1999, the Laton (California) school board removed *Bless Me, Ultima* and another book from high school English classes, expressing concern that they contained violence and profanity that might harm students. "What we're trying to do is protect the children," said board member Jerry Haroldsen. "And you've got a teacher that's trying to do what we think is not right."[111] The teacher, Carol Bennett, was using *Bless Me, Ultima* in her ninth-grade English classes when parents of some of her students complained to board members. The books were promptly pulled from the classes, and the principal was ordered to collect all copies of the book and store them in his office.

When Deidra DiMaso read *Bless Me, Ultima* to her two daughters, she was shocked by the language. The book was being studied by ninth-graders at John Jay High School in Wappingers Falls, New York. DiMaso contacted school and district administrators and went to a school board meeting in November 2000 where she urged the board to pull the book from the curriculum. "This book is full of sex and cursing," she later explained. "I asked the board members to please review all the books for any sexual content, violence or foul language prior to any book becoming required reading." Student Geoff Aung said, "It would disappoint me if the book is taken out of the curriculum, especially if it's just because of one parent." Superintendent Wayne Gersen said the district would follow its standard policy for dealing with challenged materials.[112]

21. **The Handmaid's Tale**, by Margaret Atwood. Fawcett, 1986.

Synopsis and Background: Like the modern classics *Brave New World* and *1984*, this novel suggests that a very grim future may follow from our present way of life. The author presents a haunting vision of an American society dominated by a highly ritualized, tyrannical religious cult that controls human reproduction throughout the nation. In this society, civilization has been threatened and distorted by the effects of nuclear accidents and toxic wastes, resulting in lowered birthrates, birth defects, widespread sterility, diseases, and death. The main character in the story is Offred, who is forced to serve as a "handmaid" in this stark new order, bearing children for infertile couples within society's ruling hierarchy. Offred narrates the story, alternating descriptions of her dreadful life with flashbacks to a time when she was a young working woman with a loving husband and a child. This riveting and believable story of a woman's struggle for personal freedom has implications for the role of women in modern society.

Selected Challenges, 1996–2000: In September 1998, the Richland (Washington) school board approved a list of eighty-four novels for use in high school English classes after public comment and review. However, two Richland residents, Karen Batishko and Teri Sharp, asked the board to remove *The Handmaid's Tale* and six other books from the list. Batishko and Sharp complained that the books stressed suicide, illicit sex, violence, and hopelessness. Under district policy, the principals must review the books with teachers and then forward comments to the curriculum director, after which a review committee considers the complaint and makes a decision.

Kathy Jones, a parent and social studies teacher at Chamberlain High School in Tampa, Florida, asked for a review of *The Handmaid's Tale* in May 1999 after her daughter had read the book for teacher John Fairweather's English class and complained of sexually graphic passages. This unusual dispute between two high school teachers was resolved by a school committee, which decided to keep the book on the school's reading list. The committee decided unanimously that the book was a suitable choice for advanced placement English classes. "It was the excellence of the book; it was beautifully written," said media specialist Liz Griffin in explaining the committee's decision.[113]

A Handmaid's Tale was required reading for nearly all eleventh-graders at Upper Moreland (Pennsylvania) High School until the wife of a school board member complained in June 2000 that the book was "age-inappropriate." Parents were then sent a list of alternative books that students could read instead of *The Handmaid's Tale*. Sherry Eichert, wife of board president Ed Eichert, persuaded the school administration to make the change after speaking with several parents who opposed the book. Eichert likened some passages of the book to pornography and said that students who are not in the honors English program might not understand the book's ironic tone. School board president Emily Graupner added, "The book runs far afield from the habits and mores of this community."[114]

22. The Bluest Eye, by Toni Morrison. Knopf, 1993, c1970.

Synopsis and Background: Toni Morrison has stated, "I suppose *The Bluest Eye* is about one's dependency on the world for identification, self-value, feelings of worth."[115] The main character of the novel is eleven-year-old Pecola Breedlove, a black child who is thwarted at every attempt to discover her own identity. Her greatest desire is to have blue eyes, which she feels will make her pretty and thus valued by others. Her real life is desperate and sordid. In her adolescence, she is raped by her father and bears a stillborn child. She drifts into a madness in which she believes that she has magically been given blue eyes. Her ultimate fate is life on the fringes of society, picking through garbage cans to sustain herself. The novel's early action is narrated by nine-year-old Claudia MacTeer, whose family has sheltered Pecola after her house has been burned down. Claudia and her sister Frieda become the only friends Pecola will ever have. They share gender, age, race, poverty, and ignorance, but what distinguishes them is that Claudia and her sister are confident of their parents' love, whereas Pecola is not. This emotional security allows Claudia to find her black identity in a white society. As narrator of Pecola's tragic tale of dependence and subservience, Claudia comes to a greater understanding of herself and her community.

Selected Challenges, 1996–2000: On February 10, 1998, the mother of a high school student in Montgomery County, Maryland, told the board of education that *The Bluest Eye* and four other books used in the county school system should be removed because they were at odds with the character education program taught in the schools. "I am sickened knowing that my tax dollars are being used to provide children with—and instruct them in using—lewd, adult books," said Christine Schwalm. In her presentation to the board, Mrs. Schwalm read one passage from each of the challenged books to demonstrate that they were inappropriate for high school students. The passage from *The Bluest Eye* described a preacher turned pedophile who molests children after luring them with ice cream.[116]

In March 1999, the school board in Baker City, Oregon, upheld Superintendent Arnold Coe's decision to remove *The Bluest Eye* and another novel from the Baker High School language arts program. The two novels were contained in the anthology *Seven Contemporary Short Novels*. The issue arose after parental complaints were received by the board, including one about a section in *The Bluest Eye* that describes a father raping his eleven-year-old daughter.

In June 1999, a review committee at a high school in Claremont, New Hampshire, ruled that *The Bluest Eye* was unsuitable reading for any student other than juniors or seniors. Joane Gaudette, mother of a ninth-grader who was assigned the book, said she would have preferred stronger action against the book. The school committee also decided to require teachers to send reading lists to parents early in the year so that they can decide if their children should be allowed to participate in discussions or assignments using books on the list.

23. **Flowers for Algernon**, by Daniel Keyes. Harcourt Brace, 1966.

Synopsis and Background: Flowers for Algernon is unique among the titles in our banned book list for its ever-changing literary manifestations, beginning in 1959 as a short story in a science fiction magazine, then appearing as a novelette in 1960, then as a television play, an expanded novel in 1966, and finally in 1968 as an acclaimed motion picture. Its television and film productions used different titles *The Two Worlds of Charlie Gordon* and *Charlie*, respectively. Though the story was originally written for a science fiction audience, it is a personal drama that relies on fantasy only to the extent that it assumes the existence of an experimental medical procedure that can turn a retarded person into a genius. Within this setting, the plot follows the dramatic intellectual and emotional journey of Charlie Gordon from a kind but slow-witted man to a supremely arrogant prodigy and then back again, as the medical procedure used on Charlie turns out to be temporary. In Charlie's original state, he was unable to discern the disdain with which his apparent friends treated him, but during his brief period of brilliance he sees those friends for what they are: mean spirited and rather dull. At the end of the novel, though Charlie has regressed to his retarded state, he retains an almost patronizing attitude toward those around him. In his childlike scrawl, he writes in his diary: "Everybody looked at me when I came downstairs and started working in the toilet sweeping it out like I use to do. I said to myself Charlie if they make fun of you don't get sore because you remember their not so smart like you once thot they were."[117]

Selected Challenges, 1996–2000: On February 26, 1996, the York County School Board in Yorktown, Virginia, rejected a couple's request that *Flowers for Algernon* be removed from a middle school reading list because of the novel's profanity and references to sex and drinking. The board voted unanimously to retain the book as part of the language arts curriculum. John and Tracey Crawley had requested the book's removal after their thirteen-year-old son, who attends Yorktown Middle School, expressed discomfort with reading the book. "We felt the adult themes and sexually explicit messages were inappropriate for eighth-graders," said John Crawley. Superintendent Steven Staples explained, "We feel the novel is appropriate for eighth grade under the direction of a professional teacher."[118]

When the Raybun County Board of Education in Clayton, Georgia, removed *Flowers for Algernon* from the ninth-grade curriculum on March 19, 1997, board chair Lawrence Stockton described the action as "totally illegal." A systemwide media committee had recommended that the book be retained in the curriculum and the school's media center, but several members of the board were unaware of that decision. "I beg you to at least make a public date when all people can get a chance to hear all the information and not leave it privy to a select few,"[119] Stockton told the board. That plea fell on deaf ears as the board voted 3–1 to remove the book.

In April 2000, parents in Giltner, Nebraska, had their daughter skip class assignments on the book *Flowers for Algernon*, claiming it was inappropriate reading material. Kevin and Tracy Williams said their daughter was offended by sexually explicit passages in the book, and they asked the school board to assign an alternative book for their daughter. "We're not going to be unreasonable, but this book was far out of line," said Kevin Williams, who is also a member of the school board. The teacher offered to allow the girl to skip the parts she found offensive, and promised that such material would not be covered on tests, but the girl declined the offer. Principal Doug Bandemer warned the school board against assigning an alternative novel, saying, "The problem you're getting into here is censorship."[120]

24. To Kill a Mockingbird, by Harper Lee. Lippincott, 1960.

Synopsis and Background: To Kill a Mockingbird is among the most widely read and influential books in American literature. The 1991 "Survey of Lifetime Reading Habits," conducted by the Book-of-the-Month-Club and the Library of Congress's Center for the Book, found that *To Kill a Mockingbird* was second only to the Bible among books cited as "making a difference" in people's lives. The novel sold 500,000 copies in its first year and was translated into ten languages. By 1992, 18 million paperbacks alone had been sold.[121] *To Kill a Mockingbird* provides a sensitive and insightful picture of race relations in Alabama at a time when that state was the major focus of the nation's struggle for integration and equal rights. Despite this compelling setting for the novel, its popular appeal can be attributed to its universal themes. One of those themes is that essential lessons are learned by dealing with people unlike ourselves. In the book, the children in the Finch family must learn civilizing truths as they grow, allowing them to rise above the narrowness of the place and time in which they live. The two most powerful characters in the novel are the eccentric Boo Radley and the persecuted black man Tom Robinson, both of whom are clearly outside the mainstream of Maycomb, Alabama, society. At first, the Finch children regard them as demonic and witchlike, but they eventually recognize their kinship with the "outsiders." When Tom Robinson is tried and convicted of rape, the children learn that it takes great courage to defend an outsider from community injustice.

Selected Challenges, 1996–2000: On July 8, 1996, the Lindale (Texas) Independent School District board voted unanimously to ban thirty-two books on an advanced placement English reading list after a trustee had said they were in conflict with the values of the community. Among the books were *To Kill a Mockingbird*, *Huckleberry Finn*, *The Scarlet Letter*, and *Moby Dick*. Lindale High School Principal Jim Bernard explained, "You have to remember we're in the heart of the Bible belt and this is a very conservative community that is supportive of the school system and our district has to answer to them and listen to their concerns."[122]

On July 16, 1996, the Superintendent of the Moss Point (Mississippi) School District announced that *To Kill a Mockingbird* would be reviewed by a committee of parents, educators, and community members in response to a complaint by a minister. The Reverend Greg Foster requested that the school board pull the book from classrooms because it contains a racial epithet. During a meeting with the school board, Foster also requested more parental involvement in the selection of sex education materials. Superintendent James Easton said, "If we think it's inappropriate for our community, we'll remove it. If we think it's appropriate, we'll keep it."[123]

When the Burleson, Texas, school trustees adopted a policy banning any books that contained profanity, it sparked a local controversy and charges of censorship. Teachers were particularly concerned when school officials said the policy would require them to remove books like *To Kill a Mockingbird* from reading lists. On October 27, 1997, the trustees replaced that policy with a compromise that would require teachers to send parents detailed lists of reading materials at the start of each semester. The lists would make no mention of profanity and would target no particular books. Superintendent Fred Rauschuber said he expected the compromise to please both the conservative Christian parents who supported the ban and the teachers and parents who criticized it.

25. Iceman, by Chris Lynch. HarperTrophy, 1995.

Synopsis and Background: The protagonist of *Iceman* is Eric, a fourteen-year-old whose dysfunctional family leads him to express his anger in the hockey rink. His out-of-control violence causes even his teammates to shun him, assigning him appellations like "the animal" and "Iceman." Eric's older brother Duane, 17, has renounced the violence of hockey, much to his father's displeasure. As Duane discards violence to find emotional satisfaction in music and school work, Eric becomes the center of the family's attention. The father has a demented fixation on Eric's hockey games, at which he cheers with vicious enthusiasm as Eric mauls his opponents. The mother, on the other hand, is a cold and humorless former nun, who urges Eric to turn to the church. Neither parent offers Eric the warmth and emotional support he needs. Out of touch with his feelings, Eric spends time at the local mortuary, sitting in coffins and spying on mourners. There he makes friends with the reclusive and creepy mortuary employee McLaughlin. Eric's brief friendship with McLaughlin forces him to confront his own inner darkness and eventually to quit hockey. In the end it is his brother Duane who provides the support and wisdom necessary for Eric to turn his life around. Even Eric's father comes to realize the dangers of pushing his children into violent activities.

Selected Challenges, 1996–2000: On December 3, 1996, the Haysville, Kansas, school board voted to keep *Iceman* in the Haysville Middle School library despite complaints from parents Ken and Vicki Gromala that the novel was full of profanity. Mrs. Gromala said she had counted thirty-six different places in the book where profanity was used. "I believe that most parents will feel that this is something that they don't want their sixth- to eighth-grader to read," she said. The book had been reviewed by a committee, which recommended that it be retained by the library. School librarian Janet Tibbets said the attempt to remove the book was a threat to the freedom to read.[124]

Cheryl Ward, former librarian at the Windsor Locks (Connecticut) Middle School, was transferred to another job as apparent punishment for opposing a plan to segregate "controversial" materials in the library and require parental permission to read them. The problem began in 1997 when a local parent complained that *Iceman* was included on a summer reading list. Kathy Blackburn, whose sister is on the board of education, said her twelve-year-old was bothered by the book's language and the main character's violent behavior. Blackburn wrote superintendent June Hartford-Alley asking that a policy be put in place to segregate questionable material, and Hartford-Alley asked the librarians to change their policies to address Blackburn's concerns. Ward strongly opposed changing the existing policy, which was based on the ALA's *Library Bill of Rights*, and within days she was transferred from her job.

In February 1999, a review committee set up by the Medford (Wisconsin) school board voted 4 to 2 to remove *Iceman* from the middle school library after parents Greg and Maureen Heier complained that it used "foul language" and was not "inspiring." Maureen Heier said she teaches her son not to use the kind of language found in *Iceman*, but that her main objection to the book was that "it is not an inspiring book." At the February 18 board meeting, attorney Frank Nikolay, representing the weekly *Medford Star-News*, challenged the makeup of the committee that removed the book, saying it included people who were not residents of the district. "We request that the board reverse its policy that says the committee has the right to decide that the book be removed from the library," said Nikolay. The board voted 7 to 2 to review its policy, and, if revised, to bring *Iceman* back for review. District Administrator Paul Schoenberger told the board, "If you decide to modify the policy, that does not necessarily put the book back on the shelf. All that does is recreate further consideration of it."[125]

26. The *Alice* Series, by Phyllis Reynolds Naylor. Atheneum, 1985–

Synopsis and Background: There have been a dozen books in Naylor's "Alice" series, and they are frequently banned as a series. Alice McKinley was first revealed to the public in *The Agony of Alice,* which appeared in 1985. Marketed as a children's novel, it was named an American Library Association Notable Children's Book. Because Alice quickly gained a faithful readership of upper elementary and middle school girls, author Naylor continued the story of Alice's journey into womanhood in successive books. Alice, whose mother died when she was four, lives with her father Ben and her older brother Lester. The first book in the series finds Alice in sixth grade, struggling to find an appropriate adult female role model. By the fourth book, Alice is trying to adjust to the physical changes in her body and the conflict between her desire for independence and the need to belong to a group. She has a "special friend" named Patrick, with whom she is developing a typically awkward adolescent relationship. But most of all, she is concerned about acceptance by her peers. She concludes that because she doesn't have a mother or sister, she will need the sympathy and support of a broader sisterhood, the "in group" at school. It takes Alice a while to admit that all the pretense and exclusivity are kind of boring and that she really prefers the company of her old friend Patrick. As Alice advances through the sixth, seventh, and eighth grades, she becomes a young woman who seems to have made peace with her body and has learned to think for herself. The most recent of the *Alice* books, *The Grooming of Alice* (2000), leads the series into what seems destined to become a "young adult" series.

Selected Challenges, 1996–2000: At the June 9, 1997, school board meeting in Thorndike, Maine, it was decided that *All But Alice* would be retained in the Monro Elementary School library, but it would be restricted to students in the sixth grade and above. In addition, students wishing to borrow the book must first get permission of a parent. The controversy began when the parent of a fourth-grade student complained to school officials about a passage in the book. An ad hoc committee concluded that the book was appropriate for fifth-grade students and above, but the board raised the restriction to sixth grade and added the parental approval requirement.

When a third-grader looked at the book *All But Alice,* she noticed a chapter titled "Sex." She showed it to her mother, Julie Yates, who asked her school district committee in Apple Valley, Minnesota, to remove it from all elementary school libraries in the district. The committee of parents and school staff voted to keep the book on the shelves, but the school board overruled it. Four librarians spoke in favor of retaining the book, noting that those students who are mature enough to read it should not be denied access because of a few who are not. The board disagreed with them on a 5 to 1 vote. "It's not about censorship," said board member Gene VanOverbeke, who introduced the motion to remove the book. "It's not about the First Amendment. It's about selection of age-appropriate materials."[126]

In July 1998, the Alice books were removed from the sixth-grade required reading list in Monroe, Connecticut, after the mother of a ten-year-old girl said she was shocked to discover the content of *Alice, In Between*. Jackie Feldman said, "That's not the kind of material I want my ten-year-old reading." Superintendent of Schools Norman Michaud said he decided to remove the books after he read portions dealing with what he called questionable materials. "This is not a book I would want my daughter reading," he said. The Monroe Public Library Director defended the Alice series. "I don't think these books should have been withdrawn from the list," she said. "The author is a Newbery Award–winner. You can't judge a book by a couple of paragraphs taken out of context."[127]

27. **Brave New World**, by Aldous Huxley. Bantam Books, 1958, c1932.

Synopsis and Background: When *Brave New World* was published in 1932, it was seen as a moralistic critique of the materialism and hedonism fueling modern industrial society. Huxley sees neither capitalism nor communism as the political system of the future. Instead, he sees a five-tiered caste system maintained through biogenetic engineering and devices of social control. *Brave New World* is set in the year A.F. 689 (After Ford), a time when science and technology have so dominated human thought and behavior that emotions and anxieties have been effectively suppressed. Indeed, sophisticated inhabitants of this new society snicker at words like "mother" and "father," because the only respectable way to come into the world is to be incubated in a bottle and conditioned to conformity. In the new society, conditioned reflexes take the place of thinking. Sexual promiscuity and drug use is universal, as is a compulsive involvement in games and passive entertainment. Only two characters in *Brave New World* express opposition to state control. Because of some abnormality in his birthing process, the imperfectly designed Bernard Marx is different from the other members of his caste—the dominant Alphas—generating envy and alienation in him. In an act of rebellion, he brings John Savage, a half-breed from an isolated Native American reservation, into the mainstream of the new society. John, known as "the savage," represents both a minority culture and a culture of the past. He has escaped the state-supported brainwashing, but in the novel's tragic conclusion, he falls victim to his love for Lenina Crown, a product of the modern society. He cannot remold her into the image of the beloved that he brings from his traditional culture, nor can he assimilate the new culture. His only escape is suicide.

Selected Challenges, 1996–2000: At its April 15, 1996 meeting, the Coudersport (Pennsylvania) school board debated the continued use of *Brave New World* in the senior English curriculum at the local high school. At no time during the meeting was it explained why the book was being reviewed, though after the meeting, Superintendent Ed Goulding said the matter was placed on the agenda by a board member. The board heard testimony from at least eighteen district residents expressing a wide range of opinions on the book. One speaker insisted that the book should not be allowed in the schools, but the board also requested background information on the book from Mary Boardman, who had taught *Brave New World* in her class for nineteen years. No action was taken by the board.

On January 13, 1998, the school board in Gallatin, Tennessee, tried to assure the public that a state law against providing sexually explicit or violent materials to minors would not require the board to ban literary classics with adult content. The previous week, Schools Director Merrol Hyde had said that books like *Brave New World* might violate the law, and he questioned whether the school system should have such books on its assigned reading lists. But school board member and former school principal Billy Hobbs said, "We're not in here this evening to ban any books. We're not here to have any book bannings or censorship. This whole thing has been blown out of proportion."[128] Nonetheless, the board did vote to take the state's obscenity law and turn it, nearly word for word, into an official county school board policy.

In September 2000, *Brave New World* was removed from the Foley High School library in Alabama after a parent complained that the novel's characters showed contempt for religion, marriage, and the family. "I don't think too much of assigning this to high school students," said the parent, Kathleen Stone, who said she heard about the book from a friend of her children's. "He came in and said, 'You would not believe what they're having us read in English class. They've got children having sex together in this.'" School officials insisted that the book was not banned, but had been removed pending review. The book, which is included on county and national lists for advanced-placement high school students, was assigned reading at Foley High School.[129]

28. **One Fat Summer**, by Robert Lipsyte. Harper & Row, 1977.

Synopsis and Background: Bobby Marks is an overweight fourteen-year-old boy who doesn't like his body and is the target of jokes from his schoolmates. He particularly fears the coming of summer when he can no longer shield his chubby build with heavy clothes. This summer his friend Joanie, who is self-conscious about the size of her nose, goes off to have a nose job, and Bobby takes on an exhausting job doing yard work on the estate of a Dr. Khan. Here he learns how terrifying and fulfilling one fat summer can be. He is confronted by a tough guy named Willie who harasses and threatens him. Willie drinks a lot and has problems of his own, which he takes out on Bobby. But Bobby continues to work hard at his job, and his confidence gradually grows. By the end of the summer, Bobby is dieting, has lost some weight, and even has the courage to take his shirt off, a major accomplishment for a boy with his anxieties. He discovers that a hero is not necessarily trim and tough.

Selected Challenges, 1996–2000: In March 1997, School Superintendent Herman Sirois announced that *One Fat Summer* would be removed from the required reading list at the Jonas Salk Middle School in Levittown, New York. The action ignored the recommendation of a school-appointed committee that the book remain on the list. Parent Doreen Smith had complained that the book was sexually explicit and full of violence and therefore inappropriate for her seventh-grade son. Sirois appointed an ad hoc faculty committee whose members read the book and reported back to the board. Assistant Superintendent Robert Davis admitted, "What they found was a quality book, and that no change should be made." Nonetheless, Sirois withdrew the book from the reading list. Don Parker of the Long Island Coalition Against Censorship complained, "[O]nce that happens, this is censorship," he said.

In May 1997, parents in Greenville, North Carolina, complained about *One Fat Summer* and another book, saying the books used objectionable language and should be removed from middle school libraries. Parent Georgia Bean objected to the assignment of *One Fat Summer* in her son's class at Simpsonville's Hillcrest Middle School, saying that a passage on masturbation was inappropriate for his age. A ten-member review committee was formed to consider the parental complaints and decide whether the books would remain on the shelves.

On October 25, 1999, the Rock Crusher Elementary School in Crystal River, Florida, pulled *One Fat Summer* from library and classroom shelves after a parent complained that it contains derogatory terms for African Americans, Jews, and Italians and describes a character masturbating. The book had been on the reading list at the fourth-grade level in the Accelerated Reading Program. Principal Nancy Simon said the book was inappropriate for elementary schools. "I was totally appalled," she said after reading several selected passages. "The word that describes the book is 'egregious.' " Simon said she was happy that the book was off the shelves. "We saw it. We pulled it. There was just no question," she said. "This was what we call a no-brainer."[130]

29. Always Running: La Vida Loca: Gang Days in L.A., by Luis A. Rodriguez. Curbstone Press, 1993.

Synopsis and Background: The author, Luis Rodriguez, had become a veteran of East Los Angeles gang warfare by the time he was twelve years old. In this stark biography, he describes "la vida loca" and its countless shootings, beatings, and arrests. In the course of his gang life during the late 1960s and early 1970s, Rodriguez saw the loss of friends and family members to drugs, murder, suicide, and senseless acts of street violence. In large part, he survived the violence of "la vida loca" by writing down his experiences. Rodriguez, today an award-winning Chicano poet, found a way out of the barrio through education and the power of words. In *Always Running*, he describes the shock and despair he feels when his son joins a gang, bringing back the violence and desperation of the streets. By candidly describing the hell from which he had escaped, Rodriguez hoped to save his child from the same. Though the events he recounts are sad and brutal, the story is uplifting, filled with hope, insight, and a hard-earned lesson for his son and thousands like him.

Selected Challenges, 1996–2000: In March 1996, an anonymous parent in Rockford, Illinois, condemned *Always Running* as "blatant pornography" and demanded that it be removed from the Guilford High School curriculum. Other parents soon joined the fight against the book. "This is definitely not the kind of book I would approve my child reading," said Gary Stoltz, father of a high school freshman. "It is not appropriate to make this available in a high school environment." Local alderman Frank Beach attacked the book at a city council meeting and wrote to the state's attorney asking if parts of *Always Running* were pornography. Beach complained of the book's sexual references and its descriptions of violence, guns, and drugs. In response, the district formed a review committee to make a recommendation to the school superintendent. School board member David Strommer went further, demanding that the board review every book on school reading lists. "Trash is trash and smut is smut," he said. "There are things that need to be censored. I'd like to see the people who promote this stuff be run out of town."[131]

In July 1998, *Always Running* became the focus of controversy in a number of San Francisco Bay area school districts. In San José, a series of school board discussions of whether to remove the book became so heated that school official Maureen Munroe commented: "I've had to call the police because I felt personally threatened and I think some of our employees felt threatened." A group called the Parental Rights Organization opposed the book, claiming that it is pornographic. Members of the group say that the district's refusal to remove it violates state education rules that prohibit sexual harassment and discrimination. When the school board failed to remove it from the optional reading list at district high schools, the group declared that it would work to recall the three board members who voted to keep the book.

In Santa Rosa, just north of San José, the school board decided in July 1998 to remove *Always Running* from the Fremont High School reading list, but to retain it in the library. After discovering that the book was owned by other district high school libraries, those copies were removed as well pending review. The controversy began with a complaint from parent Sarah Gama, who said her daughter brought home the book after it was assigned in her sophomore English class. Gama said the book was pornographic and offensive in its stereotyping of Latinos. In a letter to the high school principal she wrote, "I am against future young freshmen reading this garbage at school." When the school board refused to remove the book, Gama took her fight to the media, catching the attention of Sheryl Taylor, a San José parent who helped found the Parental Rights Organization, and Dennis Wolfe, an influential insurance broker in neighboring Fremont. The embattled San José school board kept the book, but added a host of restrictions, including parental warnings and required parental consent for library use. Author Rodriguez has joined the debate over *Always Running*, saying, "It's a small group of people who are targeting it. There are 100,000 copies out there and nobody has really complained about it. It's an agenda some people have. They're going to try and use it against all sorts of books. I don't think they're really after me or my book."[132]

30. **Slaughterhouse-Five**, by Kurt Vonnegut. Dell, 1969.

Synopsis and Background: Kurt Vonnegut served with the U.S. infantry during World War II, and after being captured by the Germans in the Battle of the Bulge, he was held as a prisoner of war in Dresden while the city was firebombed by Allied aircraft. After the war, he felt compelled to write about his traumatic experience. *Slaughterhouse-Five* therefore has a foundation in history and fact, but it is not a typical "realistic" novel. It mixes reality and science fiction, tragedy and slapstick, in describing the adventures of Billy Pilgrim, an American soldier lost behind enemy lines in 1944. Pilgrim is taken prisoner, and during the subsequent shock and privation, his mind wanders, "unstuck in time," revealing his postwar life, fantastic space travels, even his death, before we are transported back to the Dresden firebombing. Vonnegut describes the horrors of the firestorm, connecting it with historical or mythical events like the destruction of Sodom and Hiroshima. *Slaughterhouse-Five* is a provocative war novel that cuts through nationalistic and jingoistic stereotypes to emphasize the common bonds of humanity. Vonnegut focuses on the helpless victims of modern aerial warfare, which has shifted the battlefield to civilian cities. Professor Peter J. Reed of the University of Minnesota says:

> [T]his novel seems important not just in its ideas, or in its morality, or as an example of modern fiction, or for what it might teach about how to write, but for its lesson in thinking. It is provocative, even maddening to some, because of its irreverence. It challenges sacred cows, set ideas, merely

traditional ways of thinking. And it does not do so irresponsibly, but from the foundation of a moral human decency. This kind of invitation to openness is surely the essence of education.[133]

Selected Challenges, 1996–2000: On January 19, 1996, the school board in Round Rock, Texas, held a seven-hour meeting to consider a proposal by board member Nelda Click to remove *Slaughterhouse-Five* and several other books from reading lists at the local high schools. Some parents and schools officials had charged that the books contained too much violence. Others insisted that a system be put in place to notify parents of offensive material on reading lists. At 2:30 in the morning, the board finally concluded its contentious debate, voting 4–2 to maintain the books on the reading list.

On September 2, 1998, parent Debbie Kines told the Prince William County (Virginia) school board that she was offended by *Slaughterhouse-Five* and two other books on her sons' reading lists. Kines said she keeps "this kind of filth out of my home" by monitoring the music she allows her children to buy, having certain cable channels blocked, and imposing Internet restrictions. "I work really hard to keep this stuff from them," she said, "and the school system suggests that I bring it in and have them read it." Kines handed out excerpts from the books, and three of the seven board members agreed with her that the passages were offensive. They said school staff should reconsider the inclusion of those books on the summer reading list. "I'm completely appalled at the excerpts," said board member John Harper, Jr. "I feel that this is a degradation to the human race." Associate Superintendent Pamela Gouch said she would consider labeling such books with terms like "profanity" or "sexual innuendo" on future reading lists.[134]

In September 2000, the Rhode Island Chapter of the ACLU criticized the action of the Coventry School Department in removing *Slaughterhouse-Five* from the required reading list for high school sophomores. The high school's English Department had selected *Slaughterhouse-Five* as the one mandatory summer reading selection for sophomores, but Coventry administrators removed the book after a parent complained that it contained "vulgar language, violent imagery, and sexual content." Steven Brown, the local ACLU director, said, "School officials claim they have not engaged in censorship because the book has not been banned from the school, but only removed from a required reading list. This is of small comfort to anybody concerned about academic freedom. . . . The problem is, the school decided to allow one objection to dictate the reading for future students. I'm concerned that teachers will now think twice before placing certain books on their syllabus during a school year."[135]

31. **The Joy of Gay Sex**, by Charles Silverstein and Edmund White, Pocket Books, 1978 / **The New Joy of Gay Sex**, by Charles Silverstein and Felice Picano, HarperCollins, 1992.

Synopsis and Background: In 1978, when the original edition of *The Joy of Gay Sex* was published, it became the most sought after and controversial book for gay men. Because it was written in the pre-AIDS era, the book required an updated edition, and *The New Joy of Gay Sex* is the revised version of the gay classic. Like the original, the new edition is intended for gay men. It incorporates the dramatic implications of the AIDS epidemic and reflects the gradual assimilation of homosexuality into American society. Dr. Charles Silverstein, a clinical psychologist and psychotherapist who authored the original *Joy of Gay Sex*, has collaborated with novelist Felice Picano on the revised edition. This reference book characterizes itself as "a coming-out guide for young gay men." Its stated goals are: (1) to educate gay men about safe sex; (2) to address the emotional issues that arise in gay life, including long-term relationships, one-night stands, loneliness, and growing older; and (3) to serve as a general home reference on such diverse topics as living wills and the history of condoms. The new edition contains eight color paintings and fifty line drawings by illustrators Deni Ponty and Ron Fowler.

Selected Challenges, 1996–2000: On February 15, 1996, the Clifton (New Jersey) board of library trustees voted 4 to 2 to limit sexually explicit books to patrons over eighteen years of age, ending a three-month battle over *The New Joy of Gay Sex* and two other books. The books will now be hidden behind the circulation desk, requiring patrons to request them by name. Mayor James Anzaldi called the new policy a compromise between those who wanted the books out of the library altogether and those who wanted them to remain. Al DuBois, the city's recycling director, had begun the campaign against the books, which he characterized as obscene and pornographic. Librarians immediately began reviewing all city library books to see if they fell under the new policy. By March, another batch of books was removed.

A York Township woman quit her job at the Medina County (Ohio) Library in protest against children borrowing adult-oriented materials such as *The New Joy of Gay Sex*. Linda Pesarchick, who had worked for the library for five years before resigning in November 1996, admitted that she openly violated library rules when she refused to allow a youth to check out the book. Library Director Bob Smith said Pesarchick actually opposed checking adult-oriented material out to anyone, including adults. He explained, "The policy of the library has never changed. For children, it's the parents' responsibility to monitor what the children borrow from the library."[136]

In May 1997, a woman in Belmont, California, stumbled across *The Joy of Gay Sex* in the Belmont Public Library and decided she would take the book hostage. Linda McGeogh said she wasn't bothered by the homosexual subject matter as much as by the explicit sexual content. She asked the library branch manager to remove the book from the regular shelves and place it behind a desk or a location where it would be more difficult to find. When she was told that such action would violate library policy, McGeogh took matters into her own hands. She removed the book and has since refused to return it.

32. **Forever**, by Judy Blume. Bradbury Press, 1975.

Synopsis and Background: Forever is a story of young lovers who experience sexual intimacy for the first time and then face difficult consequences. Katherine Danziger, a high school senior, has an affair with Michael Wagner, a young man her own age, but the affair is interrupted by a summer separation and eventual breakup. Katherine's best friend, Erica, looks forward to an intimate relationship with her boyfriend, but he turns out to be a latent homosexual whose emotional torment leads him to attempt suicide. Erica's cousin Sybil has an affair that leaves her pregnant. She gives birth to the child at the time of the girls' high school graduation and puts the baby up for adoption. The title of the book comes from the pledge Katherine gives to Michael when they first say "I love you" to each other. She says she will love him "forever," and he makes the same pledge on the engraved neck piece that he gives her for her birthday. Even when they separate for the summer, they repeat their one word pledge. But Katherine soon becomes close to another man, and she begins to have doubts about the permanence of her relationship with Michael. Later, Michael drives hundreds of miles to meet with Katherine, who tells him of her uncertain feelings. Feeling rejected, Michael responds angrily, precipitating a breakup. Because of the book's focus on sexual intimacy among young people, it has aroused controversy. Nonetheless, *Forever* is extremely popular among young adults and is taught in many high school and college literature classes. Frank Battaglia, who uses the book in his college freshman composition class, says the novel is considered controversial not so much because it describes sexual intimacy, but because Katherine does not regret her love affair. In short, concludes Battaglia, "Blume's *Forever* celebrates a teenage sexuality which does not end in marriage. . . . *Forever* reflects some shifts in contemporary standards, but the novel is hardly a tract for wantonness. It gives good insight into an array of joys and pains entailed in sustaining an intimate relationship."[137]

Selected Challenges, 1996–2000: On February 12, 1996, the Board of Education in Wilton, Iowa, voted 3 to 2 to reject a proposal to restrict library access to Judy Blume's *Forever*. The book will continue to be available to all junior and senior high school students in the Wilton School District. Local parent Janet Boorne requested that restrictions be placed on circulation of the book because of its sexual content. Boorne was upset after she found her thirteen-year-old daughter reading the book.

In February 1997, after a mother complained about *Forever* being available at Eastview Middle School, a school committee in Elgin, Illinois, decided to remove *Forever* from all seven district middle school libraries on the grounds that it is too sexually explicit. The committee did recommend, however, that the book remain in high school libraries. The decision to ban *Forever* from middle schools was made in response to a complaint filed by parent Jean McNamara who said, "Unfortunately, there is still the idea out there that we don't censor children, that we have to put everything out there in front of them and let them decide what to read."[138] In July 1997, the Elgin School Board voted 6 to 1 to confirm the earlier review committee decision. Doug Heaton, the only board member who voted "no,"said the board didn't go far enough. Heaton said *Forever* should be kept out of high schools as well as middle schools. In January 1998, another committee of teachers, administrators, librarians, and parents voted 4 to 3 to affirm the removal of *Forever* from middle school libraries. On June 21, 1999, the school board once more addressed *Forever* by considering a motion to return the book to the shelves. The board rejected the motion, which kept the book banned from middle school library shelves. The board's vote was actually evenly split 3 to 3, with one member absent, but under board rules the motion was defeated. Doug Heaton, one of the board members voting against the book, said, "Parents have every right to expect that their children will not have access to sexually explicit material while browsing the shelves of a school library." Joan Devine, a middle school librarian, urged the board not to ban *Forever*. "I hope to instill in my children a love for reading and books, not a fear of books," said Devine.[139]

33. **Heather Has Two Mommies**, by Lesléa Newman. Alyson, 1989.

Synopsis and Background: Three-year-old Heather is the child of a lesbian couple. She thinks having two mommies is perfectly normal until she joins a play group and meets children who have a mommy and a daddy. The understanding adult who is in charge of the play group leads the children in a discussion of their different family structures, telling them that the most important thing about a family is that all the people in it love each other. The first part of the book deals with the events leading to Heather's conception and birth; the latter half takes a positive approach to the issue of homosexual families. As more lesbian couples are choosing to have children through alternative insemination, *Heather Has Two Mommies* has become an important title in many libraries serving both conventional and alternative families.

Selected Challenges, 1996–2000: Nampa, Idaho, resident Joe Gardner submitted a petition to the library board asking that *Heather Has Two Mommies* and *Daddy's Roommate* be removed from the children's section. On July 8, 1999, the Nampa Library Board decided to keep the books in the juvenile nonfiction section, explaining that the terms "juvenile" and "adult" referred to reading level, not content. Board chair Ed Schiller said moving the books to an adult section would be inappropriate, because they are not at that reading level. As for the complaints about the content of the books, Camille Wood, assistant director of the library, said, "Public libraries are supported by and serve all people in a community. We don't limit our selection to the view of one community section."[140]

In September 2000, a federal judge ruled that a library petition system in Wichita Falls, Texas, had the primary intent of suppressing two books, *Heather Has Two Mommies* and *Daddy's Roommate*. Linda Hughes, the city's library administrator and a defendant in the case, applauded the judge's ruling. "It puts the responsibility for censoring children's books on the parents, where it should be," she said. "And I do believe parents should be the ones who determine what books their children read." Wichita Falls mayor Jerry Lueck dismissed the judge's ruling as irrelevant. "We really don't care what his opinion is—it'll be the opinion of 51 percent of the people of Wichita Falls whether they want the books there," he said.[141]

34. Two Teenagers in Twenty: Writings by Gay and Lesbian Youth, edited by Ann Heron. Alyson Publications, 1994.

Synopsis and Background: This new edition of *One Teenager in Ten* (1983) is a collection of testimonies from gay and lesbian youth. *Two Teenagers in Twenty* retains twenty-three of the original stories and adds nineteen new ones. Young people between the ages of twelve and twenty-four tell how they came to realize that they were gay, how they explained this to their families and friends, and how their lives are affected by their sexuality. Though all are poignant and powerful, the newer stories address more timely issues, such as AIDS. The emphasis is on sexuality, not sex, and a majority of the testimonies address psychological problems such as coming out to oneself and to others. The book begins with the words of a young homosexual whose coming out was met with support and understanding, but much of the book deals with the anxiety, isolation, and sorrow that are often a significant part of growing up gay. The personal stories also convey a sense of pride, determination, and relief at discovering and accepting oneself. The book concludes with a selected annotated bibliography of relevant adult and young adult fiction.

Selected Challenges, 1996–2000: In February 1999, three Seattle, Washington, high schools were allowed to purchase *Two Teenagers in Twenty* but were forced to remove its earlier edition, *One Teenager in Ten*, from the school libraries. Acting Superintendent Joseph Ochefske said the reason for banning the first edition but not the second was that the first included a story about a sexual relationship between a student and a teacher. Linda Jordan, who filed the original complaint, said the new edition was as bad as the old one, but Ochefske said the book should be judged in the context of its purpose, to share the struggle that gay and lesbian teens face when dealing with their sexuality.

In 1998, four books on homosexual themes, including *Two Teenagers in Twenty*, were removed from the Barron (Wisconsin) High School library. The ACLU filed suit in February 1999, charging that the school district had violated the First Amendment in removing the books on the basis of their content. Under a subsequent settlement, all four books were returned to the library and will remain available to students. The district also agreed not to ban books in the future simply on the basis of concern with their content.

35. **The Drowning of Stephen Jones**, by Bette Greene. Bantam Books, 1991.

Synopsis and Background: The Drowning of Stephen Jones is based upon a real-life hate crime, whose perpetrators were interviewed by the author before she wrote the novel. The fictionalized account concerns a gay teenager, Stephen Jones, who is harassed by the popular Andy Harris and his schoolmates. Their hate eventually leads them to drown the young man. The heroine of the story is Carla Wayland, Andy's sixteen-year-old girlfriend. Before she met Andy, Carla had few friends, but she soon became part of a social circle that gave her a sense of importance and security. Yet she is uncomfortable with the insensitive attitudes of Andy and his friends. Because of her love for Andy, Carla initially makes excuses for his behavior. She cannot believe that Andy would persecute someone simply because he is different. Eventually, Andy and his friends are brought to trial for the murder, and Carla faces her own battle of torn loyalties. Her testimony will decide whether justice will prevail.

Selected Challenges, 1996–2000: In fall 1996, Penny Culliton, a teacher who had been fired for purchasing literature on homosexuality for use in her classroom, was reinstated by the Mascenic (New Hampshire) school board. Prominent among the books in question was *The Drowning of Stephen Jones*. Culliton was reinstated after the state's Public Employee Labor Relations Board upheld an arbitrator's previous decision turning the dismissal into a one-year suspension. Culliton had purchased the books with a grant that had been approved by the school superintendent and principal, but when a local newspaper reported that she had been working with a lesbian and gay support group, the books were banned.

In August and September 1998, the Barron (Wisconsin) school board removed four books from the high school library because of concern over their homosexual themes. Among the books was *The Drowning of Stephen Jones*. The books were removed despite the recommendation of a review committee to retain all four books. The ACLU filed suit against the district, claiming that it had violated the First Amendment by removing the books on the basis of their content. In February 1999, the ACLU won a temporary injunction against removing the books, and a subsequent decision allowed the books to remain in the library. The district also agreed not to ban books in the future because they disagreed with the content.

36. **Women on Top: How Real Life Has Changed Women's Sexual Fantasies**, by Nancy Friday. Simon & Schuster, 1991.

Synopsis and Background: Nancy Friday's 1973 book *My Secret Garden* was the first published compilation of women's sexual fantasies. Her 1991 sequel, *Women on Top*, uses first person fantasies submitted by readers of her earlier books to demonstrate how women's sexual lives have changed in the twenty years since she began her research. The new book centers on women's fantasies about other women, their sexual cravings, and their desire to be in control of sexual relationships. Friday says the 150 responses compiled in *Women on Top* demonstrate that there has been another sexual revolution. She says women are now in charge, in sexual posture (as the title suggests) and in every other way. "These erotic explorations of maternal dominance didn't occur in *My Secret Garden* because Mother Goddess Power was just beginning to be talked about in the 1970s," explains Friday.[142] In keeping with the author's intention to empower women to express their most secret feelings, the documented fantasies are explicit. Nonetheless, as the *Time* magazine review said, the book "has the effect of an affidavit rather than an aphrodisiac."[143]

Selected Challenges, 1996–2000: At the November 19, 1996, meeting of the Chester County (Pennsylvania) library board, several county residents demanded that sexually explicit books, including *Women on Top*, be banned from library shelves or moved to a special adults-only section. The board concluded, however, that it was the responsibility of parents to monitor what their children read. "The board and personnel cannot sit as some sort of super-censor," said board member Steve Long. "We encourage all families to be actively involved in the raising of their children . . . but the right to have information is paramount."[144] The protesters pledged to take their fight to county commissioners, state legislators, and the governor, and they called upon the library to ban sexually explicit materials from its collections. Nonetheless, at its December meeting, the board adopted a materials selection policy that reaffirmed the library's right to acquire controversial materials.

In March 1997, *Women on Top* was pulled from public library shelves in Gwinnett County, Georgia, after two residents complained about its sexually explicit content. The book was removed after being examined by a materials review committee made up of three library staff members. Connie Crosby, one of the women who complained about the book, had asked only that it be removed from general circulation. She said she never dreamed that the book would be banned altogether from the library but was pleased that the library took a hard line.

37. **The Giver**, by Lois Lowry. Houghton Mifflin, 1993.

Synopsis and Background: Best known for her realistic fiction and the comic tales of Anastasia Krupnik, Lois Lowry here presents a thoughtful science fiction novel. This Newbery Award–winning book is set in a utopian, futuristic society in which there is no poverty, crime, sickness, or unemployment and where every family seems to be happy. But this is a chilling, tightly controlled society where all controversy has been removed and family members are selected for compatibility. Twelve-year-old Jonas is chosen to be the community's "Receiver," whose unique function is to hold the community's memories. He is placed under the tutelage of an old man known as the "Giver," who begins to transfer these memories to Jonas, who for the first time learns of things like love, war, and death. Through this process, Jonas soon discovers the disturbing truth about his utopian world and the costs of a pain-free society. Thus begins his struggle for personal freedom. He plots to escape to a place called "Elsewhere," bringing with him a child he has come to love. His dangerous and desperate journey forms the exciting and disturbing conclusion to the novel.

Selected Challenges, 1996–2000: In January 1999, a city youth pastor in Avon Lake, Ohio, said sixth-grade students should not be reading *The Giver* because its themes were too mature. Curtis Bledsoe, youth pastor of Calvary Baptist Church, asked the local school board to prohibit students at Troy Intermediate School from reading the book. He said the book contains graphic descriptions and discusses topics like suicide, sexuality, and euthanasia. He recommended that the book be used only with older students, or at the very least, that parents be notified of the book's content and allowed to decide whether their children should be allowed to read it. Superintendent Daniel Ross said *The Giver* is listed as optional reading for sixth-graders and that a review committee of parents, teachers, and librarians had recommended maintaining the book on that list.

When *The Giver* was removed from reading lists in Lake Butler (Florida) public schools, a number of teachers began working to get it reinstated. On October 12, 1999, a media committee voted 4 to 1 to approve the book, despite parental complaints. Sandy Lane, mother of a junior high school student, said the book's discussion of infanticide and sexual awakening made it inappropriate for students. She had complained to School Superintendent Eugene Dukes, who sent a memo to teachers suggesting that the book be removed. The teachers complied but expressed concern over the action. Students in classes using the book had already discussed fourteen of the book's twenty-three chapters. Teacher Prudence Pate filed a formal complaint against the book's removal, and principal Bobbie Morgan supported the teachers, saying, "I'm very disheartened and so are my staff. We're trying to instill a love of reading."[145]

38. **The Witches**, by Roald Dahl. Farrar, Straus & Giroux, 1983.

Synopsis and Background: When a seven-year-old boy, presumably modeled after Dahl himself, is orphaned in an automobile accident, he goes to live with his cigar-smoking grandmother, a longtime witch-lover, who teaches the boy all about witches. The boy learns that witches all look like nice ladies, but you can spot them if you look closely. For one thing, they all wear wigs to cover their bald heads, and they have itchy scalps. When the boy and his grandmother visit a hotel, he notices that the female delegates to a conference are all scratching their heads. He soon discovers that this is a coven of witches and that the Grand High Witch is planning to destroy every child in England. The witch then turns the boy into a mouse, using her Formula 86 Delayed Action Mouse-Maker, but the boy's grandmother helps him turn the tables on the coven, turning them into mice. Some adults may consider this fast-paced adventure excessively frightening, but they will approve of the special relationship between the grandmother and grandson, a relationship that persists even when the boy is a mouse-person. The message of love and acceptance is unmistakable.

Selected Challenges, 1996–2000: On April 2, 1997, the librarian at Kirby Junior High School in Wichita Falls, Texas, announced that *The Witches* and three other books would not return to library shelves until the school board approved them. The books were in the possession of parent Steve Lane, a member of the First Assembly of God Church, who asked trustees to ban books with "Satanic" themes. Board member Steve Ayer said it was unlikely that *The Witches* and the other books would be returned to the library collections unless there was more academic value to them than he could see from excerpts. Carrie Sperling, director of the local ACLU, said, "I think it's not only censorship, but it is illegal censorship. It seems to me [the books] are not being reviewed for their academic merits . . . but probably because certain public pressure groups disagree with what they have to say."[146]

On June 8, 1998, the Dublin (Ohio) board of education decided to retain *The Witches* in the general library collections of the school district despite a request by parent Kay Koepnick to have it banned from all libraries and classrooms. Superintendent Steve Anderson had recommended maintaining *The Witches* in the libraries but discontinuing its use in class, but the board voted 3 to 2 to keep it in both the libraries and classrooms. "This is a great triumph against censorship," said board president Bert Wiser. Koepnick, who had signatures from eight other parents in her complaint, said the book expresses derogatory views toward children and conflicts with her family's religious and moral beliefs. "I find this type of material extremely objectionable and cannot understand why an educator, librarian or parent would knowingly choose this type of reading material for their students or children," she said.[147]

39. **Blubber**, by Judy Blume. Bradbury, 1974.

Synopsis and Background: Blubber provides an inside look at how insensitive some wealthy, fifth-grade children can be to each other, and to adults. Blubber is the nickname given to Linda Fischer, an overweight fifth-grader, by her mean-spirited classmates who, like a pack of dogs, follow the directions of Wendy, the class troublemaker. In addition to the name-calling, the class has tormented Linda in a variety of ways, stripping her in the girls' room, locking her in the storage closet, and forcing her to eat "chocolate ants." Blubber takes her punishment docilely. The story's narrator, Jill Brenner, goes along with this organized harassment, but she eventually crosses Wendy by standing up for Blubber at a mock trial. This, predictably, makes Jill the next target for harassment. Though Jill eventually gains an understanding of the pain of ostracism when she becomes a victim, she never really learns that it is wrong to persecute someone. This warts-and-all view of adolescent social dynamics is realistic and entertaining.

Selected Challenges, 1996–2000: In 1997, while presenting an introduction to the works of Judy Blume to third- and fourth-graders, a school librarian in Lowndes County, Georgia, happened to mention that Blume is a frequently censored children's author. Shortly thereafter, parents of a third-grader lodged a formal complaint against *Blubber*, and a review committee of teachers and administrators decided that the book contained inappropriate language for elementary school students. *Blubber* was pulled from the library shelves, and *Deenie*, another book by Blume, also came under scrutiny for appropriate content. Though the librarian concluded that *Deenie* was "not inappropriate" for elementary school students, it was nonetheless removed from library shelves. The librarian explained that in the current atmosphere, *Deenie* would have been a likely censorship target in the future.

On January 11, 1999, the board of education in Elkmont, Alabama, reversed an earlier decision to ban *Blubber* from school libraries because of two instances of the word "damn" and one of the word "bitch." The board had listened to testimony from seventh-grader Mary Saczawa, who asked them to reconsider the ban. Dr. Les Bivens, school superintendent, and Kelly Kelso, chair of the school's book review committee, also recommended lifting the ban. Ignoring an advisory committee's recommendation, the board had originally voted 4 to 3 to ban the book after receiving a parental complaint about the novel. Only after three of those voting to ban the book were defeated in subsequent board elections did their replacements produce a 6 to 1 vote to return *Blubber* to the school library shelves.

40. **A Day No Pigs Would Die**, by Robert Newton Peck. Knopf, 1972.

Synopsis and Background: The autobiographical novel *A Day No Pigs Would Die* takes place in rural Vermont in the late 1920s. The novel provides a tender picture of a close father-son relationship and a glimpse of the stark realities of farm life in a Shaker community. The story is told by a young Shaker farm boy, Rob, who describes how he passed from childhood to adult responsibility in a single year. Rob tells us of the good and bad times during this period, the happiest coming when he receives a pet piglet as a birthday present. Rob spends most of his spare time with his pet, named Pinky. But after a bad apple crop that fall and a poor hunting season, there was no food for the family, and Rob's father was forced to slaughter Rob's pig. Though his heart is breaking, Rob helps his father kill and dress his pet. Late the following spring, Rob's father dies quietly in his sleep, and Rob automatically becomes the head of the household. He makes the funeral arrangements and digs his father's grave in the valley. Late that night, Rob returns alone to the valley to say his last farewell. Because Rob's father was the area's hog butcher, this is "a day no pigs would die."

Selected Challenges, 1996–2000: On October 15, 1996, parent Scott Leonard told the board of education in Anderson, Missouri, that he objected to the profanity and violence in *A Day No Pigs Would Die*, which had been assigned to his daughter's seventh-grade honors class at Anderson Junior High School. Leonard asked the board to create a committee to review *A Day No Pigs Would Die* and other books assigned as mandatory reading. The board agreed unanimously to form such a committee, but Anderson Principal Dan Rickett said the book would remain on the suggested reading list until the committee had issued a recommendation.

On February 2, 1997, Harriet Parks, a veteran teacher at a Roman Catholic school in Utica, Michigan, said she resigned her job after administrators ordered her to stop teaching *A Day No Pigs Would Die*. Parks said school officials had told students and parents that she had retired, but she decided to publicize the real reason for her resignation. She said her students had read about half of *A Day No Pigs Would Die* when an unidentified parent complained to administrators, who confiscated the book without bothering to read it. "They made the decision to remove the book from the classroom without talking to me or other teachers," she said. "I just decided I was not going to teach there anymore."[148]

41. **Ordinary People**, by Judith Guest. Viking Press, 1976.

Synopsis and Background: Ordinary People tells the story of a family torn by the drowning death of one son, Buck, and the attempted suicide of younger brother Conrad, who blames himself for his older brother's death. The two had been thrown into rough waters when their sailboat capsized, and seventeen-year-old Conrad never forgave himself for being the only one to survive. Suffering persistent depression, Conrad slashes his wrist with a razor and is sent to a mental institution for treatment. Even after his release, he faces great difficulties in adjusting to school and family life. He isolates himself from his friends because they were his brother's friends as well, making the associations too painful for Conrad. Meanwhile, his mother's cold and distant nature prevents her from providing Conrad with the emotional support he needs. A hopeful turn of events comes after Conrad begins seeing a psychiatrist who makes him see that he is senselessly punishing himself for his brother's death. Conrad is also helped by a relationship with a young woman, and as the novel closes, he seems to have come to terms with his brother's death.

Selected Challenges, 1996–2000: At the May 1996 school board meeting in Buffalo, New York, the board voted 6 to 1 to pull *Ordinary People* from the high school curriculum until a committee reviewed it and made a recommendation. Lancaster High School student Chris Palistrant was so disturbed by the action that he took the matter to the New York Civil Liberties Union. The NYCLU sent a letter to the school board expressing their dismay that the book was removed solely on the objections of two parents. On June 24, 1996, at the urging of Superintendent Joseph Girardi, the school board voted to ban *Ordinary People* from the curriculum, citing inappropriate language and content. The vote ignored the positive recommendation of the review committee presented at the previous board meeting.

After Reverend Lee D. Sparre challenged *Ordinary People* in May 1998, citing obscene language and sexual innuendoes, the book was removed from the Fostoria (Ohio) High School library. The decision on whether to use the book in English classes was debated for a year, and a decision was finally reached by the school board on April 19, 1999. A committee appointed by Superintendent Sharon Stannard determined that today's students can easily identify with the novel and that it provides them with the opportunity to consider difficult and timely issues. In agreeing with the committee's recommendation, Stannard said that the book's sexual and profane language represented only a minute portion of the novel.

42. Julie of the Wolves, by Jean Craighead George. Harper & Row, 1972.

Synopsis and Background: The protagonist of *Julie of the Wolves* is Miyax (Julie in English), a young Alaskan girl who lives with her widowed father, Kapugen, in the true Eskimo fashion. She absorbs the culture of her people, including an understanding and respect for nature and wildlife, but when she is nine years old she goes to live with her Aunt Martha where she attends school. Prior to her departure, her father makes a traditional arrangement for her to marry David, the son of his hunting partner, when she reaches the age of thirteen. While living with her aunt, Miyax becomes gradually acculturated to a modern lifestyle, but at age thirteen she returns to marry David. She lives a harsh and miserable life, spending most of each day sewing parkas and boots for the tourist trade. A turning point comes when David attacks her sexually. She flees across the tundra, hoping to reach Point Hope where she can catch a ship to San Francisco, but she becomes lost in the snow. Upon encountering a pack of wolves, she follows her father's advice and attempts to communicate with them, imitating their sounds and body language. She becomes accepted as a member of the pack, and the wolves feed her by regurgitating the food they kill. Miyax later discovers that her father lives in a nearby village, and she sets out for a reunion. Upon her arrival she learns that he has married a white woman and has adopted the modern lifestyle. Disillusioned, she retreats to her ice house on the tundra. As the novel ends, she begins to realize that "the hour of the wolf and Eskimo is over," and she prepares to return to her father.

Selected Challenges, 1996–2000: On March 18, 1996, the school board in Pulaski Township, Pennsylvania, removed *Julie of the Wolves* from sixth-grade classes in the district. Parents Nellie and Bernie Vorderbrueggen had complained of a graphic marital rape scene in the book, and School Superintendent John Ross set up a committee of parents, teachers, librarians, and administrators to review the book. When the committee found the book appropriate for the curriculum, the Vorderbrueggens appealed to the school board, which decided by a 5 to 4 vote to remove the book.

In October 1996, the mother of a sixth-grade student at Hanson Lane Elementary School in Ramona, California, asked the school board to remove *Julie of the Wolves* from the district's required reading list. Teresa Duncan told school trustees that she was appalled to find a passage on the rape of a thirteen-year-old girl in the book. Assistant Superintendent Joe Annicharico, Jr., said Duncan's daughter was given an alternative assignment, but he questioned the appropriateness of the action. He said the district's literature review committee would probably change the book's status from "required" to "recommended" due to parental concerns about content.

43. **Jack**, by A.M. Homes. Macmillan, 1989.

Synopsis and Background: Most reviewers of *Jack* find its teenage protagonist to be clearly derivative of Holden Caulfield in *Catcher in the Rye*. Jack is a fifteen-year-old wisecracking suburban youth whose psychological vulnerabilities are, like those of Holden Caulfield, central to the plot. Jack is a likable kid caught in circumstances that are too much for him. Following his parents' bitter divorce, he lives with his mother and her boyfriend, who drinks too much. Meanwhile, his father lives in an apartment with a roommate named Bob. When his father belatedly informs Jack that Bob is actually his lover, Jack's world collapses in rage and helplessness. He wonders why he was the last one to know that his father was gay. His mother knew, and he learns that even his schoolmates knew. Within this unstable world, Jack turns to his friend Max's parents, particularly Max's mother, Elaine Burka. But during a weekend in the country with the Burkas, Jack realizes that this family has even more serious problems than his own. He sees Mrs. Burka's face purple and puffy from a beating by Max's father. The shock of encountering spousal abuse in a family he idolized leads Jack to reflect on his own life and eventually to consider that there are worse things than having a gay father. He concludes, as does the reader, that he will "be okay, permanently," that he will "make it."

Selected Challenges, 1996–2000: In 1996, for the second year in a row, the novel *Jack* was on the list of books approved for use in Fairfield (California) schools, and for the second year in a row, teachers and staff removed the book from the list just before school board members were to vote on it. The book was to be on a list of titles that high honors students could choose to read during the summer. Board member Susan Heumphreus was pleased that the book was removed from the list, but dismayed that it had appeared once more despite her opposition to it. She objected to the rampant profanity in *Jack* and its negative portrayals of characters.

After lengthy debate, the Board of Education in Spindale, North Carolina agreed on August 20, 1996, to maintain restrictions on library access to the book *Jack*. Elizabeth Blanton, a local parent, had complained that the book was inappropriate for the library because of its language. Her daughter had been assigned to do a book report, and after she chose *Jack*, her mother became aware of its offensive language. After the initial complaint, a school committee recommended that the book be placed on the library's reserve shelf. A county committee later upheld that decision, and the board of education concurred. Board member Roger Jolly, speaking for the majority, said that though he would not let his child read the book, he couldn't vote to prohibit other parents from approving it for their children.

44. **Being There**, by Jerzy Kosinski. Harcourt Brace Jovanovich, 1971, c1970.

Synopsis and Background: The central character in *Being There* is a simpleminded man named Chance, who maintains the garden and grounds for a wealthy patron called the Old Man. Chance is an orphan, born with brain damage that limits him to work in the garden and spare time in his isolated quarters. The Old Man has made it clear that Chance must do exactly as he is told or risk being institutionalized. As a result, his only contact with the outside world is through his television set. When the Old Man dies, Chance is forced to leave his home dressed in one of his late employer's expensive suits. Once on the street, he is hit by the limousine of wealthy Elizabeth Eve Rand, who takes Chance home with her to arrange for medical care. Her husband, a close advisor of the president of the United States, happens to bring the president to his home the day after Chance arrives, and when both men ask Chance for his views on the nation's economy, he responds with simple platitudes on gardening that are mistaken for profound metaphors. The president later quotes Chance in a televised speech. Chance soon begins to hobnob with important people in society and government, and his physical attractiveness results in a number of bizarre sexual encounters. Chance, who is impotent, tells both his female and male admirers that he prefers to watch, rather than participate in, sexual activity. His detachment in these sexual affairs is mistaken for experience, just as his oblivious attitude toward political and social realities is taken for sophistication. As the novel ends, the president decides to choose Chance as his running mate in his upcoming reelection campaign.

Selected Challenges, 1996–2000: On July 24, 1997, the Windsor (Connecticut) High School student council withdrew its student representative from the school board after a board member denounced *Being There*, a book on the senior reading list, as "pornographic." In a letter to the board, the student council said that Mark Cashman's comments about the book were inflammatory, self-righteous, and "offensive and insulting to staff, students and literature itself."[149]

In March 1999, the school board in Baker City, Oregon, upheld Superintendent Arnold Coe's decision to remove *Being There* and another novel from the Baker High School language arts program. The action followed parental complaints about the two novels, which were contained in the anthology *Seven Contemporary Short Novels*. The complaints about *Being There* centered on its descriptions of sexual relations.

45. ***Captain Underpants* Series**, by Dav Pilkey. Scholastic, 1997–2000.

Synopsis and Background: The Captain Underpants books are silly to the extreme, but they have been wildly popular with children. Since the appearance of *The Adventures of Captain Underpants: An Epic Novel* in 1997, Dav Pilkey has produced *Captain Underpants and the Attack of the Talking Toilets* (1999), *Captain Underpants and the Invasion of the Incredibly Naughty Cafeteria Ladies from Outer Space* (1999), and *Captain Underpants and the Perilous Plot of Professor Poopy Pants*. The central characters in these adventures are George and Harold, two misbehaving fourth-grade boys who hypnotize their school principal, Mr. Krupp, into becoming Captain Underpants, the superhero the boys created in their own homemade comic book. At the snap of anyone's fingers, Mr. Krupp, clad in jockey shorts and cape, sets out in search of villains. In the first book, the villain is the evil Dr. Diaper. In the second, George and Harold unintentionally create an army of teacher-eating toilets, and once more Captain Underpants must save the day. In the third epic adventure, Principal Krupp mistakenly hires three tentacled aliens as cafeteria ladies who turn everyone in the school into zombie nerds. Captain Underpants to the rescue. In the fourth book, our crusading hero battles the evil Professor Poopy Pants who has shrunk the entire school to miniatures, then forcing the tiny students and teachers to assume names just as silly as his own.

Selected Challenges, 1996–2000: In November 1999, a library committee at the Orfordville (Wisconsin) Elementary School evaluated *Captain Underpants and the Invasion of the Incredibly Naughty Cafeteria Ladies from Outer Space* after it had been challenged by the parents of a district student. Tom and Lauren Hartung filed a form requesting a reconsideration of the book after their fifth-grader brought it home from the library. Among the charges made by the Hartungs were that the book taught students to be disrespectful, not to obey authority or law, including God's law, to lie, and to escape responsibility. Committee members unanimously agreed that the book should stay on the library shelves.

In February 2000, the principal at Maple Hill School in Naugatuck, Connecticut, removed *The Adventures of Captain Underpants* from the school library, claiming that some fourth-graders had begun to act like the mischievous boys in the book. Superintendent Alice Carolan said, "The book was beginning to take on a life of its own." But many parents complained that the principal had overreacted, and a protest petition signed by thirty parents was submitted to the school board. "We believe that one person should not have the sole discretion to decide which books should be banned from school libraries," said parent Dorothy Hoff. "And every parent that's read it, loves it." Superintendent Carolan responded that the book had never really been fully removed, because two copies remained checked out.[150]

46. **Fool's Crow**, by James Welch. Viking, 1986.

Synopsis and Background: Fool's Crow is a novel of Native American dignity and decline. Set in 1870, the story revolves around a young Blackfoot boy whose life, like his name, is transformed by events. Originally named White Man's Dog, the young man becomes known as Fool's Crow after he kills the chief of the Crows during a raid. He then has a disturbing vision at the Sun Dance ceremony, in which he sees the end of the Indian way of life and the agonizing choice between resistance or humiliating accommodation to the white man's culture. The author uses Native American dialect and vocabulary to give the reader a sense of Fool's Crow's way of life and the importance of custom and ritual. At the same time, dreams and visions are effectively employed to reveal the fragility of Native American culture in the face of the white man's Manifest Destiny. The reader sees the relentless advance of white settlers from the point of view of the Native American, whose culture and very existence were threatened. The conclusion of the novel leaves Fool's Crow asking many of the same questions that his descendants ask today: Can Native Americans survive best by adopting the white man's ways (e.g., casinos on the reservations) or by embracing traditional culture?

Selected Challenges, 1996–2000: In March 1999, *Fool's Crow* was banned from classes in Laurel, Montana. The book was being used in an American literature class when parental complaints led the school board to vote 3 to 1 to ban it from classrooms. School Superintendent Laurel Moore had written to the board, complaining that the book was "objectionable and inappropriate for my son to read." She described the book as "disgusting" and "repulsive." When author James Welch, a Montana native, discovered it had been banned, he commented, "I just find it a surprise, and I think it's sad for the young people of Laurel. They won't get to learn more about the Indian culture."[151]

When student Dan Turvey read *Fool's Crow* in his sophomore English class in Bozeman (Montana) High School, he was disturbed by its descriptions of sex and violence. His challenge to the use of the book led to a school hearing on January 12, 2000, at which the broader issues of decency and censorship were debated. Teachers defended the book as one of the finest works of literature about the Native American experience in Montana. A district review committee then voted to keep the book in the high school, but required that parents be sent a written notice of the novel's mature content. The dispute was then carried to the full school board, which voted unanimously to retain the novel in the high school's sophomore English classes. The decision came at the end of a three-hour hearing attended by more than seventy people. Twenty-seven students, parents, and teachers spoke in favor of the novel, saying it offered valuable insights. Eight people said that teenagers should not be exposed to the novel's graphic passages.

47. **Cujo**, by Stephen King. Viking, 1981.

Synopsis and Background: Once more, Stephen King brings credibility to outrageous characters and events by setting them in Middle America. This bizarre embodiment of horror is Cujo, a placid, 200-pound Saint Bernard pet, a typical "good dog." After Cujo is bitten by a rabid bat one summer night in Castle Rock, Maine, the dog goes berserk, attacking his owner, auto mechanic Joe Cambers, and an advertising man, Vic Trenton. As if that's not bad enough, we are led to believe that Cujo is possessed by the ghost of local mass murderer Frank Dodd. There are terrifying scenes, such as when people are caught in stalled automobiles, awaiting deadly assault by Cujo. The many acts of terror are woven effortlessly into the everyday life of a small town, revealing the potential for savagery in the ordinary world around us.

Selected Challenges, 1996–2000: In April 1998, Stephen King's novel *Cujo* was thrown in the trash can by the principal of Crook County High School in Prineville, Oregon, after a parent requested that the book be removed. Principal Chris Yaeger said, "It's not what most parents would want their children to read." In a written complaint to the school district, Sue Baca cited profanity, violence, and sexual content in *Cujo* as justification for its removal. She also asked that all of King's books, as well as any other horror novels, be removed from the county's middle and high schools. "I object to any book by Stephen King as he writes horror fiction, which has no value," said Baca.[152]

On September 10, 1998, parent Ann Carver filed a complaint with the Brooksville, Florida, board of education, charging that her son had been upset by the sexually explicit scenes and vulgar language in *Cujo*. Carver not only wanted the book out of her sixth-grader's hands, but removed altogether from the school's library. Ken Pritz, principal of the West Hernando Middle School, pulled the book pending review. Susan Vaughn, the school's media specialist, said the book had been in the library since the school first opened and was very popular with the students.

48. **A Wrinkle in Time**, by Madeleine L'Engle. Dell, 1962.

Synopsis and Background: This Newbery Award–winning novel is a thought-provoking tale enjoyed by children in schools around the country. The main character, twelve-year-old Meg Murray, has an unusual family. Her father is a physicist who has disappeared mysteriously on a secret space mission. Her five-year-old brother Charles is a clairvoyant. One stormy night, Meg gets out of bed and goes down to the kitchen to get a cup of hot cocoa. She is joined by her brother Charles, her mother, and finally by an old lady seeking shelter from the storm. This is Mrs. Whatsit, who lives in a haunted house nearby. The following day, Meg, along with her brother and a friend, visit Mrs. Whatsit and meet her two companions, Mrs. Who and Mrs. Which. Using their supernatural powers, these three ladies take the children on a space ride through a "wrinkle in time." The children soon discover that their father is being held prisoner on a distant planet, Camazatz, which is controlled by the Power of Darkness. They travel alone to Camazatz and enter the Central Intelligence Building, where they are confronted by the Prime Coordinator who captures Meg's brother. Meg then locates her father trapped behind a glass wall, and by using Mrs. Who's magic glasses, she is able to pass through the wall and free him. She then proceeds to free her brother from the Prime Coordinator by repeating the words "I Love You" to him, thus releasing him from the Power of Darkness. Meg, her father, and brother then return safely to Earth. *A Wrinkle in Time* is more than an exciting science fiction adventure. It teaches the importance of individuality, respect for others, and the power of love.

Selected Challenges, 1996–2000: When a fifth-grade student at Mountain View Elementary School in Newton, North Carolina, brought home *A Wrinkle in Time* as an assignment for an academically gifted class, she told her father, Ed Palmer, that she didn't like the book. After Palmer complained to school officials, teachers allowed the girl to read an alternative assignment. But Palmer wanted the book pulled from all school libraries. On January 29, 1996, he told the school board that *A Wrinkle in Time* was inappropriate for fifth grade because it makes references to the occult, witchcraft, and mysticism. Other parents were passionate in defense of the book. "Allowing this kind of censorship to take place is far more dangerous than anything you'd find in this book," said Susan Rittiner. In the end, the board voted unanimously to keep the book in the libraries, saying that Palmer had the right to choose his daughter's reading material, but not that of other children.[153]

In April 1996, the Antioch (California) school board voted 4 to 1 against a parent's request that her daughter be given an alternative reading assignment to *A Wrinkle in Time*. Lisa Tuller had asked the board to excuse her daughter from reading the book because its references to magic and mind-reading violated her religious beliefs, but Superintendent Alan Newell said that if the district allowed each parent to set his or her own academic standards, there would be no standards at all. "Do we choose things that are so sterile nobody can object to them?" he said. Mrs. Tuller, on the other hand, felt the school was indoctrinating her daughter against her will. "My daughter is not a ward of the school and I, as her parent, want an option."[154]

49. **Crazy Lady**, by Jane Leslie Conly. HarperCollins, 1993.

Synopsis and Background: This Newbery Honor book tells the story of Vernon Dibbs, a lonely seventh-grade boy who struggles with his school work and has difficulty finding a purpose to his life. When his mother passed away two years ago, he felt he had lost the only person who considered him special. Out of boredom and aimlessness, he takes a job helping out an alcoholic woman named Maxine who is known in the neighborhood as the "crazy lady." Vernon ends up tutoring Maxine's retarded son Ronald and soon devises a money-making project to send Ronald to the Special Olympics. As Vernon becomes more and more involved in helping Maxine and her son, he gains personal confidence and learns that there is a larger world beyond him in which he can make a difference. The saddest moment comes when Maxine realizes that she must part with her son in order to ensure that he receives proper care. But even that poignant separation is an act of altruism by which Maxine seems to have transformed herself.

Selected Challenges, 1996–2000: In January 1996, Lori Parquette, the mother of a fifth-grade student at the Ann Sullivan Elementary School in Prospect Heights, Illinois, asked that *Crazy Lady* be removed from district school libraries, saying it contained inappropriate language. "Some of the sentences and some of the words [in the book] shouldn't be in the fifth grade," she said. "The kids are clamoring to get this book because of the swear words."[155] School librarian Marsha Willis defended the book, saying it had received several awards and was nominated for an Illinois children's literature award.

In October 1997, a fifth-grade teacher at Terrell School in San Jose, California, assigned *Crazy Lady* as supplemental reading for her class. The teacher held a meeting to inform parents about the book, but one parent who did not attend later challenged the book, calling it "pornography." An oversight committee assigned to evaluate the book noted five times that the book used words such as "damn," "hell," and "bitch," but said the book was nonetheless a valuable teaching tool. On December 11, the San Jose school board voted to allow teachers to continue to assign *Crazy Lady* in district elementary schools, with the stipulation that parents would be notified in advance that the curriculum included a book with some profanity. "It's not the kind of language that we're encouraging children to use, but in the real world this is the kind of language children hear all the time," said school board member Rich Garcia. "Our committee thought the overall value of the book, the lessons in the book, are greater than some of the questionable language."[156]

50. **Black Boy**, by Richard Wright. Harper, 1945.

Synopsis and Background: Black Boy is considered a classic of American autobiography and one of Wright's finest works. The book is often characterized as an autobiographical novel because of its novelistic techniques. It is a narrative of the author's journey from childhood to adulthood in the Jim Crow South. The vivid descriptions of Wright's harsh boyhood in rural Mississippi and in Memphis, Tennessee, offer an unsurpassed portrait of the struggles by African Americans against poverty and ingrained racism. Though the book is often viewed as an attack on racist Southern white society, it has also come to be understood as the story of Wright's discovery of the power of the written word. Though race was clearly a primary component of his life and work, Wright demonstrates in *Black Boy* that there were many other influences on his development as an artist. Wright, who died in 1960, has won international renown and stands alongside other great African American writers like Zora Neale Hurston, James Baldwin, and Toni Morrison. His novels *Black Boy* and *Native Son*, both of which are on our banned list, are required reading in high schools and colleges across the country.

Selected Challenges, 1996–2000: In the early hours of January 19, 1996, the Round Rock (Texas) Independent School District board voted 4 to 2 against a proposal by board member Nelda Click to remove Richard Wright's *Black Boy* and *Native Son*, along with ten other books, from reading lists at Westwood and McNeil high schools. All the books challenged by Click were used in honors or advanced placement courses. The opponents of Click's proposal noted that most of books to be banned were written by minority authors, and they suggested that her motivation was linked to a broader opposition to multicultural curricula. While rejecting the proposal to ban the books, the board did agree to create a curriculum council to develop a new policy for selecting reading material.

In May 1997, the Reverend Dale Shaw, president of the North Florida Ministerial Alliance and an associate pastor with the Mount Olive Baptist Church, attacked the use of *Black Boy* in Jacksonville's public schools. "It has historical value," he said. "But that doesn't make it right for high school students." At a Duval County School Board meeting he complained of profanity in *Black Boy* and said it may cause hard feelings among students of different races. The author's widow, eighty-four-year-old Ellen Wright, publicly defended the book. In a letter to the *Florida Times Union*, she said, "That such a record of survival against inhuman odds should be suppressed after fifty years of being fruitfully taught in our nation's schools would be tantamount to an American tragedy. *Black Boy* tells of a long-ago child who was not allowed to read books. Do we want this book denial to be repeated in today's South?"[157] In a phone interview, Ellen Wright said she also planned to send letters of encouragement to the teacher and principal who came under attack for assigning the book to students.

NOTES

1. Lee Siegel, "Harry Potter and the Spirit of the Age," *The New Republic*, November 22, 1999, p. 40.

2. David Ignatius, "The Anti-Marketing Wizard," *Washington Post*, June 25, 2000, B7.

3. "Censoring Bestsellers: Harry Potter Under Fire," *Newsletter on Intellectual Freedom*, January 2000, p. 1.

4. Ibid., p. 26.

5. Ibid.

6. Ibid.

7. Judy Blume, "Is Harry Potter Evil?" *New York Times*, October 22, 1999, p. A27.

8. "Success Stories: Schools," *Newsletter on Intellectual Freedom*, March 2000, pp. 62–63.

9. Ibid., p. 63.

10. "Censorship Dateline: Schools," *Newsletter on Intellectual Freedom*, March 2000, pp. 50–51.

11. Ibid., May 2000, p. 77.

12. "Censorship Dateline: Libraries," *Newsletter on Intellectual Freedom*, July 2000, p. 103.

13. Ibid., p. 104.

14. "Success Stories: Schools," *Newsletter on Intellectual Freedom*, September 2000, pp. 165–66.

15. "Libraries: Foley, Alabama," *Newsletter on Intellectual Freedom*, November 2000, p. 193.

16. "Libraries: Pace, Florida," *Newsletter on Intellectual Freedom*, November 2000, p. 193.

17. Ibid., p. 166.

18. "Censorship Dateline: Schools," *Newsletter on Intellectual Freedom*, January 2001, p. 12.

19. "Censorship Dateline: Libraries," *Newsletter on Intellectual Freedom*, January 2001, p. 11.

20. "Censorship Dateline: Schools," *Newsletter on Intellectual Freedom*, January 2001, p. 13.

21. Ibid., p. 15.

22. Justin Kaplan, *Born to Trouble: One Hundred Years of Huckleberry Finn* (Washington, D.C.: Library of Congress, 1985), p. 11.

23. Albert Bigelow Paine, *Mark Twain: A Biography*, vol. 3 (New York: Harper, 1912), pp. 1280–81.

24. Kaplan, *Born to Trouble*, pp. 10, 13.

25. Ibid., p. 18.

26. "Censorship Dateline: Schools," *Newsletter on Intellectual Freedom*, November 1996, p. 199.

27. Ibid., January 1997, p. 12.

28. Ibid., July 1997, pp. 97–98.

29. Ibid., May 1998, pp. 72–73.

30. Ibid., November 1998, p. 182.

31. "From the Bench: Schools," *Newsletter on Intellectual Freedom*, January 1999, pp. 13–14.

32. "Censorship Dateline: Schools," *Newsletter on Intellectual Freedom*, July 1999, pp. 94–95.

33. James Bertolino, "Maya Angelou Is Three Writers," in *Censored Books: Critical Viewpoints*, edited by Nicholas J. Karolides, Lee Burress, John M. Kean. Metuchen, NJ.: Scarecrow Press, 1993, pp. 299, 305.

34. Opal Moore, "Learning to Live: When the Bird Breaks from the Cage," in *Censored Books: Critical Viewpoints*, edited by Nicholas J. Karolides, Lee Burress, John M. Kean. Metuchen, N.J.: Scarecrow Press, 1993, pp. 306, 308.

35. Ibid.

36. Ibid., pp. 313–314.

37. "Censorship Dateline: Schools," *Newsletter on Intellectual Freedom*, May 1997, pp. 65–66.

38. Ibid., July 1997, p. 98.

39. Ibid., May 1998, p. 72.

40. Ibid., March 1998, pp. 41–42.

41. "Censorship Dateline: Libraries," *Newsletter on Intellectual Freedom*, May 1998, p. 69.

42. "Success Stories: Schools," *Newsletter on Intellectual Freedom*, January 1999, p. 20.

43. Nicholas J. Karolides and Lee Burress, eds., *Celebrating Censored Books* (Racine, Wisconsin: Council of Teachers of English, 1985), pp. 86–87.

44. Ibid.

45. "Censorship Dateline: Schools," *Newsletter on Intellectual Freedom*, May 1997, p. 63.

46. "Success Stories: Schools," *Newsletter on Intellectual Freedom*, January 1998, pp. 28–29.

47. Ibid., p. 28.

48. Ibid., July 1998, p. 120.

49. "Censorship Dateline: Schools," *Newsletter on Intellectual Freedom*, July 1998, p. 107.

50. "Censorship Dateline: Libraries," *Newsletter on Intellectual Freedom*, January 1999, p. 9.

51. "Success Stories: Schools," *Newsletter on Intellectual Freedom*, July 1999, p. 105.

52. "Censorship Dateline: Schools," *Newsletter on Intellectual Freedom*, March 2000, p. 52.

53. Kenneth L. Donelson and Alleen Pace Nilsen, *Literature for Today's Young Adults* (Glenview, Ill.: Scott, Foresman, 1989), p. 88.

54. Karolides and Burress, *Celebrating Censored Books*, p. 31.

55. "Censorship Dateline: Libraries," *Newsletter on Intellectual Freedom*, September 1998, pp. 140–41.

56. Ibid., July 1998, p. 106.

57. "Censorship Dateline: Schools," *Newsletter on Intellectual Freedom*, May 2000, p. 78.

58. "Censorship Dateline: Libraries," *Newsletter on Intellectual Freedom*, March 2000, p. 49.

59. "Censorship Dateline: Schools," *Newsletter on Intellectual Freedom*, March 2000, p. 51.

60. Stephanie Zvirin, "Starred Reviews," *Booklist*, September 15, 1994, p. 133.

61. "Censorship Dateline: Libraries," *Newsletter on Intellectual Freedom*, September 1996, p. 152.

62. Ibid., January 1997, p. 8.

63. "Success Stories: Libraries," *Newsletter on Intellectual Freedom*, March 1997, p. 49.

64. Ibid., November 1999, p. 171.

65. "Censorship Dateline: Libraries," *Newsletter on Intellectual Freedom*, September 2000, p. 143.

66. "Success Stories: Schools," *Newsletter on Intellectual Freedom*, September 1997, p. 149.

67. "Censorship Dateline: Libraries," *Newsletter on Intellectual Freedom*, January 1998, p. 13.

68. "Success Stories: Schools," *Newsletter on Intellectual Freedom*, September 1999, pp. 131–32.

69. "Censorship Dateline: Libraries," *Newsletter on Intellectual Freedom*, November 1999, p. 163.

70. "Censorship Dateline: Schools," *Newsletter on Intellectual Freedom*, July 1996, p. 121.

71. "Success Stories: Libraries," *Newsletter on Intellectual Freedom*, January 1997, p. 25.

72. "Censorship Dateline: Schools," *Newsletter on Intellectual Freedom*, July 1998, p. 110.

73. Ibid., March 1999, p. 40.

74. "Censorship Dateline: Libraries," *Newsletter on Intellectual Freedom*, March 2000, p. 49.

75. "Censorship Dateline: Schools," *Newsletter on Intellectual Freedom*, November 2000, p. 196.

76. "Censorship Dateline: Libraries," *Newsletter on Intellectual Freedom*, July 1996, p. 119.

77. "Censorship Dateline: Schools," *Newsletter on Intellectual Freedom*, May 1997, p. 62.

78. "Success Stories: Schools," *Newsletter on Intellectual Freedom*, July 1997, pp. 109–10.

79. "Censorship Dateline: Schools," *Newsletter on Intellectual Freedom*, March 2000, p. 50.

80. Ibid., November 2000, p. 195.

81. "Success Stories: Schools," *Newsletter on Intellectual Freedom*, November 1996, p. 212.

82. "Censorship Dateline: Schools," *Newsletter on Intellectual Freedom*, July 1997, p. 96.

83. "Success Stories: Libraries," *Newsletter on Intellectual Freedom*, May 2000, p. 91.

84. Ibid., May 1998, p. 88.

85. Ibid., September 1999, p. 131.

86. Ibid., March 2000, p. 61.

87. "Censorship Dateline: Schools," *Newsletter on Intellectual Freedom*, November 1997, pp. 169–70.

88. Susan Ferrechio, "A Parent Protests," *Washington Times*, February 11, 1998, p. C7.

89. "Censorship Dateline: Schools," *Newsletter on Intellectual Freedom*, November 1999, p. 164.

90. Ibid., November 2000, p. 195.

91. "Success Stories: Schools," *Newsletter on Intellectual Freedom*, September 1997, p. 149.

92. "Censorship Dateline: Schools," *Newsletter on Intellectual Freedom*, September 1998, p. 142.

93. Ibid., November 1999, pp. 164–65.

94. "Censorship Dateline: Libraries," *Newsletter on Intellectual Freedom*, January 2001, p. 36.

95. Marsha Darling, "In the Realm of Responsibility: A Conversation with Toni Morrison," *Women's Review of Books*, 5, March 1988, p. 5.

96. Ibid.

97. "Success Stories: Schools," *Newsletter on Intellectual Freedom*, May 1996, p. 99.

98. "Censorship Dateline: Libraries," *Newsletter on Intellectual Freedom*, January 1998, p. 14.

99. "Censorship Dateline: Schools," *Newsletter on Intellectual Freedom*, September 1998, p. 142.

100. R.L. Stine, *It Came from Ohio: My Life As a Writer*, New York: Scholastic, 1997, p. 114.

101. "Success Stories: Schools," *Newsletter on Intellectual Freedom*, May 1997, p. 77.

102. "Censorship Dateline: Schools," *Newsletter on Intellectual Freedom,* September 1997, p. 129.

103. "Censorship Dateline: Libraries," *Newsletter on Intellectual Freedom,* January 2000, p. 12.

104. Ibid., July 2000, p. 106.

105. Ibid., p. 103.

106. Ibid., May 2000, pp. 75–76.

107. Ibid., March 2001, p. 54.

108. Ibid., September 1999, pp. 119–20.

109. "Success Stories: Schools," *Newsletter on Intellectual Freedom,* May 2000, p. 92.

110. Rudolfo A. Anaya, "Taking the Tortillas out of Your Poetry," in *Censored Books: Critical Viewpoints,* edited by Nicholas J. Karolides, Lee Burress, and John M. Kean. Metuchen, N.J.: Scarecrow Press, 1993, p. 28.

111. "Censorship Dateline: Schools," *Newsletter on Intellectual Freedom,* September 1999, p. 120.

112. Ibid., March 2000, p. 51.

113. "Success Stories: Schools," *Newsletter on Intellectual Freedom,* November 1999, p. 173.

114. "Censorship Dateline: Schools," *Newsletter on Intellectual Freedom,* September 2000, p. 145.

115. Richard O. Moore, director, "The Writer in America," Perspective Films, 1978.

116. Susan Ferrechio, "A Parent Protests," *Washington Times,* February 11, 1998, p. C7.

117. Daniel Keyes, *Flowers for Algernon.* New York: Harcourt, Brace and World, 1966, p. 271.

118. "Censorship Dateline: Schools," *Newsletter on Intellectual Freedom,* May 1996, p. 100.

119. Ibid., July 1997, p. 97.

120. "Censorship Dateline: Libraries," *Newsletter on Intellectual Freedom,* July 2000, p. 105.

121. Claudia Durst Johnson, *Understanding* To Kill a Mockingbird: *A Student Casebook to Issues, Sources and Historical Documents* (Westport: Greenwood Press, 1994), pp. xi–xii.

122. "Censorship Dateline: Schools," *Newsletter on Intellectual Freedom,* November 1996, p. 199.

123. Ibid., p. 196.

124. "Success Stories: Libraries," *Newsletter on Intellectual Freedom,* March 1997, p. 49.

125. "Censorship Dateline: Schools," *Newsletter on Intellectual Freedom,* May 1999, p. 69.

126. "Censorship Dateline: Libraries," *Newsletter on Intellectual Freedom,* November 1997, p. 166.

127. "Censorship Dateline: Schools,"*Newsletter on Intellectual Freedom,* November 1998, p. 182.

128. "Is It Legal: Schools," *Newsletter on Intellectual Freedom,* March 1998, p. 49.

129. "Censorship Dateline: Libraries," *Newsletter on Intellectual Freedom*, January 2001, p. 11.

130. Ibid., January 2000, p. 11.

131. Ibid., July 1996, p. 118.

132. "Censorship Dateline: Schools," *Newsletter on Intellectual Freedom*, September 1998, pp. 142–43.

133. Karolides and Burress, *Celebrating Censored Books*, p. 113

134. "Censorship Dateline: Schools," *Newsletter on Intellectual Freedom*, November 1998, p. 183.

135. Ibid., January 2001, p. 14.

136. "Censorship Dateline: Libraries," *Newsletter on Intellectual Freedom*, January 1997, p. 8.

137. Frank Battaglia, "If We Cannot Trust . . . : The Pertinence of Judy Blume's *Forever*," in *Censored Books: Critical Viewpoints*, edited by Nicholas J. Karolides, Lee Burress, and John M. Kean. Metuchen: Scarecrow Press, 1993, pp. 258–59.

138. "Censorship Dateline: Libraries," *Newsletter on Intellectual Freedom*, May 1997, p. 60.

139. Ibid., September 1999, p. 119.

140. "Success Stories: Libraries," *Newsletter on Intellectual Freedom*, September 1999, p. 131.

141. "From the Bench: Library," *Newsletter on Intellectual Freedom*, November 2000, pp. 201–2.

142. Ilene Cooper, "Nancy Friday, *Women on Top*," *Booklist*, October 1, 1991, p. 201.

143. Margaret Carlson, "Batteries Not Included," *Time*, December 2, 1991, p. 78.

144. "Success Stories: Libraries," *Newsletter on Intellectual Freedom*, March 1997, p. 49.

145. "Censorship Dateline: Schools," *Newsletter on Intellectual Freedom*, January 2000, p. 13.

146. "Censorship Dateline: Libraries," *Newsletter on Intellectual Freedom*, July 1997, p. 95.

147. "Success Stories: Libraries," *Newsletter on Intellectual Freedom*, September 1998, p. 156.

148. "Censorship Dateline: Schools," *Newsletter on Intellectual Freedom*, May 1997, p. 64.

149. Ibid., November 1997, p. 167.

150. "Censorship Dateline: Libraries," *Newsletter on Intellectual Freedom*, May 2000, pp. 73–74.

151. "Censorship Dateline: Schools," *Newsletter on Intellectual Freedom*, July 1999, p. 96.

152. Ibid., July 1998, p. 110.

153. "Success Stories: Libraries," *Newsletter on Intellectual Freedom*, May 1996, pp. 97–98.

154. "Censorship Dateline: Schools," *Newsletter on Intellectual Freedom*, July 1996, pp. 120–21.

155. "Censorship Dateline: Libraries," *Newsletter on Intellectual Freedom*, March 1996, pp. 45–46.

156. "Success Stories: Schools," *Newsletter on Intellectual Freedom*, March 1998, p. 55.

157. "Censorship Dateline: Schools," *Newsletter on Intellectual Freedom*, September 1997, p. 127.

Appendixes

Between 1990 and 2000, of the 6,364 challenges reported to or recorded
by the Office for Intellectual Freedom,

- 1,607 were challenges to "sexually explicit" material (up 161 since 1999);
- 1,427 were to material considered to use "offensive language" (up 165 since 1999);
- 1,256 were to material considered "unsuited to age group" (up 69 since 1999);
- 842 were to material with an "occult theme or promoting the occult or Satanism" (up 69 since 1999);
- 737 were to material considered to be "violent" (up 107 since 1999);
- 515 were to material with a homosexual theme or "promoting homosexuality" (up 18 since 1999);
- 419 were to material "promoting a religious viewpoint" (up 22 since 1999).

Other reasons for challenges included "nudity" (317 challenges, up 20
since 1999); "racism" (267 challenges, up 22 since 1999); "sex education"
(224 challenges, up 7 since 1999); and "anti-family" (202 challenges, up
9 since 1999). Please note that the number of challenges and the number

of reasons for those challenges do not match, because works are often challenged on more than one ground.

Seventy-one percent of the challenges were to material found in schools or school libraries. Another 24 percent were to material found in public libraries (down 2 percent since 1999). Sixty percent of the challenges were brought by parents, 15 percent by patrons, and 9 percent by administrators, all down one percent since 1999.

Based on the 6,364 challenges reported to or recorded by the Office for Intellectual Freedom, as compiled by the Office for Intellectual Freedom, American Library Association, the following is a list of the 100 most frequently challenged books of 1990–2000. The ALA Office for Intellectual Freedom does not claim comprehensiveness in recording challenges. Research suggests that for each challenge reported there are as many as four or five that go unreported.

1. *Scary Stories* (series), Alvin Schwartz
2. *Daddy's Roommate*, Michael Willhoite
3. *I Know Why the Caged Bird Sings*, Maya Angelou
4. *The Chocolate War*, Robert Cormier
5. *The Adventures of Huckleberry Finn*, Mark Twain
6. *Of Mice and Men*, John Steinbeck
7. *Harry Potter* (series), J.K. Rowling
8. *Forever*, Judy Blume
9. *Bridge to Terabithia*, Katherine Paterson
10. *Alice* (series), Phyllis Reynolds Naylor
11. *Heather Has Two Mommies*, Lesléa Newman
12. *My Brother Sam Is Dead*, James Lincoln Collier and Christopher Collier
13. *The Catcher in the Rye*, J.D. Salinger
14. *The Giver*, Lois Lowry
15. *It's Perfectly Normal*, Robie Harris
16. *Goosebumps* (series), R.L. Stine
17. *A Day No Pigs Would Die*, Robert Newton Peck
18. *The Color Purple*, Alice Walker
19. *Sex*, Madonna
20. *Earth's Children* (series), Jean M. Auel
21. *The Great Gilly Hopkins*, Katherine Paterson
22. *A Wrinkle in Time*, Madeleine L'Engle
23. *Go Ask Alice*, Anonymous
24. *Fallen Angels*, Walter Dean Myers
25. *In the Night Kitchen*, Maurice Sendak

26. *The Stupids* (series), Harry Allard
27. *The Witches*, Roald Dahl
28. *The New Joy of Gay Sex*, Charles Silverstein
29. *Anastasia Krupnik* (series), Lois Lowry
30. *The Goats*, Brock Cole
31. *Kaffir Boy*, Mark Mathabane
32. *Blubber*, Judy Blume
33. *Killing Mr. Griffin*, Lois Duncan
34. *Halloween ABC*, Eve Merriam
35. *We All Fall Down*, Robert Cormier
36. *Final Exit*, Derek Humphry
37. *The Handmaid's Tale*, Margaret Atwood
38. *Julie of the Wolves*, Jean Craighead George
39. *The Bluest Eye*, Toni Morrison
40. *What's Happening to My Body? Book for Girls*, Lynda Madaras
41. *To Kill a Mockingbird*, Harper Lee
42. *Beloved*, Toni Morrison
43. *The Outsiders*, S.E. Hinton
44. *The Pigman*, Paul Zindel
45. *Bumps in the Night*, Harry Allard
46. *Deenie*, Judy Blume
47. *Flowers for Algernon*, Daniel Keyes
48. *Annie on my Mind*, Nancy Garden
49. *The Boy Who Lost His Face*, Louis Sachar
50. *Cross Your Fingers, Spit in Your Hat*, Alvin Schwartz
51. *A Light in the Attic*, Shel Silverstein
52. *Brave New World*, Aldous Huxley
53. *Sleeping Beauty Trilogy*, A.N. Roquelaure (Anne Rice)
54. *Asking About Sex and Growing Up*, Joanna Cole
55. *Cujo*, Stephen King
56. *James and the Giant Peach*, Roald Dahl
57. *The Anarchist Cookbook*, William Powell
58. *Boys and Sex*, Wardell Pomeroy
59. *Ordinary People*, Judith Guest
60. *American Psycho*, Bret Easton Ellis
61. *What's Happening to My Body? Book for Boys*, Lynda Madaras
62. *Are You There, God? It's Me, Margaret*, Judy Blume

63. *Crazy Lady*, Jane Conly
64. *Athletic Shorts*, Chris Crutcher
65. *Fade*, Robert Cormier
66. *Guess What?*, Mem Fox
67. *The House of Spirits*, Isabel Allende
68. *The Face on the Milk Carton*, Caroline Cooney
69. *Slaughterhouse-Five*, Kurt Vonnegut
70. *Lord of the Flies*, William Golding
71. *Native Son*, Richard Wright
72. *Women on Top: How Real Life Has Changed Women's Sexual Fantasies*, Nancy Friday
73. *Curses, Hexes and Spells*, Daniel Cohen
74. *Jack*, A.M. Homes
75. *Bless Me, Ultima*, Rudolfo A. Anaya
76. *Where Did I Come From?*, Peter Mayle
77. *Carrie*, Stephen King
78. *Tiger Eyes*, Judy Blume
79. *On My Honor*, Marion Dane Bauer
80. *Arizona Kid*, Ron Koertge
81. *Family Secrets*, Norma Klein
82. *Mommy Laid an Egg*, Babette Cole
83. *The Dead Zone*, Stephen King
84. *The Adventures of Tom Sawyer*, Mark Twain
85. *Song of Solomon*, Toni Morrison
86. *Always Running*, Luis Rodriguez
87. *Private Parts*, Howard Stern
88. *Where's Waldo?*, Martin Hanford
89. *Summer of My German Soldier*, Bette Greene
90. *Little Black Sambo*, Helen Bannerman
91. *Pillars of the Earth*, Ken Follett
92. *Running Loose*, Chris Crutcher
93. *Sex Education*, Jenny Davis
94. *The Drowning of Stephen Jones*, Bette Greene
95. *Girls and Sex*, Wardell Pomeroy
96. *How to Eat Fried Worms*, Thomas Rockwell
97. *View from the Cherry Tree*, Willo Davis Roberts
98. *The Headless Cupid*, Zilpha Keatley Snyder
99. *The Terrorist*, Caroline Cooney
100. *Jump Ship to Freedom*, James Lincoln Collier and Christopher Collier

Appendix A(2): OIF Censorship Database 1990–2000: Initiator of Challenge

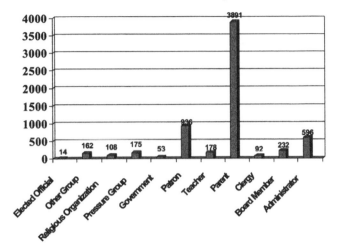

As of December 31, 2000, as compiled by the Office for Intellectual Freedom, American Library Association. The Office for Intellectual Freedom does not claim comprehensiveness in recording challenges. Research suggests that for each challenge reported there are as many as four or five which go unreported.

Appendix A(3): OIF Censorship Database 1990–2000: Institution Being Challenged

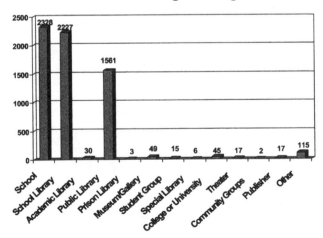

As of December 31, 2000, as compiled by the Office for Intellectual Freedom, American Library Association. The Office for Intellectual Freedom does not claim comprehensiveness in recording challenges. Research suggests that for each challenge reported there are as many of four or five which go unreported.

Appendix A(4): OIF Censorship Database 1990–2000: Challenges by Type

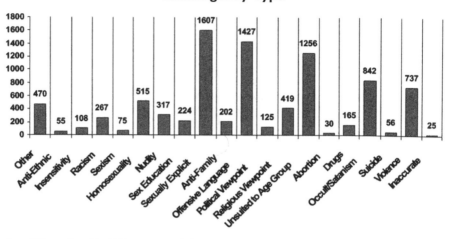

As of December 31, 2000, as compiled by the Office for Intellectual Freedom, American Library Association. The Office for Intellectual Freedom does not claim comprehensiveness in recording challenges. Research suggests that for each challenge reported there are as many as four or five which go unreported.

Appendix A(5): OIF Censorship Database 1990–2000: Challenges by Year

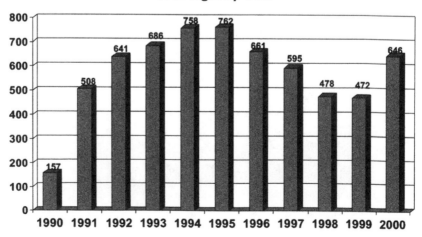

As of December 31, 2000, as compiled by the Office for Intellectual Freedom, American Library Association. The Office for Intellectual Freedom does not claim comprehensiveness in recording challenges. Research suggests that for each challenge reported there are as many as four or five which go unreported.

Appendix B: Office for Intellectual Freedom: The Most Frequently Challenged Books and Authors of 2000

The following books were the most frequently challenged in 2000:

1. The *Harry Potter* books, by J.K. Rowling, for occult/satanism and antifamily themes.
2. *The Chocolate War*, by Robert Cormier (the "most challenged" fiction book of 1998), for violence, offensive language, and being unsuited to age group.
3. *Alice* series, by Phyllis Reynolds Naylor, for sexual content and being unsuited to age group.
4. *Killing Mr. Griffin*, by Lois Duncan, for violence and sexual content.
5. *Of Mice and Men*, by John Steinbeck, for using offensive language, racism, violence, and being unsuited to age group.
6. *I Know Why the Caged Bird Sings*, by Maya Angelou, for being too explicit in the book's portrayal of rape and other sexual abuse.
7. *Fallen Angels*, by Walter Dean Myers, for offensive language, racism, violence, and being unsuited to age group.
8. *Scary Stories* series, by Alvin Schwartz, for violence, being unsuited to age group, and occult themes.
9. *The Terrorist*, by Caroline Cooney, for violence, being unsuited to age group, and occult themes.
10. *The Giver*, by Lois Lowry, for being sexually explicit, occult themes, and violence.

The most frequently challenged authors in 2000 were: J.K. Rowling, Robert Cormier, Lois Duncan, Piers Anthony, Walter Dean Myers, Phyllis Reynolds Naylor, John Steinbeck, Maya Angelou, Christopher Pike, Caroline Cooney, Alvin Schwartz, Lois Lowry, Harry Allard, Paul Zindel, and Judy Blume.

Please note that the most frequently challenged authors may not appear in the list of most frequently challenged books. For example, if every one of Judy Blume's books was challenged—but only once—not one of her books would make the top ten list, but she herself would make the most challenged author list.

Appendix C: Office for Intellectual Freedom: The Most Frequently Challenged Books and Authors of 1999

The following books were the most frequently challenged in 1999:

1. The *Harry Potter* books, by J.K. Rowling, for their focus on wizardry and magic.
2. The *Alice* series, by Phyllis Reynolds Naylor, for using offensive language and being unsuited to age group.
3. *The Chocolate War*, by Robert Cormier (the "most challenged" fiction book of 1998), for using offensive language and being unsuited to age group.
4. *Blubber*, by Judy Blume, for offensive language and unsuited to age group.
5. *Fallen Angels*, by Walter Dean Myers, for offensive language and unsuited to age group.
6. *Of Mice and Men*, by John Steinbeck, for using offensive language and being unsuited to age group.
7. *I Know Why the Caged Bird Sings*, by Maya Angelou, for being too explicit in the book's portrayal of rape and other sexual abuse.
8. *The Handmaid's Tale*, by Margaret Atwood, for its sexual content.
9. *The Color Purple*, by Alice Walker, for sexual content and offensive language.
10. *Snow Falling on Cedars*, by David Guterson, for sexual content and offensive language.

The most frequently challenged authors in 1999 were: Judy Blume, Robert Cormier, Stephen King, Lois Lowry, Chris Lynch, Walter Dean Myers, Christopher Pike, Phyllis Reynolds Naylor, J.K. Rowling, and Alvin Schwartz. Please note that the most frequently challenged authors may not appear in the list of most frequently challenged books. For example, if every one of Judy Blume's books was challenged—but only once—not one of her books would make the top ten list, but she herself would make the most challenged author list.

Appendix D: Office for Intellectual Freedom: The Most Frequently Challenged Books and Authors of 1998

The following books were the most frequently challenged in 1998:

1. *The Chocolate War*, by Robert Cormier
   The book, written for teens, is a fictionalized account of a boy's trials and triumphs at boarding school. First published in 1974, the book has often been challenged for being "sexually explicit."

2. *Of Mice and Men*, by John Steinbeck
   This short work by a Nobel Prize–winning author most often is challenged for using "offensive language" and being "unsuited to age group."

3. *Goosebumps* series and *Fear Street* series, by R.L. Stine
   These books have been challenged in schools and libraries across the country for being "too frightening for young people" and depicting "occult or satanic" themes.

4. *I Know Why the Caged Bird Sings*, by Maya Angelou
   Maya Angelou's autobiographical novel has increasingly been the focus of challenges in school libraries. Objections center on the explicit description of a rape and other sexual abuse she suffered as a child.

5. *The Giver*, by Lois Lowry
   This critically acclaimed novel has been challenged for being "violent," "sexually explicit," and using "offensive language," and for its treatment of infanticide and euthanasia.

6. *Always Running: La Vida Loca: Gang Days in L.A.*, by Luis Rodriguez
   This book has been challenged for its depiction of gang life, for being "sexually explicit," "violent," "racist," and "unsuitable for teens."

7. *Crazy Lady*, by Jane Leslie Conly
   This work often is challenged for "offensive language."

8. *Blubber*, by Judy Blume
   Back on the list this year is *Blubber*, a children's book that often is challenged for "offensive language" and being "inappropriate" for its intended age group of preteens.

The most frequently challenged authors in 1998 were Robert Cormier, Lois Lowry, John Steinbeck, R.L. Stine, Maya Angelou, Judy Blume, Robie Harris, James Lincoln Collier and Christopher Collier, and Katherine Paterson. Please note that the most frequently challenged authors may not appear in the list of most frequently challenged books. For example, if every one of Judy Blume's books was challenged—but only once—not one of her books would make the top ten list, but she herself would make the most challenged author list.

Selected Bibliography

American Library Association. *Intellectual Freedom Manual*. 6th ed. Chicago: ALA, 2001.

Bald, Margaret. *Literature Suppressed on Religious Grounds*. New York: Facts on File, 1998.

Bryson, Joseph E. *The Legal Aspects of Censorship of Public School Library and Instructional Materials*. Charlottesville, Va.: Michie Company, 1982.

Burress, Lee. *Battle of the Books: Literary Censorship in the Public Schools, 1950–1985*. Lanham, Md.: Scarecrow Press, 1989.

Burress, Lee, and Edward B. Jenkinson. *The Student's Right to Know*. Urbana, Ill.: National Council of Teachers of English, 1979.

DelFattore, Joan. *What Johnny Shouldn't Read: Textbook Censorship in America*. New Haven: Yale University Press, 1992.

Dellinger, David W. "My Way or the Highway: The Hawkins County Textbook Controversy." Ph.D. dissertation, University of Tennessee, May 1991.

Demac, Donna A. *Liberty Denied: The Current Rise of Censorship in America*. New Brunswick, N.J.: Rutgers University Press, 1988.

Foerstel, Herbert. *Free Expression and Censorship in America: An Encyclopedia*. Westport, Conn.: Greenwood Press, 1997.

Garden, Nancy. *The Year They Burned the Books*. New York: Farrar, Straus & Giroux, 1999.

Garry, Patrick M. *An American Paradox: Censorship in a Nation of Free Speech*. Westport, Conn.: Greenwood Press, 1993.

Geller, Evelyn. *Forbidden Books in American Public Libraries, 1876–1939*. Westport, Conn.: Greenwood Press, 1984.

Goff, Robert Oscar. *The Washington County Schoolbook Controversy: The Political Implications of a Social and Religious Conflict*. Ph.D. dissertation, Catholic University, Ann Arbor, University Microfilms, 1976.

Gold, John Coopersmith. *Board of Education v. Pico (1982): Bookbanning*. New York: Twenty First Century Books, 1995.

Haight, Anne Lyon. *Banned Books, 387 B.C. to 1978 A.D.* 4th ed. New York: Bowker, 1978.

Hicks, Robert D. *In Pursuit of Satan: The Police and the Occult*. Buffalo: Prometheus Books, 1991.

Hurwitz, Leon. *Historical Dictionary of Censorship in the United States*. Westport, Conn.: Greenwood Press, 1985.

Jansen, Sue C. *Censorship: The Knot That Binds Power and Knowledge*. New York: Oxford University Press, 1991.

Kaplan, Justin. *Born to Trouble: One Hundred Years of Huckleberry Finn*. Washington, D.C.: Library of Congress, 1985.

Karolides, Nicholas J. *Literature Suppressed on Political Grounds*. New York: Facts on File, 1998.

Karolides, Nicholas J., and Lee Burress, eds. *Celebrating Censored Books*. Racine, Wisc.: Council of Teachers of English, 1985.

Moffett, James. *Storm in the Mountains: A Case Study in Censorship, Conflict, and Consciousness*. Carbondale: Southern Illinois University Press, 1988.

Monks, Merri M., and Donna Reidy Pistolis. *Hit List: Frequently Challenged Books for Young Adults*. Chicago: Young Adult Library Services Association, 1996.

Moon, Eric. *Book Selection and Censorship in the Sixties*. New York: Bowker, 1969.

New York Public Library. *Censorship: 500 Years of Conflict*. New York: Oxford University Press, 1984.

Power, Brenda Miller, ed. *Reading Stephen King: Issues of Censorship, Student Choice and Popular Literature*. Urbana, Ill.: National Council of Teachers of English, 1997.

Reichman, Henry. *Censorship and Selection: Issues and Answers for Schools*. Chicago: American Library Association, 1988.

Rogers, Donald J. *Banned: Censorship in the Schools*. Columbus, Ohio: Silver Burdett Press, 1988.

Simmons, John S., ed. *Censorship: A Threat to Reading, Learning, Thinking*. Newark, Del.: International Reading Association, 1999.

Sova, Dawn B. *Literature Suppressed on Sexual Grounds*. New York: Facts on File, 1998.

Steiner, Rudolph, and Byron L. Stay. *Censorship: Opposing Viewpoints*. San Diego, Calif.: Greenhaven Press, 1997.

Vanderham, Paul. *James Joyce and Censorship: The Trials of Ulysses*. New York: New York University Press, 1997.

West, Mark I. *Trust Your Children: Voices Against Censorship in Children's Literature*. New York: Neal-Schuman Publishers, 1997.

Index

Aarons, Jesse, 167, 170
About David, 41–42, 44
Abrams, Elwin, 34
ACLU v. Reno, 112–14, 119
ACLU v. Reno II, 115
Adventure, 10
Adventures of Huckleberry Finn, The.
    See *Huckleberry Finn*
Adventures of Tom Sawyer, The, 189
After the First Death, 148, 154
Agony of Alice, The, 236
Ahrens, Richard, 11
ALA v. United States, 120
Alfred Summer, The: banning in Con-
    necticut, 50–55; interview with Jan
    Slepian, 171–73, 176–77
Alice, In Between, 237
Alice series, The, 235–37
Alice in Wonderland, 113
Aljancic, Andy, 199
Alkisswani, Halima, 192
Allende, Isabel, 216
Alter, Ann Ilan, xvi
Always Running, 239–41
Alyson, Sasha, 162
Ambach v. Norwich, 86, 96
America Reads, 1

American Center for Law and Justice,
    58
American Civil Liberties Union
    (ACLU): Arts Censorship Project,
    62; banned books list, 179; Child
    Internet Protection Act, 121–22;
    Child Online Protection Act, 115–17;
    Communications Decency Act, xxii,
    113–15; *Drowning of Stephen Jones*,
    248; *Island Trees v. Pico*, 14; *Main-
    stream Loudoun v. Board of* Trustees,
    117–19; *Slaughterhouse-Five*, 242; Jan
    Slepian, 172; *Virgil v. School Board of
    Columbia County*, 99–100; *The
    Witches*, 251
American Family Association, 58
American Library Association: *As I
    Lay Dying*, 32; banned books lists,
    xxiv, 131, 147–48; Judy Blume, 136;
    Child Online Protection Act, 115;
    Child Pornography Act of 1988, xxi;
    Communications Decency Act, xxii,
    113; *Island Trees v. Pico*, 14; *Our
    Bodies, Ourselves*, 19; Lesléa New-
    man, 164; Katherine Paterson, 169;
    Jan Slepian, 172–73
Ames, Philip, 200

Amish, 80
Amundson, Kristen, 192
Anderson, Steve, 251
Anduri, Jean, 203
Angelou, Maya, 62–66, 194–97
Annicharico, Joe, Jr., 255
Antcliff, Richard, 209
Anzaldi, James, 243
Are You There God? It's Me, Margaret, 134
Aristophanes, 99
Artist Trust of Seattle, xix
Arts Censorship Project, 62
As Good As It Gets, 161
As I Lay Dying, 31–39
Ash, Jim, 220
Ashcroft, John, 116, 171
Ashcroft v. ACLU, 117
Ashe, Arthur, 210
Attacks on the Freedom to Learn, xix–xx, xxiii
Atwood, Margaret, 229–30
Aung, Geoff, 229
Ayer, Steve, 250

Baca, Sue, 259
Back to Before, 172, 176
Bailey, Conley, 27
Bailey, Linda, 209
Baird, Sarah, 211
Baker, Dennis, 208
Bandemer, Doug, 233
Barker, Julie, 188
Barnes, John, 51–52, 54–55
Bartels v. State of Iowa, 74
Basic Reading, 23, 95
Bass, Ken, 119
Bastian, Philip, 225
Batishko, Karen, 230
Battaglia, Frank, 244
Beach, Frank, 240
Bean, Doug, 225
Bean, Georgia, 239
Beauty and the Beast, 57
Beeson, Ann, 117–18
Being There, 256–57
Belinda's Bouquet, 162–63
Bell Jar, The, 86

Bell Witch House, 146
Beloved, 220–22
Benjamin, Robert, 203
Bennett, Carol, 229
Bergen, Candice, 176
Bergen, Edgar, 176
Berkshire, James and Kathy, 200
Bernd, Mac, 226
Berry, John, 121
Bertolino, James, 194
Bethel v. Fraser, 86, 96–97
Betz, Robert, 226
Bible: The Great Gilly Hopkins, 53; invoking censorship, xv; Lesléa Newman, 165; Mark Twain, 189
Bice, Billy, 192
Bicknell v. Vergennes Union High School Board of Directors, 87–88
bin Laden, Osama, 141
Birdnow, Brad and Brenda, 185
Bivens, Les, 252
Black, Hugo, 78–79
Black, Susan, 99–100
Black Boy, 262–63
Blackburn, Kathy, 235
Blackmun, Harry, 75, 83, 89, 96
Blanton, Elizabeth, 256
Blaster's Handbook, xxi
Bless Me, Ultima, 228–29
Bloesser, Carol, 187
Blubber, xx, 131, 137, 251–52
Blucas, Walter, 228
Bluest Eye, The, 230–31
Blume, Judy: *Blubber*, 251–52; and bookbanning in Maryland, 17; on Robert Cormier, 148; *Forever*, 244–45; interview with, 131–42; on *Harry Potter* books, 183–84; Jan Slepian, 173
Board of Education, Island Trees Free School District No. 26 v. Pico: background and events, 11–15; legal analysis, 86–93, 96; *Mainstream Loudoun v. Board of Trustees*, 118–19; *Meyer v. Nebraska*, 75; *Romano v. Harrington*, 104; *Virgil v. School Board of Columbia County*, 99
Boardman, Mary, 238

Bobbsey Twins, 42
Boe, John, 57
Bolinger, Larry, 199
Bollinger, Rick, 208
Bookman, Joan, 185
Boorne, Janet, 245
Born to Trouble, 190
Bowman, George, 50–51
Bown, Robert, 55
Bowyer, Susan, 207
Boyd, Carol, 200
Bradbury Press, 135
Bradford, Shalon, 191
Branzburg v. Ohio, 122
Brave New World, 237–38
Brennan, William, 77, 79, 89–92, 96
Bridge to Terabithia, 166, 169–70
Brinkema, Leonie, 118–19
Brooks, Dan, 199
Brown, Alicia, 36
Brown, Claire, Jr., 191
Brown, Douglas and Katherine, 58
Brown, Steven, 242
Brown, Vaughan, 64
Brown v. Woodland Unified Joint School District, 58, 108, 110–12
Bruner, Gary, 185
Buchmeyer, Jerry, 216
Buchwald, Art, xvii
Buck, Pearl, 4
Buckwalter, Ronald, 113
Burger, Warren, 80, 89–92, 96–97
Burrows, Bill, 193
Burton, Richard P., Sr., 192
Bush, George H. W., xviii
Bush, George W., xxiii, 116, 171, 177
Business and Professional People's Alliance for Better Textbooks, 4
Byers v. Edmondson, xxii, 125
Byron, Margaret, 223

Cabral, Raymond, 227
Caldwell, Erskine, 7
Camp, Gary, 191
Canada, 56–57, 110
Candide, 174
Captain Underpants series, 257–58
Cardwell, Mike, 203

Carolan, Alice, 257
Carver, Ann, 259
Cary v. Board of Education Arapahoe School District, 85
Cashman, Mark, 257
Casula, Frank, 19
Catcher in the Rye, The: background and banning, xii, 212–14; Holden Caulfield, 213; Internet censorship, 113; PAW report, xx; Kurt Vonnegut, xxiv
Catch-22, 83
Cats, Cats, Cats, 165
Chadick, Jocelyn, 193
Chaffin, Denise, 215
Chamberlain, John, 205
Champion, Sam, 225
Charles V, xv
Charlie, 232
Chaucer, 99
Cheshire, Connecticut, 50–55
Chesser, Paul, 63
Child Online Protection Act (COPA), xxii, 115–16
Child Pornography Act, 1988, xx
Child Protection Act of 1998, 114
Children's Internet Protection Act (CIPA), 114, 119–22
Childress, William, 211
Chmara, Theresa, 120
Chocolate War, The: background and banning, xii, 201–4; interview with Robert Cormier, 148–52, 154–55
Christian-American Parents, 2
Christie, Agatha, xxi
Citizens Advocating the Right to Education (CARE), 27
Citizens for Excellence in Education, 56
Citizens Having Options in Our Children's Education (CHOICE), 43
Citizens Organized for Better Schools (COBS), 25, 27
Clark, Ron, 192
Clemens, Samuel. *See* Twain, Mark
Clements, Jay, 188
Clendenen, Robert, 10
Click, Nelda: *Black Boy*, 262; *Bless Me,*

Ultima, 228; *The Color Purple*, 207; *I Know Why the Caged Bird Sings*, 195; *Native Son*, 218; *Slaughterhouse-Five*, 242

Clinton, Bill: Child Online Protection Act, 115; CIPA and NIPA, 119; Communications Decency Act, xxii, 113; impeachment, 147; inaugural poem by Maya Angelou, 195

Clinton, Kip and Lisa, 223

Clippinger, Roy, 210

Coalition for Children, 15, 17–19

Cobb, Al, 35

Cobb, Tamara, 191

Coe, Arnold, 257

Coffin, Albert W., 87

Cohen, Daniel, 131, 142–48

Cole, R. Guy, 102

Coleman, Sonja, 84

Colley, Leroy and Sharolyn, 203

Collier, Christopher, 54–55, 208–10

Collier, James Lincoln, 208–10

Collins, Charles, 42–49, 153–54

Collins, Marian, 40

Color Purple, The, 206–8

Columbine High School shooting, 125

Commercial speech, 79

Communicating, 1, 5–6

Communications Decency Act, xxii, 113–16

Concerned Citizens, 2

Concerned Citizens for Better Government, 8–10

Concerned Women for America, 26, 28

Connecticut Educational Media Association (CEMA), 53

Cooke, D. M., 7–8

Cooley, Edwin, 187

Cooperative Children's Book Center, 169

Corey, David, 188

Cormier, Robert: banned books list, xii; bookbanning in Connecticut, 153; bookbanning in Florida, 40–49, 152–53; Judy Blume, 139, 148; *The Chocolate War*, 201–204; death of,

131; interview with, 131, 148–56; *We All Fall Down*, 225–26

Courage Foundation, 153

Cousins, Diana, 228

Cox, Michelle, 187

Craig, Coral Lee, 215

Crandall, Sue, 65

Crawley, John and Tracey, 232

Crazy Lady, 261–62

Creel, Joel, 40–44, 46–48, 50

Crew, Rudy, 60–61

Crosby, Connie, 249

Crouse, Rev. Tom, 206

Cujo, 259–60

Culliton, Penny, 247

Curl, Katy, 215

Curses, Hexes and Spells, 143, 145, 147

Daddy's Roommate, 162–63, 214–16

Dahl, Roald, 250

Daily Worker, 218

Daughtry, Rev. Herbert, 61

Davis, Robert, 239

Day No Pigs Would Die, A, 252–53

Dearie, Raymond, 104

Death of a Salesman, 198

Deenie, 137, 140, 252

DelFattore, Joan, 31

Deluzain, Ed, 39

Demon Lover, The, 144

Denton, James, 197

Desilets, Brien, 104–5

Detmer, Barbara, 202

Devine, Joan, 245

Dewey, John, 24

Diary of Anne Frank, 64, 95

DiMaso, Deidra, 229

Dog Day Afternoon, 87

Dogs, Dogs, Dogs, 165

Donelson, Kenneth, 201

Douglas, William O., 80

Down These Mean Streets, 81

Doyle, Jane, 64

Drowning of Stephen Jones, The, 247–48

DuBois, Al, 243

Duby, Deanna, 74

Dudley, Beverley, 209

Dukakis, Michael, 106

Dukes, Eugene, 250
Duncan, Teresa, 255
Dunfee, Mark, 211
Dynamics of Language, 1

East of the Mountains, 156
Easton, James, 234
Edict of Worms, xv
Educational Research Analysts, 56
Eichert, Sherry, 230
Electronic Frontier Foundation, xxii
Electronic Privacy Information Center (EPIC), xxiii, 23
Eliot, T. S., 190
Elliott, Juanita Davis, 38
Ellington, Jerald, 31–34
Ellis, W. Geiger, 201
Emile, xvi
Emily Just in Time, 172
English, Delorah, 33
Epperson v. Arkansas, 77–78, 81–82, 86, 90
Evans, Kristen, 219
Exon, James, 113

Facts about Sex for Today's Youth, 3
Falati, Gary, 212
Fall, Myra, 185
Fallen Angels, 219–20
Family Matters, 157
Family Research Council, 121
Farabee, David, 222
Farnsworth, Julie, 205
Farrakahn, Louis, 65
Farrell, Jennifer, 47
Farrell, Sue, 41, 46–47
Farrell v. Hall, 47–50, 100
Fat Chance, 162
Faulkner, William, 31–39
Fear Street, 122
Federal Writers' Project, 218
Feenstra, Gary, 186
Feingold, Russ, 113
Feinstein, Dianne, xxii
Feldman, Jackie, 237
Felicia's Favorite Story, 165
Feral, Rex, 123
Field of the Dogs, 166

Fike, Elmer, 4
Finch, Larry, 187
Finlayson, Sheila, 64
First Amendment: banned books list, xxiv; bookbanning in Florida, 42; bookbanning in Tennessee, 23–31; Judy Blume, 139; Child Pornography Act, xxi; Internet filters, xxiii; legal precedent in schools and libraries, 13–15; National endowment for the Arts, xviii–xix; Thomas Jefferson Center for the Protection of Free Expression, xviii
Fitzwater, Marlin, xvii
Flag salute, 76
Fleischfresser v. Directors of School District No. 200, 58, 108–12
Flowers for Algernon, 231–33
Focus on the Family, 183
Fool's Crow, 258–59
Forever, 131, 138–39, 244–45
Fortas, Abe, 78–79
Foster, Greg, 234
Fox, Paula, 55
Francois, Francis, 20
Frankfurter, Felix, 76–77
Frechette, Gary, 213
Freedom to Read Foundation, 169
Friday, Nancy, 248–49
From Watergate to Monicagate, 113
Frost, Robert, 201
Frost, Vicki, 23–24, 26, 28
Funny Talk, 176

Gabler, Mel and Norma: California censorship, 56; Tennessee censorship, 24, 31; West Virginia censorship; 1–2, 5
Galaxy, 1
Gale, David, 133
Gama, Sarah, 241
Garcia, Rich, 262
García Márquez, Gabriel, 100
Gardner, Joe, 215, 246
Gardner, John, 100
Garth, Leonard I., 116
Gaudette, Joane, 231
George, Jean Craighead, 148, 254
Ghostly Tales of Love and Revenge, 144

Gibson, Carrie, 206
Gingerbread Man, 57
Ginsberg test, 116
Girardi, Joseph, 243
Giuliani, Rudy, 142
Giver, The, 249–50
Glasser, Ronald, 93
Gloria Goes to Gay Pride, 162
Go Ask Alice, 14, 86, 226–28
God Bless You, Mr. Rosewater, 83
Goldilocks, 25
Good Earth, The, 4
Goodman, Andrew, 36, 38
Goodman, Mark, 202
Goosebumps series, 222–24
Gordon, Kimberly, 202
Gordon, Marvin, 197
Gordon, William, 17–23, 121
Gouch, Pamela, 242
Goulding, Ed, 238
Graham, Patrick, 195
Graley, Rev. Ezra, 3
Grapes of Wrath, The, xx
Grassley, Charles, 113
Graupner, Emily, 230
Graves County, Kentucky, 31–39
Graves County Baptist Association, 35
Great Gilly Hopkins, The, 50, 166–67, 169–70
Green, Cynthia, 187–88
Greene, Bette, 247
Grendel, 100–101
Griffin, Liz, 230
Grogan, John, 202
Gromala, Ken and Vicki, 235
Grooming of Alice, The, 236
Grove v. Mead School District No. 354, 26, 94, 110–11
Growing Up Female in America, 86
Grumman, Robin, 197
Guest, Judith, 253
Gursen, Wayne, 229
Gutenberg, Johannes, xv
Guterson, David, xi, 131, 156–61, 224–25
Guterson, Murray, 158
Guynn, Douglas, xxiv

Hairy Ape, 198
Hall, K.K., 6
Hall, Leonard, 40–44, 47–50
Hall, Rev. Franklin, 203
Hand, W. Brevard, 95–96
Handmaid's Tale, The, 229–30
Hans Christian Anderson Award, 170
Hansen, Chris, 117, 121
Hanson, Lisa, 211
Harkreader, Donna, 226
Haroldsen, Jerry, 229
Harp, Lonnie, 33, 35–37
Harper, John, Jr., 242
Harrell, Sue, 41
Harris, Michael, 29
Harris, Robie, 204–6
Harry Potter books, xi, 180–88
Harry Potter and the Chamber of Secrets, 180–82
Harry Potter and the Goblet of Fire, 180, 182
Harry Potter and the Prisoner of Azkaban, 180, 182
Harry Potter and the Sorcerer's Stone, 180–81, 183–85, 187
Hart, Michael, 113
Hartford-Alley, June, 235
Hartman, Diane, 51, 53
Hartung, Tom and Laura, 257
Haunted Mask, The, 222
Hawkins County, Tennessee, 23–31
Hawks, ReLeah, 39–41, 43–46
Hazelwood School District v. Kuhlmeier, 73–74, 86, 97–106
Heath, Rachel, 202
Heather Has Two Mommies, xi, 161–64, 245–46
Heaton, Doug, 245
Heier, Greg and Maureen, 235
Hein, Sarah, 211
Heins, Marjorie, 62
Heller, Joseph, 83
Helms, Jesse, xix
Hemingway, Ernest, 190
Henry, Fran, 107
Heritage Foundation, 4
Hero Ain't Nothin' but a Sandwich, A, 14

Heron, Ann, 246
Herring, Dennis, 60
Herron, Carolivia, 59, 61–62
Hetrick, Paul, 183
Heumphreus, Susan, 255
Hezbollah, xvii
Hicks, Robert,
Hill, Chris, 31
Hill, Cindy, 44–46
Hill, LaDone, 31, 34, 39
Hill, Rev. Avis, 3
Hillocks, George, Jr., 6
Hit Man, xxii, 122–26
Hitler, Adolph, 161
Hobbs, Billy, 238
Hoff, Dorothy, 258
Hogwarts, 181–82, 186
Holland, Bridges, 37
Holland, Everand, 63
Holmes, Oliver Wendell, 75
Homes, A. M., 255
Homosexuality: Daddy's Roommate,
    214–16; Heather Has Two Mommies,
    162–63; Joy of Gay Sex, The, 243–44;
    Two Teenagers in Twenty, 246–47
Hood, Joseph M., 102
Hopper, Darrell, 223
Horan, Rev. Marvin, 2–3, 6
Horn, Lawrence, 123
House of Spirits, The, 216–18
How to Make Disposable Silencers, 123
How to Rid Your Library of Books by
    Judy Blume, 136
Howard, Jeff, 31, 34, 36–39, 41
Howard, Stephanie, 216
Huckleberry Finn: background and
    banning, xii, 188–93, 233; comments
    by Ernest Hemingway, 190; influ-
    ence on The Catcher in the Rye, 213
Hugghins, Loretta, 223
Hughes, Linda, 246
Hull, Thomas G., 28–30
Humanities: Cultural Roots and Conti-
    nuities, The, 98–99
Hungry Thing, The, 175–76
Hungry Thing and the Gobler, The, 176
Husfelt, Bill, 200

Huxley, Aldous, 237–38
Hyde, Merrol, 238

I Am the Cheese: Florida bookbanning,
    40–44, 46–49; interview with Robert
    Cormier, 148, 151–53
Iceman, 234
Iggie's House, 135
I Know Why the Caged Bird Sings, 62–
    65, 194–97
Illinois Student Publication Act, 107
Images of God, 166
Impressions: background and banning,
    55–58; court decisions, 108–12; Jan
    Slepian, 175
Index librorum prohibitorum, xvi
Interaction, 1–2, 5–6
Internet: books on the Internet, 112;
    censorship, 112–13; congressional
    hearings, 113; filters, xxiii, 114–15,
    117–22; legislation, xx–xxiii, 20–23,
    113–22
Internet Filter Assessment Project, 115
Internet Free Expression Alliance, 115
Internet School Filtering Act, 114
Invisible Child, 166, 170
Irons, Peter, 125–26
Island Trees v. Pico. See Board of Educa-
    tion, Island Trees Free School District
    No. 26 v. Pico
Istook, Ernest, 114
It's Perfectly Normal, 204

Jack, 255–56
Jackson, Dick, 135
Jackson, Michelle, 219
Jackson, Robert H., 76–77
Jacob Have I Loved, 170
Jacobs, Kelly, 224
Jacobson, John, 198
Jehovah's Witnesses, 76
Jeter, Roger, 196
Johnson, Marvin, 122
Johnson v. Stuart, 93–94
Jolly, Joe, 197
Jones, Kathy, 230
Jordan, Linda, 247

Joy of Gay Sex, The, 243–44
Julie of the Wolves, 148, 254–55

Kaffir Boy, 210–12
Kanawha County, West Virginia, 1–7, 82
Kaplin, Justin, 190
Kappelman, Murray M., 19
Katz, Leanne, 54, 133
Keller, Laura, 210
Kelley, George, 188
Kelley, Tom, 123
Kelly, John, 225
Kelly, Winfield, 15–18, 21
Kelso, Kelly, 252
Kennedy, Cornelia, 30
Kennedy, John F., 14
Kennedy-Shaffer, Alan, 208
Kentucky Council of Teachers of English, 34
Kern, Lynne and David, 226
Kersey, Cynthia, 184
Keyes, Daniel, 231
Keyishian v. Board of Regents, 77–79, 86
Khomeini, Ayatollah, xvii
Kilpatrick, John, 207
Kincaid v. Gibson, 102
Kines, Debby, 242
King, Nancy, 217
King, Stephen, 259–60
Klein, Norma, 17, 133–34
Klymshyn, Debbie, 196
Knapp, Rebecca Williams, 209
Koepnick, Kay, 251
Kosinski, Jerzy, 256
Krane, Susan, xix
Kranich, Nancy, 120
Kuehlewind, Sharon, 50–52, 55

LaChance, Bert, 221
Lady Chatterley's Lover, 113
LaHaye, Beverly, 26
LaHaye, Tim, 26
Laingen, Dennis, 196
Lamb, Kurt, 205
Lamberson, Jon,
Lamont v. U.S. Postmaster General, 79
Lane, Sandy, 250

Lane, Steve, 250
Lang, Chuck, 199
Language of Man, 1
LaRue, Jan, 121
Lassley, Libby, 196
Learning Tree, 94, 110–11
LeCarre, John, xxi
Lee, Harper, 158, 233–34
Lemmer, Kathy, 205
Lemon test, 109, 111–12
Lemon v. Kurtzman, 109
L'Engle, Madeleine, 260
Leonard, Scott, 252
Leslie, Jane, 261
Lessard, Daniel, 220
Lester, Shirley, 191
Levin, Sheldon, 225
Levine, Lee, 123
Lewis, C.S., 57
Liberty Council, 186
Lipsyte, Robert, 238
Little, Sherry, 207, 219
Lively, Pierce, 30
Long, Steve, 248–49
Lopez, Ann, 185
Lord of the Flies, 158
Loring, Susan, 204
Lost Moose, 172
Lowry, Lois, 249
Lueck, Jerry, 246
Luna, Andrew, 102
Lund, Peter, 123
Luther, Martin, xv–xvi
Luttig, J. Michael, 124–25
Lynch, Chris, 234
Lysistrata, 99

Mainstream Loudoun v. Board of Trustees, 117–20
MacGoyn, Kathryn, 185
McCain, John, 114, 119–20
McCarthy, Charlie, 176
McCarthy v. Fletcher, 100–102
McClure, Linda, 191
McDaniel, Charles, 226
McGee, Molly, 222
McGinnis, Ann and Tom, 217
McNamara, Jean, 245

McReynolds, James Clark, 74–75
Malcolm X, 11, 89
Male and Female Under 18, 84–85
Malpass, Rita, 203
Manhattan Project, 147
Mansfield, Walter R., 89
Marshall, Arthur, 16–17
Marshall, John, 123
Marshall, Thurgood, 81, 89
Martin v. City of Struthers, 79
Marvin One Too Many, 166
Mathabane, Mark, 210
Matthews, Aubrey, 9
Matthews, Dave, 191
Meadows, Ivan, 217
Mein Kampf, 161
Melville, Herman, 4, 190
Mencken, H. L., 190
Meyer v. Nebraska, 74–75, 78, 86, 89
Meyerjack, William P., 51
Michaud, Norman, 237
Miesburg, John, 186
Miller, Melanie, 215
"Miller's Tale, The," 99
Millet, Kate, 3
Million Man March, 65
Milton, John, 4
Minarcini v. Strongville (Ohio) City School District, 83–85
Mind Read, The, 172, 176
Minersville School District v. Gobitis, 75–78
Moby Dick, 4, 31, 233
Moffet, James, 6
Molly's Pilgrim, 175
Molter, Kari, 212
Monsters of Star Trek, 143
Monteiro, Kathy, 193
Moore, Alice, 1–2, 4–6
Moore, Arch, 4
Moore, Jerry, 205
Moore, Laurel, 258
Moore, Monique, 210
Moore, Opal, 194–95
Mopas, Cherei, 212
Moral Majority, 15, 26, 140, 174
Moran, James B., 108

Morgan, Bobby, 250
Morris, Zane, 223
Morrison, Toni, 62–63, 220–22, 230–31
Morrow, Richard, 12–13
Mounce, Elizabeth, 183
Mowat, Farley, 47
Mozert, Bob, 25–26, 28, 31
Mozert v. Hawkins County Board of Education, 27–28, 31, 95
Ms, 86
Muccilli, Robert, 105
Mulligan, William H., 81
Munroe, Maureen, 240
My Brother Sam Is Dead, 55, 208–10
My Secret Garden, 248
Myers, Walter, 219–20

Naab, Kathie, 207
Nancy Drew mysteries, 42
Nappy Hair, 58–62
Nation of Islam, 193
National Association for the Advancement of Colored People (NAACP), 192–93
National Association of Artists' Organizations, xxi
National Coalition Against Censorship: Judy Blume, 132–33, 135–36; Connecticut censorship, 54; Lesléa Newman, 164; Jan Slepian, 173
National Council of Teachers, 136
National Council of Teachers of English, 40, 50, 169
National Education Association (NEA), 5, 56
National Endowment for the Arts (NEA), xviii–xix
National Society of Newspaper Editors, xix
Native Son, 207, 218–19
Natural Born Killers, xxii, 126
Naylor, Phyllis Reynolds, 235–36
Neal, Sue, 202
Neft, David, xix
Neighborhood Internet Protection Act, 119
Nelson, Judy, 209
Never Cry Wolf, 47

New Advocate, The, 167
New Age Religion: *Impressions,* 56–57; *New Joy of Gay Sex,* 243–44; Katherine Paterson, 169
New York Public Library, xvi
New York Is Book Country, 142
New York Times v. Sullivan, 126
Newell, Alan, 261
Newman, John O., 89
Newman, Lesléa, xi, 131, 161–65, 245–46
Newton, Jeff, xxiv
Nichols, Joe, 183
Nicholson, Jack, 161
Night of the Living Dummy, 222
Nikolay, Frank, 235
Nilsen, Alleen Pace, 201
Ninety-Five Theses, xv
Norris, Alan E., 102
Norris, Tom, 228
North, William D., 91–92

Ochefske, Joseph, 247
O'Connor, Maura, 204
O'Connor, Sandra Day, 89, 114
Of Mice and Men, xii, xx, 197–201
Office for Intellectual Freedom, xxvi, xxii, 179
One Fat Summer, 238–39
One Hundred Years of Solitude, 100
One in the Middle Is the Kangaroo, The, 135
One Teenager in Ten, 246–47
O'Neil, Robert, xviii, xxiv
Ordinary People, 253–54
Orenstein, Stephen, 16–17
Otherwise Known As Sheila the Great, 141
Our Bodies, Ourselves, 15–19, 21, 23
Owen, Katie, 196
Ownby, Richard, 188
Oxley, Michael, xxii, 115

Paladin Press, 122–26
Palistrant, Chris, 253
Palmer, Ed, 260
Panama City, Florida, 39–50, 152, 154
Paradise Lost, 4

Paradise Regained, 4
Parents of New York United (PONYU), 11, 13
Parham, Carol S., 62, 64, 66
Parker, Don, 239
Parks, Gordon, 94
Parks, Harriet, 253
Parquette, Lori, 261
Parrott, Dolores, 197
Parsons, Happy Joe, 207
Parzifal, 166
Pate, Prudence, 250
Paterson, Katherine: bookbanning in Connecticut, 50–55; Robert Cormier, 152; *The Great Gilly Hopkins,* 50–55; interview with, 131, 165–71
Patillo, Robert, 217
Paul, C., 15–18
Paxton, Jim, 37
Peck, Robert S., 252
Pellerin, Mary, 53
Penschell, Richard and Kathy, 207, 219
People for the American Way (PAW): *Attacks on the Freedom to Learn,* xix–xx, xxiii; banned books list, 179; bookbanning in Connecticut, 50–55; bookbanning in Florida, 49, 54; bookbanning in Tennessee, 23–31; Judy Blume, 136; Child Internet Protection Act, 121; Daniel Cohen, 145; *Mainstream Loudoun v. Board of Trustees,* 119; public school censorship, 74; Jan Slepian, 172
Perry, James, 123
Pesarchick, Linda, 243
Pettus, Steve, 214
Pfeffer, Susan, 41
Phillips, Elizabeth, 87
Pico, Steven, 11–14
Pierce v. Society of Sisters, 74–75, 86
Pilkey, Dav, 257
Pillsbury, Peter, 214
Pinocchio's Sister, 172, 176
Pipkin, Gloria, 39–41, 43–48, 148, 153
Places I Never Meant to Be, 132–33
Plato, xv, 4
Playboy, 113

Plopper, Bruce, 107
Pope Leo X, xv
Pornography Victims Compensation Act, xxi
Post, Suzanne, 34–35, 37
Powell, Lewis, 81, 89, 91
President's Council District 25 v. Community School Board No. 25, 81–83, 87–89
Price, Jean, 26–28
Prince George's County, Maryland, 15–23, 144
Prince George's County Educators Association, 20
Pritz, Ken, 260
Project Gutenberg, 113
Pruchniewski, Julie, 64
Purington, Sheila, 197

Quidditch, 181–82
Quigley, Rev. Charles, 3

Rabsatt, Marilyn, 199
Radice, Anne-Imelda, xviii–xix
Rainbow Curriculum, 163
Rainbows, 57
Raines, R.G., 7–10
Rauschuber, Fred, 234
Reader for Writers, 14–15
Reagan, Ronald, 13, 15, 134
Reed, Elaine, 206
Reed, Lowell, xxii, 115–16
Reed, Peter J., 241
Reid, Steve, 227
Rehnquist, William, 89–91, 114
Republic, 4
Responding, 7–10
Restless Dead: Ghostly Tales, The, 143
Rice v. Paladin Enterprises, xxii, 122–26
Rich, Toby, 20
Rich, Wayne, 4
Richards, Cecile, 221
Richardson, Patricia, 63
Richardson, Revs. W.E. and B.J., 200
Rickett, Dan, 253
Ridge, Tom, 192
Right to know, 87
Right to Read Defense Committee of Chelsea, 84, 93

Right to Read Defense Committee of Chelsea v. School Committee of Chelsea, 84–85
Right to receive ideas, 79–80
Riley, Frances, 225
Rittener, Susan, 260
Robar, Dale, 203
Roberts, Martha, 207
Robertson, Pat, 58, 142
Robinson, Ernestine, 195
Rodriguez, Luis A., 239–41
Rogers, Ron, 202
Romano, Michael, 104
Romano v. Harrington, 104
Ross, Daniel, 250
Ross, John, 254
Rotenberg, Marc, 23, xxiii
Rousseau, Jean Jacques, xvi
Rowling, J.K., 180–81
Rudolph, Paul, 66
Rushdie, Salman, xvii

Safe Schools Internet Act, 114
Salinger, J.D., xii, 212–214
Salley, Jay, 24, 26
Salvail v. Nashua Board of Education, 85
San Antonio Independent School District v. Rodriquez, 80–81, 86
Santiago, Felicita, 58–59, 62
Satanic Verses, xvii
Satanism: Daniel Cohen, 144–46; *Impressions*, 56–57; *Mozert v. Hawkins County Board of Education*, 29; PAW report, xx
Scalia, Joan, 205
Scarlet Letter, The, 233
Scarseth, Thomas, 198
Scary Stories, 272,
Schiller, Ed, 246
Schlesinger, Arthur, Jr., xv, xvii
Schmidt, Teresa and Dominic, 183
Schoenberger, Paul, 235
School Library Journal, 177
Schubb, William B., 58, 110–11
Schwalm, Christine, 231
Science Digest, 143
Scott, Tom, 222
Secular humanism, 25–29, 94

Seidler, Ann, 176
Seigenthaler, John, xix
Selverstone, Harriet, 53–54
Sexual Politics, 3
Sharp, Dan, 31–34, 36, 38
Shaw, Beverly, 219
Shaw, Rev. Dale, 263
Sheck, Michael, 93
Sheck v. Baileyville School Committee, 93
Shelton, Johnny, 31–34, 38
Sherman, Ruth, 58–62
Shuler, Judith, 205
Shumaker, Claudia and Robert, 40–42, 49
Siegel, Howard, 123
Siegel, Lee, 180
Sifton, Charles B., 88–89
Sign of the Chrysanthemum, The, 166
Silvers, Harold, 24, 28
Silverstein, Charles, 243
Simmons, Rev. Charles, 37
Simon, Nancy, 239
Simonds, Robert, 56
Simonson, Jack, 49
Simpson, O. J., 123
Sims, Rev. Charles, 191
Sims, Terry, 37
Sirois, Herman, 239
Slaughterhouse-Five, xx, 241–42
Slave Dancer, 55
Slepian, Jan: bookbanning in Connect-icut, 50–55, 174; interview with, 131, 171–77; and Katherine Paterson, 172, 177
Sloviter, Dolores, 114
Smelser, Amy and Jeff, 217
Smith, Bob, 243
Smith, Claire, 208
Smith, Doreen, 239
Smith, Robert, 161
Smith, Stan, 210
Smith v. Board of School Commissioners of Mobile (Ala.) County, 95
Smolla, Rodney, 122, 125–26
Snodgrass, Bill, 23, 25, 28
Snow Falling on Cedars, xi, 156–60, 224–25
Snow White and the Seven Dwarfs, 51

Sondheim, Stephen, xviii
Song of Solomon, 62–63
Souza, Steve, 214
Sparre, Rev. Lee D., 254
Spaulding, Bob, 32, 34, 38
Sperling, Carrie, 251
Sporkin, Stanley, xxi
Sproles, Bobby, 7–11
Stangaroni, Debby, 210
Stannard, Sharon, 254
Stansbury, Gerald, 64
Staples, Steven, 232
Starring Sally J. Freedman as Herself, 136
Staver, Matthew, 186
Steinbeck, John, xii, 197–201
Stepford Wives, The, 86
Sterling, John, 181
Stern, Gary, 105
Stevens, John Paul, 14, 89, 114
Stevens, Karen, 191
Stewart, Potter, 78
Stine, R. L., 222–24
Stinson, Ronnie, 37
Stockton, Lawrence, 232
Stoltz, Gary, 240
Stone, Harlan, 76
Stone, Kathleen, 238
Stone, Oliver, xxii
Strommer, David, 240
Student Press Law Center, 102
Summer Sisters, 132–33
Super, Marcia, 209
Superfudge, 141
Sutherland, Zena, 177

Tale of Two Cities, xxiv
Tales of a Fourth Grade Nothing, 139
Tauro, Joseph L., 84
Taylor, Chester, 214
Taylor, Mike, 214
Taylor, Sharon and Barry, 65–66, 197
Taylor, Sheryl, 241
Teller (of Penn and Teller), xxi
Terrill, Robert, 227
Tester, Tommy, 8
Theaterworks, 142
Thomas, George, 195

Thomas, Piri, 81
Thomas Jefferson Center for the Protection Free Expression, xvii, xxiv
Thompson, Barbara, 63
Thompson, Rev. Earl, 66
365 Days, 93
Three Little Pigs, 25–28
Tibbets, Janet, 235
Tiger Eyes, 137
Tinker, John and Mary Beth, 79, 107–8
Tinker v. Des Moines Independent Community School District: Ambach v. Norwich, 86; *Hazelwood v. Kuhlmeyer*, 98; legal analysis, 77–79; *Minarcini v. Strongsville (Ohio) City School District*, 84; *Sheck v. Baileyville School Committee*, 93; student press statutes, 106–8
To Kill a Mockingbird, 158, 214, 233–34
Tom Sawyer, 189
Trilling, Lionel, 190
Trotto, Beth, 15, 17–22
Tubbs, W. Grant, 9–11
Tuerkheimer, Frank, xxi
Tuller, Lisa, 261
Tuminello, Annelle, 64
Turley, Mike, 33
Turner, Harold, 200
Turvey, Dan, 259
Tutweiler, Margaret, xvii
Twain, Mark, xii, 57, 188–90
Two Teenagers in Twenty, 246–47
Two Worlds of Charlie Gordon, The, 232

Underwood, Kenneth, 4–5
University of Maryland, College Park, 65
Updike, John, 7

Vandel, Greg, 199
VanOverbeke, Gene, 236
Vaughn, Susan, 260
Vazquez, Felix, 60–61
Ventura, Jesse, 147
Verrone, Bob, 135
Vietnam War, 78
Vinson, Roger, 48–50

Virgil, Moyna, 99
Virgil v. School Board of Columbia County, 98–99
Virginia State Board of Pharmacy v. Virginia Citizens Consumer Council, 79
Vonnegut, Kurt, xxiv, 83, 241–42
Vorderbrueggen, Nellie and Bernie, 254

Waldman, Keith, 31
Walters, Ronald, 65
Wanderers, 87
Ward, Cheryl, 235
Warren Bill of Rights Project, 125
Washington County, Tennessee, 7–11
Washington Zoo, 141
Watkins, Billy, 31, 33, 36, 38
We All Fall Down, 148, 156, 225–26
Weaver, Janet, 187
Weaver, Marcia, 202
Weber, Rev. Kevin, 205
Weinberg, Stewart, 193
Welch, James, 258–59
Welles, Orson, 218
West Virginia State Board of Education v. Barnette, 76–78, 86, 91
Wetzel, Rebecca, 184
What Johnny Shouldn't Read, 31
White, Byron, 89
Whitehouse, Colette, 181
Wicca, 57, 111
Wilcox, Steve, 210
Wildmon, Rev. Donald, 58
Wilkins, Billy, 36
Willhoite, Michael, 163, 214–16
Williams, Danny, 219
Williams, J., 124–25
Williams, Karen, 200
Williams, Karen J., 200
Williams, Kevin and Tracy, 232
Williams, Rev. Tom, 9–10
Williams v. Board of Education of Kanawha County, 82
Willis, Marsha, 261
Wilson, David, 27
Wilson, DeeAnn, 225
Wilson, Donald P., 200
Wilson, Greg and Arlena, 185

Wilson, Mike, 186
Wisconsin v. Yoder, 80–81
Wiser, Bert, 251
Witches, The, 250–51
Witt, Pamela, 184
Wizard of Oz, The, 29, 53, 175, 188
Wolfe, Dennis, 241
Wolfe, Steve, 202
Women on Top, 248–49
Woor, Camille, 246
Wright, Ellen, 263
Wright, Richrd, 218–19, 262–63
Wrinkle in Time, A, 260–61

Wyatt, Robert, xix
Wyndham, Lee, 135

Yaeger, Chris, 259
Yates, Julie, 236
Young, John, 211
Young Miss, 44

Zeeman, Amy, 107
Zugay, Lucille, 19
Zykan v. Warsaw (Indiana) Community School Corporation and Warsaw School Board of Trustees, 86–87, 91–92

About the Author

HERBERT N. FOERSTEL is the former Head of Branch Libraries at the University of Maryland, College Park. He currently serves on the Board of Directors for the National Security Archives. He is a noted authority on intellectual freedom and has published seven previous books on the topic for Greenwood Publishing, including *Banned in the Media* (1998) and *From Watergate to Monicagate: Ten Controversies in Modern Journalism and Media* (2001).